Ray Raphael has taught at a one-room public high school, Humboldt State University, and College of the Redwoods. His seventeen books include *A People's History of the American Revolution*, *The First American Revolution*, *Founders*, and *Constitutional Myths* (all available from The New Press). Currently a senior research fellow at Humboldt State University, he lives in northern California.

ALSO BY RAY RAPHAEL

Constitutional Myths: What We Get Wrong and How to Get It Right

Mr. President: How and Why the Founders Created a Chief Executive

Revolutionary Founders: Rebels, Radicals, and Reformers in the Making of the Nation (co-edited with Alfred F. Young and Gary B. Nash)

The Complete Idiot's Guide to the Founding Fathers and the Birth of Our Nation

Founders: The People Who Brought You a Nation

The First American Revolution: Before Lexington and Concord

A People's History of the American Revolution: How Common People Shaped the Fight for Independence

FOUNDING MYTHS

Stories That Hide Our Patriotic Past

RAY RAPHAEL

Revised Edition

THE NEW PRESS
NEW YORK
LONDON

Originally published in hardcover by The New Press, New York, 2004

This revised edition published in the United States by The New Press, New York, 2014
Distributed by Perseus Distribution

CIP data available
ISBN 978-1-59558-949-1 (pbk)
ISBN 978-1-59558-974-3 (e-book)

The New Press publishes books that promote and enrich public discussion and understanding of the issues vital to our democracy and to a more equitable world. These books are made possible by the enthusiasm of our readers; the support of a committed group of donors, large and small; the collaboration of our many partners in the independent media and the not-for-profit sector; booksellers, who often hand-sell New Press books; librarians; and above all by our authors.

www.thenewpress.com

Composition by dix!
This book was set in Fournier MT

Printed in the United States of America

10 9 8 7 6 5 4 3 2 1

In memory of Al Young and Pauline Maier

"Who shall write the history of the American Revolution? Who can write it? Who will ever be able to write it?"

—John Adams to Thomas McKean,
July 30, 1815

CONTENTS

FOUNDING MYTHS

"Let the world admire our patriots and heroes."

Washington Crossing the Delaware.
Engraving based on painting by Emanuel Leutze, 1851.

INTRODUCTION: INVENTING A PAST

When settlers from across the Atlantic arrived on the east coast of North America, they felt they were on uncharted territory. From the Old World they imported the traditions that defined them as a people, since the New World, which they treated as a blank slate, appeared in their perspective to have no history of its own.

Slowly, over more than a century and a half, colonists developed local, homegrown histories. These remained separate and distinct until suddenly, with one cataclysmic event, they merged. The Revolutionary War provided Americans with shared stories of a common past. This past, ever since, has served the interests of nation building. For more than two centuries, the oft-repeated story of how the United States achieved its independence has bound Americans together.

All nations like to celebrate their origins, but the birth of our nation makes a particularly compelling story. The United States has a clearly defined "founding," the work of a single generation. Most nations are not so fortunate. The story of Britain's founding must cover the Norman invasion (1066), the Magna Carta (1215), the Glorious Revolution (1688), and the Act of Union (1707). China's founding includes the rise of ancient dynasties, the Nationalist Revolution in 1911, and the Communist Revolution in 1949—too much to tell in a cohesive story. Mexico has only two founding moments, independence in 1821 and revolution in the early twentieth century, but these were separated by ninety years. Canada eased into nationhood so gracefully that it hardly has a story to tell.[1]

Our story, by contrast, is simple yet grand. Its plotline is easy to follow: American colonists resisted British oppression, fought a war, achieved independence, and established their own government. Within this straightforward structure we can embellish as we please, but the storyline itself is clean and efficient. It gets the job done. It establishes a separate identity for the American people.

How we choose to tell this story helps define our nation. Daily, politicians invoke "our founders" in support of some cause totally foreign to the American experience of the late eighteenth century. They place the past—more precisely, a past they imagine—in service of a political present.

Stories of the American Revolution were first communicated by word of mouth, and these folkloric renditions, infinitely malleable, provided fertile grounds for the invention of history. Before the Revolution, angry and animated colonists gathered in taverns and meetinghouses to rail against acts of Parliament; after the fighting was done, this same crew downed pint after pint of hard cider while exchanging old war stories. For decades, men and women of the early republic told and retold what had happened, augmenting and enriching their skeletal memories of actual events, removing what was too painful to recall (no shortage there) while embellishing what could be seen as heroic (no shortage there either). At funerals or Fourth of July celebrations, orators used tales of the Revolution as grist for their rhetoric. While audiences applauded and critics ranked their performances, these civic preachers competed in the art and sport of patriotic expression. This vibrant oral tradition helped produce a history that was detailed but unfettered. Divested of any need for documentation, it went freely wherever it wanted.

The visual arts, like the oral tradition, gave the past a place in the present. During and after the Revolution, engravings and lithographs depicted the major events to popular audiences. More pliable than photography, these artistic forms allowed for leeway in interpretation. In the early nineteenth century, grandiose Romantic paintings offered indelible images of battles and key political proceedings. Subsequent generations, viewing reproductions in popular histories and textbooks, used these images to help shape a collective "memory" of the Revolution. Set to canvas long after the war had ended, they became national icons. Today, the two most dominant visual reflections of the American Revolution are John Trumbull's 1818 painting *Declaration of Independence* and Emanuel Leutze's 1851 masterpiece *Washington Crossing the Delaware*—even though there was no ceremonial signing of the Declaration on July 4, 1776, the date mistakenly applied to Trumbull's painting when it was hung in the Capitol Rotunda, and the flag displayed prominently in Washington's boat had not yet been created.[2]

Oral tradition and artistic imagination filled in the blanks left by incomplete and selective documentation. Although a handful of exceptionally literate men bequeathed volume after volume of letters, diaries, and memoirs, these writings emanated from a very small segment of the population, unrepresentative of the whole. Many of these first-person accounts were set to paper decades after the fact. Because of skewed sampling, personal bias, and the effects of time on memory, they cannot always be accepted at face value.

Selective written sources, rich but loose oral and visual traditions, and the intrusion of politics and ideology—these have presented open invitations to the historical imagination. Creatively, if not accurately, we have fashioned a past we would like to have had.

Fiction parted from fact at the very beginning. Shortly after the Revolutionary War, Charles Thomson, secretary of the Continental Congress, embarked on writing a history of the conflict. Privy to insider information, Thomson had much to reveal—but then, surprisingly, he gave the history up. "I shall not undeceive future generations," he later explained. "I could not tell the truth without giving great offense. Let the world admire our patriots and heroes."[3]

Since people like Mr. Thomson chose not to tell the truth, what might they tell instead? In 1790 Noah Webster provided an answer: "Every child in America," said the dean of the Anglo-American language, "as soon as he opens his lips . . . should rehearse the history of his country; he should lisp the praise of Liberty and of those illustrious heroes and statesmen who have wrought a revolution in his favor."[4]

So the romance began. Starting in the decades following the Revolution and continuing through much of the nineteenth century, writers and orators transformed a bloody and protracted war into glamorous tales conjured from mere shreds of evidence. We still tell these classics today—Paul Revere's ride, "Give me liberty or give me death," the shot heard 'round the world—and we assume they are true representations of actual occurrences. Mere frequency of repetition appears to confirm their authenticity.

Our confidence is misplaced. In fact, most of the stories were created up to one hundred years after the events they supposedly depict. Paul Revere was known only in local circles until 1861, when Henry Wadsworth Longfellow made him immortal by distorting every detail of his now-famous ride. Patrick Henry's "liberty or death" speech first appeared in print, under mysterious circumstances, in 1817, forty-two years after he supposedly uttered those words. The "shot heard 'round the world" did not become known by that name until 1836, sixty-one years after it was fired.

The list goes on. Samuel Adams, our most beloved rabble-rouser, lay low through the first half of the nineteenth century, only to be revived as the mastermind of the Revolution three-quarters of a century after the fact. Thomas Jefferson was not widely seen as the architect of American "equality" until Abraham Lincoln assigned him that role, four score and seven years later. The winter at Valley Forge remained uncelebrated for thirty years. Molly Pitcher, the Revolutionary heroine whose picture adorns many elementary and middle-school textbooks today, is a complete fabrication. Her legend did not settle firmly on a specific, historic individual until the nation's centennial celebration in 1876.

These stories, invented long ago, persist in our textbooks and popular histories despite advances in recent scholarship that disprove their authenticity. One popular schoolbook includes all but two of the tales exposed in this book, and several of the stories, still taken as gospel, are featured in all modern texts.[5]

Why do we cling to these yarns? There are three reasons, thoroughly intertwined: they give us a collective identity, they make good stories, and we think they are patriotic.

We like to hear stories of our nation's beginnings because they help define us as a people. Americans have always used the word "we," highlighting a shared sense of the past. Likewise, this book uses the first person plural when referring to commonly held beliefs. This usage is more than just a linguistic convenience—it pinpoints actual cognitive habits. *We* are history's protagonists. Few Americans read about the Revolutionary War or World War II without identifying with *our* side. George Washington, we are told in myriad ways, is the father of *our* country, whether our forebears came from England, Poland, or Vietnam.[6]

Like rumors, the tales are too good *not* to be told. They are carefully crafted to fit a time-tested mold. Successful stories feature heroes or heroines, clear plotlines, and happy endings. Good does battle against evil, David beats Goliath, and wise men prevail over fools. Stories of our nation's founding mesh well with these narrative forms. American revolutionaries, they say, were better and wiser than decadent Europeans. Outnumbered colonists overcame a Goliath, the mightiest empire on earth. Good prevailed over evil, and the war ended happily with the birth of the United States. Even if they don't tell true history, these imaginings work as stories. Much of what we think of as "history" is driven not by facts but by these narrative preferences.

This imagined past, anointed as "patriotic," paints a flattering self-portrait of our nation. We pose before the mirror in our finest attire. By gazing upon the Revolution's gallant heroes, we celebrate what we think it means to be an American. We make our country perfect—if not now, at least in the mythic past—and through the comforting thought of an ideal America, we fix our bearings. We feel more secure in our confused and changing world if we can draw upon an honored tradition.

But is this really "patriotism"? Only from a narrow and outdated perspective can we see it that way. Our nation was a collaborative creation, the work of hundreds of thousands of dedicated patriots—yet we exclude most of these people from history by repeating the traditional tales. Worse yet, we distort the very nature of their monumental project. The United States was founded not by isolated acts of individual heroism but by the concerted revolutionary activities of people who had learned the power of working together. This rich and very democratic heritage remains untapped precisely because its story is too big, not too small. It transcends the artificial constraints of traditional storytelling. Its protagonists are too many, and too real, to be contained within simple morality tales. This sprawling saga needs to be told—but our founding myths, neat and tidy, have concealed it from view.[7]

Traditional stories of national creation reflect the romantic individualism of the nineteenth century, and they sell our country short. They are strangely out of sync with both the communitarian ideals of Revolutionary America and the democratic values of today. "Government has now devolved upon the people," wrote one disgruntled Tory in 1774, even before war broke out, "and they seem to be for using it." Yes, indeed. That's a story we do not have to conjure, and what an epic it is.[8]

HEROES AND HEROINES

"The fate of a nation was riding that night."

Paul Revere's Ride. Drawing by Charles G. Bush,
Harper's Weekly, June 29, 1867.

1

PAUL REVERE'S RIDE

On April 5, 1860, while walking past Boston's Old North Church, Henry Wadsworth Longfellow heard a folkloric rendition of Paul Revere's midnight ride from a friend, George Sumner. The story stirred him, and the next day he began setting thoughts to paper.[1] With the United States on the verge of splitting apart, Longfellow, a unionist, was inspired by the dramatic opening to the American Revolution, when "the fate of the nation" (as he would soon write) seemed to hinge on a single courageous act. For the noted poet, Revere was a timely hero: a lonely rider who issued a wake-up call. If Revere had roused the nation once, perhaps he could do it again, this time riding the rhythmic beat of Longfellow's verse:

> So through the night rode Paul Revere;
> And so through the night went his cry of alarm
> To every Middlesex village and farm,
> A cry of defiance, and not of fear,
> A voice in the darkness, a knock at the door,
> And a word that shall echo forevermore!
> For, borne on the night-wind of the Past,
> Through all our history, to the last,

> In the hour of darkness and peril and need,
> The people will waken and listen to hear
> The hurrying hoof-beats of that steed,
> And the midnight message of Paul Revere.[2]

In close replication of Revere's own effort, Longfellow passed word of the ride to every household on America's highways and byways, issuing his alarm, line by line, as he distorted every detail of the actual deed. In the process, he transformed a local favorite into a national legend.

Longfellow himself made history in two ways: he conjured events that never happened, and he established a new patriotic ritual. For a century to follow, nearly every schoolchild in the United States would hear or recite "Paul Revere's Ride." In their history texts, students read pared-down prose renditions of Longfellow's tale, the meter gone but distortions still intact. Even today, one line remains in our popular lexicon, known to those who have never read or heard the entire piece: "One, if by land, and two, if by sea." These words, all by themselves, call forth the entire story, and Paul Revere's ride remains the best-known heroic exploit of the American Revolution.

THE EARLY YEARS

Before Longfellow, Paul Revere was not regarded as a central player in the Revolutionary saga. He was known for his engravings (especially his depiction of the Boston Massacre), for his work as a silversmith, and for his political organizing in prewar Boston. John Singleton Copley painted his portrait, which showed Revere displaying his silver work—but that was several years *before* the midnight ride.[3] Locally, Revere was also remembered as a patriotic man who climbed on a horse and rode off with a warning—but similar feats had been performed by countless others during the Revolutionary War. Although Revere was certainly respected for the various roles he played, he wasn't exactly celebrated. Schoolbooks made no mention of Revere or his derring-do.

Shortly after the fact, Paul Revere offered his own rendition of the ride that would someday make him famous. Three days after British Regulars marched on Lexington and Concord, the Massachusetts Provincial Congress authorized the collection of firsthand reports from those who were participants or observers. Paul Revere came forward to tell what he knew.[4]

Revere's version—in simple prose, not verse—differed considerably from Longfellow's. At about 10 o'clock on the evening of April 18, 1775, Revere stated in his deposition, Dr. Joseph Warren requested that he ride to Lexington with a message for Samuel Adams and John Hancock: "a number of Soldiers" appeared to be headed their way. Revere set out immediately. He was "put across" the Charles River to Charlestown, where he "got a Horse." After being warned that nine British officers had been spotted along the road, he set off toward Lexington. Before he even left Charlestown, he caught sight of two, whom he was able to avoid. "I proceeded to Lexington, thro Mistick," Revere stated flatly, "and alarmed Mr. Adams and Col. Hancock."

That was it—Revere devoted only one short sentence to his now-mythic ride. Additions were to come later. Nowhere in his statement did Revere mention the lantern signals from the Old North Church, a matter that seemed more trivial to him than it did to Longfellow. On the other hand, Revere did include much concrete information that Longfellow would later suppress, such as the fact that Dr. Warren sent a second messenger, a "Mr. Daws" (William Dawes), along an alternate route.

For Revere, the night featured a harrowing experience that Longfellow, for reasons of his own, saw fit to overlook. After giving his message to Adams and Hancock, Revere and two others set out toward Concord to warn the people there—but he did not get very far before being captured by British officers. For most of the deposition, Revere talked of this capture, of how the officers had threatened to kill him five times, three times promising to "blow your brains out." Though he had carried messages from town to town many times before, Revere had never encountered such serious danger. In his mind, this was the main event of the story.[5]

Revere's ordeal ended without personal calamity. After taking his horse, the officers released him. On foot, Revere retreated to Lexington, where he heard the first round of fire. Perhaps because he did not state point-blank that the British had fired first, the Provincial Congress thought Revere's testimony was of little consequence, and they chose not to include it in their official report, *A Narrative of the Excursion and Ravages of the King's Troops.*

Seeming to concur with the judgment of the Congress, others granted Revere no more than a place on history's sidelines. William Gordon, the early historian who conducted his own on-site interviews in the weeks to follow, did not feature Paul Revere's ride in his detailed account of the events of Lexington and Concord. "Expresses were forwarded to alarm the country, some of whom were secured by the officers on the road"—that was all he bothered to say.[6] Gordon expanded his treatment in the full-length history he published thirteen years later, but he still made no mention of any heroic exploits by Paul Revere:

> Dr. Warren, by mere accident, had notice of it [the British mobilization] just in time to send messengers over the neck and across the ferry, on to Lexington, before the orders for preventing every person's quitting the town were executed. The officers intercepted several, but some being well mounted, escaped their vigilance; and the alarm, being once given, spread apace, by the ringing of bells, and the firing of signal guns and vollies.[7]

All the early historians of the Revolution agreed: Revere was not a major player in the outbreak of hostilities. David Ramsay, writing in 1789, said only that "intelligence" was "sent to the country militia, of what was going on."[8] John Marshall (1804) mentioned Warren but not

Revere: "The country was alarmed by messengers sent out by Doctor Warren, some of whom eluded the vigilance of the patrols."[9] Mercy Otis Warren (1805) wrote simply that "a report reached the neighboring towns very early."[10] For the four most prominent contemporary historians, the transport of a message from Dr. Warren to Samuel Adams and John Hancock appeared of less lasting import than nearly everything else that happened during the historic events of April 18 and 19, 1775.

Although Paul Revere's ride was a nonstarter in the early histories, Revere's friends, neighbors, and fellow Freemasons knew of it and praised it. Joshua Fowle, who grew up near Revere in post-Revolutionary Boston, had heard of the signal lanterns and the midnight ride in his youth: "I have heard it told over many times and never doubted," he later recalled. "It was common talk." Early on, though neglected by formal history, the tale was germinating in folklore, and in 1795, a poet who signed his name "Eb. Stiles" set forth a doggerel prototype:

> He raced his steed through field and wood
> Nor turned to ford the river,
> But faced his horse to the foaming flood
> They swam across together.
>
> He madly dashed o'er mountain and moor,
> Never slackened spur nor rein
> Until with shout he stood by the door
> Of the Church on Concord green.[11]

In Stiles's poem the story took on a life of its own, richly decorated by nonexistent mountains and moors and foaming flood. Finally, twenty years after the fact, Stiles enabled Revere to reach "the Church on Concord green"—a destination that eluded him on April 19, 1775.

Perhaps in response to this emerging folklore, Jeremy Belknap, corresponding secretary for the Massachusetts Historical Society, asked Revere to provide a detailed account of his ride. Revere obliged, but he signed his paper "A Son of Liberty of the year 1775," and then added "do not print my name." When Belknap published the piece in the society's *Collections*, dated January 1, 1798, he contradicted Revere's wish and set his name in print.

In this account, delivered nearly a quarter of a century after his initial deposition, Revere abridged the once traumatic saga of his capture but included the story of the signal lanterns, perhaps by popular request. Revere also wrote at length about Benjamin Church's alleged treachery, unknown at the time of his original deposition. Since Revere's new account, like its predecessor, was undoubtedly less dramatic than folkloric renditions, it might actually have slowed the growth of the incipient legend.[12]

When Revere died in 1818, his obituary in the *Boston Intelligencer and Weekly Gazette* made no mention of his midnight ride.[13] In 1830 Freeman Hunt placed 487 popular tales of the Revolution into two volumes, *American Anecdotes: Original and Select*, yet he failed to mention Paul Revere. By contrast, Lydia Darrah, who warned George Washington about British maneuvers in 1777, made the grade, one of many heroes and heroines nationally recognized at that time.[14]

Still, local history enthusiasts kept the memory alive. Through midcentury, reports of his ride emerged and reemerged. On the fiftieth anniversary of the opening battles of the Revolutionary War, William Munroe, who had guarded the house where Adams and Hancock were staying, cited Paul Revere's role: "I told him the family had just retired, and had requested, that they might not be disturbed by any noise about the house. 'Noise!' said he, '[Y]ou'll have noise enough before long. The British are coming out.' "[15] In 1849 Richard Frothingham published the first comprehensive account of the warning of the countryside, and he included Paul Revere's role. Basing his report on depositions by Revere and other participants, Frothingham demonstrated that at least four different couriers had been sent to Lexington on the evening of April 18, including Paul Revere, and three of these had delivered their messages.[16]

With the facts laid out, Revere's story inched its way into the core narrative of the Revolution. In his 1851 *Pictorial Field-Book of the Revolution,* Benson Lossing mentioned both Paul Revere and William Dawes by name, and he included William Munroe's anecdote.[17] In 1854 George Bancroft gave a fairly accurate rendering of the story: both Revere and Dawes delivered their messages to Lexington, he said, but only Samuel Prescott was able to elude the British officers and deliver the warning to Concord.[18]

Although the story was beginning to receive attention beyond local boundaries, it was still only one of many. Three-quarters of a century after his ride, Paul Revere had not yet become a household name—and with good reason. Revere did not distinguish himself as a military hero. He was not a famous statesmen—in fact, he was not even one of the signers of the Declaration of Independence. He delivered no memorable speeches, he swayed no crowds, he made no public pronouncements of lasting significance. In the 1850s, there was no reason to suspect that Paul Revere was about to be initiated into the pantheon of Revolutionary heroes—one of the five or ten most celebrated figures of his generation.

Even so, Revere had found an appropriate niche in the annals of history. Writers during this period treated history as a series of anecdotes—distinct moments that made the past come alive—and the story of the midnight ride fit right in. Between them, Lossing and Bancroft relayed literally thousands of such tales, isolated moments featuring individual deeds in service of the Revolution.[19] That's where Paul Revere's ride might stand today—just one short scene in a giant epic—had Henry Wadsworth Longfellow not discovered the Revolutionary bit player and cast him in a leading role.

POETIC LICENSE

Longfellow's "Paul Revere's Ride" first appeared in the January 1861 issue of the *Atlantic.* The poem opened with an endearing invocation:

Listen, my children, and you shall hear
Of the midnight ride of Paul Revere, . . .

Then, in the galloping cadence of anapestic tetrameter—two slow beats followed by one long, repeated four times—Longfellow created an unforgettable tale that appealed to adults and children alike. Even in those days, nothing could thrill an audience more than an exciting chase:

A hurry of hoofs in a village street,
A shape in the moonlight, a bulk in the dark,
And beneath, from the pebbles, in passing, a spark
Struck out by a steed flying fearless and fleet;
That was all! And yet, through the gloom and the light,
The fate of a nation was riding that night;
And the spark struck out by that steed, in his flight,
Kindled the land into flame with its heat.

For Longfellow, one man alone held "the fate of the nation" in his hands. The notion that an individual hero could generate a "spark" that would "kindle the land into flame" was central to the worldview of nineteenth-century Romanticism. It also conformed to the formula for successful narratives. A storyteller par excellence, Longfellow naturally emphasized the motive force of individual action.[20]

Although "Paul Revere's Ride" has enjoyed more exposure than any other historic poem in American culture, it is riddled with distortions. These are not incidental—they are the very reasons the story has endured for a century and a half. Four historical misrepresentations are particularly significant:

(1) Strangely, in 130 lines, Longfellow says not a word about the detention by British officers, the major focus of Paul Revere's own tale. That would reveal a British presence in the vicinity of Lexington and Concord, a presence of

which some of the townspeople were already aware—what need then for a messenger? For the story to work, all British soldiers have to be stationed to the rear of Revere and his horse. "The Redcoats are coming" loses its dramatic effect if we know that some Redcoats have already arrived.

(2) To achieve maximum effect, Longfellow has Revere visit "every Middlesex village and farm." Although some allowance can be made for hyperbole, Longfellow certainly knew that his protagonist never reached Concord, the destination of the British troops and the town most in need of warning. The real Revere had tried and failed to get that far. Understandably, Longfellow did not wish to burden his story with the sober realization that the hero had been prevented from achieving his final objective.

(3) Longfellow's Revere works both ends of the signal lantern ploy, which accounts for more than half the poem. Before crossing the Charles River, Revere tells a "friend" how to work the signal; then, after arriving on the opposite shore, Revere waits to receive it, "impatient to mount and ride." For sixteen lines Revere pats his horse, gazes across the landscape, and stamps the earth, fretfully passing the time until he finally spots two lights. In reality this is not what happened. We do not know who waited to receive the signal on the opposite shore, but we do know it was not Paul Revere. After being dispatched by Joseph Warren, but before crossing the river, Revere himself arranged for two lanterns to be lit—so that someone else might see them in Charlestown and set off to warn other patriots. Someone *else*? Again, facts had to be altered to accommodate the story. There could be no other rider in "Paul Revere's Ride."

(4) Except for two bit players—his horse and the friend who lit the lanterns—Longfellow's Revere acted alone. In fact, there were many others. In 1994 historian David Hackett

Fischer reconstructed the event with a full cast of characters, including:

- A stable boy, a hostler, and at least two other Bostonians who sent word to Revere that British soldiers were readying for an offensive.
- Someone within General Gage's closest circle (possibly his own wife, Margaret Kemble Gage) who informed Dr. Joseph Warren of the offensive.
- Dr. Warren, who, on behalf of the Boston Committee, asked Revere to deliver a warning to Samuel Adams and John Hancock.
- William Dawes, who carried the same message by a different route, also at the request of Joseph Warren.
- Three different "friends" who engineered the clandestine lighting of the signal lanterns: John Pulling, Robert Newman, and Thomas Bernard.
- Two boatmen who rowed Revere across the Charles River.
- Colonel Conant and other patriots from Charlestown who waited patiently to receive the lantern signal they had arranged with Revere two days earlier.
- An unidentified messenger who was dispatched from Charlestown as soon as the signal from the lanterns was received. (Since this messenger never reached either Lexington or Concord, the entire signal lantern subplot is never consummated.)
- Richard Devens of Charlestown, who greeted Revere by the river's shore and warned him that British officers were patrolling the road to Lexington and Concord.
- Devens, Abraham Watson, Elbridge Gerry, Charles Lee, and Azor Orne, members of the Provincial Committee of Safety, who sent a note to Hancock in Lexington, warning him that British officers were headed his way.
- An anonymous courier who successfully delivered this

message at about eight o'clock in the evening, three hours *before* Revere would mount his horse.

- The innkeeper at the Black Horse Tavern in Menotomy (now Arlington), who later that night warned Gerry, Lee, and Orne that British troops had arrived, enabling them to escape out the back door.
- Solomon Brown of Lexington, who warned William Munroe, a sergeant in the town militia, that British officers were headed toward Lexington, and who later tried to alert the people of Concord to the presence of the officers, but was soon captured.
- Munroe and eight other militiamen who stood guard through the night at the house of Jonas Clarke, the Lexington minister, where Adams and Hancock were staying.
- Thirty other Lexington militiamen who gathered at Buckman Tavern at 9:00 p.m. to deal with the crisis, two hours *prior* to Revere's departure on his famous ride.
- Elijah Sanderson and Jonathan Loring of the Lexington militia, who volunteered to keep a watch on the British officers.
- Josiah Nelson, a farmer who resided on the road to Concord, who had his head slashed by the sword of one of the British officers, then alerted all his neighbors.
- John Larkin of Charlestown, who lent Revere a horse that belonged to his father, Samuel.
- Another unidentified messenger from Charlestown who set off at the same time as Revere, heading north. This rider reached Tewksbury, twenty-five miles from Boston, at about the time Revere himself was taken captive by the British officers.
- Captain John Trull of Tewksbury, who, upon receiving news from the Charlestown rider, fired three shots from his bedroom window—a signal that lacked the finesse of

the lanterns in Old North Church but that had a greater impact. The militia commander in Dracut, on the New Hampshire boundary, heard the shots and mustered his militia—several hours before the bloody dawn at Lexington.

- Samuel Tufts of East Cambridge, who embarked on a ride of his own after his neighbor, Elizabeth Rand, told him she had spotted the British column.
- Solomon Bowman, lieutenant of the Menotomy militia, who immediately mustered his town's company after viewing the British soldiers.
- Isaac Hull, captain of the Medford militia, who received word from Revere, then mustered his company.
- Dr. Martin Herrick, who left Medford to alarm Stoneham, Reading, and Lynn. These towns, in turn, sent out their own riders; by dawn, the entire North Shore of Massachusetts Bay was aroused and in the process of mustering.
- Another messenger from Medford who headed east to Malden, and from there to Chelsea.
- Yet another messenger from Medford who journeyed to Woburn, and still another from Woburn to the parish above it, now Burlington, and so on, ad infinitum, until almost every "Middlesex village and farm" had been warned by a vast network of messengers and signals—all in the wee hours of the morning on April 19, 1775.
- Finally, Samuel Prescott, a doctor from Concord, who managed to get the message to the people of his hometown that hundreds of British troops were coming their way to seize their military stores. Although Revere, Dawes, and Prescott had all been captured on the road between Lexington and Concord, Prescott alone staged a successful escape and completed the mission.[21]

Paul Revere was not so alone after all. When the main British column approached Lexington, bells and signal shots echoed from front and rear. The entire countryside was aroused and ready. This wasn't the work of one man but of an intricate web of patriotic activists who had been communicating with each other for years. Ever since the overthrow of British authority late in the summer of 1774 (see chapter 4), they had prepared for military confrontation. Anticipating just such an event as the British assault on Lexington and Concord, they had rehearsed their response. Each man within each town knew whom to contact and where to go once the time came—and now the time had come. Like Paul Revere, myriad patriots sounded their local alarms and readied themselves for action.

AN ENDURING TALE

Facts matter little when a good story is at stake. From the time of its first publication, "Paul Revere's Ride" was a national classic, and readers assumed it signified actual events. Schoolbooks confidently reiterated Longfellow's distortions. According to an 1888 text, *A History of the United States and Its People, for the Use of Schools*, Revere "waited at Charlestown until he saw a light hung in a church-steeple, which was a signal to him that the British were moving." It dutifully cited a source, referring students to "Longfellow's famous poem on the subject."[22] Although some texts noted that the poem was "not strictly historical," others blithely accepted Longfellow's altered plotline. A 1923 text, *History of Our Country, for Higher Grades*, stated fancifully, "On that night there was at Charlestown, across the river from Boston, an American of Huguenot descent holding a horse by the bridle, while he watched for a lantern signal from a church tower. His name was Paul Revere, and he is known as 'the courier of the Revolution.' "[23] Texts in 1935 and 1946 also had Revere waiting for the lantern signal—accompanied for a change by William Dawes, who in fact never went through Charlestown.[24]

Fiction, in conscientious hands, often follows history, but here history unquestionably followed fiction. Even serious scholars fell into line behind the poet. In 1891 John Fiske, one of the most prominent historians of his generation, told how Paul Revere crossed "the broad river in a little boat," then waited "on the farther bank until he learned, from a lantern suspended in the belfry of the North Church, which way the troops had gone."[25]

Starting in the 1920s, iconoclastic "debunkers" poked fun at Longfellow's Revere. William Dawes, one of the other riders, enjoyed something of a renaissance when his descendent Charles Dawes became vice president of the United States under Calvin Coolidge. Traditionalists fought back: in 1922 an army captain, E.B. Lyon, dropped patriotic pamphlets from a military aircraft following the trail of Paul Revere's ride.[26]

The most serious challenge came not from debunkers or Progressive historians, however, but from Progressive educators, who opposed rote memorization. But as recitations of Longfellow's poem began to fade from the standard curricula, Esther Forbes breathed new life into the Revere story with her Pulitzer Prize–winning *Paul Revere and the World He Lived In*. Resuscitated, her Revere is a simple artisan who leads an everyday life. Although Forbes used Revere to celebrate the common man, she reiterated the traditional view that Revere served as the "lone horseman" who saved the day for the patriots.[27]

Not until 1994 were Longfellow's errors laid to rest in David Hackett Fischer's *Paul Revere's Ride*, a masterful work of historical detection that influenced the writing of textbooks in the years that followed. No longer was Revere portrayed as the lonely messenger who rowed himself across the river, waited to receive the lantern signals, and alerted the countryside all by himself. (One notable exception was Joy Hakim's *A History of US*, which still followed Longfellow word for word.[28]) Others were involved, most revised texts stated—but they didn't say it very forcefully. "Paul Revere, a member of the Sons of Liberty, rode his horse to Lexington to warn Hancock and Adams," said one text—then, almost as an afterthought, it added, "Revere was joined by William Dawes and Samuel Prescott."[29] The visual accompaniment, of course, featured a statue of Revere, not Dawes or Prescott. According to another, "*Paul Revere* [emphasis in original], a Boston silversmith, and a second messenger, William Dawes, were charged with spreading the news about British troop movements. . . . When the British moved, so did Revere and Dawes. They galloped over the countryside on their 'midnight ride,' spreading the news."[30] In these watered-down versions, one rider turned into two or three, with Revere always in the lead.[31] The romance was gone, yet there was no hint of the elaborate web of communication that was activated on that momentous night.

Ever since Longfellow's poem, Paul Revere's ride has been part of America's heritage, and no history of our nation's beginnings would dare ignore it. All United States history textbooks at the elementary, middle school, and secondary levels, and the vast majority of college texts as well, still mention Paul Revere's ride, and this includes surveys that undertake no more than a cursory review of the American Revolution.[32] Even texts that evidence no particular desire to pass on the legend must figure a way to mention Revere somehow. According to one current secondary text, "Tipped off by men, including Paul Revere, who had ridden into the countryside to warn of the approaching British troops, the local Patriots rallied to drive the troops back to Boston." Although Longfellow's influence is reduced to a bare minimum, "including Revere" still must make an appearance.[33]

In the last few years, with memory of Fischer's work receding, there has even been a bit of backsliding. One otherwise excellent college text, while trying to broaden the story, inadvertently reverts to the signal lantern ploy, Longfellow's signature distortion: "Alerted by signal lanterns, express riders Paul Revere and William Dawes eluded British patrols and spurred their horses toward Lexington along separate routes to warn Hancock and Adams. Bells and alarm guns spread the word that the British were coming." In fact, neither Revere nor Dawes was alerted by signal lanterns, and most modern texts have long since abandoned "the British were coming" in favor of "the

Regulars were coming," since even the rebels still considered themselves British at that point.[34]

Authors of a middle-school text pass on the legend while technically avoiding a falsehood: "As the troops set out, a signal sent by the Patriots appeared in the steeple of Boston's Old North Church. Two men, Paul Revere and William Dawes, then rode through the night to warn the minutemen." Students reading this passage will of course assume that the two sentences are causally linked and that Revere and Dawes, having seen the signals, set off on their mission. This version, by pulling Dawes into the signal lantern legend, actually magnifies rather that alleviates the error.[35] Another middle-school text, also intent on featuring Dawes, garbles the story entirely: "When Revere and fellow patriot William Dawes saw two lights shine, they set off on horseback. Using two different routes out of Boston, they sounded the alert."[36] Here, both patriots are receiving the signal *within* Boston, undermining the whole purpose of the lanterns, which was to get the news across the Charles River.

Elementary- and middle-school texts still depict Revere on horseback, even if he is not always the only one: "Revere galloped across the moonlit countryside, shouting, 'The regulars are out!' to people along the way."[37] That image excites children and will not die. One current fifth-grade text presents Longfellow's poem in its entirety, then reinforces the basic premise with a question: "CAUSE AND EFFECT—What signal caused Paul Revere to begin his ride?" Then comes a map of Revere's route—no Dawes, no Prescott—and a picture of a statue depicting Revere on his horse, with the steeple of Old North Church rising in the background. "Two lanterns were hung in the church tower to signal British plans to cross the Charles River by boat," the caption says. No fifth grader could possibly doubt, after all this, that Paul Revere and his horse waited impatiently on the opposite shore, just as Longfellow said.[38]

THE FULL PICTURE

The story of "Paul Revere's ride" needs not only correction or disingenuous hedging but also perspective. One hundred twenty-two people lost their lives within hours of Revere's heroics, and almost twice that number were wounded.[39] Revere's ride was not the major event that day, nor was Revere's warning so critical in triggering the bloodbath. Patriotic farmers had been preparing to oppose the British for the better part of a year. Paul Revere himself had contributed to those preparations with other important rides. After the Boston Tea Party, he rode to other seaport cities to spread the news. In May 1774, in response to the Boston Port Act, he rode to Hartford, New York, and Philadelphia to drum up support for his hometown, and that summer he spread the call for a Continental Congress. In September 1774, seven months before his most noted journey, he traveled from Boston to Philadelphia, bearing news that the Massachusetts countryside had erupted in rebellion, and the First Continental Congress, after hearing from Revere, offered its stamp of approval. That December, four months before the shots at Lexington, he instigated the first military offensive of the Revolution by riding to Portsmouth, New Hampshire. On April 7, 1775, eleven days before his most celebrated ride, he rode to Concord (which he reached that time) to warn local patriots to conceal or move their stockpiled military stores because additional troops had arrived in Boston and would soon be making their move. On April 16, with just two days to go, he traveled to Charlestown and Lexington to fine-tune preparations with local leaders, who expected the Regulars to march any day. The ride to Lexington that Longfellow chose to celebrate continued this tradition, but, as in previous rides, it took on meaning only because numerous other political activists had, like Revere, dedicated themselves to the cause.[40]

Paul Revere was one among tens of thousands of patriots from Massachusetts who rose to fight the British. Most of those people lived outside of Boston, and, contrary to the traditional telling, these people were not country cousins to their urban counterparts. They were rebels in their own right, although their story is rarely told. We have neglected them, in part, because Paul Revere's ride has achieved such fame; one man from Boston, the story goes, roused the sleeping farmers, and only then did farmers see the danger and fight back.

In truth, the country folk had aroused themselves, and they had even staged their own revolution more than half a year before (see chapter 4). The story of Paul Revere's ride marks the end, not the beginning, of that inspiring tale. It bridges the gap between two momentous events: the political upheaval that unseated British authority in 1774 and the outbreak of formal hostilities on April 19, 1775. But ironically, in its romanticized form, the tale has helped obscure the revolution of the people that was going on both before and after. The true story of patriotic resistance is deeper and richer than Henry Wadsworth Longfellow, with his emphasis on individual heroics, ever dared to imagine.

2

SAM ADAMS'S MOB

In A. J. Langguth's popular book *Patriots: The Men Who Started the American Revolution*, one patriot stands out from the rest. Samuel Adams is the instigator of every revolutionary event in Boston, while all the other patriots are merely his "recruits," his "legions," his "roster," his "band."[1] *Liberty!*—the companion volume to a PBS series on the American Revolution—proudly proclaims, "Without Boston's Sam Adams, there might never have been an American Revolution."[2] Children's book author Dennis Fradin makes this point even more emphatically: "During the decade before the war began, Samuel Adams was basically a one-man revolution."[3]

Samuel Adams was not always the hero we make him out to be today. "If the American Revolution was a blessing, and not a curse," wrote John Adams, Samuel's cousin, in 1819, "the name and character of Samuel Adams ought to be preserved. A systematic course has been pursued for thirty years to run him down."[4] From Revolutionary times to the middle of the nineteenth century, Boston's most celebrated idol was not Samuel Adams but his close friend and colleague Dr. Joseph Warren, the nation's first martyr. John Trumbull's 1786 painting currently known as *The Battle of Bunker Hill* was in fact titled *The Death of General Warren at the Battle of Bunker's Hill*. These

"Without Boston's Sam Adams,
there might never have been an American Revolution."

Samuel Adams. Engraving based on
John Singleton Copley's portrait, 1772.

days the eminent Dr. Warren is rarely celebrated, while we take considerable pride in our most famous mischief maker, the troublesome Mr. Adams. One modern biography is affectionately titled *Samuel Adams's Revolution, 1765–1776: With the Assistance of George Washington, Thomas Jefferson, Benjamin Franklin, John Adams, George III, and the People of Boston.*

Why the shift? In the aftermath of the War for Independence, Americans were embarrassed by any radical taint, so they did not talk kindly about notorious political activists. But with the passage of time, radicals, like gangsters, can turn into heroes. Contemporary Americans, settled and secure, need not feel threatened by stories of illegal, outlandish activities such as the destruction of shiploads of tea. Indeed, we are titillated by tales of our nation's errant youth. The Boston Tea Party elicits knowing smiles, and Sam Adams, our Revolutionary bad boy and favorite rabble-rouser, brings forth fond feelings.

Ironically, this troublemaker imbues the American Revolution with design and purpose. There are two key components to his mythic story: he advocated independence many years before anybody else dared entertain the notion, and he worked the people of Boston into a frenzy to achieve his goal. These are not incidental to our telling of the American Revolution; our view of the nation's conception leans heavily upon them. Because Adams supposedly had the foresight to envision independence, we are able to perceive the tumultuous crowd actions in pre-Revolutionary Boston as connected, coherent events pointing toward an ultimate break from England. Without this element of personal intent, the rebellion would be a mindless muddle, purely reactive, with no sense of mission. Without an author, the script becomes unwieldy; without a director, the crowd becomes unruly—but Sam Adams, mastermind of independence, keeps the Revolution on cue. He wrote the script, directed the cast, and staged a masterful performance.

The beauty of the story is that Adams was not some autocrat, remote and aloof from the people he directed. He was one of the crowd—one of *us*. Perhaps that is why we like to call Samuel "Sam," although only his enemies called him that during his lifetime. Even John Adams referred to his cousin as "Mr. Samuel Adams," "Mr. Adams," or by way of abbreviation, "Mr. S. Adams" or "Mr. Sam. Adams," following the custom of the times, as in "Wm." for "William."[5] (In this book, "Sam" denotes the legend, "Samuel" the historical person.) Unlike many a Revolutionary patriarch, he was supposedly at home on the streets, mixing with the people, raising toasts in the taverns. How fitting that his face now adorns no coins or bills—only a bottle of beer.

Sam Adams, who both represents and controls the crowd, allows us to celebrate "the people." Or so it would seem. In fact, while the Sam Adams story appears to celebrate the people, it does not take them seriously. That's why the story was first invented by Adams's Tory adversaries, who wrote "the people" out of the script by placing Adams—a single, diabolical villain—in charge of all popular unrest. To understand the damaging implications of the Sam Adams story, and to see how it distorts what really happened in Revolutionary Boston, we have to examine its genesis.

THE TORIES' TALE

Not wanting to grant legitimacy to any form of protest, conservatives in the 1760s and 1770s maintained that all the troubles in Boston were the machinations of a single individual. In the words of Peter Oliver, the Crown-appointed chief justice who was later exiled, the people themselves "were like the Mobility of all Countries, perfect Machines, wound up by any Hand who might first take the Winch." Mindless and incapable of acting on their own, they needed a director who could "fabricate the Structure of Rebellion from a single straw."[6]

According to this mechanistic view, one man led and everyone else followed. At the outset, that master of manipulation was not Samuel Adams but James Otis Jr. According to Oliver, the mentally deranged Otis had vowed in 1761 "that if his Father was not appointed a Justice of the superior Court, he would set the Province in a Flame." This he proceeded to do, using the unruly yet pliable Boston rabble to fight his battle.[7] Thomas Hutchinson, the man who was chosen over James Otis Sr., told a similar tale, although less bombastically than Oliver.[8]

When Otis's insanity rendered him ineffectual, the role of puppeteer was supposedly assumed by Samuel Adams, who was also motivated by family loyalty: his father had been defeated in the progressive Land Bank scheme many years before, and Samuel vowed to seek justice by deposing the regime that terminated his father's dreams. Early on, according to Oliver and Hutchinson, Adams decided to foster a revolution that would lead to independence. The Stamp Act riots in 1765, the *Liberty* riot in 1768, the resistance to occupying soldiers, the Boston Massacre in 1770, the Tea Party in 1773, and various lesser-known demonstrations were all orchestrated by Samuel Adams, master Revolutionary strategist.

"His Power over weak Minds was truly surprising," wrote Oliver. Some of the "weak Minds" manipulated by Adams were those of lower-class Bostonians:

> [H]e understood human Nature, in low life, so well, that he could turn the Minds of the great Vulgar as well as the small into any Course that he might chuse . . . & he never failed of employing his Abilities to the vilest Purposes.

But the puppets whose strings he pulled also included Boston's most illustrious patriots, people like John Hancock:

> Mr. Hancock . . . was as closely attached to the hindermost Part of Mr. Adams as the Rattles are affixed to the Tail of the Rattle Snake. . . . His mind was a meer *Tabula Rasa*, & had he met with a good Artist he would have enstamped upon it such Character as would have made him a most useful Member of Society. But Mr. Adams who was restless in endeavors to disturb ye Peace of

> Society, & who was ever going about seeking whom he might devour, seized upon him as his Prey, & stamped such Lessons upon his Mind, as have not as yet been erased.[9]

By attributing all rebellious events first to Otis and then to Adams, disgruntled Tories like Oliver and Hutchinson exhibited the classic conservative denial of social protest: the people, if left to their own devices, will never rise up on their own. Without ringleaders, organizers, rabble-rousers, troublemakers, or outside agitators, the status quo will not be challenged because nothing is basically wrong. All protests and rebellions can be dismissed; demands and grievances need never be taken seriously.

It's easy to see why his Tory adversaries cast Samuel Adams in the leading role. Adams was a marvelous politician in every respect, equally at home in political chambers and on the Boston waterfront. An accomplished writer, he demonstrated his mastery of the art of political polemic in a steady stream of articles published in the local newspapers. He could also wheel and deal behind the scenes. As an influential member of the Boston caucus, he exerted considerable influence on the selection of local officers and the direction of the town meeting; as clerk of the Massachusetts House of Representatives, he figured prominently in that body's continuing resistance to the dictates of Crown-appointed governors. He was, in sum, an extremely effective partisan of the "popular party," and this caused his opponents in the "court party" (also called the "government party") great consternation. In the words of a contemporary Bostonian, John Andrews: "The ultimate wish and desire of the high Government party is to get Samuel Adams out of the way when they think they may accomplish every of their plans."[10]

To get Adams "out of the way," his adversaries called him a traitor. On January 25, 1769, a Tory informer named Richard Sylvester swore in an affidavit that seven months earlier, the day after a large crowd had protested the seizure of John Hancock's ship *Liberty*, he had overheard Adams say to a group of seven men on the street, "If you are men, behave like men. Let us take up arms immediately and be free and seize all the King's officers." Later, Sylvester claimed, Adams had said during one of his many visits to his home, "We will destroy every soldier that dare put foot on shore. His majesty has no right to send troops here to invade the country. I look upon them as foreign enemies." [11]

Sylvester's trumped-up allegations were sent to London, but the evidence appeared questionable, and the charge of treason was not upheld.[12] Sylvester's testimony was then archived; many years later, in the middle of the nineteenth century, the preeminent historian George Bancroft uncovered the affidavit, accepted it as fact, and repeated it word for word, no questions asked: "[Adams] reasoned that it would be just to destroy every soldier whose foot should touch the shore. 'The king,' he would say, 'has no right to send troops here to invade the country; if they come, they will come as foreign enemies.' " [13] Historians ever since have taken Bancroft at face value, just as Bancroft accepted Sylvester, and those snippets from Sylvester are repeated verbatim, as if they came from Adams himself, in textbooks, popular histories, and on the Internet today.[14] This discredited accusation continues to provide the basic "documentation" that Adams was a hellfire revolutionary, "Godfather" to the "mob," inciting riots at every available opportunity.

SAM ADAMS'S REVOLUTION

Based on the word of his Tory foes, we have granted Samuel Adams superhuman powers. This one man, we say, set Boston all ablaze—but the historical record tells a different story. Consider the various Sam Adams tales that have emerged over the years.

Stamp Act Riots: "Adams's Waterfront Gang"

In 1765 Boston crowds gathered on two different occasions to protest the new stamp tax. On August 14, a crowd of approximately three thousand colonists burned an effigy of the tax collector, Andrew

Oliver, and destroyed his office. Twelve nights later, a more violent crowd demolished the home of the wealthy Tory official Thomas Hutchinson. Following the lead of Hutchinson and other contemporary Tories, modern writers attribute these mob actions to "Adams's waterfront gang." According to William Hallahan in *The Day the American Revolution Began*, Sam Adams "had his revenge on Hutchinson for humiliating his father."[15] In fact, Adams had nothing to do with either event. He approved of the August 14 demonstration after the fact, but he did not organize it—that was the work of the Loyal Nine, a group of Boston activists that did not include Adams. He was appalled by the riot of August 26 because of its "truly *mobbish* Nature," and he acted swiftly "to assist the Majistrate to their utmost in preventing or suppressing any further Disorder."[16]

Boston Massacre: "An Adams-Inspired Mob"

In *Red Dawn at Lexington*, author Louis Birnbaum states that the confrontation that resulted in the Boston Massacre was the work of "an Adams-inspired mob."[17] A 2012 college textbook takes this one step further: the city's entire population, "some 15,000 Bostonians," was "under the sway of Samuel Adams," making a confrontation with soldiers "nearly inevitable."[18]

There is nothing in the historical record, however, that suggests Adams had anything to do with the seamen, laborers, and apprentices who threw snowballs at British soldiers and taunted them to shoot. Adams did become involved in the aftermath of the massacre. The Boston town meeting demanded that royal officials remove two regiments from the city to an island in Boston Harbor, and it appointed Adams to serve as one of its spokesmen. When the military commander offered to remove one regiment, Adams responded: "If he could remove the 29th regiment, he could remove the 14th also, and it was at his peril to refuse." According to Thomas Hutchinson, acting as governor at the time, Adams said that if the troops were not removed, "the rage of the people would vent itself"—not just against the soldiers, but against Hutchinson "in particular."[19] Later writers and historians have used this incident, as reported by Hutchinson, to prove the immense powers of Samuel Adams, for the troops did leave, and they labeled the departing Redcoats "Samuel Adams's Regiments," a term coined for political purposes back in London.[20] In truth, as Adams himself would be the first to observe, Hutchinson relented not because of one man's words, but because he feared "the rage of the people" who awaited his response.

Boston Tea Party: "The Signal"

On December 16, 1773, as three ships sat in the harbor laden with tea, several thousand angry patriots gathered in Boston's Old South Meeting House to figure out what to do. Late in the day, Francis Rotch, beleaguered owner of one of the tea-laden ships in the harbor, announced that Governor Hutchinson remained firm and would not allow his vessel to return to Britain with its cargo still on board. At that moment, Sam Adams climbed on top of a bench and announced to the crowd: "This meeting can do nothing more to save the country." According to the mythic story, everybody knew what he meant: that was the "signal" for the "Tea Party" to begin. "Instant pandemonium broke out amid cheers, yells, and war whoops," one recent narrative declares. "The crowd poured out of the Old South Meeting [House] and headed for Griffin's Wharf."[21]

This story, now included in virtually every narrative of the Boston Tea Party (including my own *People's History of the American Revolution*, published in 2001), was fabricated ninety-two years later to promote the image of an all-powerful Sam Adams, in firm control of the Boston crowd. According to several eyewitness accounts, Adams did in fact state "that he could think of nothing further to be done," but this was not some "signal," for the timing was way off. According to several eyewitness accounts, not until ten or fifteen minutes later did Indian yells trigger an exodus, and even at that point Adams and others tried to stem the tide, quiet the crowd, and continue the meeting.[22]

George Bancroft, writing in 1854, condensed the timeline of the source information, leaving out those ten or fifteen minutes: "Samuel

Adams rose and gave the word: 'This meeting can do nothing more to save the country.' On the instant, a cry was heard at the porch; the war-whoop resounded; a body of men, forty or fifty in number, disguised and clad in blankets as Indians, each holding a hatchet, passed by the door; and encouraged by Samuel Adams, Hancock, and others, and increased on the way to near two hundred, marched two by two to Griffin's Wharf."[23] The foreshortened narrative both heightened the drama and hinted at an element of causality.

A few years later, in 1865, William V. Wells, Adams's first biographer, took Bancroft's hint and created what would ever after be accepted as dogma: Adams's statement was "the signal for the Boston Tea Party," he pronounced definitively. "Instantly a shout was heard at a door of the church from those who had been intently listening for the voice of Adams. The war whoop resounded. Forty or fifty men disguised as Indians, who must have been concealed near by, appeared and passed by the church entrance, and, encouraged by Adams, Hancock, and others, hurried along to Griffin's, now Liverpool Wharf." This is the ultimate Sam Adams story—the people of Boston had been trained to follow a secret, coded message issued by their master—and Americans have been telling it ever since.[24]

The Architect of Independence

Some say 1765, others 1768, but nearly all popular renditions of the Sam Adams story state categorically that he favored independence several years before it was declared in 1776 and long before any other patriot entertained such a notion.[25] This is what supposedly made him such an effective leader—he had a vision and stuck to it. This is also why we promote him as our hero: he gives force and direction to the saga that terminates with the birth of a new nation. According to his own writings, however, Samuel Adams did not advocate independence until the winter of 1775–1776, the same time many others started favoring it. Following the lead of historian Pauline Maier, we can trace Adams's record on the issue of independence:[26]

- In 1765 Adams argued that the colonists were and always had been "good Subjects" who had "brought with them all the Rights & Laws of the Mother State"; they had never made any "Claim of Independency," he boasted, despite their geographic isolation.[27] At that time, there was no reason that Adams and his fellow colonists would even consider abandoning the country they deemed to be the freest in the world.

- In 1768, when British troops started occupying Boston, Adams wrote forcefully that colonists should be "restored to the rights, privileges and immunities of *free subjects.*"[28] Boston's problems, he asserted, were caused "by the Vile insinuations of wicked men *in America*"—not by any structural irregularities of the British Constitution.[29]

- In 1771 Adams argued, "By our compact with our King, wherein is contain'd the rule of his government and the measure of our submission, we have all the liberties and immunities of Englishmen. . . . It is our duty therefore to contend for them whenever attempts are made to violate them."[30]

- In 1773 Adams still clung to the notion that problems with the British government stemmed from "a few men born & educated amongst us, & governd by Avarice & a Lust of power." If these men—people like Thomas Hutchinson and Peter Oliver—could be "removed from his Majesty's Service and Confidence here," peace might be restored.[31]

- In 1774, writing from the First Continental Congress, Adams urged Joseph Warren, his associate in Boston, to oppose country radicals who were moving "to set up another form

> of government." Even at this late date, and while writing to his closest compatriot, he dismissed as "groundless" the charges that Adams, Warren, and other Boston patriots were aiming at "a total independency."[32]

Not until patriots and Redcoats had engaged in pitched battles for the better part of a year did Samuel Adams publicly advocate a total break from Britain.[33] By this time, as Adams himself stated, declaring independence was something of a moot point. We have no way of ascertaining when he privately started wishing for independence. Even if it was sooner than his public pronouncements indicate, his increasing radicalization probably stemmed from his frustration with British obstinacy, not from a grand vision he possessed at the outset of resistance to imperial authority.

The Man Who Made a Revolution

Sam Adams gives our Revolution some punch. The rest of the famous patriots, Patrick Henry and Tom Paine excepted, come across as cautious, rational men. Most were also very rich. These dignitaries make honorable founders but poor revolutionaries—and so we turn to Sam Adams, an allegedly true incendiary.

The real Samuel Adams does not live up to the image of a flaming revolutionary. Throughout a political career that spanned four decades, he opposed violent acts that threatened a well-ordered society:

- In 1765 Adams forcefully condemned the riots on the night of August 26, which destroyed private property. At the town meeting that followed, he agreed with the "universal Consternation" and "Detestation" of the event.[34]

- In 1768, in response to crowd action induced by the seizure of John Hancock's vessel, *Liberty*, Adams wrote in the *Boston Gazette*: "I am no friend to '*Riots, Tumults and unlawful Assemblies.*' "[35] Further, he argued that most colonists were "*orderly* and *peaceable* inhabitants" whose only aim was to enjoy the rights of Englishmen. Had Adams abandoned this stance in 1768, he would have confirmed Sylvester's claims and lost his political effectiveness.[36]

- In 1773 Adams told a compatriot, "I have long feard that this unhappy Contest between Britain & America will end in Rivers of Blood. . . . [I]t is the highest prudence to prevent if possible so dreadful a Calamity." This was a private correspondence that likely reflected his true feelings, not a public pronouncement in which he would have to be circumspect. A deeply religious Christian, Adams did not see "Rivers of Blood" as an optimum solution to the escalating conflict.[37]

- In 1774 Adams counseled his friend James Warren "to avoid Blood and Tumult" and to oppose "Rash Spirits" who would "by their Impetuosity involve us in unsurmountable Difficulties."[38]

- In 1776 Adams pronounced with great pleasure that independence had been achieved "without great internal Tumults & violent Convulsions."[39]

- In 1780 Adams served on a three-man committee that drafted a constitution for Massachusetts. While the House of Representatives, elected by the people with a minimal property requirement for the franchise, was and should be "purely democratic," he said, representatives were prone to excessive "passions and whims." The house must therefore be held in check by the "moderating power" of the senate, the governor, and his council, and that is why he supported an executive veto. This was not the stance of a revolutionary populist.[40]

- In 1786 and 1787 Adams advocated the suppression of a popular uprising of farmers and debtors, labeled by its enemies "Shays' Rebellion" after one of its many leaders. As president of the state senate, he pushed to suspend writs of habeas corpus. Afterward, when many of his contemporaries advocated leniency, Adams wanted to hang the rebels. Again in 1794, Adams endorsed the quashing of a popular insurrection in western Pennsylvania and neighboring states, tagged by Alexander Hamilton the "Whiskey Rebellion" to denigrate the rebels. In a republican government, he proclaimed, people should never break the laws, but work to change them by legal means—again, hardly a revolutionary position.

- In the 1790s Samuel Adams served three terms as governor of Massachusetts. He made no great waves during his tenure in office; instead, he continued to proclaim, as he always had, that piety and virtue were the essential ingredients of public life. Biographies, textbooks, and popular histories routinely ignore the later years of Adams's political life, which they cannot bend to fit the profile of a revolutionary.

Samuel Adams never advocated "revolution" in the modern sense, a complete overthrow of the government and a radical restructuring of the social order. He was indeed a "revolutionary" in the parlance of the times—a firm believer in the values promoted by England's Glorious Revolution of 1688, which rooted sovereignty in the people rather than in a monarch—but we read history backward when we superimpose later meanings onto earlier times.[41]

FROM SAMUEL TO SAM

Except in the minds of Tories, Samuel Adams was not perceived at the time as a one-man revolution, directing the entire affair. People did see him as a hard-hitting political force, an effective member of the radical caucus both in Boston and at the Continental Congress, but he was one among several. David Ramsay, in his two-volume history of the Revolution written in 1789, mentioned Adams three times: first, with Hancock, as one of the two men excluded by a British offer of pardon; next in a list of fifty-six signers of the Declaration of Independence; and finally as one of the twenty-two "most distinguished writers in favour of the rights of America." The cast was large, although it certainly included Adams.[42]

School texts and popular histories in the first half of the nineteenth century did not include Samuel Adams on their rosters of Revolutionary leaders; insofar as they used any radical figure to drive the story forward, they called on Patrick Henry instead. In his multivolume American history published in midcentury, however, George Bancroft placed Adams front and center, as of course did William Wells in his popular 1865 Adams biography. Drawing on Bancroft and Wells, textbook writers of the late nineteenth and early twentieth centuries depicted Adams as the prime mover of the Revolution.[43] He labored "for twelve years" to achieve independence," one said, and after that "his great work was done."[44] In this view, independence marked the end of Samuel Adams's tumultuous political career: "Although he could destroy, he did not know how to build up a state, and after 1776 he lived the most part in private, except for a brief period as governor of Massachusetts."[45] In fact, after independence Adams served until 1781 in the Continental Congress, helped draft the Articles of Confederation and the Massachusetts constitution, and then served four years as president of the Massachusetts state senate, three as lieutenant governor, and another three as governor—but in the popular imagination, he would be defined exclusively as a flamboyant revolutionary who could only tear things down.

The misreading reached its zenith with John Miller, who used the diminutive for Samuel in the title to his influential biography *Sam Adams: Pioneer in Propaganda*. Writing in the 1930s, Miller based his portrait on a conception of revolution current at the time. Since "Sam" was allegedly a rabble-rouser, he was "by nature . . . passionate, excitable, and violent." This "notorious riot lover . . . continually drenched the country with propaganda." He "summoned" the town meeting "for whatever purpose he chose." Citing Sylvester's charges as fact, Miller wrote that Adams was active in the streets, haranguing listeners "to make a bold attack upon the royal government." (According to other American statesmen at the time, Samuel Adams was not much for public speaking and would have made a poor soapbox orator; although he could certainly write and politick, he was "not very eloquent or Talkative," "neither an eloquent nor easy speaker," and "not a Demosthenes in oratory."[46]) In Miller's view, Adams's command over the people was absolute: "Boston was controlled by a trained mob and . . . Sam Adams was its keeper." By this reading, one man alone was responsible for all the unrest; the others were "brought into the revolutionary movement against their own . . . wishes."[47]

Miller's distortion of the historical Samuel Adams, like Longfellow's misrepresentation of Paul Revere, had long-lasting consequences. From the mid–twentieth century onward, meshing neatly with Cold War conceptions of revolution, it influenced not only biographical treatments of a key political figure in Boston but also the very nature and meaning of the American Revolution. Thomas A. Bailey, in his popular textbook *American Pageant*, first published in 1956, portrayed Adams as a "master propagandist and engineer of rebellion" who "appealed effectively to what was called his 'trained mob.' " (The passive voice, "was called," concealed too much: it was John Miller, echoing Adams's Tory adversaries at the time, who painted the image of Adams training his mob.) The index listing for this mastermind of revolution was "Adams, Samuel, agitator." Adams's "singular contribution," Bailey wrote, was to form local committees of correspondence in Massachusetts:

> Their chief function was to spread propaganda and information. . . . One critic referred to the committees as "the foulest, subtlest, and most venomous serpent ever issued from

> the egg of sedition." No more effective device for stimulating resistance could have been contrived, and later revolutionists have adopted some of its underground techniques in establishing "cells."[48]

Here Bailey turned history on its head. The Massachusetts committees of correspondence, organized in 1772 not by Samuel Adams alone but by a cadre of patriot activists, were hardly underground groups, prototypes of Communist cells. Quite the reverse. Earlier attempts to organize committees of correspondence had withered because they were merely private clubs, with no standing and no lasting organizational structure. This time, Adams and others cleverly piggybacked them onto existing town meetings, the local governing bodies of Massachusetts. Each town meeting appointed its committee of correspondence, which would communicate with other such committees and report back to the town. As public bodies, they could (and did) broaden the base of activists and serve as an infrastructure first for resistance and then for revolution. Finally, once British authority had vanished, these public committees, with members duly appointed by their town meetings, gathered to form a de facto government, the Massachusetts Provincial Congress. This was the dynamic of revolution in Massachusetts, not one man manipulating his trained mob and creating "underground" cells.[49]

Bailey's distortion of history was not limited to Massachusetts. The American Revolution, in fact a complex alliance of commercial interests (both South and North) and popular movements (both urban and rural), was in his view "engineered" by just "a militant minority of American radicals," with Sam Adams and a handful of other rabble-rousers calling all the shots. While denigrating revolution, he projected a simplistic view of how history works: even popular movements are said to be the work of just a few special individuals.[50]

That was in 1956. Today, in its fifteenth edition (2014), *American Pageant* offers much the same message. For the first time, Bailey's name no longer appears on the cover or the title page, but the words are his, verbatim: "master propagandist," "engineer of rebellion," "trained mob," "most venomous serpent," and so on. Only the one line about underground cells has been dropped, due perhaps to the demise of the Cold War and Communist "cells." Further, despite a half century of scholarship demonstrating otherwise, the book still states point-blank that the Revolution was "engineered" by "a militant minority of American radicals."[51]

Such distortions, which persist to this day, go back to the days preceding independence, when Adams's Tory adversaries were trying to discredit him. "Without Boston's Sam Adams, there might never have been an American Revolution," the Tories once said, and today we are saying it again.[52] This is not a good sign. The reason we can pass off Tory tales as truth is that we have unconsciously adopted their way of looking at political processes. The Tory way of thinking, which still holds sway, sees common people as "perfect Machines" who need someone with greater intelligence and drive to tell them what to do. One man leads and the rest follow adoringly.[53] A comic book sold in gift shops along Boston's Freedom Trail portrays Adams speaking to a crowd on two different occasions, and each time the crowd responds: "Adams is right!" This is the face of popular protest fostered by Sam Adams mythologies.[54]

A COLLECTIVE AFFAIR

Bostonians had all sorts of reasons to oppose British policies, and they did not need Samuel Adams to set them in motion.

Merchant-smugglers like John Rowe, William Molineaux, Solomon Davis, Melatiah Bourne, Edward Payne, and William Cooper had much to gain by opposing British mercantile policies that restricted free trade. These men, articulate and politically effective, were certainly capable of acting on their own behalf—in fact, they had been doing so for several years before Samuel Adams ascended to a position of influence in 1765. Five years earlier, they had organized themselves into the Boston Society for Encouraging Trade and

Commerce, which sent numerous petitions to Parliament. During the nonimportation movement of 1768, a resurgent group called Merchants and Traders emerged to promote the collective interests of its members. "We feel for the Mother Country as well as our selves," wrote Cooper, "but charity begins at home."[55] In 1770 this proactive organization evolved into a third group, the Body of the Trade, which reached out to include all those in town with a stake in trade issues, but Samuel Adams was not an acknowledged leader.[56]

During the Stamp Act riots, Boston's lower classes had their own motivations for ransacking the home of Thomas Hutchinson, who justified poverty because it produced "industry and frugality." According to William Gordon, "Gentlemen of the army, who have seen towns sacked by an enemy, declare they never before saw an instance of such fury."[57] This fury was their own, not Adams's.

Starting in 1768, laborers and seamen had personal reasons for resenting the presence of British Regulars in their midst. Troops routinely stopped them in the streets, roughing them up or demanding swigs of rum. Off-duty privates competed with local workers for employment on the docks. Little wonder that these people jeered the Redcoats whenever they could.

Longshoremen and sailors had good reasons for opposing British restrictions of trade. Shipping was the backbone of Boston's economy; if the ships didn't sail, "Jack Tar" would have no work. Little wonder that ordinary men who wanted jobs responded to the confiscation of the *Liberty* or the monopolization of the tea trade by British interests.

These people did not take orders from a single authoritarian leader. Patriots worked with each other in a wide array of activist groups and political organizations, and every one of these groups engaged in collaborative processes. The Boston Caucus had been meeting since the 1720s to promote candidates who were sympathetic with popular issues, such an increased availability of hard currency; by the 1770s scores of citizens were active in three caucuses, one each for North, Middle, and South Boston. In 1765 the Loyal Nine, a group of artisans and shopkeepers who met in Speakman's distillery, expanded into a group calling itself the Sons of Liberty, which met in John Marston's tavern; together with similar groups in other colonies, this group formed a fledgling infrastructure for coordinated resistance.[58] Throughout the 1760s and 1770s, the St. Andrews Lodge of Freemasons met in the Green Dragon Tavern to discuss politics and plan political actions. Like the Sons of Liberty, the community of Masons helped give some sense of cohesion and purpose to colonial unrest.

Although Samuel Adams is not known to have been a member of the groups meeting in Marston's tavern or the Green Dragon Tavern, he did belong to the Long Room Club, a group of seventeen patriots, mostly professionals, who met above the printing press of John Gill and Benjamin Edes, publishers of the patriotic *Boston Gazette*. He was also one of the founders of the Boston Committee of Correspondence, which joined with similar groups in other Massachusetts towns and other colonies to carry the torch of resistance in the 1770s. Garry Wills, one of the most respected minds of recent times, calls the committees of correspondence Adams's "own wire service,"[59] but this organization, like all the others, brought together many dedicated and talented patriots in common cause: James Warren, among the first to suggest the idea; Joseph Warren, a doctor from Harvard with great rhetorical flair; Josiah Quincy, a talented young lawyer; Joseph Greenleaf, a printer who had called the presence of British troops in Boston "an open declaration of war" against liberty; and Thomas Young, a flamboyant political activist who urged resistance at every turn.[60]

Many other tradesmen, artisans, and laborers met in the taverns of Boston to engage in collective action. Butchers, bakers, and leatherworkers sent petitions to the General Court and Boston's selectmen. Daily, during their 11:00 a.m. break, shipyard workers gathered in taverns and in the streets to talk over the state of affairs. These people, working in concert, had become political actors.[61]

All these people, and many more, came together for the Boston town meeting, the local governing organization that invited the participation of "the whole body of the people"; during the height of Revolutionary fervor, this came to include apprentices and others who were not granted the formal right to vote. Each year, the town meeting elected representatives to the Massachusetts House of Representatives, and each year these men were handed specific instructions, approved by the town meeting, as to how they should respond to the key issues of the day.[62]

The entire edifice was heavily weighted at the bottom. This was a politicized population, and that was part of the problem: British officials and local Tories found it difficult to accept, or even comprehend, the degree of popular participation in politics in Revolutionary Boston.[63]

Samuel Adams functioned within this framework. He was one of the leaders of the Boston Caucus, the Long Room Club, and the committees of correspondence. He sometimes served as moderator for the town meeting. From his position as clerk of the House of Representatives he wielded considerable power at the provincial level. More a polemicist than a street leader, he drafted many letters and resolutions, giving sentiments that were shared by many a concrete expression. He was intelligent, dedicated, persuasive, and savvy—an effective activist and master politician.[64] But Adams did not run the show, because nobody could. Revolutionary Boston did not function that way—and no self-respecting patriot, certainly not Samuel Adams, *wanted* it to function that way.

Royal officials and Tories never did grasp the Revolutionaries' distinction between "the body of the people" and a mindless mob. Because they knew no other way, they interpreted Boston's politics as a top-down chain of command. In the process, they transformed Samuel Adams into a detestable demon. Now, we honor the mythological figure his enemies created.

Mercy Otis Warren—sister of James Otis, wife of James Warren, political colleague and personal friend of Samuel Adams—knew very well that Adams owed much of his renown to the fuss made by his enemies. When General Gage singled out Adams and Hancock for proscription in 1775, she claimed, he revealed his great ignorance of "the temper of the times, the disposition of the people at large, [and] the character of the individuals":

> His discrimination, rather accidental than judicious, set these two gentlemen in the most conspicuous point of view, and drew the particular attention of the whole continent to their names, distinguished from many of their compeers, more by this single circumstance, than by superior ability or exertion. By this they became at once the favorites of popularity, and the objects of general applause, which at that time would have been the fortune of any one, honored by such a mark of disapprobation of the British commander in chief.[65]

Warren seemed amused that Adams's enemies made him into a hero—but she had no way of foreseeing that people like Gage and Hutchinson would blind later generations of Americans to the importance of democratic political behavior during the Revolutionary era. Passionately committed to the idea that government must be rooted in the people, Mercy Otis Warren, Samuel Adams, and the rest of Boston's patriots would be quite surprised to learn that America's "patriotic" history would be told centuries later from a Tory perspective.

3

MOLLY PITCHER'S CANNON

How nice it would be to discover a true heroine of the American Revolution. We have tried Betsy Ross, the woman who supposedly made the first American flag, but that story has been thoroughly discredited by serious historians.[1] We honor Abigail Adams, who cajoled her husband to "Remember the Ladies," but Abigail enters the story as the wife of a famous man, and she never went near a battlefield.[2] We would like to celebrate Deborah Sampson, who dressed as a man to enlist in the army, but if truth be told, some female soldiers were unjustly drummed out to the "whore's march" once their identity was uncovered.[3]

Our preferred heroine, if we could find her, would have braved enemy fire in a famous battle—dressed as a woman, not a man. This is not too much to imagine. Try to picture, for instance, the Battle of Monmouth, where men are suffering from the heat as well as from enemy fire. A woman passes through the thirsty and wounded troops with a pitcher of nice, cold water. Perhaps, when her husband falls while manning a cannon, our heroine takes his place and continues to fire his weapon. This, of course, inspires the rest of the soldiers to continue fighting in the face of mortal danger. In the end, after the

"Her cannon must be fired!"

Molly Pitcher, Heroine at Monmouth.
Lithograph by Currier and Ives, 1876.

battle is over, George Washington naturally bestows a medal on our lady warrior—perhaps even making her an officer.

This is the heroine we would like to celebrate—and we do. We have not only dreamed up such a tale, but we have convinced ourselves it is true. Although it would have shocked all her contemporaries, a recent middle-school textbook pronounces point-blank that Mary Ludwig Hays, a poor "camp follower" from Carlisle, Pennsylvania, was the "best known" woman to serve on Revolutionary War battlefields.[4] Another text tells her story: "Mary Ludwig Hays McCauly took her husband's place at a cannon when he was wounded at the Battle of Monmouth. Known for carrying pitchers of water to the soldiers, McCauley won the nickname 'Molly Pitcher.' Afterward, General Washington made her a noncommissioned officer for her brave deeds."[5] A third text shows a picture of two women soldiers, one wearing a long dress and the other clad in modern military fatigues. The captions read, "Past: Molly Pitcher" and "Present: Women marines served in the Gulf War."[6]

We have made Molly Pitcher, a folk legend, into a real person. The legend started in the mid–nineteenth century, receded slightly in the mid–twentieth century, but then staged a dramatic comeback in the past quarter century, filling the demand to include more women in history texts. Out of six elementary- and middle-school texts published in the early twenty-first century, five include the story of Molly Pitcher, and four feature vivid pictures, including one of Molly's dress flowing in the wind as she plunges a ramrod into a cannon.[7] These images were painted in the mid–to late nineteenth century; now, thanks to high-quality color reproduction, they provide our textbooks with visual "evidence" of a female presence in the Revolutionary War. Because these paintings appear quaint and old-fashioned, any differences between the Revolutionary and Victorian eras are easily overlooked. The key concept—what really excited the artists—is the juxtaposition of masculine and feminine imagery: a figure bearing prominent female features (in some of the paintings, Molly's breasts are partially exposed) braves the grit of the battlefield to master the ramrod and cannon. If a real woman can fight like this, these artists tell us, real men can hardly fail to follow suit.[8]

One volume of Macmillan's "Famous Americans Series," intended for a juvenile audience, reveals Molly Pitcher's perfect blend of masculine and feminine virtues. Just as thirsty soldiers at Monmouth were beginning to give up hope, they heard a woman speak:

> "Let me give you a drink," said a voice. "I'll hold up your head. Come, now, drink from my pitcher." They drank and lived. Then other fallen soldiers drank from that pitcher. And others and others until it was empty.
>
> "I will get more," the woman said. "The well is near. It is just across the road. Call me if you want another drink. Just say, 'Molly'—I will come to you."
>
> The sick men whispered her name to others. Before long many feeble voices were calling, "Molly! Molly! Pitcher! Pitcher!" Sometimes these calls were just "Molly Pitcher, Molly Pitcher." . . .
>
> A hundred fallen men were kept alive by that water. Some were able to fight again. All blessed the woman who saved them.

When her husband was also overcome by the heat, the story continues, Molly volunteered to fire his cannon in his place:

> The bullets fell around Molly. But she swabbed and loaded and fired. The hot sun blazed down on her, but she swabbed and loaded and fired.
>
> Her dress was black from gunpowder. There were smudges on her face and hands. She paid no attention. Her cannon must be fired!

Once the battle had ended, the commander in chief himself honored the army's new heroine:

General Washington took her powder-stained hand in his. He smiled at her and spoke kindly. "Mrs. Hays, the courage you showed yesterday has never been equaled by any woman. Your kindness has never been surpassed. You were an angel of mercy to suffering men. You were a pillar of strength at the cannon, with the skill of an experienced gunner. . . . Therefore, I make you a sergeant in this army. And I now pin this badge of honor upon you."

There was silence until this was over. Then a thousand soldiers began to cheer.

"Hooray for Sergeant Molly!" they cried. "Hooray for Molly Pitcher!"[9]

Here is the tale writ large. In this children's biography, Molly Pitcher takes her place beside Abraham Lincoln, Albert Einstein, Babe Ruth, and thirty other "famous Americans" featured in the same series. There is one significant difference, however, between Molly Pitcher and the others: all the rest were real people, while Molly is only a myth.

FROM CAPTAIN MOLLY TO MOLLY PITCHER

Molly Pitcher was a long time in the making. Nobody in Revolutionary times would have imagined General Washington taking the hand of a female camp follower with the Continental Army (not even a private soldier) and instantaneously making her an officer. And a common woman from Carlisle, who scrubbed houses and public buildings for several decades after the war and died without great fanfare, had no idea she would someday become "Molly Pitcher," the "best known" woman to serve in the Revolution.[10] On the other hand, contemporaries of the Revolutionary War did not have to imagine women hauling water in pails and buckets to quench men's thirst and cool the cannons; such people existed and were part and parcel of the war effort.

At least one camp follower did assume the place of her husband on an artillery team, but not at Monmouth. At Fort Washington on November 16, 1776, Margaret Corbin stood in for her husband John, who had just been killed. Margaret herself was wounded by grapeshot during the battle, and she lost the use of one arm for the rest of her life. She later became part of the "Invalid Regiment" at West Point, and on July 6, 1779, the Supreme Council of Pennsylvania awarded a lifetime pension, "one-half of the monthly pay drawn by a soldier," to the woman who had been "wounded and disabled in the attack on Fort Washington, while she heroically filled the post of her husband who was killed by her side serving a piece of artillery." [11] Corbin, it seems, picked up the nickname Captain Molly; two years after the Invalid Regiment disbanded, military records reveal that the government provided "Captain Molly" with such items as a "bed-sack" and an "old common tent." [12]

Unlike the imagined Molly Pitcher, this Captain Molly was flesh and blood—too much so, in fact, to make a good story. In the mid-nineteenth century, as the Revolution was receding from living memory, Benson Lossing tried to resurrect it by identifying the real people, places, and artifacts surviving from that time. While traveling to the Hudson Highlands near West Point, Lossing talked to three informants who claimed to have known or seen a woman named Captain Molly; one of these recalled that her Captain Molly was also called Dirty Kate and "died a horrible death from the effects of syphilitic disease." [13] Although touted in folklore, Captain Molly needed to acquire a more appealing persona before she could be enshrined as the Revolutionary War's premier woman warrior. She needed to become Molly Pitcher, who tended to thirsty soldiers as well as tending a cannon, and for that to happen, she needed to find a home at Monmouth, where soldiers literally perished from the heat. Fortunately, Molly had little trouble traveling from battlefield to battlefield. Lossing's informants placed her and her cannon-firing exploits not only at Fort Washington, where they were well documented, but also at Fort Clinton, Brandywine, and, yes, Monmouth.

We have no firsthand descriptions, recorded at the time, of a woman at Monmouth firing the cannon of her fallen husband. We might have one secondhand account. Supposedly, Dr. Albigence Waldo wrote in his diary that a wounded officer told the doctor, five days after the battle, that he had observed a woman take up the "gun" (was it a musket or a cannon?) of her fallen "gallant." [14] This evidence is questionable, however, because the original diary has not been located and because diaries or journals from Revolutionary times were sometimes altered when they found their way into print in the nineteenth century.[15]

In 1830, fifty-two years after the fact, Joseph Plumb Martin recalled seeing a women and her husband, working together, firing artillery at Monmouth. But Martin's protagonist does not match the "Molly Pitcher" description: she did not carry water to thirsty soldiers, and she did not spring to action because her husband had fallen (she had been helping all along), and she received no reward from Washington or any other officer. In fact, in Martin's tale, she was the butt of a ribald joke: "While in the act of reaching a cartridge and having one of her feet as far before the other as she could step, a cannon shot from the enemy passed directly between her legs without doing any other damage than carrying away all the lower part of her petticoat,—looking at it with apparent unconcern, she observed, that it was lucky it did not pass a little higher, for in that case it might have carried away something else." [16]

That's all we have in the written historical record—suggestive snippets, nothing more. Yet historical tales evolve through oral transmission, and they start with real-life experience. At the Battle of Monmouth, amid scorching temperatures, thirty-seven soldiers died from heatstroke. This accounted for more than one-third of the battlefield fatalities.[17] Several hundred female camp followers were either on the battlefield or close at hand. On normal days, these women cooked, washed, and hauled things about; during battles, they nursed the wounded and carried supplies to and from the lines. Undoubtedly, camp followers, so far as they could, made water available to thirsty, sweltering soldiers trying to survive the heat. Quite possibly, some of these women helped in the firing of cannons. During other battles, too, woman did what they could for struggling soldiers and aided artillery teams on the rear lines, removed from close contact with enemy soldiers. At Monmouth and elsewhere, survivors took some notice of these women's efforts when passing on stories to folks who were not there, and as the stories traveled from mouth to ear to mouth, they began to reflect a view of women quite different from that common in Revolutionary times. It was in this context that a lowly camp follower could reemerge as an iconic heroine.

Very likely, the evolution of a legendary Molly Pitcher received a boost from abroad. The first cohesive written accounts containing the key elements of the story come from the Napoleonic Wars, so its pedigree might not be entirely American. In 1808–1809, when a French army was laying siege to the Spanish town of Saragossa, a young woman named Augustina Domonech carried drinks to thirsty soldiers, then took the place of a dead artilleryman. Later, when her husband or lover was shot, she took his rifle and assumed his position in battle. This "Maid of Saragossa" became something of a sensation; unlike Mary Hays, she did not have to wait until after her death to receive her accolades. The similarity between the Maid of Saragossa and the final evolution of the Molly Pitcher tale might not be coincidental; as Molly's fame grew through the nineteenth century, she was often compared to her European counterpart.[18]

Half a century after the Battle of Monmouth, stories about an American heroine closely resembling the Maid of Saragossa emerged in print, conflated and confused but certainly vivid. One of the earliest versions appeared in a book called *American Anecdotes: Original and Select*, published in 1830:

> *Captain Molly.* Before the two armies, American and English, had begun the general action of Monmouth, two of the advanced batteries commenced a very severe fire against each other. As the warmth was excessive, the wife of a cannonier constantly ran to bring water for him from a neighboring spring. At the

> moment when she started from the spring, to pass to the post of her husband, she saw him fall, and hastened to assist him; but he was dead. At the same moment she heard an officer order the cannon to be removed from its place, complaining he could not fill his post with as brave a man as had been killed. "No," said the intrepid Molly, fixing her eyes upon the officer, "the cannon shall not be removed for want of some one to serve it; since my brave husband is no more, I will use my utmost exertions to avenge his death." The activity and courage with which she performed the offices of cannonier during the action, attracted the attention of all who witnessed it, finally of Gen. Washington himself, who afterwards gave her the rank of Lieutenant, and granted her half pay during life. She wore an epaulette, and every body called her *Captain Molly*.[19]

The story contains the basic elements of the now-classic Molly Pitcher tale: she carries water to thirsty soldiers; her husband is killed; she jumps to the cannon and saves the day; she is honored and rewarded handsomely (as no rank-and-file Revolutionary soldier ever was, whether male or female). Molly then lives happily ever after on a lieutenant's half-pay—no need for this wartime heroine to toil as a cleaning lady into her old age.

Various newspapers at the time reprinted this moving account, with its vivid image of a female war heroine. In 1835 a variation appeared in Francis Alexander Durivage's *Popular Cyclopedia of History*, this time using the name "Molly Pitcher" as well as "Captain Molly." Two years after that, New Jersey newspapers, to promote interest in the Battle of Monmouth, added further embellishments. In this version, Molly was "indignant" that her husband's cannon might lie idle, so she "flew to the gun." At the end, Congress "ratified" Molly's lieutenant's commission, a yet more fanciful construction.[20]

In 1840, George Washington Parke Custis, Martha Washington's grandson through her first marriage, repeated the basic story from *American Anecdotes* but added visual detail and a new twist on the heroine's words, as if the general had witnessed the scene himself:

> While Captain Molly was serving some water for the refreshment of the men, her husband received a shot in the head, and fell lifeless under the wheels of the piece. The heroine threw down the pail of water, and crying to her dead consort, "lie there my darling while I avenge ye," grasped the ramrod the lifeless hand of the poor fellow had just relinquished, sent home the charge, and called to the matrosses to prime and fire. It was done. Then entering the sponge into the smoking muzzle of the cannon, the heroine performed to admiration the duties of the most expert artilleryman. . . .
>
> The next morning . . . Washington received her graciously, gave her a piece of gold and assured her that her services should not be forgotten. This remarkable and intrepid woman survived the Revolution, never for an instant laying aside the appellation she has so nobly won . . . the famed Captain Molly at the Battle of Monmouth.[21]

Who could now doubt the tale? Washington had rewarded Captain Molly personally, then related the story to his grandson. With Custis's endorsement, the Captain Molly "anecdote" of Captain Molly, like the heroine herself, received the Washington stamp of approval.

One new element in the Custis version is worthy of note: "the pail of water." Other versions hadn't noted how water was delivered to soldiers, and Custis assumed the pail was the obvious vessel. According to another rendition from 1840, "A woman who was called by the troops Captain Molly was busily engaged in carrying canteens of water to the famished [and presumably thirsty] soldiers."[22] How, then, did "pail" and "canteen" evolve into "pitcher," a delicate piece of dinnerware unlikely to be found on any battlefield?

Again, we must look well beyond the Battle of Monmouth to sort this out, but there is a likely explanation. One of the best-known women during the late eighteenth century was Moll Dimond Pitcher, a fortune-teller in Lynn, Massachusetts. Sailors and ship owners would come from afar to consult Moll Pitcher before casting off to sea. Historian Emily Lewis Butterfield notes that Moll "unwittingly provided fodder for several generations of politicians, advertisers, poets, and dramatists." In 1811, for example, the Massachusetts *Scourge* joked that President Madison might find Moll Pitcher's "magic and popguns" more effective than gunboats as a defense against British harassment. John Greenleaf Whittier published an uncomplimentary poem about her in 1832, which he expanded eight years later into an epic he called "Moll Pitcher and the Minstrel Girl." A popular melodrama entitled *Moll Pitcher, or the Fortune Teller of Lynn* played on stages in Boston, New York, and Philadelphia from 1839 until after the Civil War.[23] Clearly, this Moll Pitcher had nothing to do with the Battle of Monmouth—but her name was out there, a household word, precisely at the time "Captain Molly" morphed into "Molly Pitcher," and quite fortuitously, the word "pitcher" connoted the carrying of water to thirsty soldiers. Perhaps the renown of this controversial prophetess from Massachusetts, a legend in her own right, played some role in the evolution of Revolutionary War folklore. Throughout the late nineteenth century and into the early twentieth century, the heroine at Monmouth was often called "Moll Pitcher."[24]

By the 1840s Moll Pitcher (the fortune-teller) and Molly Pitcher (formerly Captain Molly), as disparate as they were, had partially merged. When the fortune-teller's daughter died in 1841, an obituary in the *Portsmouth Journal of Literature and Politics* noted that she was "the daughter of the celebrated Moll Pitcher." A reader understandably asked *which* Moll Pitcher that might be, and the editor replied the heroine of Monmouth and proceeded to tell the story of that battle.[25] This mistaken explanation was picked up in several other papers. The female soldier's story was more appealing than that of the fortune-teller, but the fortune-teller had the more fetching name. Much as the story of a woman firing the cannon of her fallen husband migrated from Fort Washington to Monmouth, so did the name "Moll Pitcher" transfer from one female protagonist to another. Over the next few generations, Moll Pitcher and Molly Pitcher, applied to a cannon-firing woman in the Revolutionary War, were used interchangeably.[26]

At first, the name "Molly Pitcher" was merely appended to the traditional "Captain Molly" story, but in time the dainty dinnerware, with its feminine connotation, proved irresistible. Having traded in her heavy pail for a pitcher (which in later representations would display artistic ornamentation), Molly was no longer a poor, vulgar camp follower, but a respectable woman in service of men. Defined by both a cannon and a pitcher of water, she now embraced an irresistible blend of masculine and feminine attributes. That such a creature could be found in the middle of a Revolutionary battlefield was cause for wonder and celebration.

The combination of masculine and feminine imagery excited visual artists. In 1848 Nathaniel Currier, seventy years after the battle, painted a canvas titled *Molly Pitcher, the Heroine of Monmouth*. In the 1850s Dennis Malone Carter followed suit with two paintings, one of Molly by a cannon, the other of Molly being presented to Washington. By 1860 reproductions of engravings were beginning to bear the caption "Molly Pitcher" instead of "Captain Molly." With visual images now leading the way, Molly Pitcher finally prevailed over the real-life Captain Molly.[27]

THE SEARCH FOR A BODY

The legend was almost perfect, save for one element: an actual heroine, a person who had once lived and breathed. As Molly Pitcher came to life in the minds of her many fans, she demanded to be reified. People began to wonder: Who *was* this Molly Pitcher, anyway?

In the early stages of the legend, many assumed the heroic Molly Pitcher must have been married to "Mr. Pitcher," but that proved a dead-end trail. Since no Mr. and Mrs. Molly Pitcher, happily married until that fateful day at Monmouth, materialized in the historical record, some other woman, under a different name, must have been the one. The search, and the race, was on. What community, and what family, could claim Molly Pitcher as their own?[28]

How to discover the "real" Molly Pitcher, however, is a problem without a solution, for it assumes a specific historical occurrence and an identifiable protagonist. Some legends start with real events and real protagonists, which are exaggerated later to create a tale of mythic proportions, but a legend can also derive from the gradual assemblage of diverse strands that feature multiple and often anonymous protagonists. Having no definable origin, such legends are free to wander as they will, and only later will people attempt to ground the story in a real-world occurrence. This was the dynamic here. Once a fictionalized Molly Pitcher was cemented in public memory, people came forth to attach themselves, their relatives, or their communities to her tale, reveling in her fame.[29]

This brings us to Mary Hays McCauley, the eventual winner of the Molly Pitcher sweepstakes. In 1856, a local newspaper's obituary of John L. Hays, Mary's son, placed Molly Pitcher squarely in the town of Carlisle, Pennsylvania:

> The deceased was the son of the ever-to-be-remembered heroine, the celebrated "Molly Pitcher" whose deeds of daring are recorded in the annals of the Revolution and over whose remains a monument ought to be erected. The writer of this recollects well to have frequently seen her in the streets of Carlisle, pointed out by admiring friends thus: "There goes the woman who fired the cannon at the British when her husband was killed."[30]

This was a grand piece of recovered memory. Twenty-four years earlier, in the same paper's obituary of John's mother, there was no such talk—no "ever-to-be-remembered," no proposed monument, and certainly no "Molly Pitcher." Back then, before the Molly Pitcher legend had mushroomed, the description of Mary Hays McCauley had been far more modest. Being the "*widow* of an American hero" (no heroine in her own right), "she received during the latter years of her life, an annuity from the government." The piece closed with generic words applicable to nearly any local resident:

> For upwards of 40 years she resided in this borough; and was during that time, recognized as an honest, obliging, and industrious woman. She has left numerous relatives to regret her decease; who with many others of her acquaintance, have a hope that her reward in the world to which she has gone, will far exceed that which she received in this.

Had Mary Hays McCauley been celebrated during her lifetime for firing her husband's cannon, the hometown editor would have seized on the opportunity to mention what would become her singular claim to fame—but he didn't. When Mrs. McCauley died fifty-four years after the Battle of Monmouth, the legend of "Molly Pitcher" had yet to attach to this unsuspecting woman, who died with no great honors. Yet a quarter century after that, and three-quarters of a century after Monmouth, she had become in the minds of her family and community a celebrated heroine. In the life of a legend, what a difference a generation makes.[31]

Carlisle was not alone in staking a claim. In Allentown, New Jersey, during the centennial celebrations of independence, Reverend George Swain declared in a "Historical Discourse" on the history of his church that "the famous Molly Pitcher, . . . who, at the battle of Monmouth, acted the role of cannoneer in the place of her husband or some other brave who had fallen beside his gun," was reputed to be Mary Hannah, daughter of a member of their congregation. Nobody followed through on this piece of local lore, however—a lost opportunity.[32]

Citizens of Carlisle fought harder and fared better. Mary Hays, before her marriage to a laborer named John McCalla (spelled variously in contemporary records and later accounts as McKolly, McKelly, McCauly, McCauley, McAuley, McCawley, McCaley, and McCalley), does seem to have been present at Monmouth, and in 1822, forty-four years later, she did receive a pension "for services rendered" of a private's half-pay.[33] These facts provided a base upon which embellishments could be overlaid. During the prelude to the centennial, an old-time resident named Wesley Miles recalled that forty-four years earlier, he had been present at the funeral of a local woman whom he claimed had been buried with military honors. (How strange that a woman supposedly buried with military honors escaped the gaze of Mrs. McCauley's obituary writers.) Miles wrote to the local paper: "Reader, the subject of this reminiscence is a prototype of the 'Maid of Saragossa.' The heroine of Monmouth, Molly Pitcher."[34]

That's all it took. Town promoters immediately claimed the legendary figure as their own. After Miles had identified the unmarked grave site, residents of Carlisle raised $100 to place a new headstone by the bones of their forgotten heroine:

MOLLY MCCAULEY
RENOWNED IN HISTORY AS
"MOLLY PITCHER,"
THE HEROINE OF MONMOUTH.
DIED JANUARY 22, 1833
AGED SEVENTY-NINE YEARS[35]

Years later, somebody pointed out that the date of death on the tombstone was a year off. What if the site of the grave, as indicated by Wesley Miles, was off as well? In 1892, just to be sure, concerned citizens of Carlisle dug up the grave and discovered the skeleton of an adult female; they carefully placed it back, certain that those bones had once worked a cannon at Monmouth.[36]

Once Carlisle had discovered and declared the identity of Molly Pitcher, elderly residents began to come forth with tales they had never told. One former neighbor, a young girl when Mary Hays McCauley was an old woman, recalled her saying, "You girls should have been with me at the Battle of Monmouth and learned how to fire a cannon." Another suddenly remembered that she had met Mary in 1826, when "she was known as 'Molly Pitcher' "; that was actually during the reign of "Captain Molly," however, before the first recorded use of "Molly Pitcher." [37]

In a book published for the Patriotic Sons of America in 1905, local historian John B. Landis used these recovered memories to confirm Carlisle's claim to the "real" Molly Pitcher. "No imaginary heroine was Molly Pitcher," Landis wrote, "but a real buxom lass, a strong, sturdy, courageous woman." [38] Today, if elderly people suddenly came forth with stories they had heard from aging veterans of the Spanish-American War of 1898, the veracity of those stories might be questioned—but few people at the time seemed to care that more than a century had elapsed between deed and memory, and that the memories were twice removed. In 1911, when the prestigious *Journal of American History* published Landis's findings, the McCauley/Molly Pitcher connection was anointed with a quasi-official badge of approval.[39]

With her identity revealed and confirmed, Molly Pitcher began to accumulate physical artifacts. In 1903 a great-great-granddaughter of Mary Hays McCauley made a generous gift to the local historical society: "Molly Pitcher's pitcher," an ornate piece featuring oriental pagodas, some sort of fortifications, and figures floating in thin air.[40] In 1905 the Patriotic Sons of America placed a flagstaff and a cannon by Molly's tombstone; this cannon, acquired from an arsenal in Watertown, Massachusetts, had supposedly been used at Monmouth.[41] Meanwhile, at Monmouth, history enthusiasts constructed two signposts declaring "Mollie Pitcher's Well" on either side of the water source she supposedly used to fill her pitcher. Years later, Monmouth's most prominent historian, William Stryker, revealed that the marked well had been dug fifty years after the battle.[42]

Spurred by the dramatic rise to fame of her compatriot in Carlisle, Margaret Corbin—the "real" Captain Molly—staged something of a comeback. On March 16, 1926, at the urging of the Daughters of the

American Revolution, her bones once again saw the light of day. ("A few decayed fibers of wood and several rusty hand-forged nails were the only traces of a coffin," wrote a witness at the disinterment. "The bones of the skeleton were complete except the small bones of the feet and the bones of the right hand which had disintegrated.") Twenty minutes later, the remains of Margaret Corbin were placed back underground in the cemetery of the United States Military Academy at West Point, only a few miles from her original grave site. A tablet identified her definitively as "Captain Molly."[43]

And so it was. By 1926 both Captain Molly and Molly Pitcher had been identified, properly reburied, and honored with the appropriate monuments. Their legends were literally sealed in stone. One tale, however, had subsumed the other. Although the "real" Captain Molly stood in for her husband at Fort Washington, this heroic deed was not quite enough. It took the cannon and pitcher together to create the Revolution's iconic war heroine.

For a century after the town of Carlisle made Molly Pitcher its own, and for seventy years after historian John Landis legitimized that claim, her story was firmly attached to a real, dead woman. The 1948 *Dictionary of American Biography* (*DAB*) included an entry for Mary Ludwig Hays McCauley, "better known as Molly Pitcher."[44] Henry Steele Commager and Richard B. Morris, in their classic compilation of primary sources published in 1958, told the story of Mary Hays's heroic deeds at Monmouth. By way of documentation, they included Joseph Plumb Martin's recollections under the title " 'Molly Pitcher' Mans a Gun at Monmouth"—even though Martin mentions neither Molly Pitcher nor Mary Hays, and his protagonist did not lose her husband, serve water to thirsty men, or receive any reward.[45] During her unchallenged reign as the "real" Molly Pitcher, the most serious threat faced by Mary Hays McCauley was not to her identity or her good name, but to her body. In the early 1960s, the Friendly Sons of Molly Pitcher, based in Monmouth County, New Jersey, threatened to steal the heroine's bones from their resting place in Carlisle and place them at the scene of the battle.[46]

Not until the last quarter of the twentieth century, starting with the bicentennial celebrations, did historians take a more serious look at the dubious McCauley/Pitcher connection. John Todd White in 1975 and Linda Grant De Pauw and Conover Hunt in 1976 suggested that the "Molly Pitcher" story was more folklore than fact, and that Molly herself should be treated as a compilation of female camp followers.[47] For a moment, it looked as if the legend of Molly Pitcher would be expunged because of the work of diligent historians, but two contingencies turned that plotline around. First, the women's movement, at a historic peak, had correctly noted that traditional history was "his-story," and texts needed to include "her-story" as well; the hunt for historic female figures was on. Second, advances in color reproduction created a demand by textbook publishers for vivid historic images. Both demands could be satisfied by dusting off those nineteenth-century paintings of Molly tending her cannon, accompanied by a retelling of her story—and since these were textbooks, the story must be about *someone*, a real historic figure. Mary Hays McCauley's place in history was rescued after all.

Some historians continued to complain, but others let it be. The 1999 *American National Biography*, superseding the old *Dictionary of American Biography*, took the reification one step further than its predecessor had done, including an entry for "PITCHER, Molly (13 Oct. 1754?–22 Jan. 1832)." By its very structure, the article treated "Molly Pitcher" as an actual resident of Carlisle, Pennsylvania, with dates of birth and death. The details of her life, the author admitted, remained uncertain—"only her actual first name, Mary, is accepted as definite"—but like other entries that fill this twenty-four-volume authoritative reference shelved in most respectable libraries, "PITCHER, Molly" was assumed to have been a real person, even if historical disputes about her identity and her life continued.[48]

But if facts are troubling things, so are facts that don't exist. Since there is no contemporaneous evidence that Mary Hays of Carlisle carried pitchers of water to thirsty soldiers, took her husband's place at a cannon when he was killed, and was honored and rewarded by General Washington, those still wishing to tell the story have conveniently walked it backward. There is no record that a man named Hays was killed at Monmouth, so they now say Mary's husband at the time was only wounded or even just thirsty, they say, when Molly took his place. The lieutenant's commission is mostly gone, and Washington's gold pieces now appear primarily in renditions intended for children, the true holdouts. But the delicate vessels of water must remain, embedded in Mary's name of fame, Molly Pitcher—no cumbersome pails permitted.

Even with this watered-down version, those wishing to continue the tale find themselves on the defensive. Some texts published since 2012 retreat by using hedge words that get them off the hook, perpetuating the legend while disavowing any claim to its veracity: "supposedly," "may have," "according to legend," "legend says," and so on. Technically, the stories presented are only conjectural—Mary Hays "is said to have" joined her wounded husband's gun crew—but "said" by whom? When? Why? Troubling questions of authenticity raised by such diction are not explored, and textbook readers, eager to be done with their assignments, are not likely to raise them on their own. They read through the hedges, accepting story as truth.[49]

Other updated texts state flatly that Mary Hays took her husband's place, making no disclaimer, but toss in a gratuitous "legendary" or "earning folk-legend status," phrases that do not weaken the import of the statements but protect the authors against those who call Molly Pitcher a legend. The person and event are real and serve as the basis for the legend, these authors imply. This is historically incorrect. The legend came first, then promoters attached Mary Hays to it.[50]

Still others use gimmicks. "Margaret Corbin of Pennsylvania went with her husband when he joined the Continental Army. After he died in battle, she took his place. Mary Ludwig Hays McCauley also joined her husband in battle." Cleverly, the author does not actually state that McCauley's husband died and she took his place—"also" refers only to joining her husband in battle—but few if any students will catch this. This text continues: "The soldiers called her 'Moll of the Pitcher,' or **Molly Pitcher**, because she carried water pitchers to the soldiers." The altered etymology, based on no historical evidence, lends a seductive air of authenticity not in the least warranted.[51]

A few current textbooks for lower grades don't bother with hedges or gimmicks but repeat the story point-blank, walking back nineteenth-century excesses (Molly's husband is wounded, not killed, and she receives no reward from Washington) but making no further apologies: "American women also won fame for their bravery during the war. Mary Ludwig Hays McCauley earned the name Molly Pitcher by carrying fresh water to American troops during the Battle of Monmouth in New Jersey in 1778. When her husband was wounded, she took his place in battle, loading cannons." This text wraps around an image of "Mary McCauley" in a full dress, ramming a rod into a cannon's barrel.[52] One current high-school text, published in 2012, unabashedly tells the same story, but with this long-discredited addition: "Afterward, General Washington made her a noncommissioned officer for her brave deeds."[53]

The Internet, meanwhile, has helped Molly Pitcher withstand attacks based on the historical record. Like nineteenth-century paintings, it is a medium that rewards excess. As of this writing, a Google search on the Internet reveals 485,000 hits for "Molly Pitcher"—and this number is increasing rapidly. Students hoping to produce reports on Revolutionary heroines can find a wealth of information on the Net, including digitized reproductions of those flamboyant Molly Pitcher paintings. Many of these enterprising young scholars, following a folkloric tradition appropriate for our times, post their own minibiographies of Molly Pitcher on the Web.

Meanwhile, Amazon lists more than a dozen commercial biographies intended for children, two of which are cited as sources for the Molly Pitcher entry in Wikipedia. "During training, artillery and infantry soldiers would shout 'Molly! Pitcher!' whenever they needed Mary to bring water," the Wiki article says, and the claim is duly referenced to a book titled *Molly Pitcher: Heroine of the War for Independence*, for ages nine and up. Wikipedia continues: "After the battle, General Washington asked about the woman whom he had seen loading a cannon on the battlefield. In commemoration of her courage, he issued Mary Hays a warrant as a noncommissioned officer. Afterward, she was known as 'Sergeant Molly,' a nickname that she used for the rest of her life." The reference is to *They Called Her Molly Pitcher*, age range three to seven.[54]

Also for the younger set, Molly Pitcher has her own trading card in the Topps American Heritage Heroes series. The text:

MOLLY PITCHER

AMERICAN REVOLUTION

NON-COMMISSIONED SERGEANT

The image: Molly jamming her rod into the cannon's barrel, gazing intensely at her target, with an officer on horseback in the background (could it be General Washington?) looking on approvingly.

THE RETURN OF CAPTAIN MOLLY

Even if the legend is flawed, Molly Pitcher does introduce women camp followers into the core narrative of the Revolutionary War—but these women enter the story under false pretexts. In truth, they were more like the historic Captain Molly from the Hudson Highlands than the fanciful Molly Pitcher. They were poor and "vulgar," in the parlance of the times. Like Mary Hays, Margaret Corbin, and the soldiers themselves, many drank and swore. ("Molly was a rough, common woman who swore like a trouper," an elderly woman from Carlisle recalled of Mary Hays McCauley decades later. "She smoked and chewed tobacco, and had no education whatsoever. She was hired to do the most menial work, such as scrubbing, etc.")[55] These women were part of camp life, not above it.

Unlike the fabled Molly Pitcher, camp followers were not honored by Washington for their deeds. Quite the reverse. Starting on July 4, 1777—on the first anniversary of the Declaration of Independence—Washington issued orders for the women who accompanied the Continental Army not to ride on the wagons. Again and again he repeated these orders: women should walk, not ride, and they should stay in the rear with the baggage. For a general trying to put together a respectable army, camp followers were to be tolerated at best—and the fewer the better, as far as the commander in chief was concerned. "The multitude of women," he wrote in 1777, "are a clog on every movement. . . . Officers commanding brigades and corps [should] use every reasonable method in their power to get rid of all such as are not absolutely necessary."[56]

Common soldiers, on the other hand, appreciated the women among them. Contrary to general orders, they let women ride in the wagons clear to the end of the war. The only "reward" bestowed on female camp followers was the respect of their male peers. After the war, these men kept the memory of "Captain Molly" alive. When telling old stories, they recalled their own "Captain Mollies," those courageous camp followers who braved the heat of the action at Fort Washington, Fort Clinton, Brandywine, Monmouth, and other historic battlefields. Decades later, when these stories congealed into one and were set in print, veterans who were still alive came forth proudly: "Yes, that must have been her. I saw that woman. I knew the heroine myself."

While Captain Molly has a legitimate place in the story of our nation's birth, Molly Pitcher does not. The story of Molly Pitcher belongs to the nineteenth century, and it is historically significant as folklore. This appealing heroine serves men, fights tough, and is rewarded by men in high places—but she does not represent the female presence in the Revolutionary War, as some writers now contend; she distorts it. To tell history as it truly was, our heroine would be "Molly of the Buckets, Pails, and Heavy Burdens"; she would not wait till her husband died or was wounded to help with the cannons; and she would receive little if any recompense, certainly no gold or officer's commission from General Washington.

DAVID AND GOLIATH

"British professionals . . . pump[ed] shot into the backs of fleeing Minute Men."

The Battle of Lexington. Reduced engraving by Amos Doolittle, 1832, from his original engraving, 1775, based on a sketch by Ralph Earl.

4

"THE SHOT HEARD 'ROUND THE WORLD"

Every year, over one million Americans commemorate "the shot heard 'round the world" with a patriotic pilgrimage to Minute Man National Historical Park on the outskirts of Concord, Massachusetts. On April 19, the anniversary of the famous event, reenactors dress up as colonial minute men and march from nearby towns to Lexington and Concord, where they exchange make-believe musket fire with friends and neighbors dressed as British Redcoats. Throughout the state, and in Maine and Wisconsin as well, "Patriots' Day" is celebrated as an official holiday.

The story is classic David and Goliath, starring rustic colonials who faced the world's strongest army. At dawn in Lexington on April 19, 1775, several hundred British Regulars, in full battle formation, opened fire on local militiamen. When the smoke had cleared, eight of the sleepy-eyed farmers who had been rousted in the middle of the night lay dead on the town green.

In the wake of the bloodbath, to mobilize popular support, patriots proclaimed far and wide that the Redcoats had fired first. The Massachusetts Provincial Congress collected depositions from participants and firsthand witnesses, then published those accounts that conformed to the official story under the title *A Narrative of the Excursion and Ravages of the King's Troops.* British authorities countered with their own official version: the Americans had fired first. Not surprisingly, this story received little circulation in the rebellious colonies.

Because of the biases and agendas of the witnesses, we can never know for sure who fired the first shot at Lexington. But we do know that the patriots won the war of words. "The myth of injured innocence," as David Hackett Fischer calls it, became an instant American classic.[1] We have all learned that the British started the American Revolution when they opened fire on outnumbered and outclassed patriot militiamen on the Lexington Green. But this makes no sense. Revolutions, by nature, are proactive—they must be initiated by the revolutionaries themselves. The American Revolution had begun long before the battle at Lexington.

In 1836 the poet and essayist Ralph Waldo Emerson coined a catchy phrase that has signified the event ever since: "the shot heard 'round the world." Actually, Emerson's poem "Concord Hymn" commemorated the fighting at the North Bridge in nearby Concord, and his celebrated "shot" was fired by Americans:

> By the rude bridge that arched the flood,
> Their flag to April's breeze unfurled,
> Here once the embattled farmers stood,
> And fired the shot heard 'round the world.

Over time, however, Emerson's poem was relocated to Lexington, a site more hospitable to the story we wish to hear. At Lexington the farmers were clearly the victims, while at Concord they were not. The David and Goliath tale, highlighted by the image of bullying British troops mowing down Yankee farmers, has prevailed. Popular histories still repeat the story as it was first told by American patriots, making it very clear who fired the first shot: "British professionals . . . pump[ed] shot into the backs of fleeing Minute Men."[2] Current textbooks routinely locate "the shot heard 'round the world" to the standoff at Lexington, not the "rude bridge" at Concord, where Emerson placed it. One grade-school text, even as it quotes the "Concord Hymn" verbatim in a sidebar, says Emerson called the first shot fired at Lexington "the shot heard 'round the world."[3] A college text, after outlining the events at both Lexington and Concord, tries to have it both ways by misquoting Emerson, switching from the singular to the plural: "The first *shots*—'the *shots* heard 'round the world,' as Americans later called them—had been fired. But who had fired them first?" It then discusses the debate over who had fired the first shot at Lexington, showing a clear preference for that location.[4]

But what if the roles were reversed? What if American Revolutionaries were actually Goliath, and the British occupying force, greatly outnumbered and far from home, more like David? In fact, the American Revolution did not begin with "the shot heard 'round the world," wherever it was fired. It started more than half a year earlier, when tens of thousands of angry patriot militiamen ganged up on a few unarmed officials and overthrew British authority throughout all of Massachusetts outside of Boston. This powerful revolutionary saga, which features Americans as Goliath instead of David, has been bypassed by the standard telling of history. By treating American patriots as innocent victims, we have suppressed their revolutionary might.

BELEAGUERED BOSTON

At Lexington, the story goes, poorly trained militiamen, aroused from their slumber by Paul Revere, were surprised and mowed down by British Regulars. Surprised? Untrained? Unprepared? Let's take a closer look at events that culminated in "the shot heard 'round the world."

On December 16, 1773, patriots dressed as Indians dumped 342 chests of tea into Boston Harbor. On the night of April 18, 1775, sixteen months and two days later, British troops marched from Boston toward Lexington and Concord. Blood was shed, lots of it, and a war was on. What, exactly, happened during that intervening sixteen months and two days? How did an act of political vandalism lead to outright warfare?

Here is one response, repeated for generations in our textbooks and in almost all accounts of the American Revolution.

To punish Boston for what we now call the Boston Tea Party,[5] Parliament passed four bills it called the "Coercive Acts" and colonists dubbed the "Intolerable Acts." The "most drastic" of these was the Boston Port Act, which closed the port of Boston.[6] (The others are generally listed but rarely discussed in any detail.) This measure was supposed to isolate Bostonians from other colonists, but it had the reverse effect: "Americans in all the colonies reacted by trying to help the people of Boston. Food and other supplies poured into Boston from throughout the colonies."[7]

Meanwhile, leaders in twelve colonies gathered in the First Continental Congress to show support for Boston and present a united opposition to Britain's harsh move. Congress petitioned Parliament to change its course, but Parliament remained firm. Six months later, British Regulars marched on Lexington and Concord.

Most of this account is correct—as far as it goes. Colonists did help Boston and form a Continental Congress, and British soldiers did march. But why did Britain take the offensive? Was it because other colonies came to the aid of Boston or because Congress complained? Do acts of charity or written protests, in the absence of stronger forms of resistance, generally lead to war? The beleaguered Boston story does not explain why British officials used military force against British citizens living in Massachusetts in April 1775. Something critical is missing here. We need to see how political tensions resulted in actual warfare.

The problem begins with one false statement in the Boston-based narrative—namely, that closing Boston Harbor was "the final insult to a long list of abuses."[8] In fact, it wasn't so much the Boston Port Act that set one colony aflame and triggered the American Revolution, but the second of the offensive bills, the Massachusetts Government

Act. In this measure, Parliament unilaterally gutted the 1691 Charter for Massachusetts, the people's constitution. No longer could citizens call town meetings except with permission of the royal governor, and once they met, they could not discuss any items the governor had not approved. No longer could the people's representatives choose the powerful Council, which functioned as the upper house of the legislature, the governor's cabinet, and the administrative arm of provincial government. No longer could the people have any say in choosing judges, juries, or justices of the peace—local officials with the power to put citizens in jail or take away their property.

The people of Massachusetts, accustomed to home rule in local matters through their town meetings and a representative structure of government for a century and a half, were thoroughly disenfranchised by the Massachusetts Government Act. Try to imagine, today, that our Constitution was suddenly declared obsolete—not slowly eroded, but actually yanked away. This would spark considerable protest, and it did so then. Outraged citizens rose as a body to say, "No way!"

THE FIRST AMERICAN REVOLUTION

When the Boston Port Act took effect, other colonists passed the hat for relief, held days of prayer and fasting, embarked on another round of boycotts like those of the 1760s, and called for conferences to talk things over.[9] These were common forms of political action in British North America. But when the Massachusetts Government Act took effect shortly afterward, the people of that colony actually shut down the government and prepared for war. This was the stuff of revolution. Citizens of Massachusetts forcibly shed the old regime and began to replace it with their own.[10]

In June 1774, upon hearing news of the Massachusetts Government Act, patriots sprung to action. In Worcester, on July 4, members of the radical American Political Society (APS) pledged to arm themselves with "Two Pounds of Gun Powder each 12 Flints and Led

Answerable thereunto."[11] Stephen Salisbury, a local merchant, sold so much gunpowder over the next few weeks that he contemplated building his own powder house.[12] They hadn't yet figured out exactly what actions they would take to resist the Massachusetts Government Act, but they did know they would not submit to it, and they reasoned—correctly, as it turned out—that it would come to blows at some point.

The Massachusetts Government Act was due to take effect on August 1, 1774, and the first court to sit under the new provisions was scheduled to sit in remote Berkshire County, on the western edge of the province, on August 16. That court never convened. When the Crown-appointed officials showed up for work, they found themselves locked out of the Great Barrington courthouse and face-to-face with 1,500 patriots, who told them the court was closed.[13]

The next court on the schedule was to meet in Springfield on August 30, but on that day, three to four thousand patriots, marching "with staves and musick," again shut it down. "Amidst the Crowd in a sandy, sultry place, exposed to the sun," wrote one firsthand observer, the judges were forced to renounce "in the most express terms any commission which should be given out to them under the new arrangement."[14]

Patriots who closed the courts in Great Barrington and Springfield proceeded unopposed, but General Thomas Gage, the newly appointed military governor of Massachusetts, vowed to take a stand in Worcester, where the court was supposed to meet on September 6. "In Worcester, they keep no Terms, openly threaten Resistance by Arms, have been purchasing Arms, preparing them, casting Ball, and providing Powder, and threaten to attack any Troops who dare to oppose them," he wrote on August 27. "I shall soon be obliged to march a Body of Troops into that Township, and perhaps into others, as occasion happens, to preserve the peace."[15] Peace? If Gage did make good on his promise, it would look more like war—and this was more than seven months *before* Lexington and Concord.

But events soon took a dramatic turn. On September 1, taking the offensive in a rapidly escalating arms race, General Gage ordered

British troops to seize powder stored in a magazine in nearby Somerville, not far from Boston. As news spread, the story of British troops on the march took on a life of its own, and soon, across the Massachusetts countryside and proximate points of neighboring colonies, an estimated twenty to a hundred thousand angry men (this is the range of contemporary estimates, perhaps also a bit exaggerated), believing that the British Redcoats had killed six patriots and set fire to Boston, headed toward Boston to confront them.[16] In some towns, nearly every male of fighting age participated in the "Powder Alarm," as people soon called it. One firsthand observer described the frenzy of the moment:

> [A]ll along were armed men rushing forward some on foot some on horseback, at every house women & children making cartridges, running bullets, making wallets, baking biscuit, crying & bemoaning & at the same time animating their husbands & sons to fight for their liberties, tho' not knowing whether they should ever see them again.[17]

Alas, it was a false alarm. "The people seemed really disappointed," one man told John Adams two months later, "when the news was contradicted."[18]

After the patriots' showing in the Powder Alarm, Gage reasoned that his troops would be vastly outnumbered if he sent them to Worcester. "The flames of sedition," he conceded to British secretary of state Lord Dartmouth, had "spread universally throughout the country beyond conception."[19] Gage had little choice but to let the judges fend for themselves, but judges alone could not uphold the power of the Crown and Parliament against such odds. The battle was won before it raged. The day before the court was slated to meet, the APS "Voted, not to bring our Fire-arms into Town the 6 Day of Sept." Guns would not be needed; sheer numbers would suffice.[20]

At dawn on September, 6, 1774, militiamen from across the county of Worcester started marching into the town of Worcester. By ten o'clock, as the day grew hotter, 4,622 men from 37 different towns stood at the ready. (We know the numbers because Breck Parkman, one of the participants, counted the men in each militia company.[21]) Approximately half the adult male population of a county that ranged from the Rhode Island to the New Hampshire borders had mustered in force to topple British rule at the local level.

When two dozen Crown-appointed court officials showed up to work in their black suits and wigs, they found the courthouse doors barricaded. Locked out, they huddled instead in Daniel Heywood's tavern, halfway between the courthouse and the town common. There they waited, waiting for the throngs to determine their fates.

Across from the courthouse, at the home of blacksmith Timothy Bigelow, the Worcester County Committees of Correspondence tried to coordinate the day's activities, but members soon adjourned "to attend the body of the people" outside.[22] Each of the thirty-seven militia companies, which had recently elected a new military captain, now selected a political representative as well, to serve for one day only—the ultimate in term limits. These men appointed a smaller committee, which visited the court officials to work out the details of their resignations. But the plan they settled on had to make its way back to the thirty-seven representatives, and through them to the "body of the people," who rejected the first draft. The process then began anew. The apparatus was democratic but cumbersome, heavily weighted at the bottom. Things moved slowly. People became impatient.

Finally, by midafternoon, the stage was set. The militiamen arranged themselves along Main Street, half on the Mill Brook side and the other half under the embankment to the west. The lines stretched for a quarter mile between the courthouse and Heywood's tavern, each company in formation, Uxbridge in front of the courthouse, Westborough next, and so on, down to Upton and Templeton, stationed outside Heywood's tavern. When all were in place, each of the two dozen court officials emerged from the tavern with his hat in his hand, reversing the traditional order of deference, and recited his disavowal of British authority to the first company of militiamen, then walked to the next to repeat his recantation there, and in this manner made his way slowly through the gauntlet, all the way to the courthouse. Over thirty times apiece, so all the militiamen could hear, the judges, justices of the peace, court attorneys, and others whose power had been sanctioned by the Crown pledged "that all judicial proceeding be stayed . . . on account of the unconstitutional act of Parliament . . . which, if effected, will reduce the inhabitants to mere arbitrary power."[23] With this humiliating act of submission, all British authority disappeared from Worcester County, never to return.

As in Great Barrington, Springfield, and Worcester, patriots shut down the governmental apparatus in Salem, Concord, Barnstable, Taunton, and Plymouth—in every county seat outside Boston, where garrisoned British soldiers could protect the judges. From the time the Massachusetts Government Act was supposed to take effect, the county courts, which also functioned as the administrative arms of the local governments, were powerless. According to merchant John Andrews, rebels in Plymouth were so excited by their victory that they

> attempted to remove a Rock (the one on which their fore-fathers first landed, when they came to this country) which lay buried in a wharfe five feet deep, up into the center of the town, near the court house. The way being up hill, they found it impracticable, as after they had dug it up, they found it to weigh ten tons at least.[24]

Meanwhile, all thirty-six Crown-appointed Council members were told by their angry neighbors to resign. Those who refused were driven from their homes and forced to flee to Boston, where they sought protection from the British army.

In direct violation of the new law, the people continued to gather in their town meetings. When Governor Gage arrested seven men in the temporary capital of Salem for calling a town meeting, three thousand farmers immediately marched on the jail to set the prisoners free. Rather than initiate a bloodbath, Gage ordered two companies of British soldiers to retreat. Throughout Massachusetts, town meetings continued to convene. As John Andrews reported,

> Notwithstanding all the parade the governor made at Salem on account of their meeting, they had another one directly under his nose at Danvers, and continued it two or three howers longer than was necessary, to see if he would interrupt 'em. He was acquainted with it, but reply'd—"Damn 'em! I won't do any thing about it unless his Majesty sends me more troops."[25]

More than half a year before the "shot heard 'round the world" at Lexington, Massachusetts patriots had seized all military authority outside Boston. On September 21, the Worcester County Convention took it upon itself to reorganize the county militia into seven new regiments and urged each town "to enlist one third of the men . . . between sixteen and sixty years of age, to be ready to act at a minute's warning."[26] These were the famous "minute men," formed half a year before they would respond to the call at Lexington. Other counties did the same. The story of the minute men does not begin at Lexington, where we normally put it; it is part and parcel of the Revolution of 1774.

By early October patriots had seized all political authority from British officials and vested it in their town meetings, county conventions, and a Provincial Congress. Throughout the preceding decade, patriots had written petitions, staged boycotts, and burnt effigies—but this was something new. In the late summer and early fall of 1774, patriots did not simply *protest* government, they *overthrew* it. In his diary, one disgruntled Tory from Southampton summed it all up: "Government has now devolved upon the people, and they seem to be for using it."[27]

Many patriots at that point were ready to formalize the end of British rule and create an entirely new government, based not on royal authority but on the will of the people. On October 4, 1774—a full twenty-one months before the Continental Congress approved the document prepared by Thomas Jefferson—citizens of Worcester, Massachusetts, declared that they were ready for independence. Four weeks earlier, on September 6, they had toppled British authority; now they were ready to replace the old government with a new one. In a set of instructions for its representative to the forthcoming Provincial Congress, which was about to meet in defiance of Governor Gage's orders, the town meeting told Timothy Bigelow:

> You are to consider the people of this province absolved, on their part, from the obligation therein contained [the 1691 Massachusetts charter], and to all intents and purposes reduced to a state of nature; and you are to exert yourself in devising ways and means to raise from the dissolution of the old constitution, as from the ashes of the Phenix, a new form, wherein all officers shall be dependent on the suffrages of the people for their existence as such, whatever unfavorable constructions our enemies may put upon such procedure. The exigency of our public affairs leaves us no other alternative from a state of anarchy or slavery.[28]

Patriots in Worcester had a word for their dramatic move: "independency." For the British and the Tories, any mention of "independency" was considered treasonous—and even patriot leaders shied away. Samuel Adams wrote from the Continental Congress to his comrades back home, cautioning them not to "set up another form of government."[29] John Adams, also a member of Congress, wrote that "Absolute Independency . . . Startle[s] People here." Most congressional delegates, he warned, were horrified by "The Proposal of Setting up a new Form of Government of our own."[30] Perhaps Samuel and John Adams were right, for if Massachusetts moved too quickly, other colonies might balk and not come to their aid. But right or wrong, this was a revolution by and for the people of Massachusetts; even the most radical members of Congress could not keep pace.

PREPARATIONS FOR DEFENSE

The most pressing duties of the new Provincial Congress were to collect taxes and prepare for war. On October 26 delegates listed exactly what they would need to defend against a British invasion:[31]

16 field pieces, 3 pounders, with carriages, irons, &c.; wheels for ditto, irons, sponges, ladles, &c., @ £30	£480 0 0
4 ditto, 6 pounders, with ditto, @ £38	£152 0 0
Carriages, irons, &c., for 12 battering cannon, @ £30	£360 0 0
4 mortars, and appurtenances, viz: 2 8-inch and 12 13-inch, @ £20	£80 0 0
20 tons grape and round shot, from 3 to 24 lb., @ £15	£300 0 0
10 tons bomb-shells, @ £20	£200 0 0
5 tons lead balls, @ £33	£165 0 0
1,000 barrels of powder, @ £8	£8,000 0 0
5,000 arms and bayonets, @ £2	£10,000 0 0
And 75,000 flints	£100 0 0
Contingent charges	£ 1,000 0 0
In the whole	£20,837 0 0

All the political and military maneuvers of the next several months would focus on how to procure these armaments and how to keep arms and powder the patriots already possessed out of the hands of the British.

On December 14, four months before Lexington, patriots in nearby New Hampshire made the first offensive move of the war: four hundred local militiamen stormed Fort William and Mary in Portsmouth, took down the king's colors, and carried away approximately one hundred barrels of the king's gunpowder (some of which was later put to use during the Battle of Bunker Hill). The following day, one thousand patriots marched again on the fort, this time removing all the muskets and sixteen cannon. This armed attack on a British fortress was not merely a prelude to war, it was an act of war: cannons and muskets were fired. Emerson's "shot heard 'round the world" was not the first shot of the American Revolution.[32]

Although the offensive against Fort William and Mary was the first frontal military assault, it was not the first time patriots removed British arms and ammunition. Using stealth, cunning, and insider information, patriots had already taken cannon and munitions from British magazines in Boston, Providence, Newport, and New London.[33]

On February 24, 1775, almost two months before Lexington, British intelligence reported that 15,000 "Minute Men" were "all properly armed." The report noted: "There are in the Country thirty-eight Field pieces and Nineteen Companies of Artillery most of which are in Worcester, a few at Concord, and a few at Watertown," as well as ninety to a hundred barrels of powder at Concord. Further, the Provincial Congress's Committee of Supply was trying to procure more arms yet, "to be deposited at Concord and Worcester." If British soldiers tried to seize any of this cache, they were likely to trigger a massive mobilization of angry patriots.[34]

The spies also reported, though, that there were "eight Field pieces in an old Store or Barn, near the landing place at Salem," which were to be removed shortly. "The seizure of them would greatly disconcert their schemes," it concluded—and General Gage acted accordingly. On Sunday, February 26, he ordered 240 soldiers to find and remove eight field pieces and a supply of powder that patriots were hiding at Salem. Local citizens, gathered together in church, learned of the invasion in time to remove the arms and ammunition to a safer location. To stop the British advance, they simply raised a drawbridge that lay on the route of the marching troops.[35] When the British invaded Lexington seven weeks later, they would avoid the mistakes they had made in Salem: they marched by night, not on the Sabbath, and they chose a route that did not have a drawbridge.

On April 2, over two weeks before the march of Lexington, news from London arrived in Boston that set off a firestorm. Vowing to starve the errant colonists into submission, Lord North was closing the Newfoundland fisheries to Americans, cutting off all trade with anyone but the British, and mobilizing two thousand additional seamen and "a proper number of frigates" to enforce this embargo. Further, the king had dispatched four additional regiments from Ireland to Boston. Everybody in town knew immediately what this meant. Governor Thomas Gage, who was also commander in chief of the British forces in North America, had been ridiculed through the winter by his own soldiers—"Old Woman," they called him—for sitting by and letting the patriots take charge of Massachusetts without fighting back. His excuse, he said, was that he did not have sufficient troops to take the offensive. Now, with reinforcements imminent, he would certainly make a move.[36]

But where would he strike? Could he possibly attack Worcester, the very heart of resistance? There, according to a spy report written in French, patriots had accumulated fifteen tons of powder (hidden in places unknown), thirteen small cannon (proudly displayed but poorly mounted in front of the meetinghouse on Main Street), and various munitions (in the hands of a merchant named Salisbury and "un grand chef" named Bigelow). But the road there was rough, the journey arduous, and the patriots numerous, vigilant, and excessively hostile. Gage's soldiers would likely be ambushed and possibly annihilated.[37]

Concord offered better prospects, for it was much more accessible. Unlike the forty-mile trek to Worcester, this twenty-mile jaunt could be accomplished in a single night, which allowed the possibility of a surprise attack. It wouldn't be much of a surprise, however, because patriots easily surmised that Concord would be the likely target. On April 7, working with Dr. Joseph Warren and the Boston committee of correspondence, Paul Revere traveled from Boston to Concord with an urgent message: British Regulars would soon march to seize the patriots' cannons and other military stores, possibly the very next day. Even that message was not really necessary, however, because patriots in Concord, where the Provincial Congress was sitting, had figured it out themselves. Two days earlier, James Warren had informed his wife, Mercy Otis Warren: "This town [Concord] is full of cannon, ammunition, stores, etc., and the [British] Army long for them and they want nothing but strength to induce an attempt on them. The people are ready and determine to defend this country inch by inch."[38]

Ready they were, thirteen days before the Redcoats showed up. Patriots by then had been preparing for half a year for this counteroffensive by the British army, yet they continued to refine their intelligence network. On the morning of April 16, Paul Revere made a second ride westward, to Lexington this time, to confer with Samuel Adams and John Hancock, who had sought refuge there, about how to respond to Gage's imminent move. On his way back, Revere met also with patriots in Cambridge and Charlestown to fine-tune their warning systems, including the now-famous signal lantern ploy. When the big moment arrived, the minute men who had been training for months needed to get the word.

By dawn of April 19, 1775, when Regulars finally showed up at the Lexington Green, and later that morning, when they continued their march to Concord, patriot militias were as prepared as they could ever expect to be. They were willing partners in this war-in-the-making. They knew the likely consequences, and they were ready to face those consequences.

LOST IN HISTORY

The Massachusetts Revolution of 1774 was the most successful and enduring popular uprising in the nation's history, the only one to permanently remove existing authority, yet this momentous event is never highlighted and rarely even mentioned in our textbooks. A logical question to ask of any revolution would be: Where, when, and how did political and military authority first transfer from one group to another? Strangely, though, we don't ask this of our own Revolution, the very founding of our nation. If we *did* posit that fundamental question, the answer would be obvious and the Massachusetts Revolution of 1774 would become a standard and indispensable part of our national narrative, featured on every timeline and included on many a test.

Our most triumphant rebellion did not always suffer such neglect.

The British *Annual Register*, written immediately in the wake of the 1774 revolution, gave considerable attention to the forced resignations, court closures, and preparations for war throughout the countryside of Massachusetts.[39] Early American historians—William Gordon in 1788, David Ramsay in 1789, and Mercy Otis Warren in 1805—covered the response to the Boston Port Act, but they highlighted the Massachusetts Government Act as the major catalyst leading to the American Revolution. According to Ramsay, the Massachusetts Government Act

> excited a greater alarm than the port act. The one effected only the metropolis, the other the whole province. . . . Had the parliament stopped short with the Boston port act, the motives to union and to make a common cause with that metropolis, would have been feeble, perhaps ineffectual to have roused the other provinces; but the arbitrary mutilation of the important privileges . . . by the will of parliament, convinced the most moderate that the cause of Massachusetts was the cause of all the provinces.[40]

Gordon described the popular uprising in considerable and vivid detail. In response to the "obnoxious alteration" dictated by the Massachusetts Government Act, "the people at large" prepared "to defend their rights with the point of a sword," and even the moderates "became resolute and resentful."[41]

Warren went even further, calling the 1774 rebellion "one of the most extraordinary eras in the history of man: the exertions of spirit awakened by the severe hand of power had led to that most alarming experiment of leveling of all ranks, and destroying all subordination."[42]

This was too much of a revolution for conservative historians and schoolbook writers of the next generation, who argued that the "American Revolution" was not really revolutionary and that patriots were not to be construed as "rebels." Paul Allen, writing in 1819, devoted seventeen pages to the aid sent to Boston, while he assigned less than a paragraph to the resistance triggered by the Massachusetts Government Act.[43] Salma Hale's 1822 school text emphasized the themes of sympathy and solidarity, with nary a word about the overthrow of British authority.[44] The following year Charles Goodrich, in his popular *History of the United States of America*, wrote about Virginia's "expression of sympathy" with Boston, while ignoring altogether the people's rebellion in Massachusetts.[45]

The Good Samaritan approach certainly played better to children. Stories featuring neighbor helping neighbor conformed to educational goals, while those showing bullying crowds did not. Richard Snowden's school history, written in biblical style, made the events of 1774 sound like the story of the three wise men at the nativity: "Now it came to pass, when the people of the provinces had heard that their brethren in town were in a great strait, they sent to speak comfortable words unto them, and gave them worldly gifts."[46]

By midcentury, the patriotic historian George Bancroft was comfortable enough with the idea of a people's revolution to pay some respect to the uprising of 1774. Although Bancroft spoke of "sympathy" for Boston, he also devoted the better part of three chapters to the dramatic resistance to the Massachusetts Government Act. He did not, however, embrace its democratic character: it was under the direction of Boston's Joseph Warren, he claimed, who was told what to do by an absent Samuel Adams.[47] With this imaginary chain of command, Bancroft placed the first overthrow of the British firmly in the hands of America's favorite revolutionary (see chapter 2).

In 1865 William Wells followed Bancroft in placing Adams at the forefront of affairs in Boston, even though he was in Philadelphia at the time. But with no credible evidence linking Adams to the revolution in the countryside, Wells simply ignored those events. For Wells and most subsequent writers, Samuel Adams had to be the prime mover of all crowd actions—and if Adams was not present, the tale was not told. Most historians since that time have unwittingly followed the lead of British officials like Secretary of State for the Colonies Lord Dartmouth, who simply could not believe that authority had been overturned by "a tumultuous Rabble, without any Appearance of general Concert, or without any Head to advise, or Leader to Conduct."[48]

One might think that progressive historians of the early twentieth century—people like John Franklin Jameson, Charles Beard, and Carl Becker—would have taken notice of this popular uprising, but since it did not appear at first glance to be a class struggle, it eluded their attention. While "conflict" historians failed to pick up on this forgotten revolution, "consensus" historians saw no need to rock the boat. In their monumental, 1,300-page compilation of primary sources published in 1958, Henry Steele Commager and Richard B. Morris failed to document this vital episode. Instead, they included a complete section titled "All America Rallies to the Aid of Beleaguered Boston," another on the debates within the First Continental Congress, and over thirty pages on Lexington and Concord.[49]

WHY THE STORY IS RARELY TOLD

There are several overlapping reasons why we have dropped the story of America's first and most successful revolution, each deeply rooted in our national self-image and the nature of storytelling. Nationalistic and narrative demands have conspired against this saga. Ironically, on several counts, the very strengths of the Revolution of 1774 have ensured its anonymity.

This revolution was democratic by design; the people not only preached popular sovereignty but also practiced it. Although the toppling of authority enjoyed unprecedented, widespread support, there were no charismatic, self-promoting leaders to anchor the story and serve as its "heroes." There could never be too much democracy, these people believed. These rebels ran their revolution like a mobilized town meeting, each participant as important as any other; all decisions, even during their mass street actions, had to be approved by "the body of the people."[50] This made for a stronger revolution, but it simultaneously helps explain why we know so little about a popular movement that would not even tolerate individual leadership.

This revolution involved no bloodshed, for resistance was unthinkable. The *force* of the people was so overwhelming that *violence* became unnecessary. The handful of Crown-appointed officials in Worcester, when confronted by 4,622 angry militiamen, had no choice but to submit. Had opposition been stronger, there might have been violence; that would have made for a bloodier tale but a weaker revolution—indeed, more like a civil war, with the population divided. If it bleeds it leads, they say, but because of its overwhelming popularity, this revolution didn't bleed.

The Massachusetts Revolution of 1774 was ubiquitous, erupting everywhere at once. General Gage had no idea where or when he might oppose it. But a widespread uprising, not marked by a single iconic event, is difficult to chronicle; there is no clear storyline, staring with A and climaxing at Z. This revolution occurred throughout the countryside, while the media of the times were confined to Boston. Again, the broad participation led to a stronger revolution but a less compelling tale.

Like all true revolutions, the Massachusetts Revolution of 1774 was a bullying affair. Who is David, and who is Goliath, when crowds numbering in the thousands force a few unarmed officials to cower and submit? Contrast this exertion of brute strength to "helping beleaguered Boston," a far gentler tale. Particularly now, when our powerful nation is undeniably Goliath, we prefer to balance our national self-image by treating the original patriots as David, overcoming great odds.

Like conservatives of the early nineteenth century, we remain fearful of our own revolution. All narratives of early United States history include accounts of an uprising labeled by its opponents Shays' Rebellion, which was modeled after the Revolution of 1774.[51] In 1786, exactly twelve years after Massachusetts farmers had closed the courts and dismantled the established government, many of the very same people tried to repeat their earlier triumph. In Great Barrington, Springfield, Worcester—all the same places—disgruntled citizens of rural Massachusetts, calling themselves "Regulators," once again gathered in crowds to topple existing authority. There were two important differences between the uprisings of 1774 and 1786: the latter was much smaller, involving crowds that numbered in the hundreds rather than the thousands, and it failed. In our histories, we have chosen to feature the smaller, failed rebellion in preference to the larger, successful one. Although we like to commemorate the break from Britain, we hesitate to celebrate the raw and rampant power of the people who made this happen.

Finally, we don't tell this story because we prefer other stories that appear to contradict it. If Paul Revere woke the sleepy-eyed farmers, how could those farmers *already* have staged a revolution and prepared for war? If Sam Adams was commander in chief of revolutionary unrest, how could anonymous rebels throughout the countryside, on their own, have cast off British rule without him? If the "most drastic" move by Parliament in 1774 was to close the port of Boston, and if this was the "final insult" to the colonists, how could a *different* act of oppression, the Massachusetts Government Act, have been the truly intolerable act, the one that disenfranchised an entire colony and led its citizens to topple British rule? If the "shot heard 'round the world" was the true start of the American Revolution, how can there have been a successful revolution *before* that shot was fired?

EMBATTLED FARMERS: "A GREAT SPONGY MASS"

Depicting the start of the American Revolution as a single iconic moment, "the shot heard 'round the world," confuses the revolution itself with the *defense* of that revolution. Worse yet, when Emerson's "shot" migrates from Concord, where it is fired by a patriot, to

Lexington, where it is allegedly fired by a British soldier, it becomes a passive event: patriots become victims, not true revolutionaries.

Politically, patriots needed to portray themselves that way. According to a spy report sent to General Gage on April 9, ten days before Lexington, Massachusetts rebels were divided into two camps:

> The people without doors are clamorous for an immediate commencement of hostilities but the moderate thinking people within [the Provincial Congress] wish to ward off that period till hostilities shall commence on the part of the Government which would prevent their being censured for their rashness by the other Colonies & that made a pretence for deserting them.[52]

The shots fired on April 19 placed radical and moderate patriots once again on the same page.

Because blood had finally flowed, not just in dribbles but in torrents, the events of April 19, 1775, assumed great symbolic as well as political significance. The memory of that special moment in our nation's history is indelibly inscribed and frequently celebrated in American lore. The "embattled farmers," the story goes, responded to Paul Revere's alarm, grabbed their hunting guns, rushed to the scene of the action, then ran through the hills, hiding behind trees and stone walls while firing away at the arrogant Redcoats, who marched foolishly on the road below.

This simple memory does not do justice to what these men did, for it pays no heed to the collective effort that went into preparing for this momentous day, nor to the organized manner in which the patriots engaged their adversary. Those farmers did not just run off willy-nilly when aroused from their sleep by an intricate and very effective communications network; they mustered into their units, then marched together to the scene of the action. Once there, they continued to fight in as methodical a manner as the situation permitted. Historian David Hackett Fischer, the meticulous chronicler of the day's battles, concludes that, from the confrontation on North Bridge midmorning to the time British reinforcements arrived just east of Lexington at around 2:30 p.m., patriot militiamen "stood against the British force in large formations at least eight times. Six of these confrontations led to fighting, four at close quarters. Twice the British infantry was broken. . . . Altogether, it was an extraordinary display of courage, resolve, and discipline by citizen-soldiers against regular troops." Even during the final stages of the fighting, which appeared more random, militiamen traveled from one skirmish to the next in a reasonably coordinated pattern, communicating with each other and with their officers to ensure their tactical engagements would achieve maximal results.[53]

Although they functioned in organized units, the method of their organization, by military standards, was not at all conventional. Officers were elected, not appointed, and they engaged in open dialogue with common soldiers. On-the-spot strategic decisions—whether to proceed to the left or the right, to fight or withdraw—were made not from the top down, but by deliberations and debates of the body of men in arms.[54] Vocal disagreements with commanding officers, far from being punishable offenses, were the norm. By contrast, the British privates who were ordered to march through the night were never even told their purpose or destination.

This was a new kind of army, not very seasoned in fighting but well versed in the arts of collective decision making. The "embattled farmers" thought and acted as empowered citizens working in concert, not as isolated individuals taking potshots at Redcoats. The group processes of Massachusetts militiamen had been well rehearsed during the preceding decade of political protest, and beyond that, for more than a century, through their town meetings and community management of churches. Indeed, self-governance for these men had a deep religious foundation: the "covenant," an agreement among men to worship God together while acting collectively within their communities. The minute men who fought so effectively on April 19 had actually signed such a covenant, agreeing to forsake the security of their homes to secure the common good: "We whose names are hereunto subscribed, do voluntarily inlist our selves, as Minute Men, to be ready for military operation, upon the shortest notice," they had promised each other.[55]

This was not a "real" army in the European mold, but an army it was, and militarily effective. Although George Washington and others would complain repeatedly about the untrained militia, they were better trained than we have been led to believe. Back in December 1774, the Massachusetts Provincial Congress had acknowledged the unique character of its army-in-the-making by changing its drill book from a standard British text to one drawn up by Timothy Pickering, a lawyer from Salem. Patriot soldiers should be "clearly informed of the reason of every action and movement," Pickering's manual stipulated. This differed markedly from the European model, Pickering claimed: " 'Tis the boast of some that their men are mere machines . . . but God forbid that my countrymen should ever be thus regarded." Guided by this philosophy, militiamen over the next four months went through their drills, suspecting they would soon be called into action.[56]

These Massachusetts militiamen, and others who followed in their steps over the next few years, trained in their own way, but train they did, and in times of crisis, they showed up. In the words of military historian John Shy, "A reservoir, sand in the gears, the militia also looked like a great spongy mass that could be pushed aside or maimed temporarily but that had no vital center and could not be destroyed."[57] As British soldiers retreated from Concord back to Boston, they were besieged by just such a "spongy mass." Early that morning, while marching toward Lexington and Concord, Redcoats had amused themselves by singing "Yankee Doodle," a pejorative little ditty that depicted their opponents as ignorant, provincial farmers. They failed to grasp that to defend the revolution they staged many months before, these farmers had already turned themselves into soldiers. Every time we treat American patriots as no more than unsuspecting victims who needed to be aroused from their slumber, we repeat the mistake the Redcoats made. Although Emerson's embattled farmers had not opened fire until the confrontation by Concord's North Bridge on April 19, the shots, cartridges, and muskets they used had long stood at the ready, as had the men who fired them. Those months of preparation were part and parcel of the American Revolution, which was well in progress by the time the world heard the first shot.

5

THE WINTER AT VALLEY FORGE

To understand the staying power of the Valley Forge story, we need to see it through the eyes of a ten-year-old, for that is the age at which Americans first learn it in school. Other Revolutionary tales inspire images of toylike soldiers and men in wigs; they are alternately inspiring or quaint, but always remote. Not so with the suffering soldiers at Valley Forge. This is a story of elemental forces.

Nowhere is the story told better than in F. van Wyck Mason's *The Winter at Valley Forge*, one of the "Landmark Books" written for a youthful audience in the mid–twentieth century: "What a miracle was wrought at Valley Forge! This winter encampment with its pain and suffering, its heartaches and despair, might well be called the turning point of the Revolution." Mason's classic work, which introduced the story to an entire generation, depicts dedicated soldiers enduring cold and snow for the good of their country. The winter of 1777–1778, Mason writes, was "one of the cruelest winters in our country's history." As "the blizzards howled" and "the ice thickened," the rebels "found new courage, new resolve, new faith in their cause."[1] This stirring image anchors the traditional telling of the American Revolution: suffering soldiers, fueled by faith, withstood not only the wrath of the British Empire but also the worst that God Himself could deal out.

“In the midst of frost and snows,
disease and destitution, Liberty erected her altar.”

Valley Forge: March, 1777. Drawing by
Felix Octavius Carr Darley, mid-nineteenth century.

There are two important components to the story. First, the cruel hand of nature. Without the blizzards and the bitter cold, there would be little to celebrate in this wintering of the Continental Army. Militarily, the encampment at Valley Forge was merely an interlude; in terms of battlefield casualties, those were the quietest months during the entire course of the Revolutionary War.[2]

Second, patient suffering. Patriots were willing to endure extreme hardships, we are told, because they believed so strongly in their country. They were humble folk, not rich and arrogant like those British officers who lounged comfortably in nearby Philadelphia. Again, we like to see ourselves as David, doing battle with Goliath. The rebels, although outsized and outclassed, had *character.* They would do anything for the cause of freedom.

Both subplots are mistaken. Soldiers did not suffer silently. Routinely, they complained and pillaged; sometimes, they deserted; they almost mutinied. And the weather itself was hardly to blame. The winter spent at Valley Forge was milder than normal. By contrast, two years later, Continental soldiers survived the coldest winter in four hundred years on the eastern seaboard of the United States—and yet, strangely, that story is rarely told.

A LITTLE RESPECT

The Valley Forge story, in its traditional form, is disrespectful to the soldiers who endured years of hardships, endangered their lives, and in many cases actually died so that the United States could gain and retain its independence. To give these patriots the respect that is their due, we need not create idealized fantasies about how well they behaved themselves.

At Valley Forge and throughout the Revolutionary War, Continental soldiers demanded the food, clothing, and pay that had been promised them—and for good reason. Had they not tended to their own concerns and needs, they would not have been able to stay in the field and face the enemy. To appreciate this, we have to understand who these men really were and how they came to serve in the Continental Army.

Although we might like to believe otherwise, the United States won its freedom with the help of hired gunmen. At the beginning of the war, in 1775, all sorts of people showed up to fight. Farmers and artisans, rich and poor, young and old—patriots came forth with uncommon zeal. But this could not last. By the close of 1775, farmers had returned to their farms and artisans to their shops. Since most people had businesses of their own to attend to, Congress found it difficult to induce recruits to fight for their country. "The few who act upon Principles of disinterestedness," George Washington told Congress in September 1776, "are, comparatively speaking, no more than a drop in the Ocean."[3]

Reluctantly, the Continental Congress offered bounties to those who agreed to join the army. This helped, but it did not suffice. Starting in 1777, Congress fixed the number of companies that each state had to recruit for the Continental Army. States and towns, hoping to fill their quotas, added bounties of their own, but even that was not enough. Without sufficient volunteers, most communities resorted to a draft, but in those days, a draftee had only to produce a body, either his own or someone else's. Those with sufficient means, if called, hired those looking for work to fill their place. In this manner, the ranks of the Continental Army became filled with boys eager for adventure and men without property or jobs. These were the folks who hobbled into Valley Forge on December 19, 1777.

Civilians—those who had not joined up—showed no great love for either the Continental Army or the soldiers who comprised it. They feared standing armies in general (indeed, that was one of the major complaints they voiced against Great Britain), while they looked down upon the men who actually served in this one. As historian John Shy has observed, "The men who shouldered the heaviest military burden were something *less* than average colonial Americans. As a group, they were poorer, more marginal, less well anchored in society."[4] The army became representative not of the American population, but only of its lower orders: poor men and boys, laborers and apprentices, even Indians and former slaves.

This was not truly a citizens' army, as originally intended; it was far closer to the European model than Americans (both then and now) have chosen to admit. Many civilians at the time preferred to look the other way, ignoring rather than supporting the men who had become professional soldiers. Quaker farmers residing near Valley Forge had their own reasons to resent the fighting Presbyterians and Congregationalists, lads whose business it was to kill, while soldiers, on their part, grumbled about the "cursed Quakers" who were "no Friends to the Cause we are engaged in."[5] Soldiers grew to resent the lack of support they received not only from the Quakers but from "Ye who Eat Pumpkin Pie and Roast Turkeys."[6] Increasingly, the hired guns of the Continental Army saw themselves as a class apart.

At Valley Forge, it is often said, Baron von Steuben infused military discipline into the ragtag Continental Army. He turned farmers into soldiers. Although there is some truth in this, farmers became soldiers not only by marching to the commands of their officers, but also by developing a unique sense of identity, separate and distinct from all other Americans. They did indeed become a professional army, with all that that entails.

Ill prepared to support a permanent army, Congress allowed the Commissary Department to fall into a shambles. Food and clothing, much needed, never arrived. Congress, not the raw forces of nature, was accountable for the lack of provisions that caused the soldiers much grief.

Forced to fend for themselves, troops ventured forth from Valley Forge to pillage local civilians. John Lesher, who lived twenty-five miles away, complained that he was "no master of any individual thing I possess." American troops, he said, "under the shadows of the Bayonet and the appellation Tory act as they please."[7] Farmers were so discouraged that they threatened not to plant new crops. Years later, Private Joseph Plumb Martin admitted that " 'Rub and Go' was always the Revolutionary soldier's motto."[8]

At other times during the war, George Washington issued prohibitions against pillaging, but at Valley Forge he was forced to sanction the practice. Although he used the polite term "forage" rather than "pillage" or "plunder," the commander in chief ordered soldiers to strip the countryside clean.[9] Farmers were stopped on their way to market, households were raided, and magazines were depleted of all provisions. Reluctant local inhabitants, accustomed to being paid real money for their produce, grain, milk, and meat, were given only notes of questionable worth. Private Martin recalled that he received orders direct from the quartermaster-general "to go into the country on a foraging expedition, which was nothing more nor less than to procure provisions from the inhabitants for the men in the army . . . at the point of the bayonet."[10]

Soldiers tended to their needs in other ways as well. Some simply ran away. According to the traditional tale, all men remained true; in fact, eight to ten men deserted daily from Valley Forge.[11] On February 12, 1778, during a period of extreme shortages, Washington wrote: "We find the Continental troops (especially those who are not Natives) are very apt to desert from the piquets."[12]

The standard story ignores mutinies as well as desertions. On December 23, 1777, Washington reported that "a dangerous mutiny" two nights before had been suppressed "with difficulty."[13] In February, Washington reported that "strong symptoms of discontent" had appeared, and he feared that "a general mutiny and dispersion" might be forthcoming if complaints were not actively addressed.[14] In April, Washington complained that ninety officers from the Virginia line had just resigned, others were following suit, and he feared for "the very existence of the Army."[15] Although Washington might have been exaggerating for effect, it remains clear that suffering soldiers were not simply enduring their lot, silently and heroically—they were standing up for themselves. If the United States wanted an army, it would have to treat the soldiers better. Privates stated this emphatically by threats of mutiny or by simply running away. Officers threatened to resign, and many did. Actions such as these succeeded in arousing the attention first of Washington, and then, through him, of Congress and state officials. Eventually the complaints of soldiers achieved some results, even if minimal. Had soldiers not voiced their discontent and acted accordingly, the army probably *would* have dissipated.

As the war dragged on, mutinies became a real cause of concern. The famous ones—uprisings within the Connecticut, Pennsylvania, and New Jersey lines; the march on Congress on June 21, 1783; the aborted "Newburg Conspiracy"—represent only the tip of the iceberg. Firsthand accounts by both privates and officers reveal that resistance was the rule rather than the exception. Soldiers in the Continental Army repeatedly threatened to take matters into their own hands unless their basic needs were met.

The reporting of acts of resistance within the army undermines the illusion of patient suffering. Since soldiers in the Continental Army did desert in great numbers, and since mutinies were far more common than in any war this nation has ever fought against a foreign enemy, the traditional telling of the Valley Forge story requires turning a blind eye to official statistics. *Liberty!*—the book that accompanies the PBS six-hour documentary on the Revolution—announces point-blank that "desertions were relatively few" at Valley Forge.[16] Popular authors often dismiss the subject of mutiny by telling a story of George Washington and the "Newburg Conspiracy." On the ides of March 1783, at his headquarters in Newburg, New York, the beloved commander in chief allegedly defused a movement among his officers to march against Congress with a simple offhand remark: "Gentlemen," he is supposed to have said, "you will permit me to put on my spectacles, for I have not only grown gray but almost blind in the service of my country." This, allegedly, was all it took to counter all mutinous or treasonous activities: "It moved the officers deeply, and tears welled in their eyes," the story goes. "Again they felt a tremendous surge of affection for the commander who had led them all so far and long."[17] So much for mutinies in the Continental Army.

To romanticize soldiers in an attempt to honor them dishonors them instead. Rather than denying or ignoring mutinies and desertions, we should examine soldiers' grievances and how they responded to them. To this end, we have no better informant than Private Joseph Plumb Martin. Although Martin reported that he and others had made it through the Valley Forge winter by pillaging, their hardships did not end the following spring. Martin reported that two years later, in May 1780, "the monster Hunger, still attended us; he was not to be shaken off by any efforts we could use, for here was the old story of starving, as rife as ever." Continental soldiers were forced to confront the most profound dilemma any American patriot has ever had to face:

> The men were now exasperated beyond endurance; they could not stand it any longer. They saw no alternative but to starve to death, or break up the army, give all up and go home. This was a hard matter for the soldiers to think upon. They were truly patriotic, they loved their country, and they had already suffered everything short of death in its cause; and now, after such extreme hardships to give up all was too much, but to starve to death was too much also. What was to be done? Here was the army starved and naked, and there their country sitting still and expecting the army to do notable things while fainting from sheer starvation.[18]

This is the real Valley Forge story, and it lasted for eight long years. It features poor men and boys who fought in place of those who were better off. When these soldiers failed to receive adequate food, minimal clothing, or the pay they had been promised, they were forced to weigh their options: Should they endure their hardships silently, grumble among themselves, or create a fuss? If all else failed should they mutiny or simply walk away? All alternatives were possible, none favorable. In addition to staving off hunger and fighting the enemy, soldiers had to deal with this unsolvable problem day by day.

In this particular instance, Joseph Martin and his compatriots chose to act forcibly. "We had borne as long as human nature could endure, and to bear longer we considered folly," Martin continued. One day, while on parade, the privates began "growling like soreheaded dogs . . . snapping at the officers, and acting contrary to their orders." This led to a series of events sometimes labeled the "mutiny in the Connecticut line." Technically, the soldiers' behavior was mutinous, for privates did challenge the authority of officers; at one point, they even held bayonets to the chests of those in command. But the soldiers were not trying to seize power; they only wanted to gain some respect and a corresponding increase in rations. They did what they had to do, no more—and they achieved results: "Our stir did us some good in the end," Martin reported, "for we had provisions directly after."[19]

A TALE OF TWO WINTERS

The winter of 1777–1778 was not "one of the cruelest winters in our country's history." We have no record of daily temperatures at Valley Forge, but in nearby Philadelphia, only seventeen miles away, temperatures ran slightly above the historic average (see table). On more than half the winter mornings, there was no frost. Soldiers had to endure only one extended, hard freeze—from December 29 to December 31—and the thermometer dropped below double digits, briefly, only twice. Some snow did fall, but there were no memorable blizzards. Snowfall was "moderate, not heavy," according to weather historian David Ludlum. "On the basis of cold statistics," writes Ludlum, "the winter of 1777–1778 was not a severe one."[20]

Days with Low Temperature Below Freezing—Philadelphia[21]

	1777–1778	Historic Average
December	17	21
January	15	25
February	13	22
March	5	14

Ironically, soldiers in the Continental Army did have to endure a particularly cruel winter—but it wasn't during their camp at Valley

Forge. While camped at Morristown, New Jersey, in 1779–1780, they encountered what Ludlum concludes was "the severest season in all American history."[22] In Philadelphia, the *high* temperature for the day rose above freezing only once during the month of January.[23] On January 20 Timothy Matlack wrote to Joseph Reed from Philadelphia: "The ink now freezes in my pen within five feet of the fire in my parlour, at 4 o'clock in the afternoon."[24] In New York, a thermometer at British headquarters dropped to -16 degrees Fahrenheit; the lowest official reading since that time has been –15.[25] In Hartford, a daily thermometer reading revealed that January 1780 was the coldest calendar month in recorded history. On twenty-one days, the temperature dropped below 10 degrees Fahrenheit; between January 19 and January 31, subzero temperatures were recorded on nine different days, bottoming out at –22.[26]

With temperatures this low, and the cold lasting for such an extended period of time, rivers and bays froze hard. In New York, the Hudson and East Rivers turned to ice. So did New York Harbor, much of Long Island Sound, and some of the ocean itself. To the south, the Delaware River froze, as did large portions of the Chesapeake Bay. In Virginia, the York and James Rivers became solid. As far south as North Carolina, Albemarle Sound froze over. According to David Ludlum, nothing like this had ever happened since the arrival of Europeans, and it has yet to happen again:

> During one winter only in recorded American meteorological history have *all* the saltwater inlets, harbors, and sounds of the Atlantic coastal plain, from North Carolina northeastward, frozen over and remained closed to navigation for a period of a full month and more. This occurred during what has ever been called "The Hard Winter of 1780," a crucial period during the war when General Washington's poorly housed, ill-clad, and under-nourished American troops at Morristown in the north Jersey hills were keeping a watchful eye on the British army

much more comfortably quartered in New York City some 20 miles distant.[27]

For one winter only, frozen bays and rivers became new roadways. Rebel deserters walked across the Hudson, from New Jersey to British-controlled New York. Hessian deserters from the British army crossed Long Island Sound on foot to rebel-controlled Connecticut. The British carried firewood on sleighs across the Hudson River from New Jersey to Manhattan. They also sent sleighs laden with provisions from Manhattan to Staten Island, and they even rolled cannons across the ice; meanwhile, a detachment of British cavalry rode their horses across New York Harbor in the other direction. Sleighs traversed the Chesapeake from Baltimore to Annapolis. Had Washington decided to make his famous crossing of the Delaware during "The Hard Winter" instead of three years earlier, he could have dispensed with his boats—the troops would simply have marched across the frozen waters.[28]

Along with cold and ice came the snow. The first major fall in Morristown arrived on December 18, 1779, and the ground remained covered for three months afterward. In late December and early January, a series of violent storms swept through the entire Northeast. On December 28–29, the wind toppled several houses in New York City. In Morristown, several feet of snow fell during the first week of January. Joseph Plumb Martin recalled the effects of the storm on the soldiers:

> The winter of 1779 and '80 was very severe; it has been denominated "the hard winter," and hard it was to the army in particular, in more respects than one. The period of the revolution has repeatedly been styled "the times that tried men's souls." I often found that those times not only tried men's souls, but their bodies too; I know they did mine, and that effectually. . . .
>
> At one time it snowed the greater part of four days

> successively, and there fell nearly as many feet deep of snow, and here was the keystone of the arch of starvation. We were absolutely, literally starved. I do solemnly declare that I did not put a single morsel of victuals into my mouth for four days and as many nights, except a little black birch bark which I gnawed off a stick of wood, if that can be called victuals. I saw several of the men roast their old shoes and eat them, and I was afterwards informed by one of the officers' waiters, that some of the officers killed and ate a favorite little dog that belonged to one of them.—If this was not "suffering" I request to be informed what can pass under that name; if "suffering" like this did not "try men's souls," I confess that I do not know what could.[29]

As privates struggled to stay alive, officers worried about the impact on their army. On January 5, 1780, General Nathanael Greene wrote from Morristown: "Here we are surrounded with Snow banks, and it is well we are, for if it was good traveling, I believe the Soldiers would take up their packs and march, they having been without provision two or three days."[30] The following day, Greene's worst fears were almost realized: "The Army is upon the eve of disbanding for want of Provisions," he reported. On January 8 Ebenezer Huntington reported, "the Snow is very deep & the Coldest Weather I ever experienced for three weeks altogether. Men almost naked & what is still worst almost Starved."[31] Huntington, at that point, was unaware that the coldest weather was yet to come.

That same day—January 8, 1780—Washington himself offered a very bleak assessment: "The present situation of the Army with respect to provisions is the most distressing of any we have experienced since the beginning of the War"—and that included the winter spent at Valley Forge.[32] Johann de Kalb, who served as an officer under Washington, stated definitively: "Those who have only been in Valley Forge and Middlebrook during the last two winters, but have not tasted the cruelties of this one, know not what it is to suffer."[33] For all those who experienced both winters, there could be no doubt: Morristown was by far the worst.

Hardships continued. Since the snowpack hindered the shipment of supplies, soldiers had to face much of the winter cold and hungry. How long could they endure? On February 10 General Greene once again reported: "Our Army has been upon the point of disbanding for want of provisions."[34] Finally, in mid-March, the weather warmed and the snow melted. Supplies arrived, and the worst was over. On March 18 Washington summed up the experience in a letter to General Lafayette: "The oldest people now living in this Country do not remember so hard a Winter as the one we are now emerging from. In a word, the severity of the frost exceeded anything of the kind that had ever been experienced in this climate before."[35]

For the soldiers, it had never been worse than at Morristown. Yet the Continental Army made it through intact. According to those on the ground at the time, not those who would tell the story generations later, Morristown was truly the low point of the war—the real-life "Valley Forge."

Why, then, do we make such a big deal of "The Winter at Valley Forge," while the "Hard Winter" at Morristown is nearly forgotten? Revolutionary soldiers, scantily clad and poorly fed, had to brave the harshest weather in at least four hundred years; why is this not a part of our standard histories?

The answer, in a nutshell, is that Valley Forge better fits the story we wish to tell, while Morristown is something of an embarrassment. At Valley Forge, the story goes, soldiers suffered quietly and patiently. They remained true to their leader. At Morristown, on the other hand, they mutinied—and this is not in line with the "suffering soldiers" motif.

As a story, Morristown doesn't work for several other reasons as well. First of all, soldiers in the Continental Army camped there during four different winters, and this is much too confusing.[36] The "Hard Winter" was the second of these. The following winter, on

January 1, 1781, the Pennsylvania line staged the largest and most successful mutiny of the Revolutionary War. Although this did not take place during the winter of 1779–1780, any mention of Morristown would necessitate at least a nod to this mutiny, which many narrative accounts conveniently leave out. The New Jersey Brigade also camped at Morristown during that third winter, and they too had just mutinied; this uprising was unsuccessful, culminating with the execution of several mutineers. To include all this would undermine a central feature of the "suffering soldier" lesson: clearly, these patriots had not endured their plight in silence.

Furthermore, to tell the complete Morristown saga would reveal that the soldiers' hardships continued throughout the war, virtually unabated. Soldiers in the Continental Army never did receive the help they needed or the respect they deserved. To admit this would make the civilian population look bad. Why didn't other patriots come to the aid of those who did the fighting?

The story of Valley Forge, on the other hand, tells us what we want to hear. Supposedly, soldiers learned to behave themselves when Baron von Steuben whipped them into shape. There were no major uprisings. The troops were allegedly obedient and well behaved. They remained faithful to Washington when his command was challenged by intrigue. All this looks good.

Also, Valley Forge and the American victory at Saratoga happened in close succession. From the storytelling point of view, this works well. Valley Forge was the "low point," and Saratoga the "turning point," of the Revolutionary War. (Strangely, the low point occurred shortly *after* the turning point, but this technical glitch is generally overlooked.) After Valley Forge, the darkest hour was supposedly over. Come spring, once the soldiers had proved their worth, their troubles subsided. This mythic tale is based on the classic image of seasonal renewal, not historical documentation. Although hardships continued and even worsened until the end of the war, and although mutinies became rampant, the Valley Forge story serves to suppress these later difficulties. Narratives can refer to "suffering soldiers" at a precise, well-defined time, without including the more serious uprisings that followed. By telling the story of the soldiers' plight there, writers do not have to visit it later on, when a spirit of resistance swept through the Continental Army.

Finally, Valley Forge makes for a powerful story because many soldiers died. In fact, the deaths were primarily due to camp diseases—cold and hunger took few lives—but that is rarely stated because disease evokes little sense of drama or patriotic sentiment. (More soldiers actually lost their lives because of disease than at the hands of the enemy during the Revolutionary War.[37]) Still, a death toll always helps a story along. The winter at Valley Forge was so severe, we are led to believe, that people actually perished because of it—and all without raising a fuss. Such patriots they must have been!

CONSECRATED GROUND: THE STORY ENSHRINED

Nobody celebrated Valley Forge during the Revolution itself. At the time, the sorry plight of soldiers at this winter camp was a guarded military secret—kept from the ears of the British, who might seize the moment to attack, and downplayed to the French, who might deny aid if they heard too much about the ragtag Continental Army. Just before Christmas in 1777, after setting up camp in Valley Forge, Washington told Congress, "Upon the ground of safety and policy, I am obliged to conceal the true State of the Army from Public view." But the members of Congress, he confided, should be aware that there had been a "total failure of Supplies." Conditions were so bad, he reported, that "we have . . . no less than 2898 Men now in Camp unfit for duty because they are bare foot and otherwise naked."[38]

Washington's complaints to Congress, contained in his letters of December 22 and 23, 1777, comprise the basic documentation for the Valley Forge story, even though they were written just days after the army arrived there. Undoubtedly, Washington issued his bleak reports for a practical reason: he wanted to shock congressional delegates into action. The Commissary Department was in a state of collapse, unable to provide many essential items. Without "more Vigorous exertions," he warned, "this Army must dissolve."[39] Writers often quote Washington's solicitations as the definitive source on the suffering soldiers at Valley Forge, although most have chosen to ignore his repeated warnings that malcontents were on the verge of mutiny. Without his pleading words, geared for maximum effect, there would likely be no legend of Valley Forge. At Morristown, two years later, Washington painted an equally bleak picture, also geared for effect—but these words have been conveniently overlooked.

After the war, as during the war, civilians chose not to harp on the sorry state of the Continental Army, whether at Valley Forge or Morristown. The very existence of the army was something of an embarrassment to many Americans, who opposed standing armies on republican principles. The decrepit state of this particular assemblage of lower-class men and boys was particularly shameful. If anybody had spun the Valley Forge tale back then, they would have been deemed unpatriotic.

Postwar historians did not romanticize the winter camp at Valley Forge. David Ramsay (1789) devoted only one and a half sentences to Valley Forge in over seven hundred pages. Although William Gordon (1788) and John Marshall (1804) described the camp and cited Washington's letters, they did not treat it as a defining moment in the history of the Revolution or claim that soldiers always endured their hardships in silence. In fact, Marshall emphasized that soldiers seized provisions from local farmers, and all the early historians included extensive discussions of the later mutinies, indications of the soldiers' discontent.[40]

In the early 1800s, some Americans began to focus on the notion of "patient suffering" and affixed this to a particular time and place: the 1777–1778 camp at Valley Forge. In 1805, more than a quarter of a century after the fact, Mercy Otis Warren described the condition of the troops in vivid detail:

> The resolution and patience of this little army surmounted every difficulty. They waited long, amid penury, hunger, and cold, for the necessary supplies. . . . Unprovided with materials to raise their cold lodgment from the ground, the dampness of the situation, and the wet earth on which they lay, occasioned sickness and mortality to rage among them to an astonishing degree.

Warren was perhaps the first to use this experience as a key characteristic of the Revolution:

> We have seen through the narrative of events during the war, the armies of the American states suffering hunger and cold, nakedness, fatigue, and danger, with unparalleled patience and valor. A due sense of the importance of the contest in which they were engaged, and the certain ruin and disgrace in which themselves and their children would be involved on the defeat of their object, was a strong stimulus to patient suffering.[41]

Any "murmurs" of discontent, she concluded, were quickly quieted by "an attachment to their commanding officers, a confidence in the faith of congress, and the sober principles of independence, equity and equality."

To the actual troops encamped at Valley Forge, the phrase "confidence in the faith of congress" would have appeared as a joke in bad taste. Congress failed to pay them as promised, let alone feed and clothe them, and soldiers resented this bitterly. Yet Warren chose to paint a cozy picture: the bedraggled army and Congress united in common cause. Ironically, the "patient suffering" story demonstrated unity between soldiers and civilians; in truth, the suffering of the soldiers was directly attributable to lack of civilian support, and this caused no end of ill feeling.

As the notion of "patient suffering" caught on, it attached to the camp at Valley Forge. When David Ramsay came out with his *Life of*

George Washington in 1807, he included a much more extensive treatment of Valley Forge than he had in his earlier history.[42] In 1808, in the sixth edition of his immensely popular *Life of Washington*, Mason Weems told a new tale: the commander in chief, while alone in the woods at Valley Forge, was seen kneeling in prayer.[43] For more than a century, this pious image would be repeated again and again, testimony to the faith of the man, the army, and the nation.

After thirty years, civilians no longer perceived the fighting men of the Continental Army as a threat. Quite to the contrary: in the military mobilization that culminated in the War of 1812, patriotic writers and orators found it convenient to extol the virtues of the men who had prevailed in the Revolutionary War. In his July 4, 1812, oration to Congress, Richard Rush praised the "noble achievements" of Revolutionary soldiers, and he then insisted that Americans not "dishonor" their memory by failing to answer the current call to arms.[44]

Veterans who were once scorned suddenly found they were being celebrated. The sites of their brave deeds were consecrated, and this brought Valley Forge into play. The May 1812 issue of Virginia's *Monthly Magazine and Literary Journal* suggested that Valley Forge be sanctified as "classic ground to posterity" because of the "toil" and "sufferings" which the soldiers had experienced there.[45] Morristown, its legacy clouded by mutinies, was not similarly consecrated—"patient suffering" could not be attached to such a place.

Revolutionary War veterans naturally welcomed the change of attitude and gave it a practical turn. Yes, they had suffered patiently—so now, at last, they should be recompensed. Calling forth memories of mutinies, at this juncture, would have been counterproductive. Vets pushed hard to receive pensions, and in 1818, forty years after the camp at Valley Forge, Congress finally allocated money to Revolutionary soldiers who could show proof of both service and need.

From that point on, the patient suffering of the soldiers at Valley Forge became a common refrain in most American histories. Salma Hale, in his 1822 history written for schoolchildren as well as adults, romanticized the experience of the soldiers at Valley Forge: "They passed the winter in huts, suffered extreme distress from want of clothing and of food, but endured their privations without a murmur. How strong must have been their love of liberty?"[46] Charles Goodrich, writing in 1823, contrasted the Continental Army at Valley Forge with the British army in Philadelphia: "While the defenders of the country were thus suffering and perishing, the royal army was enjoying all the conveniences which an opulent city afforded."[47] This disparity between dedicated Americans and decadent Englishmen played well to a patriotic audience.

By the middle of the nineteenth century, scarcely a person was left alive who could accurately remember the severities of "The Hard Winter of 1780." In Revolutionary mythologies, the blizzards and biting cold of that winter were conveniently pushed back in time two years, to coincide with the camp at Valley Forge—the "severe winter of 1777 and '8," it was called. A newspaper in 1848 reported with an air of authority that this had been "one of the most rigorous winters ever experienced in this country. . . . So intently cold was the weather and so exhausted the soldiers when they commenced their march toward Valley Forge, that some were seen to drop dead under the benumbing influence of the frost."[48]

In 1851, Benson Lossing's travelogue of Revolutionary historic sites gave Valley Forge top billing:

> Valley Forge! How dear to the true worshiper at the shrine of Freedom is the name of Valley Forge! There, in the midst of frost and snows, disease and destitution, Liberty erected her altar; and in all the world's history we have no record of purer devotion, holier sincerity, or more pious self-sacrifice, than was there exhibited in the camp of Washington. The courage that nerves the arm on the battlefield, and dazzles by its brilliant but evanescent flashes, pales before the steadier and more intense flame of patient endurance, the sum of the sublime heroism displayed at Valley Forge. And if there is a spot on the face of our broad land whereon Patriotism should delight to pile its highest

> and most venerated monument, it should be in the bosom of that little valley on the bank of the Schuylkill.[49]

Here was the Valley Forge story full blown, much as we know it today.

By the centennial celebrations in 1876, Valley Forge had become ingrained in the national consciousness. In step with the times, the local community prepared to commemorate the one hundredth anniversary of the Continental Army's winter camp of 1777–1778. But what kind of celebration would be appropriate to honor the miserable time at Valley Forge, allegedly the lowest point in the history of the Revolutionary War?

A summer solstice party, of course. On June 19, 1878, thousands of locals joined with national celebrities to revel on the anniversary of "evacuation day," the breaking of camp. Capitalizing on the momentum, the Centennial and Memorial Association of Valley Forge gathered funds to purchase Washington's headquarters, a fixed point where tourists could pay their respects. In the years to follow, additional sites were preserved or restored, and in 1893 Valley Forge became a state park. On "evacuation day" of 1917, the federal government added its stamp of approval with the dedication of the National Memorial Arch, and on July 4, 1976, the day of the nation's bicentennial celebration, the state park was transformed into the Valley Forge National Historical Park, a shrine that remains to this day the destination point for over one million patriotic pilgrims every year.[50]

In the years following the bicentennial, a new wave of scholars challenged the "patient suffering" theme. In academic circles, this threatened the traditional telling of the Valley Forge story, but there was has been little carryover into popular history or textbook renderings. Every text at every level of education must say something about Valley Forge; by contrast, Morristown is still rarely mentioned. In some texts, Valley Forge now plays an even larger role. Conveniently inverting the discussions of Saratoga and Valley Forge to make the timing work, and borrowing the term "hard winter" from the true hard winter at Morristown, which it never discusses, one college text presents a double-page feature entitled "A National Community Evolves at Valley Forge." This section concludes: "The glue that held Americans together during the long struggle was the sense of national community that emerged in places like Valley Forge during the winter of 1777."[51] That Valley Forge was "the glue" holding people together through the remaining years of the war would be big news for Americans at the time, who did their best to ignore and even suppress the experience. True, soldiers thought of themselves in more national terms after that, but nobody else did. The mistrust between soldiers and civilians only heightened at Valley Forge, leaving the nation more disjointed than ever. It was a winter to be forgotten, not remembered.

The Valley Forge story lives on. Although Mason Weems's tale about Washington praying in the woods is no longer repeated as fact, and although blacks and Indians are now included among the barefoot soldiers, the broad strokes remain the same. When told to children, the story features the cruel hand of Nature; when told to adults, it sometimes lays the blame on Congress as well as Nature—but in either case, the soldiers proved their patriotism through patient suffering, and the values celebrated are passive obedience and blind devotion. These were deemed prime virtues in the early stages of American nationalism, and they are still seen as virtues in some modern states—but why us, and why now? In a modern democracy, such passivity seems oddly out of sync.

From the beginning, Revolutionary soldiers exhibited the freedom they were fighting for. Understandably, this caused their officers some concern. The rebel soldiers "carry the spirit of freedom into the field, and think for themselves," complained General Richard Montgomery, one of the leaders of the Quebec expedition. Montgomery could not understand why troops called "a sort of town meeting" every time a maneuver was planned. "The privates are all generals," he reported.[52] From a military point of view, this excessive spirit had to be reined in, at least to some extent. But it never disappeared, nor should it have. Supposedly, Americans cherish initiative and independence, but the traditional Valley Forge saga belittles these values; by contrast, the true story of soldiers in the Continental Army embraces them. Throughout the Revolutionary War, soldiers considered their circumstances, weighed the available options, made decisions, and took actions they deemed appropriate. Behaving like good, patriotic citizens, they made their needs known and stood up for their rights. They did not suffer in silence—instead, they devised means to make things better. They did whatever they needed to do to keep themselves alive, fed, and able to carry on.

WISE MEN

"Jefferson's Declaration of Independence was great from the moment he wrote it."

Thomas Jefferson Writing the Declaration of Independence.
Painting by Howard Pyle, 1898.

6

JEFFERSON'S DECLARATION

Since the Declaration of Independence was undeniably a great document, we naturally assume that only a great mind could have created it. That mind supposedly belonged to Thomas Jefferson, the genius of the Revolution. Jefferson's image has suffered of late because DNA evidence suggests he fathered children with his slave, Sally Hemings—but few question the quality or cogency of his thinking, or the belief that only a man of Jefferson's intellectual caliber could have drafted the momentous document that set us apart as an independent nation.

In *Liberty!* Thomas Fleming notes that Jefferson did not boast about his authorship of the Declaration of Independence. The document contained no "new principles or new arguments," Jefferson admitted. Instead, it was "intended to be an expression of the American mind." Too much "modesty," Fleming complains. There was no "American mind" at the time. The Declaration, despite Jefferson's disclaimers, was all his own doing: "Jefferson poured into it his experience as an opponent of aristocratic privilege in Virginia," Fleming argues. Only Jefferson could have said the things he did. The visuals accompanying the text underline his thesis: we see a portrait of Jefferson brooding over a candlelit draft, followed by a facsimile of the draft itself, with many of Jefferson's deletions and additions.[1]

Joseph Ellis presents a more complex version of the same argument. In *American Sphinx*, winner of the National Book Award for nonfiction in 1997, Ellis notes that Jefferson was in a position to draw on the works of many others, including George Mason, who had just drafted a very similar document, the Virginia Declaration of Rights. Ellis then lists other possible influences on Jefferson: the social contract theory of John Locke, the moral philosophy of the Scottish Enlightenment, and contemporary books on rhetoric and the art of the spoken word. At this juncture, Ellis offers an apt observation:

> The central problem with all these explanations, however, is that they make Jefferson's thinking an exclusive function of books. . . . There is a long-standing scholarly tradition—one might call it the scholarly version of poetic license—that depends on the unspoken assumption that what one thinks is largely or entirely a product of what one reads.

This point is well taken. Certainly we are more than the sum of what we read. But if not from books, where did Jefferson's ideas come from? "From deep inside himself," Ellis posits. The Declaration of Independence represented "the vision of a young man projecting his personal cravings" for a better world.[2]

Ellis's view of the creative process sets individual imagination above all else. The internal vision of the creator—a "wise man"—is not tarnished by external influences. This romantic notion ignores the political setting in which Jefferson lived. There was a revolution going on, and it had been brewing for more than a decade. People talked and wrote to each other incessantly. They engaged in hearty and contentious debate. They designed and circulated petitions and declarations. In those critical years patriots throughout the British colonies worked themselves up to the fever pitch that revolution requires. Revolutionary phrases were stated and repeated so often that they entered the very language. They became the common currency of what might very rightly be called "the American mind."

Most plain folk in America had not studied John Locke's *Second Treatise on Government*, but in any country tavern, ordinary farmers could recite the principle of the "social contract": government is rooted in the people, and rulers who forget this are ripe for a fall.[3] From first-hand experience and incessant repetition, they knew all they needed to know about popular sovereignty. For the antecedents and precedents that influenced the Declaration of Independence, Jefferson had only to look to the nearest tavern or meetinghouse, wherever patriots gathered. The most significant "source" for his forceful statement of popular sovereignty was, appropriately, the people themselves—the "American mind" that he himself rightfully credited.

THE "OTHER" DECLARATIONS OF INDEPENDENCE

On October 4, 1774, twenty-one months before the Continental Congress approved its public explanation of why it had broken from Britain, the people of Worcester, Massachusetts, declared that they were ready for independence. (See chapter 4.) Worcester was certainly in the vanguard, but patriots in other towns and other colonies also declared their willingness to break from Britain several months before a committee of the Second Continental Congress asked Thomas Jefferson to draft a formal declaration. In Jefferson's Virginia, the issue of independence preempted all others during the spring of 1776. Common folk, not just the famous patricians-turned-statesmen, came to embrace independence for political, economic, and ideological reasons.[4] Beyond noble principles, fear of slaves and Indians contributed to the desire for independence. (See chapter 9.) In the April elections voters turned out in great numbers—and they stunned the more cautious politicians. Representatives who opposed independence or a republican form of government were turned out.[5]

Before sending off their new delegates to the Virginia Convention, constituents of several counties gave them specific, written instructions to vote for a declaration of independence. Charles Lee wrote to Patrick Henry: the "spirit of the people . . . cr[ies] out for this Declaration."[6] Jefferson himself was in Virginia during that time. "I took great pains to enquire into the sentiments of the people," he wrote on May 16, 1776, just a few weeks before he would pen his famous draft. "I think I may safely say nine out of ten are for it [independence]."[7] The people had spoken, the stage was set. On May 15, 1776, the Virginia Convention instructed its delegates to the Continental Congress to initiate a declaration of independence.

Acting more swiftly than the Continental Congress, Virginia proceeded to declare independence on its own. George Mason then prepared a draft for Virginia's "Declaration of Rights," which circulated widely in June 1776. It appeared in the *Pennsylvania Gazette* on June 12, the day after Jefferson was appointed to the five-man committee that would draft a national declaration. In Philadelphia, Jefferson and the other members of the committee no doubt examined these words closely. Two weeks later, Jefferson presented his own refinement of Mason's draft:[8]

Draft of the Virginia Declaration of Rights (George Mason)	Draft of the Declaration of Independence (Thomas Jefferson)
1. That all men are born equally free and independant, and have certain inherent natural rights, . . . among which are the enjoyment of life and liberty, with the means of acquiring and possessing property, and pursuing and obtaining happiness and safety.	We hold these truths to be self-evident; that all men are created equal; that they are endowed by their Creator with inherent and inalienable rights; that among these are life, liberty, and the pursuit of happiness.

Draft of the Virginia Declaration of Rights (George Mason) (*continued*)	Draft of the Declaration of Independence (Thomas Jefferson) (*continued*)
2. That all power is vested in, and consequently derived from, the people. . . . That government is, or ought to be, instituted for the common benefit, protection, and security of the people, nation, or community.	[T]hat to secure these rights, governments are instituted among men, deriving their just powers from the consent of the governed.
3. Of all the various modes and forms of government, that is best, which is capable of producing the greatest degree of happiness and safety, . . . and that, whenever any government shall be found inadequate or contrary to these purposes, a majority of the community hath an indubitable, unalienable and indefeasible right to reform, alter, or abolish it, in such manner as shall be judged most conducive to the public weal.	[T]hat whenever any form of government becomes destructive of these ends, it is the right of the people to alter or abolish it, and to institute new government, laying it's foundation on such principles and organizing it's powers in such form as to them shall seem most likely to effect their safety and happiness.

Although Jefferson's prose flows more smoothly from point to point than Mason's, he certainly introduced no new concepts. Many key phrases were merely rearranged. Jefferson in no sense "copied" the Virginia Declaration, but he was evidently influenced by it. That should come as no surprise. This was a time of frenzied but collective agitation, and the Revolution's participants continually referred to each other's words and propositions. In all likelihood Mason himself was familiar with Jefferson's *Summary View of the Rights of British*

America, written two years earlier. Undoubtedly, both men had read classic English and Scottish works that espoused revolutionary principles, and both were privy to expressions that were common parlance among their peers. Mason and Jefferson were tapping into the same rich source.

Virginia's Declaration was only one of many. Historian Pauline Maier has discovered ninety "declarations" issued by state and local communities in the months immediately preceding the congressional declaration.[9] (She does not include the Worcester instructions, written back in 1774.) Taken together, these reveal a groundswell of political thinking in support of independence. Jefferson and Mason drafted their declarations with full knowledge that others were doing the same, even if they did not consult every state and local document.

Most of these declarations took the form of instructions by towns, counties, or local associations to their representatives in state conventions, telling them to instruct *their* representatives in Congress to vote for independence. The chain of command was clear: representatives at every level were to do the bidding of their constituents. The custom of issuing instructions to representatives did not originate with the American Revolution, but never before had local instructions expressed views of such monumental importance. Now more than ever, patriots insisted that the business of government remain under their immediate control. Witness the "Committee for the Lower District of Frederick County [Maryland]":

> *Resolved, unanimously*, That as a knowledge of the conduct of the Representative is the constituent's only principle and permanent security, we claim the right of being fully informed therein, unless in the secret operations of war; and that we shall ever hold the Representative amenable to that body from whom he derives his authority.[10]

Many of the instructions, while granting new powers to Congress, asserted that the states must retain "the sole and exclusive right" to govern their own internal affairs.[11] People were not about to relinquish any of their political "independence," even to other Americans.

Several of the local declarations offer succinct expressions of the social contract theory. Again from Frederick County:

> *Resolved, unanimously*, That all just and legal Government was instituted for the ease and convenience of the People, and that the People have the indubitable right to reform or abolish a Government which may appear to them insufficient for the exigency of their affairs.[12]

Patriots from Buckingham County, Virginia, issued a similar declaration, then followed with an optimistic vision that would have made the visionary Mr. Jefferson proud: they prayed that "a Government may be established in *America*, the most free, happy, and permanent, that human wisdom can contrive, and the perfection of man maintain."[13]

Like the later Declaration, many of these earlier documents listed specific grievances—often more concisely and pointedly than Jefferson would do.[14] Delegates at more than twenty conventions or town meetings signed off by pledging to support independence with their "lives and fortunes," foretelling the famous conclusion to the congressional declaration: "We mutually pledge our lives, our fortunes, and our sacred honor." Some of these added creative touches to this standard oath: Boston delegates pledged "their lives and the remnants of their fortunes," while patriots from Malden, Massachusetts, concluded: "Your constituents will support and defend the measure to the last drop of their blood, and the last farthing of their treasure."[15]

Thomas Jefferson was one of many scribes, not the sole muse, of the American independence movement.

A SLOW START

Because the proceedings of the Continental Congress were kept secret, Americans at the time had no way of ascertaining who was on the committee to prepare the Declaration of Independence, who among the committee penned the draft, or who edited the final version. This information, even if available, would have been deemed irrelevant. People didn't care to quibble about authorship or craft. All that really counted was the document's conclusion: the United States was declaring its independence.

During the war, even at Fourth of July celebrations, the Declaration itself was rarely quoted. On the first anniversary of independence in 1777, when William Gordon delivered the oration for the festivities in Boston, he used as his text the Old Testament. When David Ramsay delivered the oration in Charleston on the second anniversary, he used a phrase more common to the times: "life, liberty, and property," not "life, liberty, and the pursuit of happiness," the phrase used in the Declaration of Independence. In 1783, after the war had ended, Ezra Stiles mentioned Jefferson by name—but he did not celebrate the author's unique genius. Stiles said only that Jefferson had "poured the soul of the continent into the monumental act of independence."[16]

In fact, during the Revolutionary Era, George Mason's draft of the Virginia Declaration of Rights was copied or imitated far more often than the Declaration of Independence. None of the seven other states that drafted their own declarations of rights borrowed phrasing from the congressional Declaration, but Pennsylvania, Massachusetts, and New Hampshire (in addition to Vermont, which was not yet a state) lifted exact portions of Mason's text, including "all men are born equally free and independent."[17] In part this is because the state declarations of rights borrowed from each other, but Mason's wording is also more precise. What does "created equal" really mean? Years later, Stephen A. Douglas, when debating Abraham Lincoln, protested that Negroes were not the "equal" of whites, leading Lincoln to retreat by admitting they were "not my equal in many respects—certainly not in color, perhaps not in moral or intellectual endowment."[18] Had Jefferson stayed with Mason's phraseology, Lincoln could have cited the Declaration of Independence with greater authority and less apology. "Born equally free and independent" establishes clearly the nature of equality among men: it lies in their rights, not in their attributes, abilities, or achievements.

Surprisingly, the Declaration of Independence was not often cited during the drafting of the U.S. Constitution in 1787 or in the subsequent debates over ratification. Notes from the Constitutional Convention make only two references to the Declaration, while the eighty-five essays in *The Federalist* contain but one. When Patrick Henry addressed the Virginia Convention during the ratification debate, he asked rhetorically, "What, sir, is the genius of democracy?" He then proceeded to read from the Virginia Declaration of Rights, drafted by Mason, not from Jefferson's adaptation in the Declaration of Independence:

> That Government is or ought to be instituted for the common benefit, protection, and security of the people, nation, or community: Of all the various modes and forms of Government, that is best which is capable of producing the greatest degree of happiness and safety, and is most effectually secured against the danger of mal-administration, and *that whenever any Government shall be found inadequate, or contrary to these purposes, a majority of the community hath an undubitable, unalienable and indefeasible right to reform, alter, or abolish it, in such manner as shall be judged most conducive to the public weal.*

"This, sir, is the language of democracy," Henry concluded.[19]

Both David Ramsay and William Gordon, in their eighteenth-century histories, focused on the political impact of the Declaration of Independence, not the philosophy contained in its preamble. Ramsay failed to mention Jefferson as the author, while Gordon referred to him only as a member of the five-man committee that prepared the draft.[20]

During the 1790s, Jefferson's standing was determined by partisan politics. Since Federalists vilified Jefferson, they ignored his authorship and regarded the Declaration itself as suspect. Republicans, meanwhile, celebrated Jefferson's authorship in order to promote the leading figure of their own political party. Not until Republicans staged separate Fourth of July festivities in the late 1790s was Jefferson's name linked to the Declaration of Independence in public discourse.[21]

Two turn-of-the-century historians reflected these divergent stances. John Marshall, a staunch Federalist, mentioned Jefferson only in a footnote: a committee of five was appointed to prepare the document, he wrote flatly, "and the draft, reported by the committee, has been generally attributed to Mr. Jefferson."[22] Rather than focus on Jefferson, Marshall mentioned several of the other declarations of independence, and he quoted extensively from two of them.[23] Mercy Otis Warren, on the other side of the political spectrum, waxed effusive:

> [T]he instrument which announced the final separation of the American Colonies from Great Britain was drawn by the elegant and energetic pen of Jefferson, with that correct judgment, precision, and dignity, which have ever marked his character. The declaration of independence, which has done so much honor to the then existing congress, to the inhabitants of the United States, and to the genius and heart of the gentleman who drew it . . . ought to be frequently read by the rising youth of the American states, as a palladium of which they should never lose sight, so long as they wish to continue a free and independent people.[24]

Warren and other supporters of Jefferson enshrined the Declaration's author in the early nineteenth century, when memories of the Revolution were revived and put in the service of a growing nationalism. Jefferson's party, the Republicans (referred to later as the Democrat-Republicans), would remain in power for a quarter century, during which the document and its principal author were increasingly celebrated and indelibly linked.

In 1817 Congress commissioned John Trumbull to paint a large canvas commemorating the approval of the Declaration of Independence on July 4, 1776. Trumbull's masterpiece was displayed to large crowds in Boston, New York, Philadelphia, Baltimore, and Washington.[25] With the mood set, two engraved copies of the Declaration competed for public attention in 1818 and 1819. In 1823 Congress distributed an official facsimile far and wide.[26]

Jefferson fed this frenzy. As far back as 1786, he had talked of an artistic commemoration of the Declaration with John Trumbull and had provided a rough sketch.[27] He approved the distribution of the facsimile edition, hoping it would inspire greater "reverence" for the principles it espoused.[28] He even applauded the gathering of artifacts he had used while drafting the document: "Small things may, perhaps, like the relics of saints, help to nourish our devotion to this holy bond of Union, and keep it longer alive and warm in our affections," he wrote to a promoter—and he then indicated where some of these "relics" might be found.[29]

All this rankled John Adams, the only other member of the drafting committee still alive during the Declaration's revival. According to Adams, writing thirty-five years after independence, the hard-earned *achievement* of independence should be the object of celebration, not the simple act of *writing* about it, and he was the one who had successfully pushed the motion for independence through Congress. "The Declaration of Independence I always considered as a theatrical show. Jefferson ran away with all the stage effect of that," he wrote—and, he added grudgingly, "all the glory of it" as well.[30] Adams also noted that Jefferson's draft was discussed, revised, and approved by a five-member committee, then discussed, revised, and approved by the body of Congress.[31] Jefferson countered: "Mr. Adams' memory has led him to unquestionable error." In particular, Jefferson objected to Adams's claim that the two men had constituted a "sub-committee" charged with writing the document.[32]

Despite a paucity of direct sources and the differences in memory, we do know that a five-member committee was appointed to produce a draft for Congress to consider, and we can safely conjecture that the committee discussed the issues and provided some direction before sending Jefferson on his way with quill and ink. Then, when the draft reached the floor of Congress, others certainly had their say. According to Jeffersonian scholar Julian Boyd, "In all there were eighty-six alterations, made at various stages by Jefferson, by Adams and Franklin, by the Committee of Five, and by Congress.[33]

The major thrust of Adams's argument—that the Declaration of Independence was more than a one-man affair—seems correct. Even so, Jefferson won the debate. The telling of history, if not history itself, was on his side. Before he died, he proposed that "Author of the Declaration of American Independence" be inscribed on his tomb. Although he accepted and even sought credit for penning the words, however, never did Jefferson seek credit for dreaming up the ideas.[34] That unsolicited honor would be bestowed upon him by others, much later.

THE LINCOLN REVIVAL

During the Abraham Lincoln–Stephen A. Douglas debates of 1858, both participants based their arguments on the alleged authority of the Declaration of Independence. According to Lincoln, the Declaration had stated in "plain, unmistakable language" that "all men are created equal." Douglas countered that these words were never intended to apply to "the Negro or . . . savage Indians, or the Feejee, or the Malay, or any other inferior or degraded race," and he noted that many of the state and local declarations, which had preceded the congressional Declaration, had insisted that the states retain all authority over their own internal affairs.[35] Although Douglas was probably correct on the first count, and certainly correct on the second, Lincoln rebutted both arguments. The second point was easy: Lincoln noted that his quarrel was only with the *expansion* of slavery, and this involved no violation of states' rights.

But what about those slaveholding Founding Fathers? How could

Lincoln seriously maintain that they had believed in the equality of *all* men, including those they were holding in bondage?

Lincoln argued that Jefferson had included the phrase "all men are created equal" for no immediate and practical purpose, but as a "promise" for the future. The "sentiment embodied in the Declaration of Independence" was to give "hope to all the world . . . that in due time the weights would be lifted from the shoulders of all men, and that all should have an equal chance."[36] Since slavery was too firmly embedded at the time to permit practical opposition, Jefferson could do no more than issue this blanket pronouncement in favor of equality—"the father of all moral principles," Lincoln called it—for the use of future generations.[37]

Lincoln's line of reasoning had, and still has, great appeal. Because of their alleged "promise" to the future, the signers of the Declaration of Independence can be released from any charge of moral culpability or hypocrisy.

Historically, however, this is a difficult argument to sustain. Antislavery elements in the North made no mention of "equality" in instructing their delegates to state or federal conventions in 1776. Only in the slave-dependent South did the term "equality" appear. When the grand jury of the Cheraws District of South Carolina declared itself in favor of independence on May 20, 1776, it praised the new Constitution because it was "founded on the strictest principles of justice and humanity, where the rights and happiness of the whole, the poor and the rich, are equally secured," yet in Revolutionary South Carolina, slaves were not seen as part of that "whole," even though they constituted approximately half the population.[38] The grand jury of Georgetown, South Carolina, also praised the new Constitution as "the most equitable and desirable that human imagination could invent":

> The present Constitution of Government, formed by the late Congress of this Colony, promises to its inhabitants every happy effect which can arise from society. Equal and just in its

> principles, wise and virtuous in its ends; we now see every hope of future liberty, safety, and happiness confirmed to ourselves and our posterity.[39]

Not even Lincoln would have dared to suggest that back in 1776 the white citizens of Georgetown, South Carolina, intended that "promise" to extend to their slaves.

When Lincoln tried to portray the notion of "equality" as the "sentiment" of the nation's founders, he gave full credit to Thomas Jefferson, the author of the words he cherished:

> All honor to Jefferson, to the man who, in the concrete pressure of a struggle for national independence by a single people, had the coolness, forecast, and capacity to introduce into a merely revolutionary document, an abstract truth, and so to embalm it there, that today and in all coming days, it shall be a rebuke and a stumbling block to the very harbingers of reappearing tyranny and oppression.[40]

He was not the first to remake the master of Monticello—a man who preached against race-mixing and bred slaves for profit—into the architect of racial equality in America.[41] During the Senate debates on the Kansas-Nebraska Act in 1853, Benjamin Wade, a senator from Ohio, invoked the Declaration of Independence in a similar manner, and so did other opponents of slavery.[42] But because of Lincoln's presidential status and his role in ending slavery, his interpretation had an indelible, lasting impact.

In establishing Jefferson as a prophet of egalitarian principles, Lincoln displayed great political savvy. He shrewdly co-opted the founder of the opposing political party, while he recruited one of the largest slave owners in Revolutionary Virginia to argue the antislavery case. Many would agree that Lincoln played his cards well in a game that really counted. The end in this case might justify the means, but that does not make his reading of the Declaration of Independence historically correct.

The broad strokes of the Lincoln-Jefferson revival remain with us today. Routinely, current textbooks echo Lincoln's notion of a "promise" made by the founders: "All people were not treated equally in America in 1776," one states, "but the Declaration set high goals for equal treatment in the future."[43] Joy Hakim, in her popular *History of US*, writes that on July 4, 1776, "something happened . . . that changed the whole world." That "something" was not the act of declaring independence: "It was the words they used in that declaration that made all the difference. . . . Jefferson's Declaration of Independence was great from the moment he wrote it, but it has grown even greater with the passing of time."[44] With this clever turn of phrase, Hakim celebrates Jefferson's genius, his prophesy, and his ownership of the Declaration of Independence. Jefferson, like the words he penned, seems to have "grown even greater with the passing of time."

TEAM SPIRIT

It has been several years since Pauline Maier retrieved from obscurity the other declarations of independence, and although college texts are beginning to embody her research, those documents receive scant mention in elementary, middle-school, and secondary texts, and in popular histories. Though such books give some ground—they now routinely mention that Jefferson was a member of a committee, for example—they fail to acknowledge the ubiquitous revolutionary upsurge that resulted in Revolution. If they mention any widespread revolutionary feeling, they credit yet one more autonomous perpetrator: Thomas Paine. Tom Paine (as he is casually called) supposedly swayed the minds of a fickle public who could not have attained true revolutionary status without him. In the reckless rush to commemorate Paine's mastery over public opinion, some current texts list the contemporary sales of his *Common Sense* at an astounding half million, one for every free household in the thirteen colonies—even those with no literate individuals.[45] Most other texts cite Paine's own inflated numbers unquestioningly, even though he had no way of ascertaining his sales, and his three distinct estimates, offered at different times, are far from plausible.[46]

According to classic narrative structure, the wise man—whether Thomas Paine or Thomas Jefferson—persuades the rest. Yet this individualistic/heroic model does not accurately describe how history works. A better model features collaborative effort—like that between Jefferson and Mason, who were participating in an ongoing dialogue as they penned their various declarations. An entire population took part in that robust dialogue, and here, the media is indeed the message. The dialogue itself deserves celebration, not just its practical conclusion. If we disregard that public discussion, we cast a blind eye to one of history's finest examples of popular involvement in momentous decision making.

Whatever influence the Declaration of Independence has had on later history—and it has been great—at the time it was the *fact* of independence that shook the world, not the precise *words* used to justify it. Listen to what Jefferson had to say on the matter in the year before his death, for no one argues the question more persuasively:

> But with respect to our rights, and the acts of the British government contravening those rights, there was but one opinion on this side of the water. All American whigs thought alike on these subjects. When forced, therefore, to resort to arms for redress, an appeal to the tribunal of the world was deemed proper for our justification. This was the object of the Declaration of Independence. Not to find out new principles, or new arguments, never before thought of, not merely to say things which had never been said before; but to place before mankind the common sense of the subject, in terms so plain and firm as to command their assent, and to justify ourselves in the independent stand we were compelled to take. Neither aiming at originality of principle or

> sentiment, nor yet copied from any particular and previous writing, it was intended to be an expression of the American mind, and to give to that expression the proper tone and spirit called for by the occasion. All its authority rests on the harmonizing sentiments of the day, whether expressed in conversation, in letters, printed essays, or in the elementary books of public right, as Aristotle, Cicero, Locke, Sidney, &c.[47]

Later that year, while supporting the promotion of relics he had used to draft the Declaration, Jefferson again insisted that his words were to be seen as no more than "the genuine effusion of the soul of our country."[48] Unfortunately, his most ardent admirers, in their quest for a solitary visionary, have failed to take seriously Jefferson's honest and forthright pronouncement: the "authority" of the Declaration of Independence rests exclusively on the "harmonizing sentiments" of the American people.

"It is really an assembly of demigods."

Barry Faulkner, National Archives, Washington, D.C., 1936.

7

AN ASSEMBLY OF DEMIGODS

We know the story well. John Jay presented its broad outlines in the second *Federalist* essay, first published six weeks after the framers of the Constitution finished their deliberations in Philadelphia in the summer of 1787:

> This convention, composed of men who possessed the confidence of the people, and many of whom had become highly distinguished by their patriotism, virtue, and wisdom, in times which tried the minds and hearts of men, undertook the arduous task. In the mild season of peace, with minds unoccupied by other subjects, they passed many months in cool, uninterrupted, and daily consultation; and finally, without having been awed by power, or influenced by any passions except love for their country, they presented and recommended to the people the plan produced by their joint and very unanimous councils.[1]

In Jay's rendition, delegates to the Federal Convention (what we now call, in hindsight, the Constitutional Convention) were wise, dispassionate, and not in the least ambitious—in every respect, exemplars of what people at the time considered republican virtue. They did not practice interest-driven politics, in which people bicker with each other for political influence or economic gain. Jay cast the framers with a golden glow, and although slightly diffused, that light still shines today in our textbooks, popular histories, and political debates. We idolize the men who gave us our Constitution and often complain that the nation would be better off in their hands. Never a day passes without some politician, broadcast commentator, or blogger citing a founder to support his or her position on a contemporary issue totally unknown to late-eighteenth-century Americans. It's a national sport, part and parcel of our current political debates.

A PANTHEON—OR NOT?

One oft-repeated quotation characterizes the Convention itself. Back in 1787, while delegates were still trying to hammer out the details for a new plan of government, Thomas Jefferson wrote to John Adams: "It [the Convention] is really an assembly of demigods." Jefferson, though, was in Paris at the time, and he had little knowledge of what was actually transpiring within the East Wing of the Pennsylvania State House, three thousand miles across the Atlantic. Nobody outside that chamber did. Delegates had taken a vow of secrecy, which they honored. This much Jefferson knew, and it bothered him: "I am sorry they began their deliberations by so abominable a precedent as that of tying up the tongues of their members," he groused in the same letter to Adams, who was actually in London at the time, not Philadelphia. "Nothing can justify this example but the innocence of their intentions, & ignorance of the value of public discussions. I have no doubt that all their other measures will be good & wise." It was one thing to oppose secrecy from such a safe distance, but had Jefferson participated in the Convention, in all likelihood he too would have seen that public disclosure of the proceedings would likely undermine the mystique, hinder prospects for ratification, and jeopardize the entire operation. Delegates were not acting like demigods but down-to-earth politicians, grumbling, cajoling, and calling each other's bluffs.

In the end, they fashioned workable and in some cases distasteful compromises that might not be ideologically pure but that appeared the least objectionable.[2]

During the ratification debates that raged for ten months after the Convention, supporters of the proposed plan, calling themselves Federalists, lionized the framers, following the lines Jay used in his essay. Opponents, however, vilified them. Delegates had been instructed by the states to revise and amend the "Articles of Confederation and Perpetual Union," the young nation's working set of rules, but instead, on their own authority, they had unilaterally thrown that document out, opponents observed. Vastly overreaching their authority, delegates to the Convention had both violated the trust of the people and created a new government that threatened the people's liberties.

Such divergent views of the framers continued in the politically turbulent 1790s, when the various branches of government, the emerging political parties, and the people themselves squabbled over what the Constitution really meant. Signers of the Declaration of Independence, by contrast, were universally regarded as true patriots, as were the men who had fought a war to protect independence. Through much of the nineteenth century textbooks reflected this difference: the Revolutionary War and the Declaration of Independence received abundant attention, while drafting and ratification of the Constitution were typically covered in a page or even just a paragraph.

After Reconstruction, in the wake of the Civil War, that changed. The major bone of contention in the Constitution—state versus federal powers with respect to slavery—had been settled at last. In the interest of national unity, texts began promoting the Constitution and the men who drafted it in the same hagiographic manner as they did the Declaration and the men who signed that document. "[The] framers [were] a race of statesmen—patriots, with the good of the whole country at the bottom of every act—not politicians merely, not men representing and fighting for State, local, or party, or individual interests," wrote John Robert Irelan in an eighteen-volume text in 1888.[3]

No interests at stake? In 1913, reflecting the class consciousness of the Progressive Era, Charles A. Beard, a professor at Columbia University, turned that story on its head. The primary object of many framers, he claimed, was to secure their fortunes, which were tied to government bonds.[4] This theory stimulated a grand historical and educational debate that lasted through midcentury, but by the 1960s the framers were again in the driver's seat. Textbooks, which had veered toward the Progressives, backed away from Beard. While they did acknowledge the daily and sometimes contentious political debates that characterized the Convention, they reintroduced the hagiographic tone. All debates were resolved, and one was even celebrated through nomenclature: the so-called "Great Compromise" in which small states and large states supposedly buried the hatchet by allowing proportional representation in the House and representation by states in the Senate. In the end, political or economic interests were trumped by patriotism.

TROUBLE ON MOUNT OLYMPUS

True, debates at the Federal Convention did end in compromise, but how did that come to pass? Was the tone gentlemanly, as we might expect from our wise and virtuous founders? Investigating the event historically, looking at the process as well as the outcome, we are forced toward a different conclusion. There was no shortage of knockdown, drag-out battles, threats and counterthreats, and tough-minded political deal making. If these were gods, they were more of the Greek and Roman model, not above unleashing thunderbolts upon their enemies.

On May 30, the first day of debates, James Madison of Virginia, the most populous state in the Union at that time, presented what he considered to be his bottom line: "that the equality of suffrage established by the Articles of Confederation ought not to prevail in the national Legislature, and that an equitable ratio of representation ought to be substituted." That "equitable ratio," if based on population, would give Virginia nine times the power of tiny Delaware. George Read, speaking on behalf of Delaware's delegation, noted that he and his colleagues were under strict instructions from their state not to be party to any plan that changed the one-state, one-vote rule of voting under the existing Articles of Confederation, and if that rule were changed, they might well "retire from the Convention." Whether Read's statement was a bluff or in earnest, it had its effect, and the motion to change the representation in Congress was quickly tabled. Few delegates from other states wanted to chance the embarrassment of Delaware's early departure.[5]

Delaware's delegates were seemingly obstinate, but just three days later, on June 2, John Dickinson, also representing Delaware, conceded that some alteration of the equal-voting provision in the Articles of Confederation might be in order, despite his instructions to hold firm. The controversy over representation, he predicted, "must probably end in mutual concession." In particular, Dickinson "hoped that each State would retain an equal voice at least in one branch of the National Legislature," while "either the number of inhabitants or the quantum of property" could form the basis for proportional representation in the other branch. On the fourth day of debates, the broad outlines of the "Great Compromise" were already on the floor, yet delegates from large states and small states would continue to do battle for six more weeks before settling up. Intellectually, the solution was obvious, but politically it proved difficult. As Alexander Hamilton observed on June 29, the debate over representation was a "contest for power, not for liberty."[6]

The fight was furious. Delaware's Gunning Bedford Jr. warned that if the large states succeeded in overturning the one-state, one-vote provision, "the small ones will find some foreign ally of more honor and good faith, who will take them by the hand and do them justice." He then added he "did not mean by this to intimidate or alarm," but of course he did. That was the very purpose of his remarks.[7]

On the other side, Pennsylvania's Gouverneur Morris, representing the second largest state, envisioned apocalyptic consequences should "state attachments" prevail: "This Country must be united. If persuasion does not unite it, the sword will. . . . The scenes of horror attending civil commotion can not be described, and the conclusion of them will be worse than the term of their continuance. The stronger party will then make traytors of the weaker; and the Gallows & Halter will finish the work of the sword."[8]

This hyperbolic war of words was not for the timid. With each side pushing to the limits, Elbridge Gerry "lamented that instead of coming here like a band of brothers, belonging to the same family, we seemed to have brought with us the spirit of political negociators."[9]

By June 28 Benjamin Franklin had heard enough. "We indeed seem to feel our own want of political wisdom," he lamented, "since we have been running about in search of it." A month of "close attendance & continual reasonings with each other" had produced but "small progress." Unless the bickering ceased, "[w]e shall be divided by our little partial local interests" and "our projects will be confounded."

Was there any way out? "In this situation of this Assembly, groping as it were in the dark to find political truth, and scarce able to distinguish it when presented to us, how has it happened, Sir, that we have not hitherto once thought of humbly applying to the Father of lights to illuminate our understandings?" Franklin then suggested they start each day's proceedings with "prayers imploring the assistance of Heaven, and its blessings on our deliberations." Delegates could not agree even on this, and his motion was tabled.[10]

Tempers rose yet higher. Positions rigidified. "Never" was the operative word. James Wilson proclaimed "he never could listen to an equality of votes," while Luther Martin declared he would "never confederate if it could not be done on just principles." Increasingly, debate followed the classic lines of interest-driven politics: we have to defend *our* interests to prevent *others*, who defend theirs, from destroying us. Gunning Bedford claimed that because the large states were "dictated by interest, by ambition" and sought "to aggrandize themselves at the expense of the small," it was unrealistic for the small states to submit to their "proposed degradation" and act "from pure disinterestedness."[11]

George Washington, as the convention's president, could not express his views openly, but he did grouse in private. To his former aide-de-camp Alexander Hamilton, who had abandoned the Convention in frustration, he complained that "narrow minded politicians . . . under the influence of local views" were impeding all progress. "The state of the Councils," he reported, was spiraling downward, leaving "little ground on which the hope of a good establishment can be formed." The parochial interests within the convention left him uncharacteristically despondent: "I *almost* despair of seeing a favourable issue to the proceedings of our Convention, and do therefore repent having had any agency in the business."[12]

And so it continued. On July 14, exactly six weeks after Dickinson placed on the floor the outlines of the eventual compromise, delegates were still hurling insults back and forth. "The States that please to call themselves large, are the weekest in the Union," Martin pronounced. "Look at Masts [Massachusetts]. Look at Virga [Virginia]." We are left to imagine Elbridge Gerry's heated, and perhaps undignified, response; Madison reported only that he "animadverted on Mr. L. Martin's remarks on the weakness of Masts."[13]

When would this end, and how?

On July 15 delegates observed the Sabbath, and then on Monday, July 16, without any further debate, they finally decided by the slimmest of margins that the first branch of the new national legislature would be apportioned by population while each state would be represented equally in the second branch. The final vote: five states in favor, four states opposed, with Massachusetts divided.[14]

Even after the final vote, delegates from large states refused to concede. Virginia's Edmund Randolph moved that the convention adjourn for the day "that the large States might consider the steps proper to be taken in the present solemn crisis of the business." New Jersey's William Paterson called his bluff: Why just for the day? Perhaps it was time to adjourn for good, rescind "the rule of secrecy," and consult "our Constituents." That would be the end of any compromise, all delegates realized. The Convention granted Randolph's request to allow the large states to caucus, but the caucus found no alternative solution the small states would accept.[15]

To no great fanfare, and with more ill will than good, delegates had given us the now celebrated "Great Compromise."

But even so, after representation in Congress had been settled, large states and small continued to jockey for position in the new government. Who would have more say in choosing the president?

Through most of the Convention, the working draft of the Constitution stated that Congress would choose the president. But how, exactly, would it do that? Meeting separately, as usual, or meeting jointly, even though that would not happen in any other context? If they met separately, what if their selections differed? But if they met jointly, wouldn't the House, with many more members, overwhelm the Senate, with only two members per state? "A joint ballot would in fact give the appointment to one House," complained New Jersey's Jonathan Dayton, the Convention's youngest delegate. The two chambers should vote separately, he suggested, so small states in the Senate could check the large states in the House, as with normal legislation.[16]

When the Convention decided on a joint session nonetheless, New Jersey delegate David Brearly countered with another proposal: Congress would choose the president in a joint session, but the entire delegation from each state would cast a single vote, as in the old Articles of Confederation. This blatantly small-state measure, which would negate the influence of large states, also failed.[17]

But Pennsylvania's Gouverneur Morris, who had vigorously opposed congressional selection of the president all along, and disgruntled delegates from New Jersey and other small states, teamed up to revamp entirely the method of choosing the president. In a manner typical of the Convention's proceedings, Morris, Dayton, and Brearly got the matter sent to a committee consisting of one member from each state. Brearly was its president and Gouverneur Morris a member.[18]

On September 4, less than two weeks before the Convention would adjourn, the committee presented its report to stunned delegates. What had been previously decided was overturned. Congressional choice of the president was scrapped altogether; instead, state legislatures would arrange for the selection of special electors, and these people would then choose the president. What we now call the electoral college was the direct result of political finagling by a handful of delegates in committee, and small-state, large-state concerns were paramount.[19]

When trying to explain the committee's highly original method of presidential selection, Gouverneur Morris stated flatly, "It had been agreed to in the Committee on the ground of compromise." This multifaceted compromise was perhaps the most complicated political deal making of the summer, and it is never mentioned in textbooks or other renditions of our national narrative. First, the number of electors for each state would equal that state's number of representatives and senators; large states would derive an advantage, but even the smallest state would be guaranteed three electors. Because it awarded votes in large measure according to representation in the House, this measure reenforced the three-fifths compromise, giving added heft to the South and securing the support of delegates from slaveholding states. Electors were to cast ballots for two candidates, one of whom could not be from the elector's home state, and the winner would need a majority, not just a plurality, of the electors' votes; taken together, these measures prevented large states from electing favorite sons and thereby offered some protection to small states. Further, because many or most elections were not expected to produce a clear winner, runoffs featuring the five leading contenders would be determined in the Senate, where small states and large states had equal votes. (The Convention later reassigned the determination of this runoff from the Senate to the House, but with members voting by state delegations—one state, one vote—to satisfy the small states.)[20]

No coherent philosophy could encompass such divergent elements of what we might call the unheralded "little compromise." What we have, in place of coherence, is the electoral college, shaped at the

Federal Convention amid backroom wheeling and dealing. This convoluted institution, which few Americans have ever understood, has granted the presidency to the loser of the popular vote on four occasions. Forged by politicized give-and-take, it is ours to this day.[21]

"A POLITICAL LIGHT ONLY"

By deciding that representation in the first branch of the legislature, and indirectly in the presidency, should be apportioned according to population, delegates inadvertently raised a most troubling issue: Should slaves be counted as people?

Not surprisingly, since it would increase their region's influence in the federal government, Southern delegates said they should. A slave's labor, they argued, contributes to national wealth and strength, just like that of a free person.

Northern delegates, not wanting their relative influence to diminish, argued that only citizens should have a voice in the government. Counting slaves would grant enormous powers to Southern slaveholders, who would in essence cast votes on behalf of the people they held in bondage.

Since neither side would concede, delegates came to a workable but not very rational compromise: in calculating how many representatives could go to Congress, each state would include its "whole Number of free Persons," exclude "Indians not taxed," and then add "three-fifths of all other Persons," the framers' euphemism for enslaved human beings. How in the world did they come up with *three-fifths*? Why not some other fraction?

For that we need to go back to 1783, fours years before the Convention, when Congress faced an inversely related problem. At that time, while trying to make the Articles of Confederation more workable, Congress wanted to find a formula for how much money each state needed to contribute to the common treasury. Should slaves be counted in that calculation?

Southerners said no. If Congress counted slaves, who were

property, why not count horses in the North? Besides, they argued, slaves were not as productive as free people. But Northerners countered that slave labor *was* productive, so any measure of property must reflect that.

To keep the embryonic nation together, congressional delegates at that time tried to fashion a compromise. Southerners offered to count one-half (50 percent) of the enslaved population, but Northerners insisted on two-thirds (67 percent). After considerable haggling, Congress split the difference: three-fifths (60 percent).[22] In 1787, once again at an impasse, delegates to the Federal Convention simply dusted off the three-fifths fraction, even though the argument had turned into its mirror opposite. When counting slaves added an extra burden to the South's financial obligations, the North said count them, while the South said not to. But when slaves turned from a liability to an asset for purposes of representation, the South said count them, while the North said not to. *Both* sides reversed their positions. Logic? Morality? Not exactly. Delegates did whatever had to be done to move the show along. They wanted a new Constitution for the entire nation, and haggle as they might, they would do most anything to get it.

The notorious three-fifths compromise, not celebrated like the "Great Compromise," failed to settle the matter of slavery at the Convention. On August 6, after more than two months of debates, a five-man Committee of Detail fleshed out a rough draft of what would become the Constitution. In that draft, to reassure the Southern states, the committee stipulated that Congress would not be allowed to tax or prohibit "the migration or importation of such persons as the several States shall think proper to admit."

Two weeks later, when that provision came up for debate, Maryland's Luther Martin, a slave owner himself, moved immediately to strike it out. Since each imported slave would add to a state's representation, states would be rewarded politically for engaging in the slave trade. "It was inconsistent with the principles of the revolution and dishonorable to the American character to have such a feature in the Constitution," he argued.[23]

Virginia's George Mason, also a large slave owner (his plantation was very close to Washington's Mount Vernon), supported Martin's motion for both practical and moral reasons. Slavery impeded "the immigration of Whites, who really enrich & strengthen a Country," while it also produced "the most pernicious effect on manners." In words that are now often quoted, Mason boldly pronounced: "Every master of slaves is born a petty tyrant. They bring the judgment of heaven on a Country. As nations can not be rewarded or punished in the next world they must be in this."

Did these slaveholders seriously oppose the very institution that supported them? Not entirely. Neither Martin nor Mason had any problem counting enslaved people, or at least some fraction thereof, to boost the representation of their respective states. But the issue this time was the *importation* of slaves—and both Maryland and Virginia already had as many as they needed.

The profitability of rice plantations in South Carolina, on the other hand, depended on more slave labor than was currently available, so delegates from that state wanted to keep importation open. Charles Cotesworth Pinckney, a South Carolina patrician, called out Mason for his high-toned stance, alleging baser motives: "As to Virginia she will gain by stopping the importations. Her slaves will rise in value, & she has more than she wants." This surplus of slaves would allow Virginians to establish "a monopoly in their favor," setting "their own terms for such as they might sell." Mason's moralizing merely protected Virginia's local industry—breeding slaves for the market—which foreign imports would impair.

Other delegates from South Carolina and neighboring Georgia chimed in to defend the "right" to own slaves.

Charles Pinckney (Charles Cotesworth Pinckney's cousin) argued from history: "If slavery be wrong, it is justified by the example of all the world." He "cited the case of Greece, Rome & other antient States; the sanction given by France, England, Holland & other modern States. In all ages one half of mankind have been slaves."

Georgia's Abraham Baldwin (a transplanted son of Connecticut) offered an argument that defenders of slavery would repeat many times before the Civil War: slavery was "a local matter," not a "national object," and Georgia would refuse to accept any attempt "to abridge one of her favorite prerogatives." Charles Pinckney offered a similar threat: "South Carolina can never receive the plan [the Constitution] if it prohibits the slave trade." There must be no "meddling with the importation of negroes."

South Carolina's John Rutledge was particularly blunt: "Religion & humanity had nothing to do with this question—interest alone is the governing principle with nations." It was perhaps the brashest, and most honest, statement of the summer.[24]

And "interest alone" settled the manner. Delegates from the Deep South cut a deal with those from New England: in return for allowing slave importation for another twenty years and a fugitive slave law, pro-importation Southerners would cede to Northern commercial interests and drop their demand that all navigation laws require a supermajority. (The North, which depended on maritime commerce, did not want the five Southern states, a minority, to block procommerce laws.) Each side got something it wanted, although Virginia and Maryland, which opposed slave importation *and* wanted a supermajority for navigation laws, lost out.[25] In the thick of the debate over slave importation, Rufus King of Massachusetts commented, "the subject should be considered in a political light only," and that is exactly the way delegates to the Federal Convention dispatched the embarrassing matter of slavery. Philosophical talk of liberty and human rights gave way in the end to backdoor deal making.[26] When Gouverneur Morris of Pennsylvania, who favored abolition, said he "would sooner submit himself to a tax for paying for all the negroes in the U. States, than saddle posterity with such a Constitution," the other delegates simply ignored him.[27]

"THE BEST THAT COULD BE OBTAINED AT THIS TIME"

Born of politics, the Constitution is not quite the precision instrument we would like to imagine: each component functioning integrally with the others, and all consistent with some overarching philosophy. The electoral college and the vice presidency, for instance, were last-minute additions that fatigued delegates did not bother to examine carefully. The "original intent" of these and other measures was often to secure sufficient votes to comprise a majority.

This troubled George Washington, who knew all too well that the final document had been shaped by "local interests" and "selfish views"—but he endorsed it nonetheless, viewing it as a means to a greater end. One week after the Convention adjourned, he wrote to three former governors of Virginia, appealing for their support: "I wish the Constitution which is offered had been made more perfect, but I sincerely believe it is the best that could be obtained at this time; and, as a Constitutional door is opened for amendment hereafter, the adoption of it under the present circumstances of the Union is in my opinion desirable."[28] Not perfect but workable—that was the tone, and it was also the strongest argument for ratification. A national government was needed, and here were the outlines for one. The Constitution could be fine-tuned later.

Many Americans today find it difficult to treat the so-called Constitutional Convention as a rough-and-tumble affair driven as much by interest as by reason. Such honesty, they fear, would undermine the participants' credibility and the almost scriptural sanctity of the resulting document. We need not to be so timid. By altering our perspective only slightly, we might even view the contentious proceedings as a fitting start to the interest-driven constitutional democracy that soon emerged and flourished with time. Downplaying the political nature of our government's creation creates too much distance between our world and that of the framers. If we see the framers as above the fray, we cannot see them as models for how we might resolve our differences today. They become less relevant, not more so.

Historically, if we fail to explore the political dynamics that shaped the proceedings, we are left with myth and fabrication. On the word of Franklin, Washington, and others, we know that interest played its part, and thanks to James Madison, who carefully chronicled the event, we see it in practice. Whereas the gentlemen who gathered in the Pennsylvania State House in 1787, learned statesmen that they were, fully understood the historic nature of their enterprise and did their best to ground the overall structure of their plan on solid republican theory, their philosophical arguments were thoroughly entwined with push-and-pull maneuverings, as such arguments always are in real historical circumstances. There is no reason this should surprise us.

"They were America's first and, in many respects, its only natural aristocracy."

The Declaration of Independence, 4 July 1776.
Painting by John Trumbull, 1787–1820.

8

AMERICAN ARISTOCRACY

We all know their names—George Washington, Thomas Jefferson, Benjamin Franklin, Alexander Hamilton, John and Samuel Adams, Patrick Henry, James Madison. People who learned the story as children and never studied it later—which includes most Americans, as we shall see later on—will likely add John Hancock, whose name has come to represent any sort of a signature, and Paul Revere, the midnight rider of the Revolution. These were America's wise men, the great leaders who gave our nation its bearings.

Regardless of whom we cast in this role, the principal actors in the story of our nation's birth would enjoy an elevated status. They were our *creators*, so they must have been particularly honorable and judicious; that is a structural requirement of the narrative. This does not lessen the merits of the actual men we call founders or the importance of their achievements. They did what they did and that is notable, but to form a national narrative, we naturally highlight and celebrate those whom we think set the United States on its course.

THE CHOSEN FEW

Although the cast of leading characters seems set in stone, it has actually changed over time. In the newly independent nation, during and after the Revolutionary War, Thomas Jefferson, John Adams, and Alexander Hamilton (and to a lesser extent James Madison) did not make the grade. They quickly became divisive political figures, respected by some but detested by those who opposed the policies they embraced. These men we now revere were too controversial to become icons for a fledgling nation in search of a collective identity.

In those early days, two national figures stood head and shoulders above the rest: The General (George Washington) and The Doctor (Benjamin Franklin). These of course topped the list, but other heroes emerged as well.

Throughout New England, "Old Put" was a popular favorite. Almost forgotten today, Israel Putnam was already a folkloric star for his exploits in the French and Indian War, but one incident closed the deal. Supposedly, he was plowing his field in Connecticut when he heard that the British had marched on Lexington; immediately he dropped his plow, mounted his horse, and sped away to answer the alarm, not even returning to his house. Then, shortly after, he made the British pay at Bunker Hill. Such is the stuff of legend, and it earned Old Put a unique place in the hearts of his countrymen.

Two other New Englanders also became famous generals and household names: Henry Knox (now of Fort Knox fame) and the "Fighting Quaker" from Rhode Island, Nathanael Greene. So did New York's Richard Montgomery, the dazzling Irishman who rose quickly in the ranks and led the charge against Quebec, where he lost his life and gained his fame. Boston's Joseph Warren, killed in action in the Battle of Bunker [Breed's] Hill, was likewise mourned. In a militarized society that had just fought a long and troubling war for its very survival, becoming a martyr was the surest way to enter the history books.

Other military heroes, valiant warriors known for courageous deeds, were lionized. Henry "Lighthorse Harry" Lee, commander of the fabled "Lee's Legion," was more celebrated than his second cousin once removed Richard Henry Lee, who made the motion for independence in Congress. Francis Marion, the "Swamp Fox," and Thomas Sumter, the "Gamecock," achieved great renown for bogging down the British army in the South. Even the great orator Patrick Henry rose to fame in part because he was such a firm friend of war.

In the early decades of the nineteenth century, Americans began to celebrate a more cohesive group. With the enshrining of the Declaration of Independence (see chapters 6 and 15), the fifty-six men who had signed that document emerged as the nation's alleged founders. Collectively they were known as the "signers," and Americans hungered to know more about these illustrious fellows. In the 1820s John Sanderson, with the help of Robert Waln, published a nine-volume series called *Biography of the Signers of the Declaration of Independence*, and in 1827 Charles Goodrich came out with the bestselling *Lives of the Signers of the Declaration of Independence*. Others followed in a similar vein, and America had found its men. The signers ruled as the Founding Fathers through much of the nineteenth century. Every detail of their lives was uncovered, and a few additional details invented.

But what of those responsible for that other founding document, the "framers" of the Constitution? Not to be left out, the fifty-five men who attended the Federal (Constitutional) Convention crept slowly, almost imperceptibly, onto center stage, for they were the ones who wrote the law of the land. Without conscious design, Americans began to apply the term "signers" to men who affixed their names to either document. This did not happen in a moment, but today, if you hear people talking about the so-called signers, try asking them which of the two documents they are referring to. In fact, these were very distinct groups; only six men signed both the Declaration of Independence and the Constitution, and only two of these, Benjamin Franklin and Roger Sherman, had been firm advocates of independence. (James Wilson had opposed independence almost to the end, but wound up voting for it; Robert Morris and George Read actively opposed independence but signed the Declaration later; George Clymer, among several other so-called "signers," was not a member of Congress when independence was declared.) But in the popular mind, the Declaration and the Constitution have merged into one, and most people don't really care who signed what.

Taken together, however, the signers and the framers amount to over one hundred individuals, most of whom are not household names: James Smith, Jacob Broom, William Few, William Ellery, Daniel of St. Thomas Jenifer, and so on. A tale with so many heroes does not have the immediate, compelling force we expect from a creation myth. We need fewer, certainly no more than a dozen, if we expect every person in the nation to learn their stories and recite them by rote. Americans eventually settled on the small group we honor today as the "Founding Fathers." It is this elite corps, we say, who conjured the idea of independence, brought the Revolution to its successful conclusion, and then, like Solon or Moses, gave us our laws.

Adulation for the founders has evolved with the times. Today, it is no longer fashionable to be a statue. Posed, formal portraits are out as well. The informality of the late twentieth century has taken its toll on mounted riders cast in stone and the stiff, distant patricians who line up single file on the walls of echoing galleries.

But informality can be seen as irreverence, and the relaxed attitude has proved unsettling for Americans who yearn for the good old days, when the founders were properly honored. "Not so long ago," writes historian Gordon Wood, "the generation that fought the Revolution and created the Constitution was thought to be the greatest generation in American history. . . . Until recently few Americans could look back at these revolutionaries and constitution-makers without being overawed by the brilliance of their thought, the creativity of their politics, the sheer magnitude of their achievement. They used to seem larger than life, giants in the earth, possessing intellectual and political capacities well beyond our own." Yes, those were the days—"but not anymore," Wood bemoans. "The American revolutionaries and the framers of the Constitution are no longer being celebrated in the way they used to be."[1]

In fact, the Founding Fathers *are* being celebrated, although not "in the way they used to be." Popular historians such as Wood, Joseph Ellis, David McCullough, and John Ferling have managed to resurrect America's most respected statesmen by dressing them in more contemporary attire. Like modern celebrities, the founders have been humanized, personalized, and made accessible to the masses. Now, as millions read about the details of their lives, it has become fashionable once again to honor the likes of John Adams, George Washington, and Benjamin Franklin despite their human quirks, or even because of them.

The Founding Fathers were "human and imperfect; each had his flaws and failings," David McCullough wrote in a July 4 op-ed piece for the *New York Times*. In the past, flaws and failings were not to be tolerated in our most venerable public figures, but now these very imperfections work in their favor. Because they "were not gods," McCullough argues, we can admire them all the more. Were they gods, "they would deserve less honor and respect. Gods, after all, can do largely as they please."[2]

Joseph Ellis captured the modest tone in the title of his bestselling book, *Founding Brothers*. Brothers, unlike fathers, squabble and misbehave—but "their mutual imperfections and fallibilities, as well as their eccentricities and excesses" somehow manage to cancel each other out. Brothers come together in the end, as our founders did when they created a viable blueprint for the United States.

According to Ellis, the young nation's "eight most prominent political leaders" (the first four presidents plus Franklin, Hamilton, Aaron Burr, and Abigail Adams) constituted "America's first and, in many respects, its only natural aristocracy," one that can only inspire reverence:

> [T]hey comprised, by any informed and fair-minded standard, the greatest generation of political talent in American history.

> They created the American republic, then held it together throughout the volatile and vulnerable early years by sustaining their presence until national habits and customs took root.[3]

There is a troubling phrase—"by any informed and fair-minded standard"—embedded within Ellis's forthright assertion. What, exactly, might such a standard for greatness be?[4]

The *Random House College Dictionary* lists almost a score of common usages for "great," many with numerous synonyms: noteworthy, remarkable, exceptionally outstanding, important, eminent, prominent, celebrated, illustrious, renowned, main, grand, leading, highly significant or consequential, momentous, vital, critical, distinguished, famous, admirable, having unusual merit, of extraordinary powers, of high rank or standing, of notable or lofty character, elevated, exalted, dignified. Which of these meanings do we intend when we call a particular historical personage, or a particular generation, "great"? Most likely, we wish to imply some sort of ill-defined amalgamation. We do not intend specific meanings; we hope only to instill some sense of admiration for the heroes of our choosing. The term "great" serves as a grandiose but generic stamp of approval. Every time we use it, we make a momentous declaration—but without any standards, we can affix no claim of legitimacy upon our pronouncement, nor can we discuss "greatness" intelligently. In the absence of definitions and procedures, we are free to apply the term "great" promiscuously to our favorite historical personalities. Any historian or commentator can call any historical figure "great."[5]

There is no quicker route to the trivialization of history. A recent book published by American Heritage, *Great Minds of History: Interviews with Roger Mudd*, features "greatness" from three angles: a great newscaster interviews great historians about great personalities. In a chapter titled "Gordon Wood on the Colonial Era and Revolution," Roger Mudd asks Professor Wood various questions of great import about our nation's founding moment:

"Back to Ben Franklin, did he dress and speak like a gentleman?"

"What more can you tell me about Benjamin Franklin?"

"What about Alexander Hamilton?"

"What can you tell us about James Madison?"

"John Adams?"

"And what do you think about Thomas Jefferson?"

Here's how Gordon Wood responds to these questions:

"Adams was the most lovable of the Founding Fathers because he wore his heart on his sleeve."

Hamilton was ". . . the brilliant genius. . . ."

Madison was ". . . the most intellectual. . . ."

Jefferson was ". . . the most important. . . ."[6]

The problem here lies with the questions, not the summary responses they triggered. The posing of such questions leads directly to glib assessments that bear only indirectly upon the major events of the "Colonial Era and Revolution," which are purportedly under discussion. Real history—in this case, the dynamic process that led patriotic colonists toward independence—is masked by thumbnail personality profiles. Focusing exclusively on stories of allegedly great men produces little in the way of historical analysis.

CENTRAL PLAYERS

There is one use of the term "great" that does not imply adulation. If a historic personage was important and powerful enough, he (rarely she) will warrant the appellation irrespective of any moral qualities deserving of respect. Alexander the Great, Napoleon, Hitler—these people were in one sense "great," even though we might not approve of what they did.[7]

Although we would be loath to compare the "greatest generation" of Americans with great but cruel conquerors, Joseph Ellis argues that we must place our founders at the center of the story by sheer virtue of their power and significance:

> The central events and achievements of the revolutionary era and the early republic were political. These events and achievements are historically significant because they shaped the subsequent history of the United States, including our own time. The central players in the drama were not the marginal or peripheral figures, whose lives are more typical, but rather the political leaders at the center of the national story who wielded power.[8]

A key concept here (repeated three times in as many sentences) is "central"—but that notion is entirely dependent on one's field of vision. Characters who appear at the center of one story will be on the periphery of another. Were the "achievements" of Aaron Burr, an ambitious New York politician, really "central" to the "revolutionary era"? Another criterion is "wielded power," which closes and summarizes the passage. But did Abigail Adams really wield power in any sort of public way that affected history at that time? Clearly, Burr and Mrs. Adams make the list of Ellis's top eight for other reasons, Burr for the story of his duel with Hamilton, and Adams for gender balance.

Further, if wielding power were really the criterion, Ellis would have to include Robert Morris, unquestionably the most powerful civilian in Revolutionary America. Morris ran the confederated government by himself during the winter of 1776–1777 when Congress fled Philadelphia; secured supplies and arranged finances for the Continental Army at several critical moments (Washington's crossing of the Delaware and victory at Yorktown could not have been achieved without him); and assumed unprecedented executive powers, rivaling those of future presidents, during his three-year reign as superintendent of finance at the close of the Revolutionary War.[9] Even more significantly, in 1781 Morris bailed out a bankrupt nation by underwriting government notes, essentially offering his own private credit, which was good, in lieu of public credit, which people would no longer accept. By any reasonable application of Ellis's standards—"central" and "wielded power"—Morris would make the list, but he does not appear there, nor is he featured in most renditions of our nation's birth. A man who made his fortune in large measure by privateering (legalized piracy), cornering markets, and war profiteering, and who ended his career in debtors' prison, is not a top candidate for America's "natural aristocracy," no matter how much power he wielded.[10]

While promoting the importance of his eight protagonists, Ellis demotes the other three million Americans—also members of the Revolutionary generation—to the secondary status of "marginal or peripheral." But the *central* theme of the American Revolution was popular sovereignty: all power ultimately resides with the people. How, then, can "the people" be reduced to the periphery of the story? In fact, regular Americans were at the very center of the drama:

- Common farmers in Massachusetts, without any help from Ellis's featured players, were the first to overthrow British political authority.

- Poor men and boys fought the British army. Without them, the so-called Founding Fathers might all have been hanged.

- If it weren't for a popular clamoring for independence, Congress would not have unanimously passed their final declaration.

- If the people had not ratified the Constitution, it would have been one more failed proposal.

- If it weren't for the labor of hundreds of thousands of "Founding Sisters," American society could never have survived the war. Whatever the "Founding Brothers" were able to accomplish in political chambers would have proven futile.

- The political history of the American Revolution in the southern half of the fledgling nation cannot possibly be understood without reference to enslaved people and the fears they inspired among whites.

- The military history of the war in the West cannot be understood without reference to Native Americans as "central players."

Without the participation of these people, the American Revolution would have been altogether different—or, more likely, there would have been no Revolution at all.

Ellis's approach, a common one, is to place himself within the seats of power and then describe what happens when important insiders come up against each other. By ignoring the various forces acting upon insiders from the outside, however, this inside game distorts the very nature of political processes. Throughout the Revolutionary Era, representatives who gathered in deliberative bodies were expected to abide by specific, written instructions from their constituents. Their actions were also affected by military victories and defeats and other extrinsic factors not of their own doing. Political leaders did not operate in a vacuum, determining the fate of their nation by simple fiat. Lines of influence went both toward and away from the seats of power. This is always true of historical events, but especially so during the American Revolution, when outsiders insisted upon having their say.

By viewing history through this narrow prism, Ellis and other popular authors depict political leaders as causal agents who are personally responsible for the major happenings of the times. David McCullough takes this approach. It was a "miracle," he marvels, "that so few could, in the end, accomplish so much for all humankind."

Speaking specifically of independence, he conjectures: "Had they [the signers of the Declaration of Independence] been poll-driven, 'risk-averse' politicians gathered in Philadelphia that fateful summer of 1776, they would have scrapped the whole idea of a 'mighty revolution.'"[11] McCullough's founders were lonely heroes, opposing not only the British but also will of the people, the "polls." The majority of Americans during the Revolution, by this telling, are transformed into antagonists. Instead of being treated as heroes themselves, they become the lethargic masses, too slow to share the founders' forward-looking vision. The American Revolution, fought in the name of popular sovereignty, becomes strangely convoluted in stories that grant all honors to America's special aristocracy of political talent, the Founding Fathers.

But McCullough misreads the "polls" of those times. "As daunting as almost anything was the lack of popular support for independence," he writes. "By early 1776 about a third of the people were for independence, while another third remained adamantly opposed. The rest, in the old human way, were waiting to see who came out on top."[12] In his biography *John Adams*, McCullough reveals his source, a letter from Adams to Benjamin Rush in 1812: "We were about one third Tories, and [one] third timid, and one third true blue." From this single quotation, which he uses as a chapter invocation in the book, McCullough concludes, "So as yet the voices for independence were decidedly in the minority."[13] That left an uphill battle for Adams and a few radicals in Congress, who had to struggle on behalf of an unpopular cause.

But John Adams never stated that only one-third of the people were for independence in 1776. Here are the exact words he wrote to Rush:

> I lament, my dear Friend, that you were not in Congress in 1774 and 1776. A thousand Things happened there in those years that no Man now living knows but myself. . . . 1774 was the most important and the most difficult year of all. We were about one third Tories, one third timid and one third true Blue. We had a

> Code of Fundamental Laws to prepare for a whole Continent of incongruous Colonies. It was done; and the Declaration of Independence in 1776 was no more than a repetition of the Principles, the Rights and Wrongs asserted and adopted in 1774.[14]

Adams never mentioned the views of "the people" at all—he was discussing only the attitudes of members of Congress, who were divided into thirds in 1774, not 1776. The difference in dates is not trivial. His central thrust was to emphasize the importance of 1774—and to distinguish it from 1776. Writing to Thomas Jefferson in 1813, Adams repeated his assessment of "the Congress of 1774": "To draw the characters of them all would require a volume, and would now be considered as a caricature-print; one third tories, another whigs, and the rest mongrels."[15] No statement about Congress in 1774 can demonstrate that only a minority of the American people favored independence two years later. The notion that there were as many Tories as patriots in 1776 is highly implausible; had this been so, the Tories, allied with the most powerful army on earth, would certainly have prevailed in a war that was well underway. Further, no estimate made by one man thirty-six years after the fact can be accepted as proof of the sentiments of an entire population.[16]

McCullough's contention that there was "no sweeping support for rebellion"[17] does not jibe with Adams's own writings at the time. On July 3, 1776, the day after Congress voted for independence, he wrote to his wife Abigail:

> Time has been given for the whole people maturely to consider the great question of independence, and to ripen their judgment, dissipate their fears, and allure their hopes, by discussing it in newspapers and pamphlets, by debating it in assemblies, conventions, committees of safety and inspection, in town and county meetings, as well as in private conversations, so that the whole people, in every colony of the thirteen, have now adopted it as their own.[18]

According to Adams's reporting at the moment, no matter what he might write later, independence resulted from a months-long national conversation—and the people themselves, in overwhelming numbers, decided to make a clean break from Britain.

Adams's assessment on July 3 is confirmed by other evidence. Pauline Maier's list of state and local declarations of independence (see chapter 6) includes fifty-eight towns that issued instructions endorsing independence, while she uncovered only one that instructed its representative not to vote for independence. By June 1, when Congress took up Richard Henry Lee's tabled motion to become a separate nation, nine of the thirteen states, under intense popular pressure, had told their congressional representatives to support independence, while only one state delegation (New York) was under instructions to refrain from voting for independence. In Maryland, after the provincial convention had forbidden its congressional delegates to support independence, four county conventions instructed their representatives to overturn that decision and tell delegates to push for independence. That's precisely what happened, and on the morning of July 1, just as Congress was set to resume its deliberations on independence, John Adams received a letter from Maryland's Samuel Chase: "I am at this moment from the house to procure an express to follow the post, with an unanimous vote of our convention for *independence*, &c. See the glorious effects of county instructions. Our people have fire if not smothered."[19]

Yet McCullough writes, "It was John Adams, more than anyone, who made it [independence] happen."[20] Here is a clear implication of causality: if Adams "made it happen," without him there might never have been a Declaration of Independence. This seems highly implausible. There were several political figures within Congress working toward independence, in addition to all those promoting independence on the state and local levels. Adams played an important role, but he did not run the show, nor is it fruitful to compare his contributions to those of Samuel Adams, Samuel Chase, Thomas Paine, and any number of political activists who threw themselves into the project. Adams allied himself with these people, and together they accomplished the task. Neither he nor anybody else owned independence; the American people did. Without John Adams, chances are the Continental Congress would still have broken ties with Britain in the summer of 1776; without a preponderance of popular support for independence, chances are Congress would have chosen a different path.[21]

John Ferling, like McCullough, places Adams not only above the people but also in opposition to them. In his comparative biography of Washington, Adams, and Jefferson, he states, "Washington and Adams achieved historical greatness in the American Revolution. In some ways, Adams's achievement was the more impressive. His was the more lonely struggle." Adams was "more impressive," he argues, precisely because he bucked the tide.[22] But if this is to be our standard for "historical greatness," a person is less likely to become great if he or she chooses to engage in common cause with others. Any form of collective action, by definition, is not worthy of the adulation we bestow on solitary heroes who oppose the will of the people—a strange notion for an avowedly democratic society.

"Why is it," Joseph Ellis asks rhetorically, "that there is a core of truth to the distinctive iconography of the American Revolution, which does not depict dramatic scenes of mass slaughter, but, instead, a gallery of well-dressed personalities in classical poses?"[23] If there is a core of truth to this, it is a dangerously partial one. The Revolution did include scenes of slaughter; per capita, it was the bloodiest war in our nation's history save for the Civil War, killing more than twice the percentage of the American population as World War II and thirty-five times the percentage as Vietnam. The iconography of the war should certainly incorporate this "truth," and also the "truth" that everyday Americans were directly involved in the political activities that led to the war, more so than at any other time in our nation's history with the possible exception of the Civil War. The "well-dressed personalities in classical poses" did engage in actions of momentous and lasting import, but so did tens of thousands of Massachusetts farmers who first broke from British rule, 25,000 soldiers who perished while fighting for the patriot cause, 300,000 soldiers who placed their bodies on the line, and 3,000,000 people—the entire population—whose lives were severely disrupted for eight years as the United States labored in birth. To say that the story of a very select group of "well-dressed personalities in classical pose," an aristocracy of political talent, supersedes all the rest, that their deliberations were somehow on a higher order than the profound deeds of others, is a grievous error. It takes the American Revolution, and with it the nation it created, out of the hands of the people.

DOING BATTLE

" 'Tis true he could talk—Gods how he *could* talk!"

"Give Me Liberty or Give Me Death!" Engraving, 1876.

9

"GIVE ME LIBERTY OR GIVE ME DEATH!"

The time: March 23, 1775. The place: the "New Church" of the Henrico Parish in Richmond, Virginia—the largest building in town, but still too small to hold all those who wished to attend the second session of the extralegal Virginia Convention. Patriots were gathering in Richmond rather than Williamsburg, the capital, for fear the royal governor might try to disband them.

The reason: Armed hostilities had not yet commenced, but Britain was beefing up its military presence in America with more troops and ships. While moderate patriots were still trying to avoid an armed confrontation, Patrick Henry introduced a series of resolutions that would raise a militia and place the colony in a state of preparedness. In defense of these resolutions, Patrick Henry delivered the most famous speech of his illustrious oratorical career. He addressed his remarks to the president of the Convention, as was the custom. Here are the final passages of his remarkable call to arms:

> Let us not, I beseech you, sir, deceive ourselves longer. Sir, we have done every thing that could have been done, to avert the storm which is now coming on. We have petitioned—we have

remonstrated—we have supplicated—we have prostrated ourselves before the throne, and have implored its interposition to arrest the tyrannical hands of the ministry and parliament. Our petitions have been slighted; our remonstrances have produced additional violence and insult, our supplications have been disregarded; and we have been spurned, with contempt, from the foot of the throne.

There is no longer any room for hope. If we wish to be free—if we mean to preserve inviolate those inestimable privileges for which we have been so long contending—if we mean not basely to abandon the noble struggle in which we have been so long engaged, and which we have pledged ourselves never to abandon, until the glorious object of our contest shall be obtained—we must fight!—I repeat it sir, we must fight!! An appeal to arms and to the God of Hosts is all that is left us!

They tell us, sir, that we are weak—unable to cope with so formidable an adversary. But when shall we be stronger? Will it be the next week or the next year? Will it be when we are totally disarmed, and when a British guard shall be stationed in every house? Shall we gather strength by irresolution and inaction? Shall we acquire the means of effectual resistance by lying supinely on our backs, and hugging the delusive phantom of hope, until our enemies shall have bound us hand and foot?

Sir, we are not weak, if we make a proper use of those means which the God of nature hath placed in our power. Three millions of people armed in the holy cause of liberty, and in such a country as that which we possess, are invincible by any force which our enemy can send against us.

Besides, sir, we have no election. If we were base enough to desire it, it is now too late to retire from the contest. There is no retreat, but in submission and slavery! Our chains are forged. Their clanking may be heard on the plains of Boston! The war is inevitable—and let it come!! I repeat it, sir, let it come!!!

It is in vain, sir, to extenuate the matter. Gentlemen may cry

> peace, peace—but there is no peace. The war is actually begun! The next gale that sweeps from the north will bring to our ears the clash of resounding arms! Our brethren are already in the field! Why stand we here idle? What is it that gentlemen wish? What would they have? Is life so dear, or peace so sweet, as to be purchased at the price of chains and slavery? Forbid it, Almighty God!—I know not what course others may take; but as for me, give me liberty, or give me death![1]

These words are stirring indeed, but it is highly unlikely that Patrick Henry uttered them. The speech was invented many years later, based on distant recollections of those who were present at the time. Although we know people were moved by Patrick Henry's oratory on March 23, 1775, we have no text of what he actually said.

In 1805 an attorney named William Wirt resolved to write about the life of Patrick Henry. This would not be an easy task. Although Henry had figured prominently in the events leading up to the Revolution, and although he went on to become governor of the nation's then-largest state, he left few records for historians or biographers to ponder. He was an orator, not a writer, and there are no transcriptions, recorded at the time, for any of his flamboyant prewar speeches, including this one, that led to his renown.

In 1815 Wirt wrote to a friend of the difficulties he was having in finding reliable material about the subject of his book:

> It was all speaking, speaking, speaking. 'Tis true he could talk—Gods how he *could* talk! but there is no acting the while. . . . And then, to make the matter worse, from 1763 to 1789 . . . not one of his speeches lives in print, writing or memory. All that is told me is, that on such and such an occasion, he made a distinguished speech. . . . [T]here are some ugly traits in H's character, and some pretty nearly as ugly blanks. He was a blank military commander, a blank governor, and a blank politician, in all those useful points which depend on composition and detail.

In short, it is, verily, as hopeless a subject as man could well desire.[2]

Undaunted, Wirt filled in the blanks according to his own discretion. He wanted to write a tale that would inspire American youth, and for that he did not need to stick too closely to the historical record. "The present and future generations of our country can never be better employed than in studying the models set before them by the fathers of the Revolution," he wrote to John Adams.[3]

In 1817, twelve years after he started his project, William Wirt published the first biography of Virginia's Revolutionary folk hero: *Sketches of the Life and Character of Patrick Henry*.[4] He dedicated his book "to the young men of Virginia," whom he hoped would emulate the hero of his tale. No matter that he invoked poetic license; his goals were to stimulate patriotism and sell books, and he was successful on both counts. Wirt's book immediately became a mainstay of popular history. Reprinted twenty-five times in the next half century, it furnished much material that would be used in promoting a nationalist spirit—including the famous "liberty or death" speech, which finally appeared in print forty-two years after it was delivered and eighteen years after the great orator's death.[5]

How accurate is Wirt's rendition?

Three decades after Henry delivered his inspirational call to arms, Wirt corresponded with men who had heard the speech firsthand and others who were acquainted with men who were there at the time. All agreed that the speech had produced a profound impact, but it seems that only one of Wirt's correspondents, Judge St. George Tucker, tried to render an actual text. Tucker's letter to Wirt has been lost, but we do have a letter from Wirt to Tucker that states, "I have taken almost entirely Mr. Henry's speech in the Convention of '75 from you, as well as your description of its effect on you verbatim."[6]

Scholars have argued for years whether the speech we know is primarily the work of William Wirt or St. George Tucker.[7] But what about Patrick Henry? How much of the speech is his?

Some of those favoring the Tucker hypothesis suggest that the speech published by Wirt is a fairly accurate rendering, since Tucker himself was there at the time. By his own admission, however, Tucker's account of the speech was based on "recollections," not recorded notes. "In vain should I attempt to give any idea of his speech," he wrote. Tucker attempted a reconstruction of only two paragraphs (the first two in the selection included here), which constitute less than one-fifth of the speech.[8] Even this much is suspect. It seems improbable that St. George Tucker could commit Henry's words to memory, then reproduce them accurately several decades later. He might have captured the basic gist, but what about the diction and cadence, so crucial to the art of oratory? And what about the rest of the speech, which amounted to 1,217 words? Where did all those words originate?

Imagine, in our own times, the task of trying to re-create the words of a speech delivered forty-two years ago if we had no written record. That was the same amount of time between the first printing of *Founding Myths* in 2004 and when John F. Kennedy, on October 22, 1962, delivered one of the most striking and fateful addresses in the history of this or any nation. Then, President Kennedy told the American people that the Soviet Union was trying to place missiles in Cuba, just ninety miles from the United States shore, and that he had just ordered a "quarantine" of Cuban waters. If Soviet ships attempted to make any deliveries, they would have to fight American ships. Kennedy's action, which brought the world to the brink of a nuclear holocaust, was a pivotal moment of the Cold War and among the scariest moments in history, when the very existence of human life on earth seemed threatened.

But forty-two years later, who, without prompting from the record, could remember Kennedy's exact words? They too were stirring—something about the path being full of hazards, but the greatest danger would be to do nothing at all—but was that really the way he said it? And what else did he say? Millions watched and heard the speech, some might have even jotted down some notes, but who could reconstruct the speech decades later if they had not taken notes at the time?[9]

Those of us old enough to remember the speech will recall the emotions—the fears and apprehensions of the moment—much better than the words. We might also recall Kennedy's deportment and tone. So it was with Patrick Henry. He had delivered an inspiring and very hawkish speech with great dramatic flair—people could remember that. But to recall the exact words he used to excite those patriotic feelings is another matter altogether.

FEAR AND LOATHING

Henry's speech, as we know it, owes much to the oratorical genius of William Wirt and St. George Tucker, in some combination, and it reflects the agendas of nineteenth-century nationalists who were fond of romanticizing war. To idealize war, however, much has to be left out. In the "liberty or death" speech that these men supposedly resurrected, key components of Patrick Henry's popular appeal are mysteriously absent. Henry's sentiments, and those of the men he addressed, were not always so noble as Wirt wanted his readers to believe.

In fact, we do have one account of Henry's speech that was recorded at the moment, not years later—and this version is seriously out of sync with Wirt's later rendition. In a letter dated April 6, 1775, James Parker wrote to Charles Stewart,

> You never heard anything more infamously insolent than P. Henry's speech: he called the K——— a Tyrant, a fool, a puppet, and a tool to the ministry. Said there was no Englishmen, no Scots, no Britons, but a set of wretches sunk in Luxury, that they had lost their native courage and (were) unable to look the brave Americans in the face. . . . This Creature is so infatuated, that he goes about I am told, praying and preaching amongst the common people.[10]

Even allowing for the bias of an unsympathetic observer, Parker's account is plausible. As in any era, hawkish patriots during the American Revolution probably questioned the enemy's courage, descended to name-calling, and appealed to widespread fear. Demagoguery is the underbelly of oratory, yet "wretches sunk in Luxury" did not make it into Wirt's rendition.

Less than one month after Henry delivered his "liberty or death" speech, fear of slave uprisings helped trigger the onset of the Revolution in the South. In the spring of 1775, white citizens of Virginia believed that African Americans held in bondage were planning to rise up, rebel, and go on a murderous rampage against them. Fearful whites panicked and prepared for the worst—and Patrick Henry, one of the largest slaveholders of his county, was among them. Before dawn on April 21 the royal governor of Virginia, Lord Dunmore, dispatched a party of marines to seize gunpowder stored in the magazine at Williamsburg. Later that day, infuriated patriots gathered to protest. One newspaper reported their reasoning:

> The monstrous absurdity that the Governor can deprive the people of the necessary means of defense at a time when the colony is actually threatened with an insurrection of their slaves . . . has worked up the passions of the people . . . almost to a frenzy.[11]

Governor Dunmore at first claimed he had seized the powder so the slaves couldn't get to it. Shortly afterward, however, he changed his stance: if the patriots harmed a single British official, he pronounced, he would "declare Freedom to the Slaves, and reduce the City of Williamsburg to Ashes."[12]

This only kindled the flames of rebellion. Within the next few days at least seven counties hastily formed "independent companies," partly because the British had just shed blood at Lexington and Concord, but also in response to Dunmore's threat. In Fredericksburg on April 29, more than six hundred members of these companies prepared to march against the governor in Williamsburg. Dunmore reiterated his threat to raise the slaves, saying he would do so immediately if the companies proceeded with their plans.

Moderates convinced most of these companies to disband, but two companies persisted: Albemarle and Hanover. The Albemarle volunteers voted to continue to Williamsburg "to demand satisfaction of Dunmore for the powder, and his threatening to fix his standard and call over the negroes."[13] But they too soon turned back, leaving the field to the company from Hanover—under the leadership of Patrick Henry, a slave owner with much to lose.[14]

The Hanover County committeemen were not of one mind, but Henry, with many friends and relatives on the committee, carried the day. Because of "apprehension for their persons and property," they decided to march on the capital. Since Dunmore had threatened to raise the slaves while simultaneously seizing gunpowder that whites could use to defend themselves, Henry and the majority of the Hanover men felt they were likely to suffer "calamities of the greatest magnitude, and most fatal consequences to this colony" unless they went on the offensive.[15] In the end, the incipient rebellion triggered by Dunmore's actions reached a negotiated (albeit temporary) settlement: the British paid for the powder they had seized, and the Hanover company went home.

Later that year, when Lord Dunmore formally offered to free any slaves who joined the British army, Colonel Patrick Henry of the First Virginia Regiment took it upon himself to publicize Dunmore's action far and wide. (For more on Dunmore's offer of freedom, see chapter 11.) This time Henry's exact words were set in writing, and there can be no doubt he used fear as a rallying cry:

> As the Committee of Safety is not sitting, I take the Liberty to enclose you a Copy of the Proclamation issued by Lord Dunmore; the Design and Tendency of which, you will observe, is fatal to the publick Safety. An early and unremitting Attention to the Government of the SLAVES may, I hope, counteract this

dangerous Attempt. Constant, and well directed Patrols, seem indispensably necessary.[16]

Slaves were not the only objects of fear—Indians might cause trouble as well. One of the independent companies that threatened to march on Williamsburg noted that Dunmore had tried "to render (at least as far as in his power so to do) this colony defenceless, and lay it open to the attacks of a savage invasion, or a domestick foe [a common euphemism for enslaved people]."[17] This theme was repeated often in complaints about British policies issuing from the Southern states: the king, Parliament, and royal governors were inciting Indian attacks as well as slave insurrections. The following summer, Congress formalized these complaints in the Declaration of Independence. The king, it said, "has excited domestic insurrections amongst us and has endeavored to bring on the inhabitants of our frontiers the merciless Indian savages."

Patrick Henry, like many white Virginians, speculated in western lands. In 1767 he acquired two tracts from his father-in-law that he couldn't even find when he went looking for them. According to notes he made in his fee book, he knew these were cut off by territory that had been "allotted to the Indians by a treaty," but he purchased them anyway, "hoping that line would be altered." Eventually it was: "After many contests and much altercation with the Indians," as well as with other colonists and British officials on both sides of the Atlantic, the line was changed so he could secure most of the land. Henry knew, as did other white Virginians, that both native people and imperial officials stood in the way of land speculation and white settlement of the West.[18]

With access to land at issue, it is little wonder that Henry advocated military invasions of Indian country. In 1778, as governor of Virginia, he increased the military support for frontier settlements and sanctioned a company of "Volunteers" who set out to raid Indian territory.[19] The following year he authorized an expedition into distant territory inhabited by the Chickamaugas, militant Cherokees who resisted white domination.[20] Following the Revolutionary War, while arguing for American rights to navigate the Mississippi River, he declared he would sooner part from the Union than with the Mississippi.[21] Before, during, and after the Revolution, Henry was an avid expansionist. His own self-interest, as well as the interest of many other Virginians, demanded it.

In his efforts to arouse public opinion against Britain, which had tried to shut down white settlement of the trans-Appalachian territories, Patrick Henry likely made some appeal to the prevailing anti-Indian sentiments. Since western lands would be easier to acquire with Britain out of the way, playing to fears of a British-Indian alliance would aid Revolutionary recruitment (see chapter 14). Likewise, it is difficult to imagine that Henry did *not* play the "slave card"—his ace in the hole—in his politicking. Yet nowhere in any of his speeches, as rendered by later writers, do we see even a hint of pandering to instincts less noble than the love of liberty. His speeches, quite literally, have been whitewashed.

ANOTHER DOCTORED SPEECH

"Liberty or death" was not the only speech to receive a touch-up. Ten years earlier, in his first year as a representative to Virginia's House of Burgesses, Henry had stepped forth to offer a dramatic denunciation of the Stamp Act. According to William Wirt:

> It was in the midst of this magnificent debate, while he was descanting on the tyranny of the obnoxious act, that he exclaimed, in a voice of thunder, and with the look of a god, "Caesar had his Brutus—Charles the first, his Cromwell—and George the third—('Treason,' cried the speaker—'treason, treason,' echoed from every part of the house.—It was one of those trying moments which is decisive of character.—Henry faltered not for an instant; but rising to a loftier attitude, and fixing on the

> speaker an eye of the most determined fire, he finished his sentence with the firmest emphasis)—*may profit by their example.* If *this* be treason, make the most of it."[22]

In this version of the story, reconstructed a half century after the fact, Patrick Henry dramatically defied his detractors. At the time, however, a French traveler who observed the event firsthand noted that Henry responded to the charge of "treason" quite differently:

> Shortly after I Came in one of the members stood up and said he had read that in former times tarquin and Julius had their Brutus, Charles had his Cromwell, and he Did not Doubt but some good American would stand up, in favour of his Country, but (says he) in a more moderate manner, and was going to Continue, when the speaker of the house rose and Said, he, the last that stood up had spoke treason, and was sorey to see that not one of the members of the house was loyal Enough to stop him, before he had gone so far.
>
> [U]pon which the Same member stood up again (his name is henery) and said that if he had affronted the speaker, or the house, he was ready to ask pardon, and he would shew his loyalty to his majesty King G. the third, at the Expence of the last Drop of his blood, but what he had said must be attributed to the Interest of his Country's Dying liberty which he had at heart, and the heat of passion might have lead him to have said something more than he intended, but, again, if he said anything wrong, he begged the speaker and the houses pardon. Some other Members stood up and backed him, on which that afaire was droped.[23]

The discrepancies between these two accounts are striking. While nineteenth-century Romantics depicted Henry as defiant in the face of numerous critics, the firsthand witness stated clearly and emphatically that Henry apologized for his excess not once but twice, and that the charge of "treason" came only from the Speaker of the House, not from a chorus of members. Henry was not a solitary hero standing tall in the face of numerous adversaries; instead, he tried to cover his bases when it appeared he had overreached his bounds. By backpedaling, Henry acted wisely and astutely—but not heroically.

The Romantic versions of both these speeches—"liberty or death" and "Caesar had his Brutus"—glorify bold defiance. They also glorify oratory itself. At a time when many Americans did not have the ability to read learned dissertations on politics, everybody could hear and respond to a speech. Oratory was crucial to the creation of American nationalism. It is no surprise that William Wirt was something of an orator himself: he served as the keynote speaker to commemorate the fiftieth anniversary of the Declaration of Independence in Washington, D.C., on July 4, 1826.

Oratory has its uses, but it can also drown out compromise, reasoned consideration, and dissent. Hawkish oratory, taken at face value, functions as military recruitment. Noble sentiments lead impressionable boys and young men to offer up their lives in service to their nation or cause. This danger intensifies when one orator pumps up the words of another, as with Wirt and Henry. Patriots of the early republic sanctified their nationalism and expansionism by appealing to the hallowed tradition of the Revolution. Even if the words came from Wirt, the "liberty or death" speech played better when attributed to the "Son of Thunder," the legendary orator from a generation past.

Through much of the nineteenth century, countless schoolchildren practiced memorization and recitation by delivering and dramatizing the "liberty or death" speech. Little did they know that the words they spoke did not come from Patrick Henry, or that the noble sentiments they expressed concealed baser motives. Today, we do know these things, yet Henry's call to arms is still featured in many current texts. Students no longer recite the speech, but "give me liberty, or give me death" still tells them that marching off to war is admirable and patriotic. In her *History of US*, Joy Hakim provides a complete stage set for the speech, which she repeats verbatim with no credit to Wirt: "Henry stepped into the aisle, bowed his head, and held out his arms.

He pretended his arms were chained." After quoting several sentences, she concludes, "Then Patrick Henry threw off the imaginary chains, stood up straight, and cried out, 'Forbid it, Almighty God! I know not what course others may take, but as for me, give me liberty or give me death!' "[24]

This story works because the words have been teased and the context ignored. A speech that called the king a "fool," and Englishmen, Scots, and Britons "wretches," would not be so celebrated today, and a man who catered to fears of slaves and Indians would not be quite so honored.

“ ‘Don’t throw away a single shot,
my brave fellows,’ said old Putnam,
’till you can see the white of their eyes.’ ”

The Battle of Bunker Hill. Engraving, 1850s,
based on painting by Alonzo Chappel.

10

THE WHITES OF THEIR EYES

During the Battle of Bunker Hill, the story goes, Israel Putnam (some say William Prescott) issued a command: "Do not fire till you see the whites of their eyes!" Displaying great courage and discipline in the face of advancing Redcoats, the untested patriots stood their ground and withheld their fire until they could gaze into the eyes of the enemy.

According to depositions of those who participated in the battle, American officers issued many commands: "Fire low." "Aim at their waistbands." "Pick off the commanders." "Aim at the handsome coats." "Powder must not be wasted." "Wait until you see the white of their eyes."[1] What is so special about the last one? Why has this particular idiom, which now exemplifies the story of Bunker Hill, been included among the classic tales of the American Revolution?

Soldiers who see the whites of the eyes of their adversaries must be fighting a very personalized, intimate sort of war—not like the industrialized warfare of later years. Man-to-man and honorably, a soldier could prove his valor by facing off against his adversary. This is what "the whites of their eyes" story gives us. It sets the Revolutionary War in a class by itself. Those were the days, we imagine, when a man could look the enemy directly in the eyes before shooting him down.

AN EXPERIMENT

The "whites of their eyes" command was not new to the American Revolution. Prince Charles of Prussia supposedly issued it in 1745, as did Frederick the Great in 1757. They were probably not the only ones. During the Revolution itself, other officers at other battles were said to have spoken these words.[2] "Do not fire until you see the whites of their eyes" was a figure of speech, a common idiom used by eighteenth-century officers to gain control over their soldiers' fire.

Let's imagine Revolutionary soldiers *did* obey the order exactly as stated. When would they be allowed to shoot? At what distance can a person see the whites of another person's eyes?

Try this experiment. Have someone charge at you, then signal when you can see the whites of the aggressor's eyes. Have a third party note the spot and measure how close it is to you. If you actually do see the whites of eyes at more than ten yards, you have unusually keen vision.

Now repeat the experiment in a battlefield simulation. Have hundreds of people march toward you in full battle gear and kicking up dust, or if that is too difficult to arrange, settle for just a dozen or two marching toward you with long sticks to represent muskets and bayonets, finally breaking their rhythmic gait into a rapid assault. At what point, exactly, can you see the whites of the eyes of the enemy? Five yards? Perhaps less? Certainly not much more. Do you really wish to wait that long until you fire? How could you and your compatriots possibly reload for a second volley?

Clearly, the command was not meant to be taken literally, as we infer now. When officers issued this order, as many did, they were telling their soldiers to focus hard on the enemy and hold their fire until further command. They were not telling them to fire only when the enemy had advanced to within five or ten yards.

Once, an American officer did insist that soldiers hold their fire till the enemy was only about ten yards away. On May 29, 1780, at Waxhaws, South Carolina, Colonel Abraham Buford ordered his troops not to shoot until the British legion, commanded by Banastre

Tarleton, was almost upon them. The single volley proved insufficient to stop the charge, and the patriots were immediately overrun.[3] One hundred thirteen patriots were killed immediately and another 203 were captured, most of whom had been wounded. British losses, by contrast, were only five killed and twelve wounded. This real-life experiment at close firing failed miserably.

Americans often point to the "massacre" at Waxhaws as an example of British cruelty (see chapter 12). Whether or not Tarleton's men killed soldiers trying to surrender, as patriots later claimed, the battle certainly revealed the ugly face of close combat. When soldiers fought each other with swords, musket butts, and bayonets, battles were likely to turn into slaughters. If "the whites of their eyes" were actually sighted, things could turn nasty indeed.

"CANNONS ROARING MUSKETS CRACKING DRUMS BEATING BUMBS FLYING ALL ROUND"

Sometimes, a Revolutionary soldier could see into the whites of the eyes of the enemy; far more often, he could not. Most men who died never even saw their slayers. In fact, the majority of soldiers who perished did so from diseases or while languishing in prisons. With soldiers coming together in crowded and often unsanitary conditions, typhoid fever, typhus, dysentery, and smallpox ran rampant. Close contact with one's fellow soldiers took more lives than close contact with the enemy. According to military historian Howard Peckham, approximately 10,000 patriots died in camp. Another 7,000 died as prisoners of war, primarily by catching diseases from each other. By contrast, Peckham recorded 6,824 deaths from battle casualties.[4]

Those who succumbed in battle were often mowed down by cannons or muskets fired in their general direction by men from afar. The war that brought our nation into existence did not feature direct man-to-man combat nearly so often as we would like to believe; conversely, it did feature distant killing much more often than we prefer to imagine. While soldiers in the infantry were making or resisting a charge, their counterparts in the artillery, working in teams of three to fifteen, were loading cannons, mortars, and howitzers and letting them loose on an anonymous enemy. These weapons featured not only solid shot but also grapeshot, canister shot, and bombs that exploded—antipersonnel ammunition designed to maim or take human life. The point of soldiering, then as now, was not only to display individual valor but to kill strangers from as safe a distance as possible—the farther away the better. Consider these firsthand accounts by participants in the Revolutionary War:

> Cannons Roaring muskets Cracking Drums Beating Bumbs Flying all Round. Men a dying woundeds Horred Grones which would Greave the Heardist of Hearts to See Such a Dollful Sight as this to See our Fellow Creators Slain in Such a manner.
>
> —Private Elisha Stevens, the Battle of Brandywine[5]

> At length we fired the first gun, and immediately a tremendous cannonade—about one hundred and eighty, or two hundred pieces of heavy cannon—were discharged at the same moment. The mortars from both sides threw out an enormous number of shells. It was a glorious sight to see them, like meteors, crossing each other, and bursting in the sky. It appeared as if the stars were tumbling down. The fire was incessant almost the whole night, cannonballs whizzing, and shells hissing, continually among us, ammunition chests and temporary magazines blowing up, great guns bursting, and wounded men groaning along the lines. It was a dreadful night! It was our last great effort, but it availed us nothing. After it, our military ardor was much abated.
>
> —William Moultrie, the first Battle of Charleston[6]

> During the whole night, at intervals of a quarter or half an hour, the enemy would let off all their pieces. . . . I was in this

place a fortnight and can say in sincerity that I never lay down to sleep a minute in all that time. . . .

The cannonade was severe, as well it might be, six sixty-four-gun ships, a thirty-six-gun frigate, a twenty-four-gun ship, a galley and a sloop of six guns, together with six batteries of six guns each and a bomb battery of three mortars, all playing at once upon our poor little fort, if fort it might be called. Some of our officers endeavored to ascertain how many guns were fired in a minute by the enemy, but it was impossible, the fire was incessant. . . .

The enemy's shot cut us up. I saw five artillerists belonging to one gun cut down by a single shot, and I saw men who were stooping to be protected by the works, but not stooping low enough, split like fish to be broiled. . . .

When the firing had in some measure subsided and I could look about me, I found the fort exhibited a picture of desolation. The whole area of the fort was as completely ploughed as a field. The buildings of every kind hanging in broken fragments, and the guns all dismounted, and how many of the garrison sent to the world of spirits, I knew not. If ever destruction was complete, it was here.

—Private Joseph Plumb Martin, the siege of Fort Mifflin[7]

Even at Bunker Hill, patriots had to brave bombardment from across the river in Boston and from men-of-war and gun batteries anchored offshore. All the firsthand accounts by patriots feature the terror caused by the enemy's distant fire. The cannon shot "buzzed around us like hail" and "were incessantly whistling by us," wrote John Chester.[8] "From Boston and from the ships," wrote Peter Brown, the British were "firing and throwing bombs, keeping us down till they got almost around us." The "brisk" fire from distant weapons "caused some of our young country people to desert."[9] William Prescott complained about the "very heavy cannonading and bombardment" and the "very warm fire from the enemy's artillery," which the patriots had to endure while working on their fortifications.[10] "Our men were not used to cannon-balls," William Tudor confessed to John Adams, "and they came so thick from the ships, floating batteries, &c., that they were discouraged from advancing."[11]

One of the most vivid accounts of the Battle of Bunker Hill comes from Issachar Bates, who had just enlisted in the army at the age of seventeen:

> We had to take our full share of their hot metal—of Cannon Balls—Grape and Cannister shot— . . . I could see them great nasty porridge pots flying thro' the air & cramed as full of Devils as they could hold, come whispering along with its blue tail in the day time, and its firey tail by night and if it burst in the air it would thro its hellish stuff all about ones ears, and if it fell to the ground it would hop about just as if the verry Devil was in it, until it bursted and then look out for shins and all above and at the same times cannon balls flying about once a minuit.[12]

Such was the terror of impersonal warfare. Deeply affected by "these wicked inventions of men to shed blood and bring destruction upon their fellow creatures," Bates became a pacifist and later joined the Shaker sect. Many others of the Revolutionary generation, like Bates, detested the brutalities of war. Approximately eighty thousand people, one in every thirty free Americans, were members of pacifistic religious sects that opposed the taking of human life.[13]

All this killing-from-afar is left out of the traditional telling, with its emphasis on a more proximate style of warfare. Listening to accounts of those who were there places the Battle of Bunker Hill in a different perspective. Nearly all firsthand descriptions feature the heavy bombardment by British artillery. American soldiers did hold their fire until an appropriate time, and, in the end, a few who had not managed to escape did face hand-to-hand combat. But the notion that the patriots did not engage in battle until they could look the enemy in the eyes is not a fair or adequate characterization of the fighting, either at Bunker Hill in particular or in the American Revolution in general.

THE BATTLE OF BREED'S HILL

Here's what happened at the so-called Battle of Bunker Hill. After a disastrous retreat from Concord on April 19, 1775, the British army garrisoned within Boston, a peninsula attached to the mainland only by a thin neck. A large array of colonial militias, quickly transformed into an actual army, surrounded the city and laid siege to the British Regulars within it. After a stalemate that lasted almost two months, colonial rebels received intelligence that the British were preparing to break out and take command of a promontory across the Charles River. American officers issued orders to construct fortifications on Bunker Hill, but the officers charged with executing these orders decided that Breed's Hill would be easier to defend. This is how the Battle of Breed's Hill became known as the Battle of Bunker Hill.

Throughout the night of June 16, 1775, farmers-turned-soldiers worked the soil for military purposes; by dawn on June 17, they had constructed a redoubt "eight rods square." All morning they continued to labor on a series of breastworks that would shield them during an attack, but once the British had spotted their fortifications, patriots had to brave an incessant cannonade while they worked. Approximately 1,500 patriots prepared to defend the position on Breed's Hill against an attack of almost 3,000 British Regulars.

British ships fired not only on the patriots' redoubts, but also on the nearby town of Charlestown, which they committed to flames. Issachar Bates described the conflagration: "And Oh! What a horrible sight, to stand and behold their hot balls, carcases and stink-pots flaming thro' the air for the distance of more than a mile, and in less than an hour that beautiful town was all in flames!" [14]

In the early afternoon, as patriot soldiers braced for the British advance, their officers fired commands like grapeshot. "Do not fire till you see the whites of their eyes," or some variation thereof, was among these last-minute directives hurled at the farmers-turned-soldiers during this crash course on battlefield discipline.

At around three in the afternoon on June 17, a vanguard of British soldiers advanced up the hill. Most of the patriots held their fire as commanded; a few did not. (Later, one American officer stated that he had purposely shot early, hoping to induce premature and ineffectual fire from the enemy.[15]) When the British were close enough that musket fire might be reasonably effective—approximately sixty yards, according to contemporaneous reports—the patriots commenced their first volley. The deadly fire continued unabated, causing the Redcoats to retreat.

The British regrouped and charged the hill once again. This time the patriots held their fire until the enemy was only thirty yards away, still not close enough to gaze into the eyes of the soldiers who were trying to kill them. Since the second charge was not as concerted as the first, there was not as much danger of being overrun, so patriots could wait longer before discharging their muskets. Again the shots hit their marks, and again the British retreated.

Through heavy cannonading, however, the British were able to force the patriots to abandon their breastworks. When the Redcoats charged the third time, the weary and shell-shocked patriots decided to abandon the redoubt. They had not received the reinforcements they had expected. Most patriots were able to run; a few who could not leave the redoubt quickly enough were forced to deflect bayonets with the butt ends of their muskets. This was the only fighting in close quarters during the battle.

The retreat was itself fraught with hazard. Offshore batteries continued to pound away at the narrow Charlestown Neck, which the Americans were forced to cross. "I was not suffered to be touched," wrote Peter Brown, "although I was in the fort when the enemy came in, and jumped over the walls, and ran a half a mile, where balls flew like hail-stones, and cannon roared like thunder."[16]

Technically, the British won the Battle of Bunker Hill, for they took new ground—but their victory came at a horrific cost: 226 killed and another 828 wounded, some of whom later perished. Most of these young men from poor families on the other side of the Atlantic were hit by bullets fired from muskets at midrange. Patriot losses were also significant: 140 killed and 271 wounded.[17] Today, we celebrate this bloodbath with a quaint little story about "the whites of their eyes," which demonstrates how valorous war can be.

THE "EYES" PREVAIL

How did the crude, impersonal slaughter at the Battle of Bunker Hill come to satisfy our yearning for a more intimate form of combat?

Contemporaneous accounts referred to Bunker Hill as a defeat for the Americans. Patriots, however, placed an interesting spin on this defeat. Soon after the battle, the Massachusetts Committee of Safety issued a report that claimed a moral victory: "Though the officers and soldiers of the ministerial army meanly exult in having gained this ground," wrote the committee, "they cannot but attest to the bravery of our troops." The carnage inflicted upon the British, it claimed, had "blasted" all previous records. "Such a slaughter was, perhaps, never before made upon British troops."[18]

Crucial to the positive spin placed on the defeat was the willingness of the rebels to hold their ground against thousands of disciplined Redcoats. Despite glistening bayonets pointed at them, the committee declared, the inexperienced American troops had not panicked. They had obeyed their officers' orders to withhold fire. With ammunition scarce, no shots had been wasted. Not until the British "came within ten or twelve rods," wrote the Committee of Safety, did the Americans commence their first volley; on the second charge, they waited till the enemy was "five or six rods" away. (One rod is 16.5 feet, so "ten or twelve rods" translates to 165 to 198 feet, or 55 to 66 yards, and "five or six rods" to 82.5 to 99 feet, or 27.5 to 33 yards.)[19]

Those numbers would figure prominently in the early histories of the Revolutionary War. William Gordon and David Ramsay repeated the Committee of Safety's estimate verbatim. John Marshall stated more conservatively that the British had advanced "within less than one hundred yards" when the Americans opened fire.[20] Virtually all the early accounts specified the distance that separated the opposing forces at the time of the first and second volleys, for this constituted proof that the patriots had both followed orders and displayed great courage in the face of the advancing Redcoats. But those distances, although varying somewhat from one account to the next, were always several times greater than five yards, the point at which the whites of the enemy's eyes might first become visible in combat situations.

Cold, hard numbers confirmed the patriots' discipline; a figure-of-speech command by American officers would have proved nothing. None of the Revolutionary Era historians—William Gordon, David Ramsay, John Marshall, or Mercy Otis Warren—mentioned anything about "the whites of their eyes." In 1788 David Humphreys published a biography of Israel Putnam, the officer from Connecticut who was later said to have issued the order. Humphreys said not a word about the command at Bunker Hill that would later be tied to Putnam's name, but he did tell another story that would become enshrined in Revolutionary lore: "Putnam, who was ploughing when he heard the news [about Lexington and Concord], left his plough in the middle of the field, unyoked his team, and without waiting to change his clothes, set off for the theatre of action."[21] (In later versions of the tale, still with us today, "Old Put" jumped immediately on his horse without even bothering to unyoke his team.) Here was a tale worth telling—this single incident exemplified the eagerness of New England farmers to answer the call to arms. "The whites of their eyes," by contrast, was hardly a story at all in the minds of contemporaries.

The story first found its way into print in Mason Weems's popular biography of George Washington, a quarter century afterward:

> *"Don't throw away a single shot, my brave fellows,"* said old Putnam, *"don't throw away a single shot, but take good aim; nor touch a trigger, till you can see the white of their eyes."*

> This steady reserve of fire, even after the British had come up within pistol-shot, led them [the British] to hope that the Americans did not *mean to resist*! . . . But soon as the enemy were advanced within the fatal distance marked, all at once a thousand triggers were drawn, and a sheet of fire, wide as the whole front of the breast-work, bursted upon them with most ruinous effect.[22]

Over the next half century, although a few writers echoed Weems's tale, most preferred to state specified distances at which the patriots fired: Paul Allen in 1819 followed Marshall's estimate of one hundred yards; Charles Goodrich in 1823 wrote "within twelve rods"; Salma Hale in 1822 shortened it to "within ten rods"; Noah Webster in 1833 used the official Committee of Safety numbers, ten to twelve rods. Richard Hildreth, a conscientious scholar writing in 1849, set the distance at "within a hundred yards." Even George Bancroft, a popular historian fond of direct quotations and folksy dialogue, said nothing about "the whites of their eyes." Instead, he offered two contemporaneous estimates: "within eight rods, as [William] Prescott afterwards thought," and "within ten or twelve rods as the committee of safety of Massachusetts wrote." Setting a prescribed distance was deemed critical to the moral of the story, but the precise words of the commanding officer were of little account in most renditions.[23]

Richard Frothingham, in an exhaustive study of Bunker Hill written in 1849, presented a thesis that would set Weems's story back even further: Israel Putnam was not even in charge at the time. That honor, he wrote, went to William Prescott, a colonel from Massachusetts.[24] In the middle of the nineteenth century, a furious debate raged through academic circles: who *was* the commander at the Battle of Bunker Hill? Both Putnam and Prescott had their defenders.[25]

One would think that uncertainty over the identity of the commander would have interfered with any story about what this mystery man actually said. Not so. Following Frothingham's passing reference to the "whites of their eyes" in 1849, the story picked up steam—and it has never lost its momentum. In the first half of the twentieth century, specific distances began to disappear from school texts; instead, students were told that "untrained militia . . . coolly stood their ground until they saw the whites of the enemy's eyes."[26] A figure of speech had been taken literally and enshrined in the official lexicon of the Revolutionary War. Students had little trouble drawing the obvious conclusion: American patriots, like knights of the Middle Ages, fought their foes eye to eye and hand to hand.

The "whites of their eyes" tale has shown remarkable endurance. In the most recent *American National Biography*, a twenty-four-volume compilation that represents state-of-the-art history, the entry for Israel Putnam states definitively: "As field commander of the troops at Bunker Hill, Putnam gave one of the most famous orders in American military history: 'Men, you are marksmen—don't one of you fire until you see the white[s] of their eyes.' " But what does the *American National Biography* say about William Prescott? "Tradition has him [Prescott] calling, 'Don't fire until you see the whites of their eyes.' " Although this statement is guarded in tone and not incorrect ("tradition" does say this), the story is passed on nonetheless. Putnam said it, Prescott said it, they both said it—one way or the other, or both ways at once, the legend continues.[27]

Significantly, most modern renditions leave out the actual distance between the armies at the time the Americans opened fire.[28] In the absence of concrete numbers, which the early accounts had scrupulously included, we are left only with the evidence of our senses to interpret the now-famous command. Advancing British soldiers must have been at extremely close range, we assume, if the patriots could see into their eyes. Since the distances mentioned in contemporaneous accounts would contradict this assumption, they are conveniently omitted.

When the story is repeated in school texts, it is often accompanied by reproductions of Romantic paintings, such as John Trumbull's famous *The Death of General Warren at the Battle of Bunker's Hill*, which show British and American forces within arm's length of each other.

If only we could believe that our nation was born in this manner, with no man firing his Brown Bess musket before establishing a kind of personal (albeit adversarial) relationship with the enemy. That's the way they did it in the old days. That's how wars are supposed to be. People do not state this directly, but unthinkingly, and by including the "whites of their eyes" tale within the popular narrative of our nation's founding, Americans find it easier to justify and even celebrate the purposive killing that occurred in the Revolutionary War, and by informal proxy, in wars generally.

GOOD V. EVIL

"The relations between master and slave in Virginia were so pleasant that the offer of freedom fell upon dull, uninterested ears."

Life of George Washington the Farmer. Lithograph by Claude Regnier, 1853, based on painting by Junius Brutus Stearns, *Washington as a Farmer at Mount Vernon*, 1851.

11

PATRIOTIC SLAVES

In the popular movie *The Patriot,* which remains to this day the most viewed dramatic presentation of the Revolutionary War, a British officer rides up to Benjamin Martin's South Carolina plantation and offers freedom to any slaves who will fight in His Majesty's army. This is rooted in historical fact. Early in the war Lord Dunmore, the royal governor of Virginia, pronounced: "I do hereby declare all indented Servants, Negroes, or others (appertaining to Rebels) free, that are able and willing to bear Arms, they joining His Majesty's Troops as soon as may be."[1] Later on, British general Henry Clinton made a related offer, although stopping short of promising freedom: "Every Negro who shall desert the Rebel Standard" would enjoy the "full security to follow within these Lines, any Occupation which he shall think proper."[2]

In fact, several thousand bondsmen from South Carolina took these offers seriously and fled to the British in search of their freedom.[3] Not so in *The Patriot*. In the Hollywood version of history, the officer who offered freedom to slaves at Martin's plantation received a most unexpected response from the black field hands he addressed: "Sir, we're not slaves. We work this land as freed men." Here begins a serious stretch of poetic license: we see happy blacks working plantations as freed men in Revolutionary South Carolina, the very heart of the Deep South.

A bit later in the film, an enslaved man named Occam enlists in the militia, serving in place of his master. Although this never happened in South Carolina, Occam proceeds to bear arms on behalf of the patriots in an integrated militia unit. Not until the Korean War, says Dean Devlin, one of the film's producers, would black and white Americans again serve side by side.

Midway through the story, Occam sees a notice posted on a bulletin board in camp. Since Occam, like most of his peers, can't read, someone else reads it aloud:

> By order of GENERAL GEORGE WASHINGTON and the CONTINENTAL CONGRESS, all bound SLAVES who give minimum ONE YEAR SERVICE in the CONTINENTAL ARMY will be GRANTED FREEDOM and be paid a bounty of FIVE SHILLINGS for each month of service.

Occam then looks wistfully into the air as he whispers to himself: "Only another six months."

The document read to Occam, which is seen onscreen and appears visually authentic, contains more historical errors in a single sentence than at first seems possible. A complete concoction, it seriously misrepresents the participation of African Americans in the Revolutionary War. Neither George Washington nor the Continental Congress issued anything like this emancipation proclamation, which allegedly preceded Lincoln's famous decree by more than fourscore years.

When Washington first assumed command of the Continental forces, he banned the enlistment of all Negroes, both slave and free. Because of serious manpower shortages, however, he soon had to rescind a portion of his order: free blacks who had previously served were permitted to reenlist, but those held in bondage were still banned. Enslaved soldiers were viewed as an embarrassment to a republican army fighting in the name of freedom.[4]

Soldiers were recruited by individual states, not by the Continental Congress, as implied in the notice read to Occam. Later in the war some states permitted blacks to serve as substitutes for whites who had been drafted, but in South Carolina, not a single black is known to have enlisted in the Continental Army during the entire course of the Revolutionary War. Upon the urging of John Laurens, Congress had indeed suggested that the state recruit enslaved men, but the notion of arming those held in bondage was preposterous to most white South Carolinians, who rejected the proposal out of hand. "We are much disgusted here at Congress recommending us to arm our Slaves," wrote Christopher Gadsden. "It was received with great resentment, as a very dangerous and impolitic Step."[5]

Unwilling to militarize the enslaved population, white Southerners confronted their manpower shortages by offering special bounties. Bondsmen did figure in the bounty policy, although not by *receiving* a bounty, as suggested in Washington's alleged emancipation proclamation; instead, they *were* the bounties. In April 1781 the "Carolina Gamecock," Brigadier General Thomas Sumter of the South Carolina militia, offered to each private "one grown negro"; officers received more according to their rank, up to "three large and one small negro" to a lieutenant colonel.[6] Late in 1780, with British forces threatening Virginia from the south, the legislature tried to attract three thousand new recruits by offering each one a "healthy sound negro" between the ages of ten and thirty.[7]

Had Washington and the Continental Congress truly offered freedom for a single year of service, when the standard term for everyone else was "three years or the duration of the war," enslaved men by the tens of thousands would have rushed to sign up.[8] This would have seriously disrupted Southern society, already reeling from the mass exodus fleeing to the British. George Washington lost at least seventeen (and likely more) of the people he claimed as slaves when they escaped to the British; he was not likely to weaken his command over the remaining 200+ bondsmen claimed by him or his wife during the war years by offering freedom to those enlisting in the Continental Army.[9]

Further, if Washington and the Continental Congress had truly offered freedom to enslaved people, who would compensate the masters? Already broke, Congress would not be able to afford the expense—but to liberate the workforce without paying off masters would surely have provoked an outright rebellion among Southern whites. The Union would have collapsed at the very beginning had Washington and the Continental Congress followed the plotline of *The Patriot*.

Why did the creators of *The Patriot* manufacture this specious document, with all the lies it embodied? "The great and painful irony of the American Revolution is the fact that this was a war fought for freedom," explains the screenwriter, Robert Rodat, in an interview featured on the DVD. White Americans, while pursuing their own freedom, denied freedom to the men, women, and children they enslaved. The only way to resolve this inherent contradiction is to make the freedom struggle for blacks coincide with that of their white masters—but to achieve such an unlikely wedding of interests required the makers of *The Patriot* to break, not merely bend, historical truths.

The desire to reconcile the inherent contradiction of the Revolution tempted Rodat to create a highly implausible story. Toward the end of the film, Benjamin Martin's family is sheltered by a black Maroon (escaped slaves) community, composed of his slaves-who-were-not-really-slaves. These joyous people even host a wedding party, to the beat of African drums, for Martin's son Gabriel. This is how we would like to imagine our Revolutionary past: a happy union between former black field hands and a white plantation family.

The conclusion to Occam's tale is even more incredible. As the soldiers prepare to fight and perhaps die at Cowpens, a fellow who has formerly been a bigot observes that Occam has already served his time. (Even by the film's own terms, this does not hold: the alleged emancipation notice applies only to Continental soldiers, while Occam is a militiaman.) Although Occam, unlike white soldiers, is free to go, he refuses to leave, for he has become a true patriot: "I'm here now on my own accord," he announces. The reformed bigot replies: "I'm honored to have you with us. Honored." Then, in the concluding scene, Occam and his new white friend set out to "build a whole new world," starting with a house for Benjamin Martin.

Although the story is made up, *The Patriot* purports to historical authenticity. Viewers are encouraged to treat the movie as a reasonable simulation of actual events, and most do. "We felt that while we were telling the fictional story," says producer Mark Gordon, on the DVD, "the backdrop was serious history." That's why Gordon and his team decided to consult the Smithsonian Institution, whom they credit in the closing titles. "When you hear the words 'Smithsonian Institution,' " Gordon explains, "you think serious, you think important."

The mystique of "history" is marshaled in support of fiction, and *The Patriot* tells a story we wish to believe: the American Revolution was the first step along the long road to the termination of slavery. The War for Independence, with its promise of freedom and its suggestion of equality, supposedly served as a blueprint for black independence as well as white.

In truth, the contradiction between slavery and the American Revolution was not so easily resolved as it was in *The Patriot*. During the war, Southern white patriots united in opposition to the seemingly diabolical designs of the British, who threatened the very roots of their society by offering freedom to people enslaved to rebel masters. After the war, the institution of slavery solidified throughout the South, even as it gradually disappeared in the North. During the Revolutionary War, many thousands of enslaved people had managed to escape from their masters, seriously threatening the very existence of slavery in regions dependent on slave labor, and in response, white owners clamped down. The rigid slave codes we associate with the period before the Civil War were a direct outcome of the Revolutionary War. *This* is "serious history." The notion that blacks and whites in South Carolina pulled together in the wake of the Revolution to "build a whole new world" is a self-serving fantasy.

HISTORY IN BLACK AND WHITE

The celebration of black patriotism is itself a historical phenomenon. At the time of the Revolution and for decades after, little was said about the black presence in the Revolutionary War. Early historians assigned no special role to black patriots, while they either ignored or downplayed the flight of enslaved people to the British. When they did happen to mention this, they emphasized the loss inflicted on white masters. "It has been estimated that between the years 1775 and 1783 the state of South Carolina was robbed of twenty-five thousand negroes, valued at about twelve million five hundred thousand dollars," wrote Benson Lossing in his *Pictorial Field-Book of the Revolution*, citing the early historian David Ramsay.[10]

In the middle of the nineteenth century, however, the notion of "colored" patriotism assumed great political significance. Abolitionists pointed to the participation of blacks in the American Revolution to make a strong argument: if these people helped white Americans win freedom, how could they be denied their own?

In 1855 a black abolitionist from Boston, William Nell, authored a book called *The Colored Patriots of the American Revolution*. Nell's work, according to an introduction written by fellow abolitionist Wendell Phillips, was intended "to stem the tide of prejudice against the colored race" and "to prove colored men patriotic."[11] Harriet Beecher Stowe, in a second introduction, claimed that black patriots should be honored even more than whites: "It was not for their own land they fought, not even for a land which had adopted them, but for a land which had enslaved them, and whose laws, even in freedom, oftener oppressed than protected. Bravery, under such circumstances, has a peculiar beauty and merit."[12]

As his title suggested, Nell focused exclusively on the five thousand blacks who fought on the side of the Americans. He made no mention of enslaved African Americans who fled to the British; this would scarcely have won converts to the abolitionist cause. Since he could not point to any black patriot soldiers when discussing South Carolina, he cited the celebrated revolutionary Charles Pinckney: "In the course of the Revolution, the Southern States were continually overrun by the British, and every negro in them had an opportunity of running away, yet few did."[13] Instead of running, Pinckney said, South Carolina's slaves worked side by side with their masters to fortify against British attacks. Ironically, abolitionists at that time were in no position to dispute this idyllic picture of happy slaves during the American Revolution.[14]

Following the Civil War and Reconstruction, during the Jim Crow era, blacks in the Revolution once again took a backseat. In 1891 one of the country's foremost historians, John Fiske, spoke for his age when he ignored the historical record and stated bluntly that happy slaves had declined Lord Dunmore's offer of freedom:

> The relations between master and slave in Virginia were so pleasant that the offer of freedom fell upon dull, uninterested ears. With light work and generous fare, the condition of the Virginia negro was a happy one. . . . He was proud of his connection with his master's estate and family, and had nothing to gain by rebellion.[15]

One writer during this time, Edward Eggleston, made an intriguing use of the "happy slaves" myth in his argument for Negro inferiority. Negroes were so lacking in mental capacities, he claimed, that they would die out from natural evolutionary processes; this was the "ultimate solution" to the "Negro problem." As proof of their inability to fend for themselves, Eggleston offered the example of early emancipation efforts around the time of the Revolution: these resulted from "the improved moral standards" of whites, not the efforts of a "black race" too feeble to "assert its rights." By failing to acknowledge the many and varied efforts that blacks had made to gain their freedom during the Revolution, Eggleston perpetuated one of the greatest of all historical lies: "The Negro possessed no ability whatsoever to help free himself. So long as he had plenty of food, and outlets for his ordinary animal passions, he remained happy and content." [16]

Edward Eggleston also wrote textbooks for children, and these texts included no mention of these allegedly passive blacks when discussing the American Revolution.[17] Neither did any of twenty-two other school texts I surveyed that were written from the end of Reconstruction to the beginning of the civil rights movement.[18] From the time of Ulysses S. Grant to Dwight D. Eisenhower, textbook writers totally excluded one-sixth of Revolutionary-Era Americans.[19]

So did most professional historians. With only a few exceptions (most notably Herbert Aptheker, a Communist writing in the 1940s and 1950s), white authors ignored the black presence in the Revolution for a full century, from the Civil War to the 1960s. It fell upon black historians to tell the story.

In 1883 George W. Williams included in his comprehensive *History of the Negro Race in America, from 1619 to 1880* an extensive discussion of the Revolutionary Era. He started by exposing the hypocrisy of white Revolutionaries:

> The sentiment that adorned the speeches of orators . . . was "the equality of the rights of all men." And yet the slaves who bore their chains under their eyes, who were denied the commonest rights of humanity, who were rated as chattels and real property, were living witnesses to the insincerity and inconsistency of this declaration.[20]

Then, rather than limiting his attention to the contributions of black patriots, Williams undertook a serious investigation of the racial politics involved in military recruitment. He showed step by step how Washington and his War Council came to prohibit the enlistment of blacks during the siege of Boston, and he then explained how Dunmore's proclamation of freedom forced them to reverse themselves. He chronicled the flight of enslaved people to the British and the feeble attempts to quell this exodus by white patriots who claimed to be "true friends" of the people they held in bondage. Suddenly, however, Williams interjected into his forthright analysis a pat display of traditional patriotism: "The struggle went on between Tory and Whig, between traitor and patriot, between selfishness and the spirit of noble consecration to the righteous cause of the Americans," he wrote.[21] Williams tried to negotiate a difficult course: he wanted to tell the story from the black perspective, but he could not evidence anti-American or pro-British sentiments.

Despite his hesitations, Williams arrived at a truly radical conclusion:

> Enlistment in the army did not work a practical emancipation of the slave, as some have thought. Negroes were rated as chattel property by both armies and both governments during the entire war. This is the cold fact of history, and it is not pleasing to contemplate. The Negro occupied the anomalous position of an American Slave and an American soldier. He was a soldier in the hour of danger, but a chattel in time of peace.[22]

This sobering assessment would not be echoed by white writers for three-quarters of a century.

Although Williams's work was ignored by white scholars, two black scholars writing in the 1920s, Carter G. Woodson and W.E.B. Du Bois, took up where Williams had left off. Woodson, often labeled "the father of Negro history," organized the *Journal of Negro History* in 1916, and in 1922 he published a comprehensive survey that became the standard text for a quarter of a century, *The Negro in Our History*. Woodson treated the flight of enslaved people to the British in a straightforward manner, without apologies; he also added that "a corps of fugitive slaves calling themselves the King of England's Soldiers harassed for several years the people living on the Savannah River, and there was much fear that the rebuffed free Negroes of New England would do the same for the colonists in their section."[23] At the close of the war in the South, Woodson concluded, "There followed such a reaction against the elevation of the race to citizenship that much of the work proposed to promote their welfare and to provide for manumission was undone."[24] Gone was the fairy tale with a happy ending. The American Revolution had done as much harm as good.

In 1924 Du Bois, a socialist and founder of the NAACP, followed Woodson's basic line in his informal history *The Gift of Black Folk: The Negroes in the Making of America*. Du Bois discussed openly the idiosyncratic "patriotism" of black soldiers:

> His problem as a soldier was always peculiar: no matter for what her enemies fought and no matter for what America fought, the American Negro always fought for his own freedom and for the self-respect of his race. Whatever the cause of war, therefore, his cause was peculiarly just. He appears . . . always with a double motive,—the desire to oppose the so-called enemy of his country along with his fellow white citizens, and before that, the motive of deserving well of those citizens and securing justice for his folk.[25]

In 1947 John Hope Franklin discussed black flight to the British in his popular college text *From Slavery to Freedom*—but the story remained ghettoized, told only as "Negro history." Despite the work of Williams, Woodson, Du Bois, and Franklin, blacks were still not included in the standard telling of the American Revolution.[26]

Not until the 1960s were blacks once again counted as "present" at our nation's founding. In 1961 another black scholar, Benjamin Quarles, published an account that was both penetrating and thorough, *The Negro in the American Revolution*.[27] The broad lines of argument had been made before, but Quarles added significant detail, and his timing was perfect. Within the history profession, Quarles's masterpiece was considered "a bombshell of a book."[28] Young white historians, influenced by the civil rights movement, embraced and built on Quarles's work. In the decades that followed, black and white scholars have produced a wealth of monographs and in-depth studies chronicling how African Americans experienced the Revolution and the impact of their actions on the politics of war. Some but not all of this new information has made its way to popular audiences. Today, as in the 1850s, Northern blacks who found freedom by fighting with the patriots are celebrated, while their Southern counterparts who fled to the British are not.

A TALE OF TWO STORIES

(1) In Northern states during the American Revolution, some enslaved people earned their freedom by fighting side by side with white patriots. Further, a war fought in the name of freedom triggered a gradual end to the nefarious institution of slaves from Pennsylvania northward.

(2) In Southern states during the American Revolution, other enslaved people, many more than those who found freedom by fighting for the Americans, escaped from patriotic masters to join the British.[29] After the war, white masters, having witnessed a partial breakdown of their power over the people they held in bondage, cracked down, hardening the institution of slavery in the South.[30]

These are true statements, but the first set has considerable appeal for our times, while the second has none.

If we try to cast the American Revolution as a battle between good and evil, we are faced with the undeniable fact that many of the most prominent patriots owned slaves. Slavery is America's original sin—but when we stick to the story we like the best, we beautify this blemish on a perfect America. We preserve the good name of the founders by portraying the Revolution as a progressive force that dealt a serious blow to the institution of slavery.

The first story appears to absolve the Revolutionaries of their sins, while the second holds them fully accountable. But to tell the first while ignoring the second requires mining the historical evidence selectively. This is done consciously, not innocently, for ever since the publication of Quarles's *Negro in the American Revolution* fifty years ago, the story of the black exodus at the moment of our nation's inception has been known and embraced within the scholarly community.

The simplest technique is to stonewall. Of thirteen textbooks for elementary, middle-school, and high-school students surveyed for the 2004 edition of *Founding Myths*, only one mentioned that more blacks sought their freedom with the British than with the patriots.[31] None stated that some who fought for the patriots were sent back into slavery at war's end, or that patriot leaders in the South offered enslaved people as bounties to entice white recruits.[32] Not one admitted that enslaved people fled from Washington's Mount Vernon plantation and from Jefferson's Monticello, or that white patriots used the fear of slave flight and slave uprisings to recruit for their cause (see chapter 9). As a partial concession to the facts, some did mention Lord Dunmore's proclamation, but none named any individuals who fought with the British, whereas they did feature particular individuals who fought with the patriots.

The record since that time is mixed. One high-school text published in 2013 makes clear distinctions between North and South, telling the story with great precision: "Because slaveholders led the revolution in the Southern colonies, their slaves saw the British as the true champions of liberty. Thousands of enslaved people sought their freedom by running away to join the British forces." In the long run, the authors continue, the Revolution triggered emancipation in the North, "where slavery was not critical to the economy and slaves numbered only 5 percent of the population," yet "although laws eventually banned slavery in the northern states, many northern masters sold their slaves to the South before they could become free. Emancipation failed in the South, where slaves amounted to about one-third of the population and were essential to the plantation economy."[33]

This is refreshingly honest, yet several recent texts, published between 2012 and 2014, continue with skewed presentations. Through selectivity of evidence, authors lead students to believe that more blacks found freedom with the Americans than with the British. A fifth-grade text, which emphasizes individuals, speaks of James Armistead ("a spy for George Washington"), Peter Salem ("among at least five African Americans who fought the British at the Battle of Concord"), and James Forten ("just 14 years old when he joined the Continental Navy"), but it features no enslaved people who went to the British, even though we know many names and several life stories. The same text also displays a dramatic illustration depicting the all-black First Rhode Island Regiment in combat. (The faces on individual soldiers do not look *too* black, however.) "Close to 5,000 enslaved African Americans fought for the Continental Army," the authors explain. By contrast, when "the British governor of Virginia promised freedom to all enslaved people who fought for the British, "more than 300" responded, wearing "patches that said *Liberty to Slaves*."[34] Yes, both strands are included, but the numbers tell a story in themselves. Although many more than five thousand enslaved people would seek freedom with the British by war's end, fifth-grade readers, understanding that five thousand is greater than three hundred, will infer a conclusion based on the evidence presented: slaves preferred the patriots.

By taking facts out of context, authors present false impressions without making false statements. A middle-school text states, "Washington pleaded with the Continental Congress for more troops. He even asked that the Congress allow free African Americans to enlist."[35] This is true, but it ignores the fact that General Washington, upon taking command of the Continental Army in July 1775, had *banned* new enlistments of "any stroller, negro, or vagabond." After that, in November, he proclaimed that even free blacks already serving in the army would be ineligible for reenlistment. Only when Lord Dunmore recruited slaves for the British, and when the Continental Army failed to attract enough white recruits, did Washington rescind his order. To relate the final act without providing the relevant background is not a forthright rendering of history.[36]

Even some college textbooks mislead. After telling of Dunmore's proclamation to liberate slaves willing to serve in the British army, one states categorically: "In fact, the British treated slaves as captured property, seizing them by the thousands in their campaigns in the South." Again, this is partially true: enslaved people who worked plantations seized by the British were treated as property. But the phrase "in fact" leads readers to believe that those who responded to Dunmore's proclamation were not freed but treated as property, which is not true. (The text conflates and confuses three distinct scenarios: Dunmore's offer of freedom in 1775; General Henry Clinton's Philipsburg Proclamation in 1779, which did not actually promise freedom but still triggered a far greater flight than did Dunmore's proclamation; and the plight of enslaved people still working on plantations seized by the British in 1779–1781.) Then, after producing the impression that the British reneged on their deal, the text relates how the Revolution placed slavery "on its way toward extinction," even in Virginia.[37]

By applying a double standard, these texts are able to tell one story and suppress the other. They pronounce proudly that the Revolution, with its rhetoric of "freedom" and "slavery," cracked the institution that held half a million Americans in bondage. In 1777 Vermont stipulated that all slaves born thereafter would be freed upon reaching their maturity (age twenty-two for males and eighteen for females). In 1780 Pennsylvania followed suit with more conservative age limits (twenty-eight for men, twenty-one for women), and by the early nineteenth century all Northern states had taken steps toward the termination of slavery.[38]

The makers of *The Patriot* were so taken with the Northern version of the African American saga that they used it in South Carolina, where it has no place. They did not wish to tell the Southern story, even though their movie was set in the South. Slaves fleeing from famous patriots like Washington and Jefferson would not play so well to a modern audience. Imagine an alternate plotline: halfway through the movie, Benjamin Martin's slaves run off to fight under Colonel Tavington, the film's sinister British villain; in the next battle scene, Martin, the patriot hero of the tale, kills three of his former bondsmen along with the usual seven Redcoats. This is not what we wish to see.

SEEKING FREEDOM ANY WAY THEY CAN

There is another way of looking at these stories. If we focus on the black experience rather than how the stories portray whites, the two suddenly blend into one.

African Americans in both the North and South used the Revolution to foster the cause of black freedom. In a war between whites, they sided with whichever side offered the best hope of emancipation. They acted strategically in their own best interests, not from any prior commitment to the Americans or the British. In the North, where the British were weak and where the patriots were looking for soldiers, they cast their lot with the Americans. In the South, where the British offered them new lives and appeared (at least in the later years) to be able to make good on that promise, they flocked to the royal standard. Freedom was the name of the game, and they played it however they could.

That's the simple version; the actual plotline has many twists and turns. In the North, slaves had to negotiate carefully to ensure that their contributions to the patriots' cause would actually result in their freedom; in many cases, whites tried to renege on their promises after the war.[39]

In the South, the risks were far greater and more difficult to assess. Enslaved people in 1775–1776 and again in 1779–1781 were under the general impression that if they could escape and offer their services to the invading British army they would be freed. They had no assurances, however, nor was it certain that the British would prevail. What if they ran to the British army but were later defeated and returned to their original owners? What if the British proved not to be liberators after all, but just one more set of white men ready to exploit black labor? Perhaps they would free some but not all of those who came to them. Perhaps families would be torn apart.

On the other hand, what would happen if enslaved people decided *not* to join the British? Patriot masters, fleeing the British army, might haul them away to places unknown, where they would be sold or hired out to strangers. If their masters ran and left them behind, they would have to survive on their own amid economic chaos. Even worse, how would they be treated if they were *captured* by the British, rather than joining them willingly? As prizes of war, they would belong to the conquerors. Very likely, they would be sold and sent to the West Indies.

Perhaps they should just run away without seeking support from either side. They could try to blend in with the small communities of free blacks in Savannah, Charleston, Wilmington, or Williamsburg. But in such numbers? How would they make a living? Maybe they'd do better in the backwoods of the Dismal Swamp, but wherever they went, they would have to support themselves, and settling in one place to raise food would increase the risk of being captured.

Their fates were in the balance: they might wind up free or dead. In the fields or huddled in small groups at night, wary of informers among their peers, they pondered the alternatives, projecting the possible consequences of their actions, trying to predict the most likely outcomes. They considered various outcomes and evaluated strategies. Such decisions to make—and with such consequences![40]

As it turned out, many trying to escape were captured by patriot slave patrols. Sometimes, when the British were inundated with runaways, fugitives were turned away. Thousands succumbed to diseases—primarily smallpox, to which they had no immunity. Those who reached the British and survived were often turned into laborers, servants, or soldiers. They toiled on plantations not unlike the ones they had left; they served the personal needs of British officers, who became their new masters; they joined the king's army for indefinite terms of service—some later served in the West Indies and even the Napoleonic Wars. Many were given as slaves to white loyalists in compensation for lost property.

On the other hand, many did find freedom. At the close of the war, the British transported three thousand men, women, and children, formerly enslaved, from New York to Canada. As free persons, they were granted plots of land—the worst available, of course. Others went to London, where they faced hard times. Some managed to escape to deep woods and dank swamps, where they survived for years in their own Maroon communities. (Despite what we see in *The Patriot,* there are no records of white gentry putting on elaborate wedding ceremonies in these enclaves of black refugees.) Many eventually wound up in Sierra Leone, the African colony established for formerly enslaved blacks.

From the black perspective, such stories are indeed "epic," as reflected in the title of Cassandra's Pybus's book *Epic Journeys of Freedom: Runaway Slaves of the American Revolution and Their Global Quest for Liberty*, which chronicles a mass black exodus from slavery that preceded the more famous Underground Railroad of the mid–nineteenth century.[41] But where are they in our textbooks? We hear about James Armistead Lafayette, Peter Salem, and James Forten, so why not Boston King, David George, Thomas Peters, or other refugees whose journeys are well documented and whose stories we could relate if we chose to?[42]

Liberty! (the book and PBS series) features James Armistead Lafayette as one of the five key "portraits" to represent the American Revolution; the others are King George III, George Washington, Benjamin Franklin, and Abigail Adams.[43] Enslaved to the Virginian William Armistead, James volunteered for the army and worked as a double agent under the Marquis de Lafayette; after the war, he petitioned the Virginia Assembly for his freedom and received it. His story, a good one, is certainly enhanced by the prestige of the officer he served, but we could paint an even broader canvas by featuring the pursuit of freedom by Harry Washington, who had worked involuntarily for a man of even greater renown, George Washington.

In 1763, George Washington helped form a company called Adventurers for Draining the Great Dismal Swamp, hoping first to cut and sell the timber and then to farm the drained area. Each partner was to contribute five enslaved workers to perform the tedious task of swamp dredging, and to this end, Washington purchased a man listed in the records as Harry, born in West Africa. In 1766, after working the mosquito-infested swamp for over two years, Harry was removed to Mount Vernon, a more livable environment. Five years later Harry escaped from his master, but after George posted a reward, the man he claimed as his property was captured and returned. Harry continued at Mount Vernon until 1776, when he and two others made their way to a British vessel in the Potomac River. By that time, his trade was listed as "hostler."

Taking the name of his famous former master, Harry served behind British lines during the invasion of New York just two months after he fled. Later, during the British invasion of the Carolinas, he served as a corporal in a unit called the Black Pioneers, attached to the Royal Artillery Department. At the conclusion of the war in 1783, Harry was once again stationed in New York, where he had to elude the "slave catcher" his former master sent to retrieve his escaped slaves. Also, as commander in chief of the Continental Army, General Washington tried to enforce the Treaty of Paris, which stipulated that the British return all former slaves to their masters—but to no avail. Harry safely shipped out aboard a British vessel headed to Nova Scotia.

There, in a much different land, Harry and his peers were given their own plots of minimally productive land, which they tried to work for almost a decade. Late in 1791, Harry shipped out once again, this time across the Atlantic to Sierra Leone. Leaving behind a house, two town lots, and forty acres, he and his wife Jenny sailed off with an ax, a saw, a pickax, three hoes, two muskets, and some furniture to what they believed to be the Promised Land in Africa.

But they were not exactly returning to their homeland. Sierra Leone was not the place of Harry's origin, nor was it under the control of the black settlers. The émigrés from North America confronted disease and hardships of all kinds, including the autocratic rule of the London company that had sponsored them. In 1800 Harry and others, seeking to control their own destinies, staged a rebellion that failed. Tried and convicted by a military tribunal, Harry was exiled to a neighboring land, where he died. Yes, Harry Washington had escaped slavery to find "freedom," but exploitation by other humans and the ravages of nature took their tolls.[44]

As narratives, the overlapping but very different sagas of George Washington (whom we know so well) and Harry Washington (whose life is obscure but still discernable) are full and rich, depicting two amazing quests for freedom. George grew from the revolutionary experience, not only leading his country to freedom but also, at his death, freeing the people he had once held in bondage; Harry grew as well as he fought for and explored the complex dimensions of freedom in an often hostile world. Presented together, they reveal significant historical trends and events. These sorts of multifaceted stories are worth telling. The celebration of our nation's birth becomes deeper yet if we choose not to censor some of the intrepid struggles for freedom that the Revolution made possible.[45]

"British parties, . . . the most brutal of mankind, were . . . robbing, destroying, and taking life at their pleasure."

Drawing by Felix Octavius Carr Darley, mid-nineteenth century.

12

BRUTAL BRITISH

We can all picture the enemy in the Revolutionary War: the Redcoats, in full battle formation. In our minds, we view these people as "foreign." They were soldiers sent from across the seas, bent on putting Americans down.

The enemy, once identified, is easy to vilify. The handiest way to justify intentional killing is to portray the opposition as brutal. In any war, stories abound of atrocities committed by the other side; violent acts committed by the protagonists are merely retaliations for these foul deeds. This is the basic logic of warfare, and the American Revolution was no exception.

GOOD GUYS AND BAD GUYS

The simple juxtaposition of good versus evil gives the movie *The Patriot* its raw power. At the outset of the film, Benjamin Martin, played convincingly by Mel Gibson, does not want to fight against the British. Although he was once a hero in the French and Indian War, now he is trying to raise six children (his wife is deceased) and he wants no part of politics or war. "I am a parent," he says at a meeting of patriots. "I haven't got the luxury of principles."

Martin's political apathy does not last long. After a battle is fought in their front yard, Martin and his children and their slaves-who-are-not-really-slaves tend to the wounded, patriots and British alike. Right at this moment Colonel Tavington gallops onto the scene, leading his fearsome British Dragoons. Grinning insidiously, Tavington orders all wounded patriots to be shot on the spot. He also arrests Benjamin's oldest son, Gabriel, for carrying messages. As Gabriel is being dragged away to be hanged, Benjamin protests that his summary execution would violate "the rules of war." Tavington responds: "Rules of war! Would you like a lesson in the rules of war?" He then points his pistol at the rest of Martin's children. Martin backs off, but when Gabriel's younger brother Thomas bursts forth with a feeble and ill-advised rescue attempt, Tavington shoots Thomas in the back.

Colonel Tavington, we see, is a very bad man. Benjamin Martin is understandably very angry, and he becomes a patriot after all. The cold-blooded killing of his son Thomas must be avenged.

Shortly afterward, Tavington is called to task for these and other barbarous deeds by his superior, General Cornwallis. But after Martin outwits Cornwallis with a cunning scheme, the general abandons his preference for gentlemanly warfare and gives Tavington permission to pursue "brutal" tactics. Sanctioned brutalities become a cornerstone of official British policy.

Tavington, now operating according to orders, proceeds to commit even greater outrages. He gathers the entire population of a village into a church, seals off the door and shutters, then burns it to the ground. Every man, woman, and child—including Gabriel's new bride—perishes in the flames. (Gabriel had earlier been rescued from the gallows by his dad and his two youngest brothers, ages about eight and ten.) A little later, Tavington uses some cunning of his own to kill Gabriel. By now, the viewer is as outraged as Benjamin Martin, who has lost two sons at the hands of the sinister British officer. Tavington and the British must be stopped! We are rooting furiously as our hero, using an American flagpole for a bayonet, faces off against his nemesis in the concluding Battle of Cowpens.

In *The Patriot,* we learn that the British were the bad guys, and that their Colonel Banastre Tarleton (upon whom the character of Tavington was based, according to the film's writer, Robert Rodat) was the personification of evil. Patriots, by contrast, were the good guys. Americans did not slaughter their prisoners, and they killed no civilians—certainly not a churchful all at once.

At one point, *The Patriot* does show Benjamin Martin's militiamen on the verge of hacking to death British soldiers who had just surrendered—but these excesses are immediately put to a halt by Commander Martin: "Full quarter will be given to British wounded and any who surrender," he commands. Gabriel delivers the moral of this scene: "We are better men than that." That's the basic message of the film: the Americans were better men than those British bullies, like Tarleton, who didn't think twice about hacking prisoners to death.

One scene does equivocate. Back in the French and Indian War, Benjamin Martin had proved himself a hero at "Fort Wilderness." Throughout the film, men praise him for this—but nobody will say what he did. One night at camp, Gabriel asks his father to tell him what happened at Fort Wilderness. Reticent at first, Benjamin finally responds. French and Cherokee raiders had killed some settlers, including women and children. To avenge this slaughter, Martin and company tracked down the offenders and butchered them. "We took our time," he says softly but deliberately. "We cut them apart, slowly, piece by piece. I can see their faces. I can still hear their screams." He then proceeds with a graphic description of how they mutilated the bodies. "We were . . . heroes," he concludes sardonically.

"And men bought you drinks," Gabriel adds.

"Not a day goes by that I don't ask God's forgiveness for what I did."

Such an admission, coming from the hero of the story, produces a stunning effect. Everything else that happened or will happen in the film takes on an added dimension, for this man is real. But Martin's atrocities were all committed in the past, out on the frontier. He had been fighting for the British at that point—but during the

Revolutionary War, at the birth of our nation, no such atrocities could be tolerated. American patriots were simply too *good* to engage in barbarous behavior. The British thereby serve as scapegoats for the horrors of war.

A simple but deft twist of costuming confirms this thesis. The dreaded Green Dragoons—mostly American Tories commanded by Briton Banastre Tarleton—wore green jackets with white pants, shirts, and collars; only their sashes and helmet plumes were red. The "special feature" added to the DVD version of the film shows a brief image of this uniform, but in the film itself, green is traded in for a more familiar red. "There were many different kinds of uniforms in the British army," says costume designer Deborah Scott. "We basically settled for one very strong look." Strong and recognizable: the Redcoats. All the men commanded by Colonel Tavington are unquestionably British. All the evil deeds are performed by foreigners, not Americans.

This is the way most Americans today have heard the story of the Revolutionary War: the opposition wore no green, only red. In the telling of the war that has evolved over time, the men who fought on the other side were the Redcoats, British antagonists familiar to us all.

THE FIRST CIVIL WAR

The Patriot draws on the interpretation of the war put forth at the time by American patriots. On May 29, 1780, in the Waxhaws district of North Carolina, soldiers under the command of Banastre Tarleton killed American prisoners rather than granting them quarter. For the remainder of the war, the Waxhaws incident provided a rallying cry for angry patriots as they prepared to terminate the lives of other human beings: "Tarleton's Quarter!" they would yell furiously as they stormed into battle. (Sometimes, the cry was "Remember Buford!"—referring to Abraham Buford, the American commander at Waxhaws.) For patriots toward the end of the Revolutionary War, as for the fictional Benjamin Martin, the enemy's butchery provided reason enough to fight against the British.

This story, proof positive of the enemy's cruelty, has endured for over two centuries. But there has been one important alteration. At the time, the patriots' greatest fury was directed at their local adversaries, the Tories. Now, the adversaries have exchanged green uniforms for red. They must be seen as foreigners, not "us."

In fact, it was Americans who did the slaughtering at Waxhaws—maybe not patriots, but our countrymen nonetheless. There, Banastre Tarleton led a force of 40 British Regulars and 230 American Tories, primarily from New York. "The British Legion, Americans all, began butchering their vanquished countrymen," writes military historian John Buchanan.[1] This was no isolated event. British officers, on their part, often tried to restrain their American recruits, sometimes to no avail. "For God's sake no irregularities," pleaded British general Henry Clinton, trying in vain to curtail the excesses of Tories who fought under him.[2]

The Revolution in the South was a bloody civil war—even more internecine than the Civil War of the nineteenth century, for no geographic boundaries separated the combatants. (Even when patriots fought the Redcoats, they viewed them as "Regulars," not foreigners, as we do today.) In South Carolina alone, local historian Edward McCrady tabulated 103 different battles in which Americans fought Americans, with nary a Brit in sight.[3] At King's Mountain, one of the great victories for the patriots, over one thousand American loyalists fought under a single British officer.

The impact of this first civil war was devastating. "The whole Country is in Danger of being laid waste by the Whigs and Tories who pursue each other with as much relentless Fury as Beasts of Prey," wrote the American general Nathanael Greene.[4] In some regions all civil society came to a halt. Whenever a band of partisans raged through, inhabitants had to "lay out" in the woods, abandoning their homes to the ravages of soldiers—whatever side they happened to be on. On July 20, 1781, the American major William Pierce wrote to St. George Tucker:

> Such scenes of desolation, bloodshed and deliberate murder I never was a witness to before! Wherever you turn the weeping widow and fatherless child pour out their melancholy tales to wound the feeling of humanity. The two opposite principles of whiggism and toryism have set the people of this country to cutting each other's throats, and scarce a day passes but some poor deluded tory is put to death at his door.[5]

Partisans on both sides believed they were fighting for their homeland. Many, like the fictional Benjamin Martin, had lost relatives who were to be avenged. Fighting was localized and personalized—and thereby more impassioned. These were not professional soldiers just doing their jobs, but men with scores to settle.

In tales such as *The Patriot,* the fight is between the British, who are cruel or indifferent, and the Americans, who are forced to respond. History was far more complicated than that. Consider: Who is the hero and who is the villain in each of the following tales?

- After Tories had beaten his mother, William Gipson of South Carolina admitted that he took "no little satisfaction" in torturing a prisoner who was placed in his charge: "He was placed with one foot upon a sharp pin drove in a block, and was turned round . . . until the pin run through his foot."[6]

- A Tory from Georgia, Thomas Brown, was accosted by a patriot mob. Trying to defend himself, he shot one of the patriots in the foot. The mob subdued him, tarred his legs, branded his feet, and took off part of his scalp. Brown lost two of his toes and could not walk for months. Once he had recovered, he organized a band of Tories and Indians that raided patriot plantations for the remainder of the war.[7]

- Moses Hall, a patriot from North Carolina, suffered a "distressing gloom" when he observed his comrades murder six defenseless prisoners: "I heard some of our men cry out 'Remember Buford,' and the prisoners were immediately hewed to pieces with broadswords." Reeling with "horror," Hall retreated to his quarters and "contemplated the cruelties of war"—but not for long. On a subsequent march, he came upon a sixteen-year-old boy, an innocent observer, who had been run through with a British bayonet to keep him from passing information to the patriots. "The sight of this unoffending boy, butchered . . . relieved me of my distressful feeling for the slaughter of the Tories, and I desired nothing so much as the opportunity of participating in their destruction."[8]

In cases such as these, how can we portray one side as filled with virtue, the other with vice? Barbarous acts, and the retribution they inspired, crossed political boundaries. Real-life patriots participated in this gruesome game of retribution. Frequently, they too slaughtered men who were trying to surrender or had already been taken into custody. In the aftermath of the patriot victory at King's Mountain, Colonel William Campbell tried to "restrain the disorderly manner of slaughtering and disturbing the prisoners."[9] His orders were not heeded; prisoners were prodded and trampled to death when they couldn't keep up with the march. A late-night mock trial ended in the summary execution of nine Tories. "It is impossible for those who have not lived in its midst, to conceive of the exasperation which prevails in a civil war," explained Colonel Isaac Shelby, one of the executioners, as he justified his actions years later. "The execution . . . was believed by those who were on the ground, to be both necessary and proper, for the purpose of putting a stop to the execution of the patriots in the Carolinas by the Tories and the British."[10]

MY COUNTRY, RIGHT OR WRONG

Early American historians, members of the Revolutionary generation, could not ignore the obvious: the war for independence from Britain was also a civil war among Americans, particularly in the South. Tories who had "embodied" as soldiers, wrote William Gordon in 1788, "marched along the western frontiers of South Carolina. They had such numbers of the most infamous characters among them that their general complexion was that of a plundering banditti." Some of the patriots, he admitted, were little better: "Many of the professed whigs disgraced themselves, by the burnings, plunderings and cruelties, that they practiced in their turn on the royalists."[11] Gordon cited General Nathanael Greene, who bemoaned the "embarrassments" caused by the patriot militia's "savage disposition" and "mode of conducting war." While Gordon confessed that patriots engaged in wrongdoing, his admission contained a disclaimer: officers like Greene and Francis Marion, the good patriots, tried to put an end to the misbehavior of bad patriots.[12]

David Ramsay, in his 1785 *History of the Revolution in South Carolina*, attributed all sorts of foul deeds to Thomas Brown, the Tory who had been tortured by patriots. Brown had hanged prisoners without trial, Ramsay said, and he had turned some over to Indians to be scalped. When a mother offered a passionate plea to spare the life of her son, Brown had turned a deaf ear.[13] The following year, Brown complained directly to Ramsay, denying the atrocities and explaining the hangings: he was under direct orders to hang prisoners who had violated their parole, and the son of the pleading mother had recently engaged in the systematic torture of Tory prisoners before they were executed.[14] In his 1789 *History of the American Revolution*, Ramsay removed all reference to Thomas Brown's villainy—but the rumors he had helped to spread four years earlier did not disappear. In his magnum opus, Ramsay covered the civil war with a more balanced approach:

> Individuals whose passions were inflamed by injuries, and exasperated with personal animosity, were eager to gratify revenge in violation of the laws of war. Murders had produced murders. Plundering, assassinations, and house burning, had become common. Zeal for the King or the Congress were the ostensible motives of action; but in several of both sides, the love of plunder, private pique, and a savageness of disposition, led to actions which were disgraceful to human nature. Such was the exasperation of whigs against tories, and of tories against whigs; and so much had they suffered from and inflicted on each other, that the laws of war, and the precepts of humanity afforded but a feeble security for the observance of capitulations on either side.[15]

Ramsay went on to philosophize about "the folly and madness of war," and he concluded that "war never fails to injure the morals of the people engaged in it"; the patriots were no exception.[16]

Mercy Otis Warren, writing in 1805, admitted that the Revolution had included a "domestic war" and that patriot soldiers, like their adversaries, had evidenced barbarous behavior, but she added a stronger disclaimer: patriotic Americans were never as bad as the British and Tories. Fortunately, she stated, they had lacked "a fierce spirit of revenge." In her concluding remarks, Warren commended the Revolutionaries for their moderation:

> Great revolutions ever produce excesses and miseries at which humanity revolts. In America . . . the scenes of barbarity were not so universal as have been usual in other countries that have been at once shaken by foreign and domestic war. . . . The United States may congratulate themselves on the success of a revolution which has done honor to the human character by exhibiting a mildness of spirit amid the ferocity of war, that prevented the shocking scenes of cruelty, butchery, and slaughter, which have too often stained the actions of men, when their

> original intentions were the result of pure motives and justifiable resistance.[17]

Patriotic writers of the following generation did not focus much attention on the barbaric civil war in the South. Charles Goodrich, writing in 1823, said not a word of it; the war was only a struggle for independence from Great Britain, not a true "revolution" featuring domestic upheaval here in America. When writers in the early and mid–nineteenth century did mention the civil war in the Southern backcountry, they, like Warren, issued an immediate qualification:

> But censure ought not to rest equally upon the two parties. In the commencement of the contest, the British, to terrify the people into submission, set an example which the tories were quick, but the whigs slow, to follow; and in its progress the American generals, and they alone, seized every occasion to discountenance such vindictive and barbarous conduct.[18]

The chain of blame was never more clearly stated: the British were the worst, followed in order by Tories and common patriots. Only patriot leaders were beyond reproof. In 1838 John Frost stated flatly, "The British generally conducted the war with cruelty and rancour."[19]

George Bancroft, in the mid–nineteenth century, wrote that British leaders were "the most brutal of mankind," while Americans were "incapable of imitating precedents of barbarity." He singled out Banastre Tarleton and Thomas Brown for particular blame. "The line of [Tarleton's] march could be traced by groups of houseless women and children," he wrote—although in fact this was true in the wake of any march at the time, no matter what the army. He repeated and embellished the rumor that prisoners taken by Brown had been delivered to Cherokee Indians, who tomahawked them or threw them into fires. Any questionable behavior on the part of the patriots, meanwhile, was excused as justifiable retaliation. After their victory at King's

Mountain, patriots had hanged several of the prisoners they took. When describing these executions, Bancroft wrote:

> Among the captives there were house-burners and assassins. Private soldiers—who had witnessed the sorrows of children and women, robbed and wronged, shelterless, stripped of all clothes but those they wore, nestling about fires kindled on the ground, and mourning for their fathers and husbands—executed nine or ten in retaliation for the frequent and barbarous use of the gallows at Camden, Ninety-Six, and Augusta; but Campbell at once intervened, and in general orders, by threatening the delinquents with certain and effectual punishment, secured protection to the prisoners.[20]

Bancroft wanted to have it both ways: the "house-burners and assassins" deserved the worst, yet benevolent patriot officers still protected them—at least those who had not yet been hanged.

Starting in the mid–nineteenth century, some academic historians challenged the traditional patriotic wisdom by refusing to lay greater blame on the British or Tories. "Whigs and Tories pursued each other with little less than savage fury," Richard Hildreth wrote in 1851. "Small parties, every where under arms, some on one side, some on the other, with very little reference to greater operations, were desperately bent on plunder and blood."[21] Forty years later, John Fiske stated bluntly: "There can be no doubt that Whigs and Tories were alike guilty of cruelty and injustice."[22] By the turn of the century, a few American historians were displaying definite sympathies for the loyalists, who had suffered "lawless persecution" at the hands of "irresponsible mobs" of patriots.[23] All crowd actions, even those of the American Revolution, were to be discredited, for they were disruptive to the social order.

Histories that did not favor patriots over loyalists, however, were not always greeted favorably outside academic circles. During the first half of the twentieth century, the views of Progressive historians were perceived as a threat to traditional American values. Attempts by the Progressive education movement to introduce a spirit of relativism in the schools caused traditionalists to recoil. Patriots and loyalists should never be placed on an equal footing, they claimed. An officer of the Daughters of the Colonial Wars, for instance, complained about books that "give a child an unbiased viewpoint instead of teaching him real Americanism. All the old histories taught my country right or wrong. That's the point of view we want our children to adopt. We can't afford to teach them to be unbiased and let them make up their own minds."[24]

In the 1960s, scholars practicing "the new social history" began looking long and hard at the brutal fighting in the South during the later stages of the Revolutionary War, trying to decipher the peculiar local logic that led to the breakdown of civil society. Why, they asked, did particular individuals or groups become partisans to this side or that? How did the differences among neighbors escalate so quickly to such a fever pitch? Professional historians have found no easy answers—and in the absence of any clear alternatives, the simple morality tale lives on.

Indeed, the tale has been embellished. No nineteenth-century writer depicted the brutal British burning a church, with all the inhabitants of a village inside. But the makers of *The Patriot* did, even though there is nothing in the historical record to suggest such a horrific occurrence during the War for Independence. As historian David Hackett Fischer observes, "Something remarkably like this event actually happened, but not in South Carolina during the American Revolution. It happened in the French village of Oradour-sur-Glane on June 10, 1944, during World War II. . . . There were atrocities enough on both sides in the American Revolution, but the German director has converted an 18th-century British and American loyalist army into the S.S."[25]

Sometimes, as in *The Patriot*, the good-versus-bad theme is deafening; often, it is muted but still audible. Popular writers today, in a tone reminiscent of Mercy Otis Warren, give some notice to the brutal civil war, but they find ways of qualifying any condemnation of the patriots. In *Liberty!* Thomas Fleming refers to "the savage seesaw war," but the only examples of savagery he presents were committed by the other side. Thomas Brown, he reports, hanged thirteen wounded patriots "in the stairwell of his house, where he could watch them die from his bed."[26] The reporting of such callousness is calculated to leave a firmly biased impression on the reader. Fleming fails to note that the hangings did not take place in Brown's *own* house, as implied; that if Brown was in bed, it was because he had just been wounded; that the hangings had been ordered by his superiors; and that the man who originally spread the rumor, David Ramsay, later disavowed it. Instead, he restates without question the conventional story about this Tory villain, treating him as the "devil incarnate," in the words of one nineteenth-century historian.[27]

Robert Leckie, in *George Washington's War*, offers a vivid description of patriots mowing down loyalists who were trying to surrender at King's Mountain:

> The rebel blood was up, their vengeance fed by the memory of the Waxhaws. "Buford! Buford!" they shouted. "Tarleton's Quarter! Tarleton's Quarter!" They pursued their frightened victims as they ran to a hollow place on the hilltop and cowered there in horror. One by one, the frontiersmen cut them down, sometimes singling out neighbors by name before they fired. Many of the Patriots thirsted to revenge themselves on the deaths of relatives and friends who were murdered by the Tories. Their eyes glittered maniacally as they loaded and fired . . . loaded and fired . . . At last Major Evan Shelby called on the Loyalists to throw down their arms. They did, but the rebel rifles still blazed. [Ellipses as in the original.][28]

But were these *real* patriots who acted so savagely? Not exactly. They were illiterate "Irish and Scots-Irish" who called their rifles "Sweet

Lips" or "Hot Lead." "None of them could have quoted a line from Tom Paine's *Common Sense*," Leckie writes, "and the phrase *Declaration of Independence* meant about as much to them as it did to their livestock."[29] They were animals, not Americans; their deeds need not reflect poorly on the cause. Undue cruelties attributed to Americans must somehow be deflected, if they cannot be defended.

Many of today's textbooks continue to slant their coverage of the brutal civil war in the South. "Loyalist bands roamed the backcountry," reports a middle-school text. "They plundered and burned Patriot farms, killing men, women, and children." Treatment of the other side, by contrast, is far more respectful: "Francis Marion led his men silently through the swamps. They attacked without warning, then escaped. Marion's guerrilla attacks were so efficient that he won the nickname 'Swamp Fox.' " One side plunders, burns, and kills, but when the other side does likewise, it is merely being "efficient." The language tells us very clearly how we should react.[30] Another middle-school text announces that "the southern war was particularly brutal" and "pitted Americans—Patriots versus Loyalists—against each other in direct combat." This much is true, but it says no more about American brutality; instead, it states clearly that the British "destroyed crops, farm animals, and other property as they marched through the South" and mentions only one man by name: Banastre Tarleton, the British officer who "sowed fear throughout the South by refusing to take prisoners and killing soldiers who tried to surrender."[31] A college text tips its hand with an adverb: "The colony of Georgia was *ruthlessly* overrun [by the British] in 1778–1779." (Emphasis added.) Significantly, this text describes no American advance—not even the purposive "scorched earth" annihilation of Iroquois lands, villages, and people in the North (see chapter 14)—as "ruthless."[32] Such biased language is not new; in fact, this exact same sentence appears in the first edition of the textbook, published in 1956.[33] But due to "textbook lag" (see Afterword), the words persist and still have force, despite cultural changes in sensitivities since the mid–twentieth century.

Some textbooks now display more balance, attributing blame to both sides. In South Carolina, says one college text, "Most of the upcountry was stripped bare. As each side took control, neighbors attacked each other, plundered each other's farms, and carried away each other's slaves."[34] Another college text offers the usual fare—"Banastre Tarleton led one especially vicious company of loyalists who slaughtered civilians and murdered many who surrendered"—but follows this with a parallel account of an American leader: "In retaliation, planter and merchant Thomas Sumter organized 800 men who showed a similar disregard to regular army procedures, raiding largely defenseless loyalist settlements near Hanging Rock, South Carolina, in August 1780."[35]

Such passages convert what used to appear as liabilities—the uncivilized acts committed by some Americans, which undercut the national image of moral superiority—into teachable moments. Unbiased reporting of the brutal civil war in the Southern interior exposes the cycle of revenge and its unseemly consequences. Insofar as this message is received and internalized, senseless wars become less likely. On the other hand, pointing to atrocities committed only by the enemy panders to instincts of revenge, always the fodder of war hawks. Retributive violence becomes viewed as rational, leading otherwise decent people to sanction brutal acts they would normally condemn.

HAPPY ENDINGS

"Everyone realized that this surrender meant the end."

The Surrender of Lord Cornwallis at Yorktown, 19 October 1781.
Lithograph by Nathaniel Currier, 1852,
based on painting by John Trumbull, 1787–circa 1828.

13

THE FINAL BATTLE: YORKTOWN

On October 19, 1781, Lord Cornwallis formally surrendered his entire army—some 8,000 troops—to George Washington at Yorktown, Virginia.[1] When Lord North, the British prime minister, heard the news, he exclaimed, "Oh, God, it is all over!" So ended the Revolutionary War.

This story is repeated in virtually every narrative account of the American Revolution. The notion of a decisive final battle constitutes a neat and tidy conclusion to the war, placing America firmly in control of her own destiny. "The great British army was surrendering," writes Joy Hakim in her popular textbook. "David had licked Goliath. . . . A superpower had been defeated by an upstart colony."[2]

"CARRYING ON THE WAR"

Not everybody at the time saw it that way. In the wake of Yorktown, George Washington insisted that the war was not yet over, and King George III was not ready to capitulate. In fact, the fighting continued for over a year—but this part of history is rarely told. To stick to the story we like, we declare that people who engaged in subsequent battles were somehow mistaken—their fighting was some sort of illusion. "Washington considered the country still at war," writes A. J. Langguth in his bestselling book *Patriots*, "and George III was under that same *misapprehension*."[3]

When King George III heard of Cornwallis's surrender at Yorktown, he did not respond as fatalistically as did Lord North. "I have no doubt when men are a little recovered of the shock felt by the bad news," he said, "they will find the necessity of carrying on the war, though the mode of it may require alterations."[4]

Washington was worried that the British Crown might respond this way—so worried, in fact, that he redoubled his efforts to build up the Continental Army. On October 27, only ten days after the victory at Yorktown, the commander in chief urged Congress to continue its "preparation for military Operations"; a failure to pursue the war, he warned, would "expose us to the most disgracefull Disasters."[5] In the following weeks, Washington repeated this warning more than a dozen times.[6] "Yorktown was an interesting event," he wrote, but it would only "prolong the casualties" if Americans relaxed their "prosecution of the war." Candidly, he confessed:

> My greatest Fear is that Congress, viewing this stroke in too important a point of Light, may think our Work too nearly closed, and will fall into a State of Languor and Relaxation; to prevent this Error, I shall employ every Means in my Power.[7]

Heeding Washington's advice, Congress called on the states to supply the same number of soldiers they had furnished the preceding year. But the states were financially strapped, and their citizens were tiring of war. They failed to meet their quotas, and Washington did not receive enough men to undertake the offensive operations he had contemplated.[8]

Meanwhile, the British and French continued to battle for control of the seas. In the West Indies, six months after Yorktown, British seamen defeated the French fleet that had cut off the lines of supply during the siege of Yorktown. With the French naval presence weakened, the British would be able to regroup and take the offensive; they could move their vast armies by sea to support any land operation they chose.

Washington was not the only American general worrying about this. Nathanael Greene, who had hoped to lead an attack on Charleston, suddenly expressed concern that the British might attack him instead.[9] On June 5, 1782, more than seven months after Yorktown, Washington wrote to the United States secretary of foreign affairs about the need to undertake "vigorous preparations for meeting the enemy."[10]

Finally, on August 4, the commanders of the British army and navy in North America informed Washington that the Crown was prepared to recognize "the independency of the thirteen Provinces," providing only that loyalists receive full compensation for seized property and that no further property be confiscated. It seemed the war was coming to an end at last—but Washington was not buying it.[11] Not until a peace treaty was signed and British troops had returned home would he relax his guard. In his general orders for August 19, 1782—ten months after Yorktown—he wrote: "The readiest way to procure a lasting and honorable peace is to be fully prepared vigorously to prosecute War."[12]

The British then offered to suspend all hostilities, but Washington still wouldn't bite. Right at this moment, he received word that Lord Rockingham, the British prime minister believed to be responsible for the peace overtures, had died. The American commander in chief, who placed little stock in the fickle nature of British politics, assumed Rockingham would be replaced by a hard-liner. On September 12 he wrote: "Our prospect of Peace is vanishing. The death of the Marquis of Rockingham has given shock to the New Administration, and disordered its whole System. . . . That the King will push the War as long as the Nation will find Men or Money, admits not of a doubt in my mind."[13] A full year after Yorktown, Washington warned Nathanael Greene:

> In the present fluctuating state of British Councils and measures, it is extremely difficult to form a decisive opinion of what their real and ultimate objects are. . . . [N]otwithstanding all the pacific declaration of the British, it has constantly been my prevailing sentiment, the principal Design was, to gain time by lulling us into security and wasting the Campaign without making any effort on the land.[14]

A preliminary peace treaty was signed on November 30, 1782—but even that was not enough to satisfy the ever-suspicious American commander. On March 19, 1783, one year and five months after Yorktown, Washington was still keeping his guard up: "The Articles of Treaty between America and Great Britain . . . are so very inconclusive . . . that we should hold ourselves in a hostile position, prepared for either alternative, War or Peace. . . . I must confess, I have my fears, that we shall be obliged to worry thro' another Campaign, before we arrive at that happy period, which is to crown all our Toils."[15]

Washington saw what we do not. He knew well that Cornwallis did not command and surrender *the* British army in North America, as most Americans now assume. In fact, Cornwallis served under General Henry Clinton, commander in chief of the British army in America, who still had at his disposal some 40,000 soldiers stationed in Halifax, New York, Charleston, Savannah, St. Augustine, and the West Indies, five times as many British soldiers as he lost for service at Yorktown and three-and-one-half times as many as were available for service under George Washington.[16] Although a fraction of Clinton's forces had surrendered, the vast majority remained ready for battle. The Americans had recently sustained a significant loss, the surrender of over five thousand at Charleston, yet they had continued to fight. So had the British in 1777, after the British commander John Burgoyne lost some 8,000 men in his ill-fated expedition down the Hudson River. By sheer numbers, Cornwallis's defeat at Yorktown was not that different from these earlier battles.

Great Britain still maintained a strong presence in and around the United States. It controlled the St. Lawrence Valley to the Great Lakes, East Florida, several islands in the West Indies, and the Atlantic ports of Halifax, New York, Charleston, Savannah, and St. Augustine. After the defeat at Yorktown, General Clinton could have unleashed forces from any of these enclaves. New York's Hudson Valley was particularly vulnerable, since Washington had weakened its defense when he moved his army south. The West was still not secured from Native inhabitants, who were now aided by Spanish as well as British forces. Tory bands ruled much of the Southern backcountry. Most important, once the French fleet had sailed southward, the British navy controlled the coastal waters. "Without a decisive Naval force we can do nothing definitive," Washington complained shortly after Yorktown.[17]

Washington understood that the outcome of the Revolutionary War depended on continuing French support. The war was being waged with French money. The siege at Yorktown had been conducted with French equipment, and over half the regular forces had been French. The siege had been successful only because French ships were able to keep British ships from resupplying the troops. If French support were suddenly withdrawn for reasons beyond the control of the Americans—say, a separate treaty of peace between France and Britain—the Americans would never be able to dislodge the British from their coastal strongholds. If Britain then decided to unleash its vast army against Washington's struggling Continentals, the fledgling United States might well be crushed.

This was not idle speculation. Back in London, upon hearing the news from Yorktown, Secretary of State Lord George Germain argued that Britain should at least hold onto its coastal enclaves, which could service the West Indies trade and provide a foothold on the continent. Perhaps, if French-American relations turned sour, and if Americans tired of their wartime governments, the opportunity would present itself to mount another offensive. Although the war's popularity was on the wane, the British ministry opted to continue the defense of positions it securely held.[18]

Because of military realities and diplomatic uncertainties, the outcome of the Revolutionary War was still very much in doubt after Yorktown. Had they displayed resolve, the British certainly possessed the resources to continue the fight. Only by reading history backward can we conclude that total British withdrawal was a foregone conclusion. Under the circumstances, Washington had no choice but to continue the war, pushing the temporary advantage the Americans had gained from Yorktown until Britain actually removed all its troops and ships.

He did just that. Immediately following the victory at Yorktown, Washington dispatched a force southward, hoping to put pressure on the British stationed in Charleston and Savannah. While placing control of the Chesapeake in French hands, he sent the main contingent of the Continental Army northward to counter any offensive by Clinton and the troops under his command in New York. Meanwhile, in the Southern backcountry, the war between local loyalists and patriots continued even without a British presence, each side seeking vengeance for atrocities committed by the other. Across the Appalachians, frontiersmen continued to battle against Native nations, who were still supported by the British.

Warfare continued on all these fronts. According to military historian Howard Peckham, 365 Americans lost their lives in the fighting after Yorktown. (As a percent of the population of the United States, this would amount to over 36,500 today, several times the American death toll in any comparable period of time in the Vietnam War or the entire eight years of the Iraq War.) This is undoubtedly a conservative estimate; because of the decentralized nature of the conflict in the South and West, many encounters were never reported. By contrast, during the Battle of Yorktown, only twenty-four American soldiers had been killed. The post-Yorktown death toll exceeded that of the first twelve months of the Revolutionary War, from April 1775 to April 1776, which included the battles of Lexington, Concord, Bunker Hill, and Quebec.[19] Family and friends of the deceased, were they alive today, would be taken aback to discover that we think the deaths of their loved ones had not occurred during the Revolutionary War. Henry Laurens, former president of the Continental Congress and one of the negotiators of the peace treaty, would have been particularly surprised: his son John, an aide-de-camp for Washington, perished in battle against British Regulars on August 27, 1782—more than ten months after the war had supposedly been over.

Just as the story of "the shot heard 'round the world" hides the dramatic revolution that preceded it, so does the story of "the final battle" suppress all that came afterward. Our telling of the American Revolution is astoundingly incomplete, leaving out both its true beginning and its true ending.

There are at least three major reasons for this hushing up of the historical record. First, we want our stories to have neat beginnings and endings, and we are willing to bend the evidence to make this happen. Second, we prefer to view the war as a bipolar struggle between Americans and their oppressors, without acknowledging that the brutal civil war in the South and fighting in the West continued unabated after Yorktown. Third, we remain blind to the global nature of the conflict. With no interest in the broader picture, we fail to comprehend why the war went on long after we believe it did.

THE AMERICAN REVOLUTION: A GLOBAL WAR

The French navy and army that enabled the victory at Yorktown were no strangers to their British adversaries. The American Revolution marked the fifth time in less than a century that Britain and France had been at war with each other. For thirty-six years (1689–1697, 1701–1713, 1744–1748, 1754–1763, 1778–1781) these two colonial powers had battled for dominance in Europe and around the world. The debt Britain accrued during the previous conflict, known in this country as the French and Indian War, led to increased British taxation of her American colonies. This met great resistance, culminating in the Revolutionary War. American rebels, realizing they could not win the war alone, declared their independence in large measure so they could receive aid from France; the French government could not openly support the United States unless there *was* a United States, an actual nation. With French money, French troops, French arms and ammunition, and French ships, Americans were able to counter British attempts to quash their rebellion. The causes, the politics, the fighting, and the outcome of the American Revolution were integrally linked to the ongoing struggle for supremacy first between two European nations and ultimately among all European powers.

In 1763, British victory in the French and Indian War had caused France to lose its stake on the North American mainland. When British colonists declared independence from their mother country thirteen years later, the French monarchy—no great friend to the cause of "liberty"—saw an opportunity to strike back. Once the rebels had proved their mettle with the victory at Saratoga, France jumped into the fray. France had not been able to beat Britain alone, but with the help of others, it might be able to cripple, or at least maim, its archrival.

France tried to get Spain to oppose Britain. Initially, Spain declined; governmental leaders did not wish to give credence to the American rebellion, fearing it might inspire Spanish colonies to follow suit. But Spain had many good reasons for joining the fight against the world's dominant naval power. Britain had seized Gibraltar, the Spanish fort that controlled the entrance to the Mediterranean. It had also taken the island of Minorca, off Spain's eastern coast. It held the former Spanish colony of Florida, and by controlling Honduras, Jamaica, and several smaller islands, it vied with Spain for dominance in the West Indies, key to its empire in Central and South America. Following the French defeat in 1763, Spain and Britain were the only colonial powers competing for the mainland of North America. If Britain could be expelled, Spain might gain control of the Mississippi and extend its hegemony throughout most of the continent.

In April 1779, Spain allied with France against Britain. It did not formally ally with the United States, but by waging war on Britain, Spain played a major role in the American Revolution. Troops, ships, and money that Britain might have used to quell the rebellion had to be used against Spain instead. In the later years of the war, Spain battled against Britain on the American frontier, dislodging the British from West Florida and challenging their control of the Mississippi.

In the summer of 1779, a combined French-Spanish force—sixty-six ships of the line and ten thousand men—prepared to invade southern England. For several weeks the allies cruised the English Channel, sending British communities along the coast into a panic. But the allies could not overcome logistical problems caused by poor communications, and they called the invasion off. Also near home, early in 1781, a French force invaded the British-held island of Jersey in the English Channel, closer to France than to Britain. The invasion was repulsed, but over two thousand men remained stationed there, along with another two thousand on the neighboring small island of Guernsey. In southern Britain (England and Wales), some 25,000 cavalry and infantrymen, along with an average of 35,000 militiamen, remained on duty in case of another attack from the English Channel, while in Scotland, some 6,000 Regulars protected the North Sea coastline. Meanwhile, British generals in America kept asking for more manpower to stage their offensives, but with the homeland itself in jeopardy, they had to make do with the soldiers they already had.[20]

In fact, British troops and ships at this time were scattered all over the globe. At Gibraltar, French and Spanish forces began a siege that would last for years. Five thousand soldiers remained stuck there, and worse yet, the British navy needed to devote considerable resources to break through the blockade periodically to supply the beleaguered garrison. So too with Minorca and the two thousand troops besieged there. The battle for control of the West Indies demanded constant attention, siphoning off some ten thousand soldiers and a hefty portion of the British navy. To the east, local rebellions in India were trying to expel British who had colonized the coast, and French vessels and soldiers aided the rebels, as they had the Americans. British soldiers and sailors needed to fight on all these fronts simultaneously.

Diplomatically, because it was perceived as the strongest world empire, Britain found itself isolated. In December 1780, the Netherlands formally allied with France and Spain against Britain. The Dutch, major commercial rivals of the British, controlled the Cape of Good Hope, a key supply station for ships on their way to India or the East Indies. Now that France and the Netherlands were allies, French ships could make use of this station while British ships could not, thereby allowing France to compete for hegemony in the Indian Ocean. Early in 1781 Britain tried to take the Cape, but the Dutch, reinforced by French ships on their way to India, prevailed. In August, just before the Continental Army and the French converged on Yorktown, British ships engaged Dutch ships in a fierce sea battle for control of the North Sea and command of the critical Baltic trade, rich with naval stores.

Aside from German states that rented out soldiers, Great Britain had no friends. Other governments—Russia, Denmark-Norway, Sweden, Prussia, Portugal, and even the Holy Roman Empire—formed a League of Armed Neutrality to protect their vessels, which traded with the allies, from predatory British ships. Russia, though, deemed the League too weak and was thinking of declaring war on Britain. The American Revolution, originally a contest between thirteen colonies and their home government, had evolved into another global war of empire that echoed the so-called Seven Years' War of 1754–1763, known only in this country as the French and Indian War, which also originated in America.[21]

This was the state of European affairs when Cornwallis surrendered the troops under his command at Yorktown. To see things through British eyes, we have only to consult the official *Annual Register*, an official contemporaneous publication of Parliament that documented the political scene in London. Here is the introductory abstract for a section it calls "Retrospective View of affairs in Europe to the close of the year 1781":

> Second attempt of France upon the island of Jersey. Baron de Rullecourt lands his troops in the night and surprises St. Helier

the capital. Compels the lieutenant-governor to sign a capitulation. Summons Elizabeth Castle. Is gallantly attacked in the town by Major Pierson. French commander falls, and his remaining troops surrender prisoners of War. Major Pierson unfortunately slain in the instant of victory. Necessities of the inhabitants and garrison of Gibraltar. Extraordinary prices of provisions and necessaries. Admiral Darby sails with a grand fleet and a convoy to its relief. Spanish fleet retires into Cadiz at his approach. Gunboats. Dreadful cannonade and bombardment of the town and garrison from the Spanish camp. Town destroyed, and many of the inhabitants perish. Convoy from St. Eustatius taken by M. de la Motte Piquet. Secret expedition [to India], under Commodore Johnstone, and Gen. Meadowes. Fleet attacked in Port Praya Bay by M. de Suffrein. French repulsed. M. de Suffrein's timely arrival at the Cape of Good Hope, frustrates the design upon that place. Dutch ships taken by Mr. Johnstone in Saldanha Bay. General Elliot's grand sally from Gibraltar, by which he destroys the enemy's batteries and works. Invasion of the island of Minorca. Combined fleets return from that service, to cruise at the mouth of the Channel. Proposal for attacking Admiral Darby at Torbay, overruled in a council of war. Enemy, frustrated in all their views, retire to their respective ports. State of the war with Holland, in Europe. Admiral Hyde Parker fails with a small squadron for the protection of the Baltic trade. Upon his return, falls in with Admiral Zoutman, with a great Dutch convoy, and a superior force. Desperate engagement at the Doggar-Bank. Dutch Fleet and convoy return in great disorder to their own coasts. *Hollandia* of 68 guns sunk. Consequences of the action. Royal visit to Admiral Parker at the Nore. Admiral Kempenfeldt fails to intercept a great convoy fitted out at Brest, with troops, stores and supplies, for the French fleets and armies in the East and West Indies. Falls in with and takes several of the convoy; but discovers the enemy to be so greatly superior in force, that he could not prosecute the design farther.[22]

Such was the Revolutionary War from a British perspective. This array of military operations across continents shaped British policy in the fall of 1781, when Yorktown fell. Had the American rebellion been their only concern, British officials might well have regrouped, sent more soldiers and ships, and continued the war. They might have staged more offensives, but even if they did not, they could have decided to hold on to the coastal enclaves they already controlled, thereby maintaining a strong presence on the eastern shore of North America. They were then holding Gibraltar, part of the Spanish mainland; soon, they would hold a port on the mainland of China—Hong Kong—that could withstand both the Nationalist and Communist revolutions. New York, Charleston, and Savannah, like Gibraltar and Hong Kong, might have remained in the British Empire for decades or even centuries.

It didn't happen that way because the British people had tired of fighting—and financing—a global war. With European powers lined up against them and strong anti-imperial movements in both the United States and India, the government was overextended and falling ever more deeply in debt. Throughout the war, a strong opposition within the British Parliament had been predicting this outcome, and now the prediction was coming true. It was time to scale back the British Empire to more manageable proportions.

The defeat at Yorktown helped tip the political scales and trigger a change in the British ministry, but that didn't happen immediately; not until March 22, 1782, not long after the British learned they had lost Minorca but five months after Cornwallis's surrender, did Lord North's government finally crumble. Even then, although Parliament resolved not to continue *offensive* measures in the United States, it did not voluntarily relinquish the ground it already held there, nor, of course, did it cease fighting elsewhere.

The war continued across the globe. Battles were lost and won in the West Indies. In April, at the Battle of the Saints, British ships avenged the loss of Yorktown by defeating the French fleet under Admiral de Grasse. In September, the British garrison at Gibraltar repulsed a massive French-Spanish assault. But on the east coast of India, Hyder Ali, Sultan of Mysore, raised a large army to fight the outnumbered British garrisons, while a French fleet disrupted shipments of supplies. This situation was reminiscent of that at Yorktown, but there was one essential difference: from the standpoint of British imperialists, India and the East Indies were even more important than the rebellious American colonies. The East India Company, which had triggered the American Revolution by trying to unload tea on the American market, considered the sources of that tea more valuable than one particular market for it, and it kept its own private army on the job to augment the government's forces.

The writing was on the wall, and Britain finally engaged in peace negotiations, securing the best terms it could. On February 21, 1783, in defending the proposed settlement in the House of Commons, William Pitt the Younger, soon to become prime minister, laid out the pragmatic calculus of a strategic retreat. Carefully, he detailed how Britain faced steep odds against the combined forces of the "four powerful States" of the alliance in engagements across the globe, from the West Indies to the English Channel, the "Northern Seas," and the Mediterranean, and now even in India. Further, the war had created "an unfunded debt of thirty millions," seriously weakening the empire. To achieve "the dissolution of that alliance" and "the immediate enjoyment of peace," negotiators had had to make concessions, but it was the only way, and it was time to move on: "Let us examine what is left with a manly and determined courage. Let us strengthen ourselves against inveterate enemies; and reconciliate our antient friends." Those "antient friends," of course, included the former British colonies in North America.[23]

Peace came just in time. On June 28, 1783—one year and eight months after the Battle of Yorktown—British garrisons in India found themselves in a precarious position. The French fleet had bested its scurvy-weakened British counterpart to control the coastline. A showdown loomed, with control of India hanging in the balance, but just at that moment, news arrived from back home: five months earlier, a preliminary peace treaty had been signed with Britain's various adversaries (America, France, Spain, and the Netherlands). With hostilities officially terminated, French commanders were obliged to call off their assault.[24]

By treating with its enemies separately, British diplomats had been able to secure many existing possessions. Gibraltar, their islands in the West Indies, and colonies in India remained in British hands. (Lord Cornwallis, after his defeat at Yorktown, would go on to become governor-general and commander in chief in India.) Best of all, war was over and the threat of an allied assault on England itself had passed. In the peace that was to follow, British ships were free to go wherever they pleased and trade with whomever they liked—including the newly formed United States. The empire, although diminished, had been salvaged thanks to the tactical retreat from thirteen rebellious colonies on the North American mainland.

The full story differs markedly from the one Americans tell themselves. According to our texts and popular histories, America was in command of its own destiny, defeating the mightiest empire on earth. "The world was amazed at what the Americans had done," one high-school text proudly pronounces.[25] Although we often give a grateful nod to France, rarely do we present the American Revolution as part of a global war. Only by ignoring the international context can we tell the story we like.

REMEMBERING AND FORGETTING GLOBAL HISTORY

Historians of the Revolutionary generation, having grown up as Englishmen, took more of an interest in events overseas. They kept a sharp gaze on British politics, after Yorktown as much as before. Nobody at the time would have thought that events leading to the conclusion of the war were somehow irrelevant to the main story. To understand the actions that resulted in the final settlement, early historians paid considerable attention to the global context, which clearly affected Britain's decision to abandon its claims on the thirteen rebellious colonies in North America. They also recognized that in 1782, the year following Yorktown, the British maintained a formidable military presence along the coast, while the civil war in the Southern interior continued unabated.

William Gordon (1788) devoted almost two hundred pages to the post-Yorktown events that led to the final settlement.[26] David Ramsay (1789) covered both "the campaign of 1782" and actions of "the other powers involved in the consequence of the American War."[27] Mercy Otis Warren (1805) discussed the Battle of Yorktown in the opening chapter of her third and final volume; in the subsequent 394 pages, she discussed in considerable detail the continuing fight in America, naval battles in the West Indies, the war in the Mediterranean, British politics, mutinies in the Continental Army, negotiations for peace, and the consequences of American independence.[28] John Marshall (1804–1807) followed Washington word for word: after Yorktown, the war was still on. Once the French fleet had gone, he wrote, Americans had little hope of dislodging the British from their coastal strongholds.[29] Reporting on the final year and a half of the war, for these contemporary observers, was more than a mere afterthought.[30]

Popular writers of the nineteenth century began to play tricks with the historical record. Mason Weems, who in 1806 invented the story of Washington and the cherry tree, wrote that King George III, instead of wishing to continue the war, was "graciously pleased" to change leadership in Parliament and pursue peace.[31] Noah Webster (1833) emphasized the "inexpressible joy" experienced throughout the United States upon hearing the news from Yorktown. The celebration of victory, he wrote, was so pervasive that Washington himself, instead of heightening his resolve to fight, "liberated all persons under arrest, that all might partake in the general joy."[32] With Washington celebrating and the king graciously conceding, Yorktown was presented as a happy ending to the war.

Not all authors simplified the story to this extent. John Frost (1838) quoted the king's speech to Parliament, in which he indicated his resolve to continue the war after Yorktown. Frost also discussed the continuing involvement of France, Spain, and the Netherlands.[33] As late as 1874, in the final volume of his monumental history, George Bancroft engaged in a lengthy discussion of the international context of British politics, crucial to an understanding of the end to the war.[34]

But to extend the story beyond Yorktown, and to include a global sweep, presented several problems. First, a story this broad was not very elegant. The intrigues of international politics were more difficult to follow than a simple battle, winner take all. Second, any serious discussion of the Revolution in 1782 would entail an admission that the war in the South was essentially a civil war (see chapter 12). If Britain had supposedly capitulated after Yorktown, and yet the fighting had continued, who, exactly, was the "enemy"? This raised more questions than could comfortably be answered in simple narrative form. Third, taking the global context in earnest would require the admission that Americans did not control their own destinies. The basic premise of the favored story—that patriots were able to overthrow the mightiest empire on earth because their cause was so noble—would be called into question.

For all these reasons, popular historians and textbook writers began to ignore the final year and a half of the American Revolution. Resorting to the simplest of narrative devices, they simply decreed that their histories ended at Yorktown. There, the Americans won and the British lost. The Americans celebrated, while the British, following Lord North, declared, "Oh God! It is all over." End of story.

Early twentieth-century textbooks followed this line.[35] One popular text in 1913 stated flatly, "The surrender of Cornwallis ended the Revolutionary War."[36] Another in 1935 pronounced authoritatively, "In both England and America everyone realized that this surrender meant the end."[37] No student would ever have suspected that "everyone" did not include either George Washington or King George III, both of whom endeavored to continue the war.

In 1956, at least one major textbook broadened and deepened the story. At that point, military alliances were very much in the forefront of the Cold War—NATO (North Atlantic Treaty Organization), SEATO (Southeast Asia Treaty Organization), and the so-called Soviet Bloc—as they had been during World War II and the United Nations action in Korea. Wars fought by Americans were now seen in a more international context, and Thomas A. Bailey, in his popular college text *The American Pageant*, reflected this. Starting in 1778, he explained, what had been a colonial war evolved into a world war. Dutifully, Bailey listed not only members of the anti-British alliance but also those of the armed neutrality, which adopted "an attitude of passive hostility toward England." The rebellious Americans, he explained, "did not achieve their independence until the conflict erupted into a multi-power world war that was too big for Britain to handle"; that was why Britain, which by his count still had over fifty thousand troops in North America and the West Indies, chose not to pursue the war further. "To say that America, with some European aid, defeated England is like saying, 'Daddy and I killed the bear.' " Here was a dramatic reversal of the classic national narrative.[38]

But Bailey's depiction of the American Revolution as a "world war" did not root deeply in the American mind. For a national narrative to work, the nation itself, with just a little help from "daddy," had to be the cause of its own independence. After the Cold War, the United States did indeed seem to determine both its own fate and the fate of the world, and the international context that permitted it to prevail in the Revolutionary War was for the most part ignored, save for later editions of Bailey's text.

In 2002, of thirteen elementary, middle-school, and secondary textbooks displayed at the annual convention of the National Conference for Social Studies, not one stated that both Washington and King George III vowed to pursue the war after Yorktown, or that a bloody civil war persisted in the South, or that fighting continued across the globe. Instead, eight of the texts concluded their chapters on the Revolution by highlighting Lord North's statement: "Oh God. It is all over," while eight concluded with another tale indicating a final resolution: the surrendering troops marched to the tune of "The World

Turned Upside Down." (Four texts included both stories, while only one had neither.)[39] Typically, the final year and a half of the Revolutionary War was abridged to a single subordinate clause, and reduced even further by qualifying adjectives: "Although some fighting continued, Cornwallis's surrender effectively marked the end of the war."[40] All texts gave the impression that the surrender of Cornwallis involved the whole British army, not just a small fraction of the British forces stationed in North America: "On October 19, 1781, Cornwallis surrendered his entire army of 7750 regulars, together with 850 sailors, 244 cannon, and all his military stores."[41] Few students, or even teachers, would even think of asking whether *Cornwallis's* "entire army" and the entire *British* army were one and the same.

Today, elementary, middle-school, and secondary texts still disregard the international context, and only a handful of college texts do better. In my survey of twenty-three college texts published since 2009, only five discuss the global sweep of Britain's entanglements that informed its decision to give up the fight for its thirteen rebellious colonies in America.[42] Of the remaining eighteen, three discuss British concerns in the West Indies but nowhere else,[43] and the other fifteen remain silent—no Gibraltar, Minorca, English Channel, Cape of Good Hope, India, or the East or West Indies.[44] Some of these do mention that Britain still had many troops stationed nearby; some discuss briefly the political debates in Parliament; a few even observe, "The British could have fought on."[45] But why did they *not* fight on, if they had the resources to do so? This is the obvious next question, and it would lead to an investigation of Britain's defense of a global empire and how this affected its policy with respect to America. But these texts don't go there.

This is surprising. For a decade now, Colonial and Revolutionary Era academics have been exploring and dissecting what they call "the Atlantic World": the cultural, social, political, economic, and military interplay among peoples and governments of Europe, Africa, and the Americas. Yet even this has not significantly broadened the narrow parameters in which we tell the Yorktown story, not only for younger students but at the college level as well.[46] One recent college text is subtitled *U.S. History in a Global Context*, but here is all it says about the impact of Yorktown: "When British prime minister Lord North heard the news of Yorktown, he reportedly exclaimed, 'Oh God! It's all over!' The British government decided to pursue peace negotiations." So ended "the final phase of the Revolutionary War."[47]

Another recent college text, sophisticated in other respects, announces proudly, "The *Continental Army* had managed the impossible. *It* had defeated *the British* army and won the colonies' independence" (emphases added)—no mention of help from the French fleet, French army, or French finances, and acknowledgment of only a single British army, Cornwallis's.[48] It's a simple tale and still the one we still prefer: by besting Great Britain, our nation shaped its own destiny. Americans have always done their best to avoid European entanglements, and this applies to the telling of history as well as to history itself.

"We said, The whole west, clear to the Mississippi, is ours; we fought for it; we took it; we hoisted our flag over its forts, and *we mean to keep it*. We did keep it."

Daniel Boone Escorting Settlers through the Cumberland Gap.
Detail of painting by George Caleb Bingham, 1851–1852.

14

MARCH OF THE AMERICAN PEOPLE

The American Revolution, with its happy ending, set us on our path: first a Constitution, then expansion across the continent, and finally the ascendancy to international prominence. But the story ended happily for only some. For others, the Revolutionary War signaled a loss, not a gain, of popular sovereignty. When we tell the story of the American Revolution from the standpoint of those who lost their land and their sovereign status, it takes on an entirely different aspect.

In 1958 two of the nation's most prominent historians, Henry Steele Commager and Richard B. Morris, concluded their 1,300-page compilation of primary sources for the American Revolution on a bright, optimistic note:

> The American Revolution . . . did little lasting damage, and left few lasting scars. Population increased throughout the war; the movement in the West was scarcely interrupted; and within a few years of peace, the new nation was bursting with prosperity and buoyant with hope.[1]

This view prevailed for two centuries. The Revolutionary War, by freeing white Americans from their shackles to the east, allowed them to look—and move—to the West. The rest, as they say, is history: the United States grew and thrived as it stretched across the North American continent.

We like to think of the Revolution as a war for independence. It was that, but it was simultaneously something very different: a war of conquest. Commager and Morris were partially correct—the Revolution did promote westward expansion—but the march of white settlers across the Appalachians did not leave all Americans "buoyant with hope." For many indigenous people, it signaled the end, not the beginning, of independence.

The American Revolution was by far the largest "Indian war" in our nation's history. Other conflicts between Euro-Americans and Native Americans involved only a handful of Indian nations at a time, or even just a single one—but all nations east of the Mississippi River were directly involved in this war. Most fought actively on one side or the other; more sided with the British, but some, particularly those east of the Appalachians, thought they would gain by joining the rebels. Before and during the Revolution, Indian played off one set of whites against the other as they sought to maintain their own lands. Afterward, with the power of competing European nations on the wane and the fledgling United States tilting westward, their options became more limited: resist at all costs; retreat to the West, where other native people lived; or negotiate a surrender as best they could.

DIVIDE AND CONQUER

According to one recent high-school textbook, "Native Americans remained on the fringes of the Revolution."[2] What constitutes a "fringe," however, depends on one's vantage point. The Revolutionary War looks very different if we stand on Indian lands and look east.[3] Narratives told from the perspective of the Iroquois or Delaware,

Cherokee or Shawnee bear little resemblance to those most Americans have incorporated, without question, into our national narrative.

Iroquois. Not all Iroquois were of one mind about the Revolutionary War. Both British agents and American patriots courted the Iroquois, the British using presents, the Americans veiled threats. Reasoning that American expansion posed a greater threat to their own interests, four of the six nations—Senecas, Cayugas, Onondagas, and Mohawks—cast their lots with Britain. Influenced by a missionary named Samuel Kirkland, the other two nations—Oneidas and Tuscaroras—allied with the Americans.[4]

In 1777 the grand council fire for the League of Six Nations was extinguished. Instead of coming together, Iroquois fought each other as well as their white foes. On August 6 at Oriskany, New York, several hundred Seneca, Cayuga, and Mohawk warriors joined with British rangers and loyalist volunteers to ambush patriot militiamen and their Oneida allies. Angry that their traditional allies had fought against them, Senecas attacked an Oneida settlement, and the Oneidas, in turn, plundered nearby Mohawks. A civil war among whites had become a civil war among Native people.

Pro-British Iroquois were far more numerous than their pro-American counterparts, and they figured more prominently in the war. In 1778 they staged numerous raids on white settlements, most memorably at Wyoming Valley and Cherry Valley. The following year, Congress responded by authorizing a force of some four thousand soldiers, commanded by General John Sullivan, to conduct a scorched-earth campaign against Indian villages. On July 4, 1779, Sullivan's officers offered a toast: "Civilization or death to all American Savages."[5] Then, for the remainder of the summer, they burned every village, chopped down every fruit tree, and confiscated every domesticated plant they could find. In the name of civilization, they tried to wipe out the developed civil society of people they called savages. At the end of the campaign, Sullivan reported triumphantly to Congress:

> The number of towns destroyed by this army amounted to 40 besides scattering houses. The quantity of corn destroyed, at a moderate computation, must have amounted to 160,000 bushels, with a vast quantity of vegetables of every kind. Every creek and river has been traced, and the whole country explored in search of Indians settlements, and I am well persuaded that, except one town situated near the Allegana, about 50 miles from Chinesee there is not a single town left in the country of the Five nations.[6]

The Sullivan campaign, which was followed by the "Hard Winter" of 1779–1780—the coldest on record for the eastern United States—created great hardships among the Iroquois people. (For more on the "Hard Winter," see chapter 5.) It did not, however, terminate Iroquois resistance. The following summer, more than 800 warriors staged raids in the Mohawk Valley, killed or captured 330 white Americans, and destroyed six forts and over 700 houses and farms. Senecas, Cayugas, Onondagas, and Mohawks also forced Oneidas and Tuscaroras off their lands, causing them to seek refuge on the outskirts of white settlements.

The war continued in 1781, with angry Iroquois warriors continuing their raids on whites who tried to occupy their lands. When Cornwallis surrendered at Yorktown, the Iroquois were still fighting, but they couldn't continue forever without British support. In 1782 that support was withdrawn, and in the Treaty of Paris the following year, Britain recognized United States sovereignty not only in the thirteen rebellious colonies but over the trans-Appalachian region as well, land which was still owned by the Iroquois and other Indian nations. Indians who had fought by the side of the British felt deceived and forsaken. Meanwhile, Euro-Americans felt entitled to settle land that Native Americans regarded as their own.

Delaware and Shawnee. The fate of other Indian nations paralleled that of the Iroquois: the Revolution caused internal divisions, while the termination of the war triggered an onslaught of white incursions.

Initially, chiefs from the Delaware and Shawnee pledged friendship with American patriots, hoping to work out some sort of accommodation with whites who bordered on their lands. Patriot officials offered these people assurances of support and protection, and they even suggested they would allow friendly Indians "to form a state whereof the Delaware nation shall be the head, and have a representation in Congress"—one of the most disingenuous promises in the history of white-Indian relations.[7] Patriots never did come through with any significant support, and white settlers continued to harass rather than protect indigenous people, friendly or otherwise, whom they encountered. After Indian-hating frontiersmen murdered four friendly Shawnee who were being held as hostages, the rest of the Shawnee joined with their militant neighbors—the Mingo, Miami, Wyandot, Chippewa, Ottawa, and Kickapoo—in support of Britain.[8]

American acts of aggression alienated the Delaware as well. When white Americans invaded their land and burned their villages, most of the Delaware joined the resistance. A few Christian converts tried to remain out of the fray, but this proved impossible. On March 8, 1782, volunteers from the Pennsylvania militia massacred ninety-six men, women, and children—none of whom were warriors—at the Gnadenhutten mission. As justification for their deeds, the militiamen alleged that their victims had given aid to the British by harboring enemy warriors. This was the crude underbelly of the American Revolution in Indian country.

Cherokee. To the south, the Cherokees waged their own war for independence during the (white) American War for Independence. When Henry Stuart, a British agent, visited the Cherokees early in 1776, he found them in heated debate over how to deal with the advance of Virginians and Carolinians onto their lands. Young warriors argued for immediate resistance: it was "better to die like men than to dwindle away by inches," they argued. Cherokee elders, on the other hand, favored caution. The young hawks were "idle young fellows" who should not be listened to, they told Stuart. Warriors, on the other hand, told Stuart that their elders were "old men who were too old to hunt."[9] The threat to Native lands was producing serious stress within Cherokee society.

The warriors prevailed. In the summer of 1776 angry young Cherokees staged numerous raids on frontier white settlements, but their timing could not have been worse. Patriots had just repelled a British attack on Charleston, and since there was no other threat in the region, rebels from the four southernmost states were free to vent their rage on the Cherokee. Six thousand armed men, having trained and mobilized for war against the British, marched against Indians instead. David Ramsay, a South Carolina patriot, explained how the campaign against the Cherokee was used as a training ground for the Revolutionary War:

> The expedition into the Cherokee settlements diffused military ideas, and a spirit of enterprise among the inhabitants. It taught them the necessary arts of providing for an army, and gave them experience in the business of war. . . . [T]he peaceable inhabitants of a whole state transformed from planters, merchants, and mechanics, into an active, disciplined military body.[10]

This war had a particularly Southern bent. As in the Sullivan campaign against the Iroquois, the object was to starve Indians into submission—but once they did submit, some of these Indians were taken as slaves. William H. Drayton, one of South Carolina's leading patriots, instructed members of the expedition against the Cherokees: "*And now a word to the wise*. It is expected you make smooth work as you go—that is, you cut up every Indian cornfield, and burn every Indian town—and that every Indian taken shall be the slave and property of the taker."[11] Enslavement of captured Indians, however, proved controversial; since this might result in Indians enslaving their white prisoners, the practice was eventually banned. Although whites were forced to turn over Indians they hoped to keep as slaves, this Southern scorched-earth campaign still accomplished its desired result: a total disruption of Cherokee society. Colonel Andrew Williamson, commander of the South Carolina forces, reported back to Drayton on the success of the mission: "I have now burnt every town, and destroyed all the corn, from the Cherokee line to the middle settlements."[12]

The impact on Cherokee society was profound. Elders signed two treaties in which they relinquished over five million acres of land (an area the size of New Jersey) and agreed to end their hostilities—but young warriors, the ones who initiated the conflict, refused to give in. Instead, many moved to the South and West, and they vowed to continue fighting. These people, called the Chickamaugas after their new home, refused to recognize the treaties negotiated by Cherokee elders. The Cherokee, like the Iroquois, became divided by differing responses to the American Revolution. Further, as some native people were forced from their homes, competition for land increased among multiple Native nations. By the war's end in 1783, these sorts of internal and external tensions had affected all indigenous people in the vast stretch of land between the Appalachian Mountains and the Mississippi River.

After the Treaty of Paris. For many Indian nations, the War for Independence—*their* independence—continued long after the British conceded defeat. They continued to fight because so much was at stake. Before the war, Britain had restrained white Americans from settling in the West. After the war, unrestrained, settlers streamed over the mountains at a breakneck pace and claimed Indian land. It had taken Euro-Americans more than a century and a half to settle the thin strip of land east of the Appalachians, but it took them scarcely a decade to extend their reach across a broader area to the west of the mountains. The Revolutionary War had made that possible.

Indian resistance did not fall away, even in the face of this onslaught. In the South, factions within the Creek, Choctaw, and Cherokee nations, including the breakaway Chickamaugas, formed a pan-Indian confederacy dedicated to fighting white encroachments on all of their lands. By procuring arms from Spain, which controlled the mouth of the Mississippi and lands to the south and west, they made a show of force that slowed, but did not stop, white advances. White Americans assumed they now owned the western lands—but many Indians thought otherwise. Alexander McGillivray, a half-Creek, delivered the message of the pan-Indian Confederacy to the United States Congress:

> We Chiefs and Warriors of the Creek Chickesaw and Cherokee Nations, do hereby in the most solemn manner protest against any title claim or demand the American Congress may set up for or against our lands, Settlements, and hunting Grounds in Consequence of the Said treaty of peace between the King of Great Britain and the states of America declaring that as we were not partys, so we are determined to pay no attention to the Manner in which the British Negotiators has drawn out the Lines of the Lands in question Ceded to the States of America—it being a Notorious fact known to the Americans, known to every person who is in any ways conversant in, or acquainted with American affairs, that his Brittannick Majesty was never possessed either by session purchase or by right of Conquest of our Territorys and which the Said treaty gives away. . . .
>
> The Americans . . . have divided our territorys into countys and Sate themselves down on our land, as if they were their own. . . . We have repeatedly warned the States of Carolina and Georgia to desist from these Encroachments. . . . To these remonstrances we have received friendly talks and replys it is true but while they are addressing us by the flattering appellations of Friends and Brothers they are Stripping us of our natural rights by depriving us of that inheritance which belonged to our ancestors and hath descended from them to us Since the beginning of time.[13]

To the north, nations from the Great Lakes region—the Mingo, Miami, Wyandot, Chippewa, Ottawa, Kickapoo, Shawnee, and

Delaware—continued to fight as well. Officially, the British in Canada could give them no support, but Indians were still able to get unofficial aid in the form of arms and favorable trade. In 1790, Miami fighters defeated an onslaught of soldiers led by Josiah Harmar, commander of the United States Army. In 1791, when white militiamen marched in full force into the Ohio country, warriors from across the North, and even some from the South, stood up to the intruders and killed 630 troops in a single battle along the banks of the Wabash River.

Until recently, these successful acts of Indian resistance were rarely noted. White victories, on the other hand, have not only been noted but celebrated. Historically, American history texts have seen fit to include the story of Fallen Timbers, when Washington sent "Mad Anthony" Wayne and 2,600 soldiers of the United States Army to confront a force of 2,000 Indians—the largest and most diverse force of Native Americans ever assembled against the United States government. This time the whites won and the Indians lost, and that triumphant story gets told.

From an Indian perspective, the American Revolution was pivotal, a global war that encompassed all people proximate to their known world. Fighting continued nonstop for two decades in the Native fights for independence that swept one-third of the way across the North American continent, from the Great Lakes to the Gulf of Mexico. If we view those fights as "fringe," we undermine the whole concept of a people's independence.

"WHO DEFENDED SETTLERS IN THE WESTERN LANDS?"

Of the many narratives featuring Native people in the Revolutionary War, which do we choose to tell—and why? Consider these two alternatives:

(1) In what is now Kentucky, a local militia leader, George Rogers Clark, hatched a scheme to end Indian raids on white

settlements: strike the British outposts that supplied the arms. In the summer of 1778 and the winter that followed, Clark led a band of fewer than two hundred frontiersmen down the Ohio River to the Mississippi Valley. This small group of patriots captured three British forts along the Mississippi and Wabash Rivers, placing a wedge between Native people and their British patrons and thereby "winning the West" for the fledgling United States.

(2) In the summer of 1779, the Continental Congress trained and outfitted some four thousand soldiers to take control of the countryside occupied by four Iroquois nations that had allied themselves with the British. This expedition, under the command of General John Sullivan, was by far the largest campaign conducted by the Continental Army in 1779. It destroyed forty Iroquois towns and a major portion of the food supply for the Iroquois people.

Textbooks through much of the nineteenth century included the latter story, a major military operation, but ignored Clark and his small band. Sullivan's purposive destruction of farms, orchards, and towns presented no ethical problem; it was done in "retribution" for the "horrible massacres" and "dreadful atrocities" committed by "bands of ferocious Iroquois," who had attacked "defenceless mothers, wives, and children" and tortured "prisoners in every way that savage cruelty could devise" in Wyoming Valley (Pennsylvania) and Cherry Valley (New York).[14] In a businesslike manner, authors reported that Sullivan, "according to his instructions, proceeded to lay waste their country."[15] After stating that "Sullivan marched to and fro through that beautiful region, laying waste their corn-fields, killing their orchards, and burning their houses," one author added a descriptive footnote: "The Indians, in the fertile country of the Cayugas and Senecas, had towns and villages regularly laid out. They had framed houses, some of them well finished, painted, and having chimneys. They also had broad and productive fields, and orchards of apple, pear, and peach trees." Destroying all this was perfectly legitimate because "the atrocities of the Indians had kept the inhabitants of the Wyoming and Mohawk valleys in continued terror."[16]

Toward the end of the nineteenth century, after Indian nations from coast to coast had been defeated, textbooks shifted. Sullivan's destruction of an obviously civilized society undermined the principal justification for displacing Indians: they were allegedly "savages." No longer proud of Sullivan, authors dropped him from their rosters, filling his spot with George Rogers Clark. The "Indian massacres" remained, but through narrative sleight of hand, a new hero took the stage:

> In the summer and autumn [of 1778] horrible Indian massacres were committed by bands of ferocious Iroquois led by Tory captains at Wyoming, Pennsylvania, and Cherry Valley, New York; there were also towns attacked and burned to ashes along the coast; but no great battle was fought. In the West, Captain George Rogers Clark of Virginia by his resolute bravery drove the British out of Illinois and later from Indiana, thus securing that immense region to the United States.[17]

No matter that Clark's exploits had nothing to do with Wyoming or Cherry Valleys; his "resolute bravery" served as a narrative counter to those "horrible" massacres. In a survey of twenty-three textbooks published between 1890 and 1955, every single one featured Clark, dubbed the "Washington of the West," while only three made any mention of Sullivan.[18] "Clark's expedition deserves to be ranked among the world's great military campaigns," boasted *A History of Our Country for Higher Grades*, published in 1923.[19]

From a storytelling point of view, Clark's tale seems preferable to Sullivan's. Clark can be portrayed as a David, battling against formidable odds, while Sullivan is undeniably a Goliath. Clark's story appeals precisely because his force was so small. In the traditional telling, Clark and his men braved flooding rivers in the dead of winter to surprise Henry Hamilton, the British commander at Vincennes. The Americans, supposedly outnumbered, yelled and marched back and forth to give the illusion of a much larger army. The ploy worked, and Hamilton surrendered. "Clark belonged to the men of genius who persist in accomplishing tasks which men of judgment pronounce impossible," stated the popular textbook writer David Saville Muzzey in 1934.[20] The authors of a 1942 text pronounced proudly: "The final result of this exploit was to give the Americans the territory that now forms the states of Ohio, Illinois, Indiana, Michigan, and Wisconsin."[21] The story here is that so few—just "a small but effective force of backwoods riflemen"—could accomplish so much. "Clark's victories opened the way for the march of the American people across the continent," wrote William Backus Guitteau in 1919.[22]

The Sullivan story, by contrast, has little appeal. His expedition conducted a terrorist campaign against a civilian population. Until just recently, textbook writers preferred to stay with the romantic image of valiant frontiersmen while suppressing the genocidal policies of the United States government. All six of the elementary and middle-school texts displayed at the 2002 National Council for Social Studies convention featured Clark, while not one mentioned Sullivan. Five of the seven high-school texts at that time included Clark's tale, and, again, none said a word about Sullivan's scorched-earth campaign, sanctioned by the Continental Congress.[23]

All these texts whitewashed the story of George Rogers Clark, who in fact engaged in dubious practices rarely mentioned. Clark tortured and scalped his prisoners. When they captured Indians outside Vincennes, he and his men tomahawked them and threw them in the river. To avenge the "Widows and Fatherless," he claimed afterward, "Required their Blood from my Hands."[24] Clark, like Sullivan, systematically destroyed Indian food sources, and he allowed his men to plunder Indian graves for burial goods and scalps, but such details did not find their way into the usual telling.[25] Instead, Clark has now become a "protector" rather than a "conqueror." Here is a question posed to wiki.answers: "Who defended the settlers in the western lands?" And the answer: "George Rogers Clark helped protect settlers in the western lands." In this one question and answer, a war of conquest is turned on its head.[26]

WE MEAN TO KEEP IT

The late-nineteenth- and early twentieth-century texts, unabashed, told a bolder tale that was closer to the truth. George Rogers Clark, they proclaimed proudly, was "the conqueror of the Northwest."[27] Authors assumed that Americans—white Americans, that is—had not only the right but also the moral imperative to take over the continent. In 1899 D.H. Montgomery, one of the most popular writers of his time, wrote in his *Beginner's American History*:

> General George Rogers Clark . . . did more than anyone else to get the west for us. . . . By Clark's victory the Americans got possession of the whole western wilderness up to Detroit. When the Revolutionary War came to an end, the British did not want to give us any part of America beyond the thirteen states on the Atlantic coast. But we said, The whole west, clear to the Mississippi, is ours; we fought for it; we took it; we hoisted our flag over its forts, and *we mean to keep it*. We did keep it. (Italics in the original.)[28]

Today, such outright jingoism would seem too crude—but the jingoism persists, even if it is no longer advertised as such. Routinely, current texts follow their chapters on the Revolutionary War with a brief section on "settling the western frontier." Once Britain ceded the West in the Treaty of Paris, they say, settlers ventured across the mountains to stake their claims. In the Land Ordinance of 1785, Congress ordered that a rectangular grid be superimposed on all newly acquired possessions of the United States to facilitate the private acquisition of land. Two years later, in what is now called the Northwest Ordinance, it established a procedure by which settlers in the new territories could form new states. Together, the Ordinances of 1785 and 1787 "opened the way for settlement of the Northwest Territory in a stable and orderly manner."[29] These measures are treated as Congress's crowning achievement during the interval between the Revolution and the drafting of the Constitution. "If you got the impression that the Congress under the Articles of Confederation was a total washout," writes Joy Hakim, "that isn't quite true. That Congress did a few things right, and the Northwest Ordinance was one of them."[30]

This storyline looks quite different from an Indian perspective. Just as the Revolution was the largest conflict between whites and Indians in our nation's history, so was the Ordinance of 1785 the most significant and damaging piece of legislation. It turned open spaces into lines on a map, harnessing the earth so land could be bought and sold. In the Treaty of Paris, signed in 1783, the British had ignored Indian rights to the land by stating that the "boundaries" of the United States extended clear to the Mississippi; now, Americans effectively ignored Indian tenure by providing that all lands be labeled so they could be distributed to Euro-American speculators and farmers.[31] This "happy ending" to the Revolution spelled only doom to Native inhabitants.

Right at this crucial juncture, with their fates being sealed by lauded acts of Congress, Indians have curiously disappeared from the traditional narrative. In thirteen elementary, middle-school, and high-school texts surveyed in 2002, not one discussed the pan-Indian resistance to white expansion in the wake of the Revolutionary War.[32] Indian resistance reappeared in later chapters, which described their rearguard struggles for survival in the nineteenth century—but nary a word at the critical moment, our nation's founding, when Indian claims to their homelands were bypassed and the earth was divided into property that whites could own.

Very recently, a few textbooks have adopted a more balanced approach, viewing that pivotal time from both white and Indian perspectives. One fifth-grade text, immediately following a discussion of the Land Ordinance of 1785 and the Northwest Ordinance of 1787, presents a two-page spread, with a timeline, on Indian resistance in the 1790s.[33] At a similar point in the narrative, after outlining the two ordinances and the opportunities they offered for settlers and speculators, a high-school text comments, "But freedom and opportunity for Americans came at the expense of the region's 100,000 Indians, who were expected to give up their lands and relocate elsewhere."[34] A college text adds significant detail:

> Indians knew well that the pressures of war always threatened to deprive them of their homeland. "You are drawing so close to us that we can almost hear the noise of your axes felling our trees," one Shawnee told the Americans. Another group of Indians concluded in 1784 that the Revolutionary War had been "the greatest blow that could have been dealt us, unless it had been our total destruction." Thousands fled the raids and counter-raids, while whole villages relocated. Hundreds made their way even beyond the Mississippi, to seek shelter in territory claimed by Spain. The aftershocks and dislocations continued for the next two decades; an entire generation of Native Americans grew up with war as a constant companion.[35]

Treating the Revolutionary War as a war of conquest in this manner can be troubling. Former colonists were subjugating other peoples, even as they resisted subjugation by Britain. These contradictory realities, like slave owners fighting a war for freedom, challenge our national narrative. What kind of people are we, anyway?

There is an answer, and we are moving toward it. Americans are and always have been a diverse people with diverse histories, and nothing defines our nation better than that. Increasingly, purveyors of public history embrace this truth, but it presents a new set of challenges. With multiple protagonists and perspectives, what happens to *the* American narrative? How can any textbook, curriculum, or sweeping historical account capture the full experience of the Revolutionary War, much less the broad range of American history?

The challenge is great, and it is little wonder we so often retreat. Two of the college textbook authors who showed so forcefully how the Revolutionary War had been "the greatest blow" to Native people sound a different tone when writing for middle-school students. In a section titled "Defending the Frontier," they tell an old story: "Seeking to defend against attacks on the frontier, Virginia sent George Rogers Clark. . . ."[36] The language conveys what the authors do not really intend, that Americans in the West were the innocent ones, not the aggressors. Viewing the rebellious colonies as the afflicted party is a default mode in chronicles of the American Revolution, and such talk will not cease in an instant.

15

STORYBOOK NATION

Our history texts tell us that colonists became "Americans" by sharing the experience of the Revolutionary War, but this is not altogether correct. Soldiers and civilians, Northerners and Southerners, whites and blacks—these people experienced the war in very different ways, and by the end they seemed less enthusiastic about joining together as Americans than they had been at the outset.[1] Our magical beginning was already lost in the past—but this past would soon rebound and take on a life of its own. Rediscovered and reconstituted, it would become a vibrant force in the shaping of a nation. It was not the Revolution itself but the use of its image that created a unified, national experience to be shared by all Americans.

HARNESSING THE PAST

To "remember" their Revolution, the people who lived through it first had to learn to forget. "Much about the event called the Revolutionary War had been very painful and was unpleasant to remember," wrote historian John Shy. "Only the outcome was unqualifiedly pleasant, so memory, as ever, began to play tricks with the event."[2] This did not come about in a day. The past needed time to *become* a past before it

“Let the youth, the hope of his country,
grow up amidst annual festivities,
commemorative of the events of the war.”

American Independence, 1859. Anonymous lithograph.

could be selectively recalled in a more positive light and form the basis for national traditions.

Despite bad memories of war, all patriotic Americans could share one remembrance of unequivocal joy: the declaring of independence. Other war stories would take years of seasoning before assuming their final form, but the recollection of that special moment was put to work from the start. Every year, Americans could revive their commitment to their nation by celebrating the instant of its inception.

John Adams, for one, had a very definite notion of how Americans could commemorate their nation's birth. On July 3, 1776, the day after Congress voted for independence, he wrote to his wife, Abigail:

> The second of July 1776 will be the most memorable epocha in the history of America. I am apt to believe it will be celebrated by succeeding generations as the great anniversary festival. It ought to be commemorated as the day of deliverance, by solemn acts of devotion to God Almighty. It ought to be solemnized with pomp and parade, with shows, games, sports, guns, bells, bonfires, and illuminations, from one end of this continent to the other, from this time forward forevermore.[3]

Adams certainly had the spirit right, but he guessed wrong on the date. He had no way of knowing that the official record would soon be altered to change the timeline of history.

Like John Adams, other members of Congress entertained notions of a national celebration, so they conjured an event worth celebrating. Americans were primed to celebrate on July 4 rather than July 2 because the broadside of the Declaration, which circulated widely in July 1776, bore the heading "In CONGRESS, July 4, 1776." The following spring, the committee that printed the official *Congressional Journal* fabricated an entry for July 4 to reflect this preference. The printed journal, unlike the original one, included a signed version of the Declaration of Independence in its July 4 entry, while it omitted the crucial entries for July 19 (the day the New York delegation finally gave its assent and Congress ordered that an engrossed copy be "signed by every member of Congress") and August 2 (the first day anybody other than President John Hancock and Secretary Charles Thomson actually signed the document).[4] According to the official but contrived record, the "Unanimous Declaration of the Thirteen United States" was entered into the books fifteen days *before* it became unanimous, signed even by delegates from New York, who, following their colony's instructions, had *not* voted in favor of independence in early July. This clever invention gave Americans the Fourth of July.

In our nation's first "photo op," an engrossed copy of the Declaration of Independence was presented for signing on August 2. Many members of Congress signed on that day, and over the course of the next several months, others who had been absent or were newly elected affixed their signatures as well.[5] At least fourteen men who were not even present on July 4, 1776, signed their names to the document that appears in the *Congressional Journal* for that date. Eight of these—Matthew Thornton of New Hampshire, William Williams of Connecticut, Charles Carroll of Maryland, and Benjamin Rush, George Ross, James Smith, George Clymer, and George Taylor of Pennsylvania—had not yet become delegates. Oliver Wolcott of Connecticut had taken leave of Congress to assume command of his state's militia, while Lewis Morris and Philip Livingston went home when the British threatened to invade New York. William Hooper of North Carolina, Samuel Chase of Maryland, and George Wythe of Virginia were helping their states constitute new governments. Later, these men would return to sign their names, some not until late that fall. One delegate, Thomas McKean of Delaware, did not sign until after the "official" journal had been doctored the following year.[6]

The signing of the Declaration of Independence was a manufactured event, consciously designed to produce a sort of "overnight antiquity," in the words of historian Garry Wills.[7] The sleight of hand worked. By 1786, the tenth anniversary of independence, Fourth of July rituals in the major cities had assumed an air of tradition. Early in the morning, bells or cannons announced the beginning of commemorative festivities. Militia or volunteer units marched in parade; then, in ritualistic procession, citizens joined the march toward the site of the official oration. There, a prominent citizen preached a secular gospel; often these speeches were placed in print, and some became bestsellers. After the oration, people would join in song, much like parishioners responding with hymns. The Fourth of July was celebrated as a holy day—"the Sabbath of our Freedom," according to one contemporary participant.[8]

Following the formal commemoration, people adjourned to various inns and taverns to break bread and drink. Each group offered thirteen toasts in honor of the body assembled, the state, the nation, and the republican ideal of popular sovereignty. After dinner, with their patriotism revived and their spirits lubricated, Americans caroused in the streets, where they gathered around bonfires and set off fireworks.

Toward the end of the eighteenth century, this "holy day" turned into a "holiday." For the first time, unencumbered by any religious obligations, workers were given a day off. To celebrate the birth of their nation, Americans neither labored nor went to church. The Fourth of July became the liveliest day of the year.

Early Fourth of July rituals helped define the evolving American character. While orators highlighted the "superior advantages" of republican government and "public virtue," the parades and festivities showcased the military aspects of the "American" experience.[9] In 1786 a writer for the *Independent Gazetteer* commented on the proper celebratory mores:

> Let the youth, the hope of his country, grow up amidst annual festivities, commemorative of the events of the war. . . . Let this young hero, at frequent intervals, quit the toils of husbandry, to kindle his public spirit amidst war like exercises; let him learn the use of arms and accustom himself to discipline in the sight of the most respectable citizens. Let him, in their presence, pledge himself to defend his country and its laws.[10]

While the Revolutionary War receded into the past, military men marched in Fourth of July parades, cannons fired, and all paid homage to the Revolutionary dead, creating national martyrs. As Boston poet Barnabas Binney wrote: "With Blood they seal their Cause, / Died to save their Country's Laws." [11]

By paying tribute to the past, Americans affirmed their commitment to the nation that was emerging in the present. The Fourth of July conferred upon the nation a "history," even if it was recent and brief. That was a start. In time, that history would be embellished, set to paper, and codified into a narrative that every American would be expected to learn.

Not coincidentally, two of the orators at early Fourth of July celebrations—William Gordon and David Ramsay—were the first Americans to pen narratives of the Revolution. Gordon led the way with his four-volume tome entitled *The History of the Rise, Progress, and Establishment of the Independence of the United States of America*, published in 1788.[12] The following year, David Ramsay published his two-volume *History of the American Revolution*.[13] Both Gordon and Ramsay wrote with political purpose. By chronicling the struggle for independence, Gordon hoped to promote his republican ideals. Ramsay, an active Federalist, tried to unify the nation by developing an "American" sense of identity through a shared history. "Joining foot to foot, and hand to hand, . . . with one mind," Ramsay wrote, the American people presented "a solid phalanx opposing their energies and resources to the introduction of arbitrary power." [14]

Other contemporary historians wrote with acknowledged agendas. John Marshall (*The Life of George Washington*, 1804–1807) was a leading political figure in Virginia in the 1790s and chief justice of the United States Supreme Court for more than three decades, starting in 1801.[15] As a staunch Federalist, Marshall wished to minimize regional differences and promote a stronger sense of national pride; to do this, he focused on Washington as a symbol of unity. Mercy Otis Warren (*History of the Rise, Progress, and Termination of the American Revolution*, 1805) was an ardent anti-Federalist, and she too wrote with purpose. Warren's brother, James Otis, and husband, James Warren, had been prominent Massachusetts patriots, and she herself had been an active and communicative Revolutionary. Warren, who still viewed herself as a patriot, tried to revive a sense of public virtue in the post-Revolutionary generation.[16]

The prominent early historians of the Revolution were similar in three respects. First, while professing to seek only the "truth," they consciously promulgated civic values. Although Warren and Gordon focused on public virtue and Ramsay and Marshall on strengthening the nation, their goals certainly intermeshed. All four promoted "America" as the embodiment of republican ideals. Together, they laid the foundations for a coherent narrative of the Revolutionary War, although this rough draft of an American Genesis did not yet include most of the tales featured in these pages. (Gordon's rendition of Samuel Adams, and Warren's celebration of Jefferson's genius and the "patient suffering" at Valley Forge, were notable exceptions.)

Second, they all borrowed liberally from an even earlier work, a narrative set in print years before by an Englishman. Throughout the Revolutionary Era, an official publication of the British Parliament, the *Annual Register*, chronicled events in the rebellious colonies as part of its annual news-of-the-world report. As luck would have it, during this period the *Register* was under the editorship of Edmund Burke, who wrote many of the entries himself. An outspoken Whig member of Parliament, Burke embraced a perspective that was easy for American patriots to accept: actions adopted by the British government to keep the colonists under tight reins were ill-advised and self-defeating.

Few Americans bothered to read the *Annual Register*, but those who took the trouble perused it carefully—they must have, for they copied it word for word. Sentences, paragraphs, and entire pages reappeared verbatim in the works of Gordon, Ramsay, Marshall, and, to a lesser extent, Warren. In 1789 the *Columbian*, a staunchly patriotic journal, published a "concise history of the late war in America" that lifted large sections from Burke's *Register*, admittedly copied "without change" because of "the superior eloquence of its composition." [17] In 1899 a scholar named Orin Libby exposed this so-called "plagiarism," although during Revolutionary times, intellectual property was not so jealously guarded, and all the alleged culprits had freely acknowledged their sources.[18]

Third, none of the early historians was as successful as he or she had hoped.[19] Only cultured literati, who already knew the basic story, actually purchased their multivolume tomes; the masses of people whom the authors had wanted to inspire never took much notice. For every person who read their ponderous works, scores of others heard about the glorious deeds of the original patriots only by word of mouth. While Fourth of July rituals celebrated the past in a style accessible to all, written history needed to come down a notch if it was ever to be embraced by common Americans.

ROMANCING THE REVOLUTION

Like his more learned and renowned contemporaries, an itinerant preacher and traveling book salesman named Mason Locke Weems wanted to promote patriotism, but he took the pulse of the American people more accurately. Weems could deliver a sermon, fashion a speech, or play the fiddle—whatever would draw an audience. For thirty years he peddled his "Flying Library" up and down the eastern seaboard. From New York to Georgia, he worked the crowd at court days and revival meetings. At first he sold books for Matthew Carey, a Philadelphia publisher; later, he pushed his own wares as well—biographies of George Washington, Benjamin Franklin, William Penn, and Francis Marion.[20]

Mason Weems gave the reading public what it wanted: virtuous heroes, lively prose, and cheap books. In 1797 he outlined to Carey the basic strategy that would catapult him to fame:

> Experience has taught me that small, i.e., quarter of dollar books, on subjects calculated to *strike* the Popular Curiosity,

> printed in very large numbers and properly *distributed*, would prove an immense revenue to the prudent and industrious Undertakers. If you could get the life of General Wayne, Putnam, Green &c., Men whose courage and Abilities, whose patriotism and Exploits have won the love and admiration of the American people, printed in small volumes and with very interesting frontispieces, you would, without doubt, sell an immense number of them.[21]

Following his own formula, Weems embarked on his personal writing career. In the spring of 1799, as George Washington's health began to fade, Weems propositioned Carey:

> I have nearly ready for press, a piece to be christened "The Beauties of Washington." . . . The whole will make but four sheets and will sell like flax seed at quarter of a dollar. I could make you a world of pence and popularity by it.[22]

Washington died six months later, and Weems wrote immediately to Carey: "Millions are gaping to read something about him. I am nearly primed and cocked for 'em." And so he was: by February 1800 Weems had published his first edition of George Washington's biography, an eighty-page pamphlet which did indeed sell like flaxseed at planting time.[23]

Over the next few years Weems peddled his own pamphlet from his "Flying Library." He also took subscriptions for John Marshall's forthcoming *Life of George Washington*. When Marshall's laborious volumes appeared, subscribers complained that there was too much history and too little Washington. Weems listened. He wanted to deliver God and country at an affordable price, but he also knew that his little pamphlet would not serve as a substitute for a full-scale biography, so he started gathering and inventing more material. In 1806, for his fifth edition, he added the fictive "I cannot tell a lie" story about cutting down the cherry tree, and in 1808, the sixth edition, he expanded his product into the full-length book that would introduce the Father of our Country and the Revolutionary War to generations of Americans (*The Life of George Washington; With Curious Anecdotes, Equally Honorable to Himself and Exemplary to His Young Countrymen.*)

To establish his credibility, Mason Weems identified himself on the title page as "Formerly Rector of Mount-Vernon Parish." Although there never was a "Mount-Vernon Parish," the preacher had occasionally delivered sermons at Pohick Church, which Washington might have attended many years before. This supposedly gave the writer an inside connection, and he undoubtedly picked up on some local folklore, but "Parson Weems" (as he was now called) did not hesitate to invent a story from scratch if it could produce the desired result.

Weems's challenge was to present Washington as picture-book-perfect, and to do it in grandiose style. William Gordon had complained that extravagant writing made the reader feel he was "in company with a painted harlot"; if so, Weems was among the most promiscuous of writers.[24] By magically conjuring fantastic and even outrageous images, he entertained as he preached. "He is a most delightful mixture of the Scriptures, Homer, Virgil, and the back woods," wrote Sydney Fisher over a century later. "Everything rages and storms, slashes and tears."[25] For example:

> Then sudden and terrible the charge was made! Like men fighting, life in hand, all at once they rose high on their stirrups! while in streams of lightening their swords came down, and heads and arms, and caps, and carcasses, distained with spouting gore, rolled fearfully all around.[26]

Weems set the standard, and others followed suit. Biography was the name of the game, and the rules were clear: choose a military hero or prominent Revolutionary statesman, build up his virtues while suppressing his vices, and above all, entertain. So it was, in the early 1800s, that fading memories of the Revolution came back to life for the American people. Biographies of Patrick Henry, Thomas Sumter (the Gamecock), and Francis Marion (the Swamp Fox) delighted and inspired. Even David Ramsay jumped onboard, penning a biography of Washington that outsold his original history.[27] During the 1820s John Sanderson came out with a nine-volume series of eulogies entitled *Biography of the Signers of the Declaration of Independence*. All these bestsellers were buttressed by lofty sentiments. Heroic biographies, which provided moral instruction for the young, also promoted a sense of national identity at a time when the United States, still in its adolescence, needed to counter the centrifugal forces of regionalism and rapid westward expansion.

The War of 1812 both reflected and furthered an increased militarism in American culture. Revolutionary War veterans, once scorned, were suddenly celebrated, and the myth of "patient suffering," focused on Valley Forge, now flourished. In 1817 William Wirt promoted military values with his re-creation of Patrick Henry's speech. Since the United States had been created through acts of war, military virtues became synonymous with patriotism.

The emphasis on military struggles, along with the rage for popular biographies, reduced history to a series of isolated stories with individual protagonists and straightforward plotlines. Battles had definite beginnings and endings, and nobody could mistake a hero for a villain. Events were shaped by personal acts of courage and valor, not by collective action. Separate scenes—"anecdotes," in the parlance of the times—were connected only by the sense of morality they instilled. One book was titled *Anecdotes of the American revolution: illustrative of the talents and virtues of the heroes and patriots, who acted the most conspicuous parts therein*;[28] another presumptuously labeled itself "a complete anecdotal history" of the Revolution.[29] Leading characters assumed godlike proportions in order to serve as appropriate role models for young Americans. The Revolution, in a word, lost all of its dimensions but one.

As those documenting the Revolution searched for heroes, they eyed the fifty-six delegates to the Continental Congress who had signed the Declaration of Independence. In fact, the Declaration of

Independence had been approved by thirteen state delegations, and most delegations were responding to specific instructions from their constituents. In the popular mind, however, the courageous patriots assembled in Philadelphia had taken the fate of the nation upon themselves. Although countless patriots operating on the state and local levels had also pledged their lives and their fortunes (see chapter 6), these people, along with the collective bodies through which they operated, were eclipsed by "the Signers."

Responding to similar impulses, academic as well as popular writers rendered versions of the past intended to unify the nation. Between 1833 and 1849 Jared Sparks, soon to become president of Harvard, edited a monumental twenty-five-volume series entitled *The Library of American Biography*. He also published a twelve-volume collection of Washington's writings, introduced by a scholarly biography. Here at last were serious works that appealed to the public: altogether, Sparks sold more than half a million volumes. Although Sparks toned down the language and stepped up the documentation, he still dressed up the Revolutionary pantheon for public inspection. Sparks routinely doctored the documents to eliminate offensive material or undignified language. A man of Washington's stature, he reasoned, should not be remembered for such folksy expressions as "not amount to a flea bite."[30]

If the marketplace made its mark on the telling of history, so did the advent of public education. Back in 1790 Noah Webster had argued persuasively that "in our American republics, where government is in the hands of the people, knowledge should be universally diffused by means of public schools."[31] The logic was irrefutable, and by the early decades of the nineteenth century, public education was becoming the norm rather than the exception. Since the need for an informed citizenry necessitated the study of history as well as the "three Rs," early children's texts included elementary renderings of the American Revolution. One book, *The American Revolution Written in the Style of Ancient History*, imitated biblical language and assigned each of the central characters a biblical name.[32]

In 1820 the American Academy of Language and Belles Lettres offered a prize of $400 plus a medal of solid gold for the best history of the United States designed for schools.[33] Salma Hale, who produced the winning entry, outlined the objectives for his book:

> [T]o exhibit in a strong light, the principles of political and religious freedom which our forefathers professed, and for which they fought and conquered; to record the numerous examples of fortitude, courage, and patriotism, which have rendered them illustrious; and to produce, not so much by moral reflections, as by the tenor of the narrative, virtuous and patriotic impressions on the mind of the reader.[34]

Hale's book and many others like it were produced in tiny formats, four inches by six inches or even less, small enough to fit in a mechanic's apron or a frock pocket. Reprinted in mass quantities and sold for a pittance, they presented a child's version of history to a population that was minimally literate. Addressing two audiences—young students and adult citizens of a young nation—they performed double duty: character building and nation building.

In their treatments of the American Revolution, books such as Hale's tread a thin line: they needed to celebrate the break from Britain, but they could not preach the virtues of rebellion to children who ought to obey their elders. Coincidentally, this was the same thin line followed by many Americans of the times. In the decades after the Revolutionary War, upheavals in France and Haiti, with their infamous massacres, had given revolution a bad name. The earlier meaning of "revolution," prevalent during the War for Independence, connoted a "revolving turn of events," not an overthrow of the established order; specifically, it referred to the Glorious Revolution of 1688 in England. This is why members of the colonial elite could consider themselves "revolutionaries."[35] In the early nineteenth century, once the meaning of the word had changed, conservatives faced the task of de-revolutionizing the American Revolution. Paul Allen, writing in 1819, argued that the patriots should not even be called "rebels." Since they were fighting for no more than "the rights secured by Magna Charta," they were simply upholding ancient law and tradition.[36] Drawing on folkloric material and the letters of famous leaders collected by Sparks and others, popular writers presented a sanitized version of the Revolution, an amalgamation of simple morality tales depicting courageous displays of valor and great individual achievements. It was at this point that the critical 1774 revolution in Massachusetts, a popular uprising that established a dangerous precedent, began to disappear from the saga.

At midcentury, writer-artist Benson Lossing gave this idolatrous, anecdotal history a concrete physical expression. Embarking on an eight-thousand-mile pilgrimage through the "Old Thirteen States and Canada," Lossing visited "every important place made memorable by the events of the war" in a quest to discover "the history, biography, scenery, relics, and traditions of the War for Independence." His aim was to rescue the "tangible vestiges of the Revolution" from oblivion, before they were swept away by "the invisible fingers of decay, the plow or agriculture, and the behests of Mammon."[37] While researching his historical travelogue, Lossing listened to the tales of countless old-timers, people who had been raised on stories of the Revolution told by firsthand participants. He tapped into an oral tradition strongly linked to a sense of place. Everywhere he went, locals would usher him through battlefields that had turned back to meadows, calling forth the ghosts who still prowled about.

In 1851 and 1852 Lossing published his folkloric compilation, *A Pictorial Field-Book of the Revolution*, accompanied by more than one thousand illustrations. In two large and impressive volumes, Lossing turned his readers into historical tourists. He provided no organizing principle other than plain geography; the narrative simply followed his journey from one place to the next. This conformed to the "antiquarian" approach to history prevalent at the time: the past survived in the present through physical relics and the stories of individual lives.

Such was the state of historical writing when George Bancroft, a prodigy who had graduated from Harvard at the age of sixteen, commenced his serious and comprehensive history of the British colonies in North America and their War for Independence. Bancroft combined the talents of scholar, writer, and political advocate. He drew on all traditions, written and oral, and geared his history to scholars and laypeople alike. Gifted with a marvelous eye for detail, he could spin a yarn or eulogize a hero as well as any writer of his times—but he also believed in primary source documentation. Like Jared Sparks, with his biographical collections, and Peter Force, with his monumental compilation of newspaper accounts and official records,[38] Bancroft gathered a wealth of material from the colonial and Revolutionary eras; unlike Sparks and Force, he synthesized what he read into a coherent story with a definite perspective. Through some 1,700,000 words, Bancroft held fast a single perspective: that from the very beginning of colonial settlement, the colonists had moved toward independence. America was the promised land, and this was her age. European monarchies and aristocracies were old and corrupt; America, young and vital, represented humanity's best hope. Whatever Americans did to foster freedom and democratic values was commendable, while anyone who opposed America must be considered malevolent.[39]

Bancroft defined the American experience for the American people. His history, published serially between 1834 and 1875, told the story of our nation's founding from a passionately patriotic perspective. Later, learned professors would take him to task for his excesses, but the vibrant nationalism he espoused still permeates our popular culture today. Bancroft wove images of a perfect America into a rich mosaic with a strong narrative thread.

But there was some dissent. Richard Hildreth, a contemporary of Bancroft, took a different tack:

> Of centennial sermons and Fourth-of-July orations, whether professedly such or in the guise of history, there are more than enough. It is due to our fathers and ourselves, it is due to truth and philosophy, to present for once, on the historic stage, the

> founders of our American nation unbedaubed with patriotic rouge, wrapped up in no fine-spun cloaks of excuses and apology. . . . The result of their labors is eulogy enough; their best apology is to tell their story exactly as it was.[40]

Hildreth was not a commercial success. Precise but dry, his prose failed to excite. The public seemed to prefer history wrapped in "fine-spun cloaks." In scholarly circles, on the other hand, Hildreth received a warm response. Historians of the late nineteenth century's "scientific school" preferred Hildreth's tempered tone to Bancroft's hyperbole. The American Historical Association, founded in 1884, saw no need for "Fourth-of-July orations . . . in the guise of history." The history profession tried to remove itself from the peddling of patriotism. According to John Fiske, labeled the "Bancroft of his generation," the job of history, like that of science, was only "to emphasize relations of cause and effect that are often buried in the mass of details."[41]

Most common citizens, however, could not have cared less about cause and effect. They looked to history for different and more personal reasons: to connect with the past, often through tangible legacies, and to buttress the present with a sense of tradition. In 1876, triggered by the centennial celebrations, communities throughout the eastern states returned to Benson Lossing's physical, on-site approach. By consecrating particular locations, they claimed the Revolution as their own. During and after the centennial, almost every town with some stake in the Revolution formed its own historical society, dedicated to preserving the relics and traditions of the past. "George Washington slept here" had a more immediate ring than scholarly debates over abstract causes. The lay alternative to "scientific history" was clearly expressed in the first "objective" of the Daughters of the American Revolution, as stated in its bylaws of 1890:

> To perpetuate the memory and spirit of the men and women who achieved American Independence; by the acquisition and

> protection of historic spots and the erection of monuments; . . . by the preservation of documents and relics, and of the records of individual services of Revolutionary soldiers and patriots; and by the promotion of celebrations of all patriotic anniversaries.[42]

Popular history and academic history were parting ways. Scholars dismissed popular history as "nostalgia"; laypeople regarded academic works as irrelevant at best, irreverent at worst. The central scholarly debate during this time—whether the Revolution had been caused by the wrongdoing of select individuals or by a fundamental flaw in the concept of empire—played to deaf ears outside academia. Recently divided by the Civil War and Reconstruction, Americans now reminded themselves that South and North had fought side by side at our nation's inception. It was time to gather inspiration from the "Heroic Age" of the founders, "one equaling in interest and grandeur any similar period in the annals of Greece and Rome." The Revolution, according to a magazine editorial, was characterized by "a strange elevation of feeling and dignity of action" which furnished "a treasury of glorious reminiscences wherewith to reinvigorate . . . the national virtue." The editor continued:

> What political utility can there be in discovering, even if it were so, that Washington was not so wise, or Warren so brave, or Putnam so adventurous, or Bunker Hill not so heroically contested, as has been believed? Away with such skepticism, we say; and the mousing criticism by which it is sometimes attempted to be supported. Such beliefs have at all events become real for us by entering into the very soul of our history and forming the style of our national thought. To take them away would now be a baneful disorganizing of the national mind.[43]

By the end of the nineteenth century, romantic stories of the nation's founding had been fine-tuned and firmly implanted in the mainstream of American culture. Revolutionary mythologies, including but not limited to those featured in this book, helped create and support jingoistic attitudes. These stories portrayed war as a noble experience, and they praised Revolutionary soldiers as particularly valorous. Patrick Henry's "Liberty or Death" speech, conjured long after his death, made young Americans feel good about fighting for their country. Patriots had looked into the whites of the eyes of their foreign foe. They had suffered patiently at Valley Forge, remaining true to their cause and their leader. Tales of the Revolutionary War, fashioned to reflect military values, taught Americans the logic and language of expansive nationalism: you fight a war, win it, and thereby become more powerful.

While these stories touted militarism, they failed to acknowledge the revolutionary nature of the American Revolution. In fact, revolutions are the work of groups, not individuals, and ours was no exception. The dominant mode of the original patriots was collaborative action, and the ultimate end was to place government in the hands of a collectivity, the "body of the people." Yet the tales that emerged, with the notable exception of the Boston Tea Party, ignored that. Instead, they romanticized deeds of individual achievement. The story of the Massachusetts Revolution of 1774, in which ordinary farmers overthrew British rule, was replaced by the tale of Paul Revere, the lone rider who rousted farmers from their slumber. Rather than revealing the intricate web of patriotic resistance organizations in Boston, the tales showcased a charismatic mastermind, Sam Adams. Instead of unveiling the rash of state and local declarations of independence, which demonstrated a revolutionary groundswell, they bestowed all attention on Thomas Jefferson, the creative genius who allegedly conjured the ideas for the nation's sacred scripture "from deep within himself."

We owe our very existence, the stories said, to the wisdom and courage of a small cadre of leaders who worked closely together, as a separate and distinct group, to determine the fate of the nation. In fact, these men did not act in a vacuum. Outside official chambers, a host of local activists, working in committees, tended unrelentingly to the business of the new nation. Meanwhile, poor men and boys of the Continental Army, together with countless local militiamen, repulsed British advances. The so-called founders *reflected* the fervor of the people—they did not create it. By ignoring or downplaying the widespread participation of ordinary people in Revolutionary affairs, stories that claimed to be patriotic subverted the very essence of popular sovereignty, the explicit reason for the nation's existence. Four score and seven years after the United States declared its independence, Abraham Lincoln gave poetic voice to this central theme by boasting that our original patriots had established a nation "of the people, by the people, and for the people." When we say our nation was created by a mere handful of Founding Fathers, we lose a key component of this democratic trinity.

CONCLUSION: WHY WE TELL TALL TALES

Despite advances in historical scholarship that show them to be mistaken or misleading, the fanciful tales featured in this book continue to anchor the telling of the American Revolution. They endure because they engage and excite and please, and a story, if it pleases, will generally trump hard evidence.

History, of course, can never adequately re-create the past. Back then, people didn't know how things would turn out; now, we do. Try as we might, we will always be reading history backward. This in itself places an impenetrable barrier between past and present. There are other barriers as well, differences in culture and circumstance. Added to all this, the sheer multiplicity of events, always chaotic, belies our attempts at neat packaging.

Inevitably befuddled, we unravel the tangle of the past by substituting a series of comprehensible stories that draw on important elements of traditional Western storytelling. The past has no beginning, middle, and end, but our stories must. The past has multifarious players, more than we can possibly meet, so we make the acquaintance of just a few, giving preference to heroes and heroines who embody virtue and represent our collective ideals. Documents abound, but these atomic elements tell us little until we organize them and assign meanings. As one philosopher of history put it, the past is "immense, sublime, and gone."[1] The stories we tell of the past, on the other hand, are contained, manifest, and present. People in all cultures tell such tales. The problem lies not in the act of conjuring them, but in failing to acknowledge their purpose and limitations. In practice, they are subject to several common fallacies.

Individual agency. Assuming undue agency for one's subject is the biographer's great temptation, and the historian's as well. Samuel Adams, it is said, single-handedly steered the United States toward independence—as did John Adams, Thomas Jefferson, and Thomas Paine. Each of these allegedly indispensable protagonists, in the hands of admiring authors, not only drives the story but *becomes* the story. The committees of correspondence, by definition collective endeavors, become "Sam Adams's committees," and the Declaration of Independence "Jefferson's Declaration." The fallacy of protagonist-as-primary-agent sustains historical mythologies while relegating great numbers of people and groups to the sidelines, or simply discarding them.

Presumed consistency. In most textbooks and popular historical narratives, protagonists shape events more than events shape protagonists. For this to happen, a protagonist functions as an engine chugging through time, the track always straight. The inner Samuel Adams, hell-bent from the outset on separation from Britain, eventually achieves his goal. Any notion that his position *evolved* as he reacted to circumstances beyond his control would appear to negate the power of that engine. James Madison, so-called Father of the Constitution, envisioned that document and then made it happen; never mind that at the Constitutional Convention, the very model of a collective deliberation, Madison lost out on forty of seventy-one issues on which he took a stand, or that the Constitution he envisioned at the start—including an absolute federal veto over all state legislation—was very, very different from the one that emerged, or that by 1798 his view on federal versus state authority had turned upside down. To this day, scholars as well as laymen make free use of the term "Madisonian," as if it that denoted a consistent, unwavering philosophy that placed its indelible stamp on how things turned out.[2]

Faulty representation. Heroes and heroines, selected for their uncommon features, are marshaled forth to represent all the people, including those who are common, not special. History is supposedly revealed through stories of protagonists who are "giants" or "larger than life." Their exploits are "amazing" or "unbelievable." "Never before or since," we like to say, "has there been such a man or woman"—and yet, strangely, we present these exceptional people as "representative" of historical movements. George Washington, Benjamin Franklin, Thomas Jefferson—we speak of these illustrious individuals as *the* Revolutionaries, and we use them as stand-ins for all the *other* Revolutionaries, although we have just proclaimed they are not like the rest.

Iconic events as protagonist-agents. Special events subsume other events, in the same way that heroes and heroines subsume other characters. Three such events drive and define the traditional story of the American Revolution, but each in fact hides critical features:

- The British never would have marched on Lexington and Concord unless the people of Massachusetts had shed British rule the previous year, yet the iconic tale of "the shot heard 'round the world," which allegedly initiated the American Revolution, effectively conceals the revolution that happened before it.[3]

- Congress voted for independence on July 2, 1776, only because a groundswell of public pressure, including instructions by state and local bodies to declare independence, had made that move viable—yet the later event has subsumed the others, reversing cause and effect. "The Declaration launched a period of energetic political innovation, as one colony after another reconstituted itself as a 'state,' " one recent college text states emphatically. In fact, Congress had requested the emerging states to form new governments back on May 10, almost two months earlier, and by July 2 several states were in the process of doing so. These were key steps in making the congressional declaration possible, not consequences of it.[4]

- The Battle of Yorktown proved to be pivotal, but only because other world powers, acting in various theaters across the globe, circumscribed Britain's options in response to this particular military defeat. When we isolate the Battle of Yorktown and treat it as the definitive end of the war, we lose the global context, critical to all international events. We do not see the elephant but only the tip of his tail.

All events, iconic and otherwise, exist in webs, not in isolation. Stories that ignore such webs not only misrepresent history but blind us to the fluid and interconnected dynamics of how human societies function.

LANGUAGE THAT DECEIVES

The construction of our sentences, like the structure of our stories, leads to individualistic misinterpretations of history. Sentences written in the active voice require subjects, just as stories require protagonists. The problem is, we don't always know the exact identities of the subjects of our sentences. Composites suffice only for a while. So when we tire of saying "Republicans opposed" or "rebels demanded," we turn to a slightly more personalized alternative: "Republican spokesmen opposed" or "rebel leaders demanded." These subjects are still generic, but at least they refer to individual people rather than to abstract groups. We like that, and we revert to it unconsciously. It's a default mode in the writing of history. "Rebels" and "rebel leaders" are used interchangeably, as if there were no difference between them.

But the casual use of the term "leaders" has a perilous side effect:

if some are leaders, all the others become followers. A few important individuals make things happen, the rest only tag along; a few write the scripts, the rest just deliver their lines. Adopting and extending this default grammar, writers cast about for "leaders" to serve as subjects for their sentences and protagonists for their narratives. James Otis "persuaded" the Massachusetts Assembly to call for a Stamp Act Congress, a college text states. Taken as face value, this means that Otis actually convinced others to change their positions and vote his way, but we have no evidence this happened. Instead, "persuaded" is a linguistic convenience, linking Otis to the assembly's action in some generic way and claiming him as an individual agent. James Madison "devised the Virginia Plan, and he did most of the drafting of the Constitution itself," the same text states. Even though the first statement is doubtful and the second demonstrably incorrect, this author believes that drafting the Constitution needs a protagonist and assigns the role to Madison, "generally known as the father" of that document.[5]

If a leader is not immediately evident, authors often invent one. All American history texts, for instance, discuss a farmers' uprising they call "Shays' Rebellion," which occurred in the wake of the American Revolution. Readers naturally assume that this rebellion was led by a charismatic individual named Shays, who held great sway with his followers. It wasn't that way. Daniel Shays, an unassuming character, filled an important role because of his military experience, but he in no way owned or even led the movement—in fact, he was not even active during the early stages of the uprising.[6] The appellation "Shays' Rebellion," first used by authorities who opposed the uprising, belittles the significance of the insurgents themselves, steering us away from the people's real grievances. One recent text says that Shays "issued a set of demands" while the rebellious farmers "rallied behind" him, becoming "Shaysites" as if they belonged to some cult. Another states that "Daniel Shays organized protestors," whom it characterizes as "Shays' supporters."[7] The rebels never thought of themselves as "Shaysites" or "Shays' supporters." They called themselves "Regulators" because they hoped to regulate the functioning of government.[8]

In this manner, storytellers turn history on its head. Since each sentence needs a subject and each tale a protagonist, groups are signified and subsumed by their alleged leaders. The famous founders, we are told, *made* the American Revolution. They dreamed up the ideas, spoke and wrote incessantly, and finally convinced others to follow their lead. In this trickle-down telling of history, as in trickle-down economics, the concerns of the people at the bottom are addressed by mysterious processes not often delineated. Supposedly, hundreds of thousands of Revolutionaries risked their lives on behalf of independence simply because they had been told by others to do so. They were not agents acting on their own behalf.

When this process is spelled out, it fails to convince. One proposed model breaks down all of humanity into six groups: Great Thinkers, Great Disciples, Great Disseminators, Lesser Disseminators, Participating Citizens, and the Politically Inert. Ideas filter down from one group to the next until they finally reach the bottom. In the American Revolution, the Great Thinkers were the philosophers of the European Enlightenment; Great Disciples included men like Thomas Jefferson, Benjamin Franklin, and Thomas Paine; Great Disseminators were regional political organizers like Samuel Adams and Patrick Henry; Lesser Disseminators were the leaders of politically active groups such as the local committees of correspondence; Participating Citizens were the members of those groups; the Politically Inert were all the people who started out as neither patriots nor Tories. Ideas, like military orders, supposedly drifted down this chain of command until enough people were willing to engage in revolution.[9] There is no provision here for any movement *up* the ladder. The people themselves, in whose name the Revolution was fought, were no more than passive receptors. Dissemination theories such as this, when laid bare, appear ludicrous, but they buttress much of the prose in textbooks and popular histories. A few gifted historical actors convince others what to do, and that is how history happens.

THROUGH THE EYES OF A CHILD

The simplistic model—a few individuals make history happen—works well with children. Fortuitously, that is the primary audience for stories of our nation's founding. What most Americans know about the Revolution they learned in the fifth grade, for at no later time do students undertake an in-depth study of the subject in the majority of public schools. Because most middle-school and high-school curricula focus on more recent events, they require no more than a cursory review of Revolutionary history.

This quirk in curriculum is fortunate in some ways, unfortunate in others. On the one hand, fifth graders are at the peak of their learning curve. Ten-year-olds read and converse intelligently, they are delightfully curious, and they are not yet distracted by the trials of pubescence. On the other hand, these young students have little worldly knowledge. Few can compare the American Revolution, the French Revolution, and the Russian Revolution or understand the complex struggles for power that dominate political affairs, past and present.

So how do we purvey the American Revolution to these ten-year-olds? We enlist the basic elements of successful storytelling: heroes and heroines, with an emphasis on wise men; battles that pit good against evil and David against Goliath; and, of course, happy endings.

History aimed at children is dominated by the study of particular men and women who are portrayed as "special." Although fifth-grade texts are structured around a narrative thread, their abundant minibiographies leave readers with a sense that history is some sort of amalgamation of the lives of memorable personalities. Over the past few decades, the choice of protagonists has changed: Abigail Adams is sometimes featured over her husband, John, and a Latino, Bernardo de Gálvez, now appears in nearly every text for young people. But the Founding Fathers, very wise men, still occupy a prime position. Schoolchildren learn that their nation, at its birth, was in trustworthy hands.

Battles are the most concrete manifestations of historical conflict.

Children, with their sense of well-defined "teams" and of definite winners and losers, intuitively understand them. The struggles between soldiers and civilians that continued throughout the war and daily shaped it, on the other hand, would be more difficult to grasp. Battles of the Revolutionary War have a particular appeal to children. Clever and dedicated to their cause, ragtag Americans, acting the role of David, outwitted and outfought Goliath, overconfident British soldiers dressed up in fancy red uniforms. "Discover how a few brave patriots battled a great empire," beckons the cover copy of *American Revolution*, published by DK Eyewitness Books "in association with the Smithsonian Institution," with an age range advertised as "8 and up."[10] Resolution is important for children, and this military conflict had the best ending possible: the birth of an independent nation, *our* nation.

Through the study of history, young people learn about political processes, present as well as past. In California, students study state history in fourth grade, early United States history in fifth grade, ancient world history in sixth grade, not-so-ancient world history in seventh grade, and nineteenth-century United States history in eighth grade. Ninth grade is open, although many students opt to take geography or other electives. Sophomores study modern world history and juniors, modern United States history. Most states follow a similar pattern. By the time seniors get around to studying politics, government, and economics, they have been reading and hearing stories for seven years about individuals and social groups who struggled for power in the past.

Along the way, students internalize a "grammar" they will use to decipher political events. All too often that grammar is individualistic, linear, and devoid of context. The History and Social Science Standards for the California Public Schools, for example, require teachers to "describe the views, lives, and impact of key individuals (e.g., King George III, Patrick Henry, Thomas Jefferson, George Washington, Benjamin Franklin, John Adams)."[11] This directive assumes that individuals influence events but ignores a reverse truth, that events influence individuals. Such a skewed perspective hides real-life political processes. Students do not address hard but instructive questions embedded in authentic historical investigation: How do certain individuals come to represent groups and constituencies? How do some people gain access to positions of power, thereby determining the fates of others? How do people come together to resist domination and stand up for their own interests?

History, if rendered responsibly, can direct and instruct students toward such high-level inquiry, but at what point can we start young people along that path? Even ten-year-olds can understand that during Revolutionary times, leaders did not act alone but depended on local committees and congresses. Samuel Adams and other Boston activists organized a local committee of correspondence. This group reached out to towns in the hinterlands, which then formed similar committees that communicated with each other, as the name suggests. They strategized. They organized. Even George Washington, the commander in chief, consulted his Council of War on significant military maneuvers. This shift in focus promotes a civics lesson appropriate for young children. It urges collective, spirited participation by the many, not dominance by the few. It demonstrates that leaders lead best when acting in concert with others. Why *not* teach such things early on, when students are beginning to look at the wider world and imagining ways to make it better? And why not confirm the original meaning of American patriotism: government must be based on the will of the people?

Studying the revolutionary behavior of common citizens would also reveal some of the dangers inherent in majoritarian democracy, particularly the suppression of Tory dissent or the use of jingoism to mobilize support. Here is "bullying" on a grand scale. The forthright examination of human suffering in the American Revolution can counterbalance the unquestioning celebration of war. As students follow the conflicts in the 1760s and early 1770s, they can see how imperial suppression, intended to break the resistance, only increased it, and how peaceful resolutions broke down. These sorts of lessons reveal rather than conceal the dynamics of political struggle, both past and present. Individual protagonists can and will feed into this drama within the curricula, but they should not define it. Washington needed his soldiers as much as they needed him. Ten-year-olds or high-school students can readily comprehend that history—everything that happened in the past—is a team sport. No single player determines the outcome.

HISTORY AND HERITAGE

To tell historical tales uncritically, believing them to be literal representations of real events, is like treating paintings on a museum wall as photographic reproductions. Unless we acknowledge the hand and mind of the artist, we mistake fiction for fact. This can be dangerously self-serving. By choosing stories specifically tailored to make us feel good, we turn people who once lived and breathed, with their richly textured lives, into stick figures. We pay a high price for the illusion that we can bring the past to bay.

Sometimes, this illusion is put to political uses. The hero-worship that passed as history in the early nineteenth century served the interests of a developing nationalism. The telling of history was itself of historical import: shared stories of the Revolution helped people feel like "Americans." Today, the power of illusion is even greater. Storytelling has become a science, not just an art. Audacious professional marketers use sophisticated techniques to manipulate public opinion. The overarching reach of broadcast and electronic media makes these strategies particularly insidious. Contrived stories, self-serving interpretations of public events, are not just incidental—they are anathema to the functioning of democracy, which depends on the free flow of accurate and often complex information.

Although we must always remain vigilant, some stories are more suspect than others. As a rule of thumb, the better the story, the more we should be on guard. Certain tales play so well they demand to be told, regardless of the evidence. So it is with traditional stories about the American Revolution, which appear immune to critical complaint. Some are contradicted by hard evidence: Paul Revere did not wait to see whether one signal lantern or two would flash from Old North Church. The stirring call to arms that ended with the phase "Give me liberty, or give me death," although inspired by Patrick Henry, was conjured decades later by someone else. Thomas Jefferson did not gather the ideas for the Declaration of Independence "from deep inside himself." Other stories fall short because they lack perspective and mask key events. Common farmers in Massachusetts had already shed British rule before Lexington and Concord. The war did not screech to a halt at Yorktown. David did not lick Goliath all on his own. And yet, whether true or not, traditional tales such as these have been certified by ceaseless repetition. Collectively, the litany is our identifying American story, our *heritage*.

But heritage is not history, even if they sometimes overlap. Heritage places the past in service of the present; history receives the past on its own terms. History looks beyond traditional stories and seeks only primary evidence, contemporaneous to the times being studied. Heritage embraces stories of later derivation because others have done so before us. Such tales, even if only imagined, provide continuity to our national narrative, one generation to the next.

Heritage has critical importance and is essential to human society. Others before us have shaped the world we live in now, and we must appreciate that as we take our own place in the grand sweep of events. In many ways we belong to the past, to our heritage—yet the past does not belong to us. We don't own it. To own something is to control it, and we cannot control what actually happened in a time gone by. Nor should we pretend that we can by substituting an imaginary past that is more to our liking.

Although facts sometimes challenge heritage, evidence-based history is not for that reason unpatriotic. The Revolutionary Generation did in fact create a nation. To discover just how people pulled that off, we do best to consult original, contemporaneous sources and build our narrative upon these alone. The highest honor we can give to

Revolutionary Americans is to try to understand them on *their* terms, without undue intervention from *other* Americans who lived between then and now. This requires constant attention. Unless we examine the distortions passed on by previous renderings of our national narrative, we will not discern how these might be clouding our vision today. Those who do not learn from the mistakes of history-telling are doomed to repeat them.

AFTERWORD: WHICH MYTHS PERSIST—AND WHY

Ten years have passed since the initial publication of *Founding Myths*. Much can change in a decade—or not. Today, in current renditions of our national narrative, does Paul Revere still wake up those sleepy-eyed farmers? Does Molly Pitcher bring water to thirsty soldiers and fire the cannon of her fallen "gallant"? Does Thomas Jefferson find the ideas for the Declaration of Independence "from deep within himself?" Have such tales remained fixed in our historical imaginations, or do we now pay closer attention to the historical record?

Story by story, the answers are mixed. By comparing school textbooks published from 2001 to 2004 with those published from 2011 to 2014, we can get some sense of which tales show the greatest resiliency and which are more malleable. These answers, in turn, can provide insights into why some mythologies stand firm in the face of countervailing evidence while others cede at least some ground.

Let's start with the tales that show some indication of weakening. Today, more attention is being paid to enslaved people who sought their freedom by fighting with the British, undermining the myth of the patriotic slave in the Deep South. So too with Native Americans: nearly all texts now mention that more sided with the British than with the Americans, and often they explain why. Women are presented front and center more than ever. One college textbook, for instance, features letters written by five women during the Revolutionary War but not a single letter from a male Revolutionary soldier.[1] Louisiana governor Bernardo de Gálvez, meanwhile, is a fixture in nearly every text, giving the narrative a Latino protagonist.

These changes are not just happening of their own accord; constituencies are pushing for them. Concerted action on the part of specific communities is the clearest path to changing the historical narrative in our textbooks. Conversely, mythologies that remain unchallenged by any particular constituency are less likely to give way. Even if backcountry patriots in the South were as brutal as Tories, no current backcountry Tory constituency demands equal treatment.

Without a constituency, can evidence alone provide the thrust for change? The short answer: yes, but only occasionally, and even then the myth will often find ways to adapt and survive.

Take Molly Pitcher, a clear fabrication. Word is getting out, and our favorite Revolutionary heroine appears less often than she did a decade past—but she does surface still. Some texts, unaware of research that lays the myth bare, carelessly repeat the tale verbatim, while several others, knowing better, have devised ways to feature Molly nonetheless. With a wink and a nod, they offer a sweeping qualifier—"reportedly," "allegedly," "according to legend," "according to tradition," or "the story goes," open invitations to repeat the tale without making any claim to authenticity. This classic textbook hedge allows the "legend" or "tradition" to continue intact, immunized against any and all evidence to the contrary. Never do we see the more honest formulation of what these texts are actually saying: "There is no historical documentation for this story, but we are passing it on nonetheless because it's just so good and it meets our need to feature Revolutionary women."

Another strategy is to back off just an inch or two, then continue as before. Paul Revere was not the only rider, they say, but was joined by William Dawes and perhaps Samuel Prescott. Instead of a single rider waking the slumbering farmers, we now have two or three. There is still no hint, however, of the elaborate intelligence network that was set into motion that night, or of the seven months of preparation for just such an event, or of the revolution throughout the countryside that had already occurred. Revere rides on. No textbook would dare omit him.[2]

Similarly, most school texts now acknowledge that Thomas Jefferson, when drafting the Declaration of Independence, worked with a five-man committee. Even so, Jefferson directs the drama: "In the heat of the Philadelphia summer, Jefferson struggled to find the words that would convince Americans and the world of the rightness of independence. The result was masterful. John Adams and Benjamin Franklin, who were also on the committee, suggested only minor changes."[3] By this account, Americans still need convincing and Jefferson is a master at persuasion. If Revere now has two sidekicks, Jefferson has four.

Many college texts, on the other hand, acknowledge the state and local declarations in favor of independence during the spring of 1776, responding to recent research. According to one, Jefferson "drew on language used in the dozens of local 'declarations' written earlier by town meetings, county officials, and colonial assemblies. The Virginia Declaration of Rights drafted by Mason in May 1776, for example, claimed that 'all men are equally free and independent, and have certain inherent natural Rights.' "[4] And another: "Many years later Jefferson insisted that there was nothing original about the Declaration of Independence, and he was not entirely wrong. The long list of accusations against King George, which formed the bulk of the Declaration, contained little that was new, and even some of the stirring words in the preamble had been used by the radicals time and again."[5]

While new evidence has broadened the Jefferson story at the college level, not one of the textbooks I surveyed mentions that the town meeting in Worcester, Massachusetts, pushed for independence a full twenty-one months before the congressional Declaration and eighteen months before the rash of declarations starting in April 1776.[6] Why not? Unlike the ninety declarations uncovered by Pauline Maier (see chapter 6), this one is an outlier. It precedes by far the iconic Declaration and does not fit neatly within the traditional storyline. Although the evidence is conclusive, contained within the Worcester Town Records housed in the basement of Worcester City Hall, evidence and the historical significance of events do not guarantee that those events will make their way into a textbook.[7] Even if a constituency emerges to push Worcester's declaration into the story, obstacles will emerge. This document, along with the 1774 revolution that drove it forward, turn the story around, making any rewrite arduous.

If evidence can be inconvenient, the absence of evidence can be very convenient. A case in point: the "Liberty or Death" speech, drafted by William Wirt but attributed to Patrick Henry. Those words have become an irresistible motto that will not be readily relinquished. To admit that William Wirt conjured his hero's speech forty-two years later would be to concede too much. Henry himself has to have delivered that memorable pronouncement or it is not worth celebrating. A too-much-to-lose mythology, Henry's authorship remains impervious to deconstruction or dismissal.

Two other myths have proved surprisingly durable. One features Samuel Adams as the flaming rabble-rouser, and the other the final battle at Yorktown, in which David finally bests Goliath. For very distinct reasons, I expected that each of these would give some ground, but their grip on our national narrative remains as strong or stronger than ever.

The increased attention to popular protest in the Revolutionary days, I conjectured, would lead people to question the top-down dynamic that underlies the Sam Adams mythology: Adams calls the shots and the people do his bidding. Instead, while devoting more attention to popular movements, authors feel an even greater need for decisive protagonists to drive such stories. Waving the banner of a popular movement, Adams consequently leads the pack *more* often rather than less so. Only a handful of upper-level texts treat him as more than a caricature "firebrand."

I also conjectured that the scholarly community's focus on the "Atlantic World" during Colonial and Revolutionary times would raise awareness of Britain's global perspective following the defeat at Yorktown. Just a short passage could summarize Britain's options at the time: with the empire threatened on many fronts, a strategic retreat from America appeared the best way to preserve what was left. Very few texts follow this route, however (see chapter 13). On one level, this can be explained by the continued demand for tidy endings; a major battlefield loss seems a natural conclusion to a war. But that goes only so far. Yorktown was indeed a pivotal event, but why did this particular defeat lead to an end of the war while the surrender at Saratoga, of similar proportions, did not? The answer to that question would require some attention to Britain's global situation—yet to feature the global context would take America out of the driver's seat, so the question is not asked. Keeping the United States in command of its destiny is an intrinsic component of the traditional narrative. We must remain the protagonists of our own story.

SAME AS IT EVER WAS: IMPEDIMENTS TO CHANGE

Constituent pressure is the surest path to a reconsideration of mythologies, but *who*, exactly, would want to nudge our heroes, heroines, and iconic events aside—and why? In the words of a critic who objected to my deconstruction of the Molly Pitcher tale: "Myth or not, it's still a nice story which does no harm to anyone. Why not just let it alone?" Here is the default rationale for orthodoxy. Traditional stories are, in fact, our tradition. Having invested in them for all these years, we don't *want* them to change. Familiar and comfortable stories have always held sway, yet today the forces of inertia are buttressed by the realities of twenty-first-century media and the move toward uniform standards in education.

Textbooks and tests. Elementary, middle-school, and secondary texts thrive on tradition. Because these texts require approval by public bodies, publishers must satisfy a broad cross section of citizens, including many who cling fast to the stories they already know. Authors are selected more for their writing talents than for their familiarity with the latest historical research, and editors and publishers have their say as well. Textbook professionals, not people with expertise in the field, typically design timelines and review questions. Such aids are geared to standardized tests, and standard, in history, translates to traditional. For more than a decade we have witnessed a national crusade for excellence in education, but so-called "excellence" is based on historical narratives all Americans should presumably know. Testing reflects this:

- "Who exhorted the Boston crowd?" Better say Sam Adams, not Ebenezer MacIntosh, Thomas Young, or William Molineux, actual street leaders at the time.

- "Who wrote the 'Give me liberty, or give me death' speech?" William Wirt will not be listed as a multiple-choice option, so you might as well go with Patrick Henry, even if you suspect otherwise.

- "Where and when did the Revolution start?" Lexington and Concord on April 19, 1775—no matter that Massachusetts patriots had already overthrown British rule the previous year.

- "What was the coldest, hardest winter of the Revolutionary War?" If you choose Morristown in 1779–1780 you will be marked wrong, although of course you are correct.

Some authors and editors might question the narrative they are expected to produce, but they hesitate to put themselves too far ahead of the curve. Caught in the crossfire between story and evidence, they split the difference to satisfy both masters. "Reportedly," "according to tradition," and related terms are the most obvious hedges, but there are others, chief among them the passive voice: "became known as," "was heard to say," and so on. Texts written for older students also evidence such practices, although perhaps not as often. One college text, excellent in many other ways, describes the crowd actions in Boston in 1768: " 'Let us take up arms immediately and be free,' Sam Adams was heard to say; 'We shall have thirty thousand men to join us from the Country.' "[8] The key question masked by "was heard to say" is: by whom? In this case, by Richard Sylvester, trying unsuccessfully to frame Samuel Adams.

Publishers, for commercial reasons, release new editions every few years, but their revisions are generally minimal. One popular title—*American Pageant*, first published in 1956—is now in its fifteenth edition. For the first time, the original author, Thomas A. Bailey, no longer appears on the cover or the title page, but the overwhelming majority of the text for the Revolutionary Era is reprinted verbatim, just as he wrote it in the middle of the past century. In three chapters covering the Revolutionary period, the only difference in the central narrative between the fourteenth edition, published in 2010, and the fifteenth, in 2014, is the addition of one short paragraph (fifty-six words) on "women's role in the Revolutionary War."[9]

Internet. Increasingly, the Internet is not merely supplementing textbooks but replacing them. In theory, the Net's immediacy would encourage newer, more accurate renditions of history. In practice, repetition is rewarded and old stories frequently prevail. If you search for "Molly Pitcher," some half-million results appear. Most people will select from the first page, where the myth is immediately confirmed. The Internet's Free Dictionary states flatly: "Noun 1. Molly Pitcher—heroine of the American Revolution who carried water to soldiers during the Battle of Monmouth Court House and took over her husband's gun when he was overcome by heat (1754–1832)." This is followed by a link to Mary Ludwig Hays McCauley.[10] Wikipedia backs off just a tad—"Molly Pitcher (1754–1832) was a nickname given to a woman said to have fought in the American Battle of Monmouth, who is generally believed to have been Mary Ludwig Hays McCauley"—but it includes two mid-nineteenth-century graphic illustrations, a photograph of "Molly Pitcher Spring," and several citations to children's biographies that affirm and appear to validate the standard story.[11] Scrolling down a Google search, and on the next few lists of ten, we find several commercial establishments (mostly inns and alehouses), the Molly Pitcher rest stop on the New Jersey Turnpike, a horse race, and some grade-school student papers. Not until far down, after several groups of ten, do we begin to see an occasional article that discusses the myth and how it came to be.

The Internet lends its digital wealth to anybody with a point to prove and the time to mine for supporting material, to be manipulated as one pleases. All sources are treated as equal, whether they are contemporary documentation or the distant memories of aging men and women, often influenced by intervening events. In this manner, statements by the founders rendered in the first quarter of the nineteenth century, after several mythologies had already taken root, are treated as trustworthy, even if contradicted by hard contemporaneous evidence.[12] The Internet didn't initiate this flimsy method of historical research, but by making the practice so much easier, it facilitates the spread of the misinterpretations the mythologies produce.

If the Internet is an agent of orthodoxy, it is also an agent of change. A generation ago, scholars needed a major research library to access published historical records that are now available electronically. The Internet has expanded the field of "*public*ation"—that is, making source materials available to the public. Not so long ago, documents needed to be set in print in order to be read outside their respective repositories; in the mid–twentieth century they could be photographically reproduced and shipped to research institutions; now, they can be scanned and accessed from any computer across the globe. This greatly facilitates the research necessary to correct historical mistakes.[13]

On the one hand, easy access to information has fueled history's many partisans. On the other hand, it has enabled amateurs to become true scholars. Some of the best historical research in Revolutionary Era history is now conducted by people with no university affiliation. This has taken popular narratives of the Revolution to a new level, more firmly rooted in contemporaneous documentation.[14]

NEW DIRECTIONS?

Back to the source. In educational circles, the Internet is beginning to transform the very nature of textbooks. Previously, school texts provided a running narrative, to be swallowed whole by their readers; now, that narrative is often accompanied by links to digital documentation. Because texts are reissued every few years, they are synchronizing swiftly with electronic media. Documents are moving front and center, with students themselves helping to create the narratives.

The new Common Core State Standards, adopted by forty-five states at this writing (although opponents in a few states are trying to stop their implementation), are overwhelmingly text centered. For a generation, innovative history educators have been featuring what they call "DBQs," or document-based questions, to increase critical thinking and interpretive skills, and Common Core is establishing this approach as the professional standard. Fifth graders are being asked to "analyze multiple accounts of the same event or topic, noting important similarities and differences in the point of view they represent." Middle-school students are expected to "identify aspects of a text that reveal an author's point of view or purpose (e.g., loaded language, inclusion or avoidance of particular facts)." Finally, juniors and seniors in high school must learn to "evaluate authors' differing points of view on the same historical event or issue by assessing the authors' claims, reasoning, and evidence" and "corroborating or challenging them with other information."[15]

Such skills are critical to establishing historical literacy, yet the rise of document-based learning does raise questions. How are documents selected? Are narrative accounts in textbooks subject to examination? How deeply do the DBQs penetrate? And perhaps most critically, how is the context of each document presented? Without context, we cannot understand texts, but without texts, we will never be able to establish context. This conundrum, fundamental to the practice of history, comes to the fore with document-based learning.[16]

Examining texts without context can perpetuate mythologies. For example: Revolutionary Era curricula based on the Common Core will likely feature the Declaration of Independence. Students, in examining that document, will naturally highlight Jefferson's "all men are created equal," not realizing its connection with Mason's "all men are born equally free and independent." They will also note the dramatic conclusion, in which congressional delegates pledged "our lives, our fortunes, and our sacred honor," courageously placing themselves on the line. Without context, they will not see this as standard practice for the genre, based on similar pledges from hundreds of lesser-known patriots who ascribed to earlier declarations in favor of independence. Consequently, the famous document presented for examination, and by association its primary author, will carry the full load of the narrative. Careful examination of this one iconic text, in isolation, masks as much as it reveals.

Students might also be asked to examine the famous "liberty or death" speech, attributed to Patrick Henry. As they do, they will certainly note the noble sentiments, including the argument that oppressed patriots had exhausted all available options except war. They will never dream to ask what the author of this speech avoided, arguments dear to the heart of white Virginians at the time: British officials are prepared to free your slaves and set "savages" against you. Nor will they ask questions critical to the understanding of the words they are reading: Who was the real author, and when was this speech actually written? What emerges from their study is not a fair representation of military mobilization in the South in March 1775.

DBQs can even create mythologies. In 2005, the AP United States

History test presented a historical image in which a woman wears a tricorn hat, grasps a powder horn in one hand, and supports a musket with the other; in the distance, a flag waves from a fort. No context is provided except for the title: "Woodcut of Patriot woman, Marblehead, MA, 1779." Students were expected to use this image when constructing an essay on the question "To what extent did the American Revolution fundamentally change American society?" The official "Scoring Guidelines" explained the "document inferences" students were expected to draw from this single image:

- Women participated in the American Revolution.

- Women's roles were expanded during the American Revolution; women performed tasks previously done solely by men.

- Hints at the potential for revolutionary change in women's roles.[17]

Yet women did not participate in the American Revolution in the manner depicted, bearing muskets for military reasons. The war did expand their roles and their worries, but not in that direction. Indeed, the original publication of the image accompanies an explicitly antiwar poem, "A New Touch on the Times, well adapted to the distressing situation of every Seaport Town." With men "gone the ocean wide" (Marblehead was a fishing center), women were left on their own to face wartime shortages and exorbitant prices: "It's hard and cruel times to live, / Takes thirty dollars to buy a sieve." How did "every Seaport Town" fall upon such hard times, the author asks?

> For sin is the cause of this,
> We must not take it then amiss,
> Wan't it for our polluted tongues,
> This cruel war would ne'er begun.

We should hear no fife and drum,
Nor training bands would never come:
Should we go on our sinful course,
Times will grow on us worse and worse.

Then gracious GOD now cause to cease,
This bloody war and give us peace!
And down our streets send plenty then
With hearts as one we'll say Amen![18]

Not only did the AP program present the Marblehead woodcut out of context, but it also erred by assuming the image was descriptive rather than normative. This is a common mistake: images and words can have many purposes, and reporting is only one. They can praise or condemn, ridicule or scold, and often they are meant to cajole. Not understanding the genre or the intent, we cannot draw inferences from an isolated document—yet that is exactly what the AP asked students to do. Most likely, test takers followed the errant path the test makers cleared for them and assumed the image was presented as a true representation of real women. Presented with evidence this scanty, students are not merely encouraged but forced to jump to conclusions. They have no choice but to practice hasty history.

The example might be extreme, but the problem is common. Since teaching to the test requires a fast-moving curriculum, document-based lessons must be brief. On any given subject, students are presented with minimal evidence and little context with which to evaluate that evidence. On the basis of this small sample they are asked to make snap judgments, undermining the very intent of document-based learning.

Thinking historically. This is not to say we shouldn't teach with documents. To reveal mythologies for what they are, we do need to start by evaluating sources. The Common Core Standards are on to this, and DBQs can be of great service. But *how* do we evaluate sources?[19] And how do we weave these strands of evidence into historical narratives? We need standards for our standards.

Mythologies can thrive only when we don't think clearly about how we know—and don't know—the past. We can dispel myths one by one, as I do in this book, but we can also create a climate of learning hostile to the development of attractive but misleading narratives. We can learn the art of "historical thinking," as educators and historians now say. But to practice and teach historical thinking—and that is the aim of the Common Core—we must first accept our limits and proceed from there. By approaching the past cautiously rather than hastily, we can attack mythologies at the roots.

Learning to think historically, in my mind, involves five basic tenets that build on each other:

(1) *We don't know the past.* As historian Richard White puts it, "Any good history begins in strangeness. The past should not be comfortable. The past should not be a familiar echo of the present." Because of differences in time, circumstance, and perspective, we can never create a one-to-one correspondence between the actual past and the narrative we use to represent it.

This is not a difficult lesson to convey. In fifth grade, or even earlier, a teacher can arrange to video some event the students all witness or experience. A month or two later, students are asked very specific questions about this event, such as how many people there were, the exact time, and so on. Responses will likely differ, but which of the answers are wrong and which correct? The video is played back, a contemporaneous answer book, and students learn that memory can play tricks with history. Then comes the kicker. A month or two after another shared event, students are asked to respond once again to specific questions. This time, though, there is no video to determine who is correct. What to do now? What sorts of contemporaneous documents might we look to for answers? Did anybody keep a journal at that moment? Interview participants? Issue reports at the time? Welcome to the practice of history.

(2) *While no constructed narrative can claim to be "true," some are clearly better than others.* We do have standards: all claims to historical authenticity must conform to the available evidence from the times. We observe the past through spotty remnants. While these will never tell the whole story, they can shape its parameters.

Again, this is easily taught even at the elementary level. Lay out some facts, then weave two or more narratives around those facts. To make one story interesting, bend a fact or two. Weave another narrative, perhaps more mundane, that conforms to all the facts presented. Then weave a third story, from a slightly different perspective, that also conforms to the facts. Students will see that one story is demonstrably wrong, even if they can't say for sure that either of the others is a true representation of what actually happened.

(3) *Things might have happened differently.* Humans are historical agents. They make decisions and take actions, not fully knowing how things would turn out. To grasp this, we need to disregard all that has occurred since and view matters in light of the circumstances at a specific point in time, using only the information available to people then as they pondered their options and tugged with each other to produce desired outcomes. Our past was their present. Before it was history it was life in the moment, one thing after the next, the future uncertain.

Simulated debates can demonstrate that historical outcomes are not fixed. People do make decisions; they act one way or another. Debating any hot topic from the past, with time and circumstance clearly established and all arguments based on later happenings strictly banned, will reveal the contingency of history.

(4) *Things didn't happen differently. They happened the way they happened.* After we come to realize that multiple options were possible, we need to go one step further and ask, "Why *wasn't* it otherwise?" If we don't pose this question, history will remain incomprehensible. The political processes that steered history on the course it took need to be viewed carefully and in sequence. History happened *when* it happened. We need to see how decisions made and actions taken, day by day, influenced subsequent events, leading to new sets of contingencies and opening some options while closing others. We watch history unfold, not in real time but as closely to it as we can.

Here, unfortunately, there are no quick and easy methods. Teachers and students, authors and readers have no choice but to engage each subject on its own terms. Here is the daily grind of history, and it requires scrutiny and patience. Since sequencing is key, all events must be viewed strictly in the context of when they happened. If we try to short-circuit time to prove some point, we will likely get the story wrong.

(5) *Historical inquiry never ceases.* New evidence, or new perspectives on old evidence, can produce new insights and new conclusions. Part and parcel of every document-based lesson should be: "What related questions might we ask to clarify matters? What other types of sources might we seek to deepen our inquiry and/or test our hypotheses?" Historical thinking is not limited to *answering* questions; we must also learn to *ask* questions that might reveal what has been hidden.

Following this path, and asking questions few have thought to pose, mythologies begin to wither. For example:

- During the Revolutionary Era, when and where did both political and military authority first transfer from British officials to colonials? This is a logical question to ask for any revolution, but it is not often posed for this one. If it were, those sleepy-eyed farmers whom Paul Revere allegedly awoke would be restored to their place in history.

- In 1777, Britain lost a force of some eight thousand in its failed Hudson River expedition. Four years later it lost a similar number at Yorktown, but it still had forty thousand troops in North America and the West Indies stationed in nearly impenetrable strongholds. Why did one defeat trigger the end of the war, while the other did not? Posing this question requires us to examine Britain's struggles to maintain its vast empire, challenged on many fronts by other world powers. The question itself—again quite logical but rarely asked—would lead to an expanded look at the end of the war and lay to rest the David-bested-Goliath mythology surrounding Yorktown.

- At Valley Forge soldiers suffered in the cold. Did they suffer from the cold during other winters as well? Was Valley Forge in fact the coldest? These are questions curious fifth graders might ask but textbooks don't. If they did, we would hear about Morristown as well, and soldiers who mutinied. The Valley Forge story would not disappear, but its triumphalism would be tempered. We would see that the everyday problems faced by soldiers in the Continental Army were not solved by the winter at Valley Forge.

The questions continue, or at least they should. That's the only way we can clear the air. We might not learn exactly how it was in Revolutionary times, but we can free the people who lived back then from shackles placed upon them by later generations.

ACKNOWLEDGMENTS

As usual, I thank my wife, Marie Raphael, for sharing her ideas, conjuring key phrases, and editing portions of the manuscript. Gilles Carter gave the original work a careful reading and offered many useful suggestions. Marc Favreau and Cathy Dexter gave excellent editorial assistance. Anthony Arnove, Jeff Pasley, Howard Zinn, and Hugh Van Dusen nurtured the idea in its formative stages, and Jeff Kleinman persuaded me to broaden the scope. Several scholars commented on portions of the manuscript pertaining to their fields of research: Al Young, Pauline Maier, Gary Nash, Colin Calloway, James Merrell, Andrew Burstein, and Cassandra Pybus. I hope I have done justice to their suggestions; my own views are not always the same as theirs. Others gave friendly words of advice or encouragement: Mike McDonnell, Eric Foner, David Hackett Fischer, and Gary Kornblith. David McCullough provided a key reference. Gilles Carter helped locate and identify pictures, as did Jessica Reed from the Granger Collection, while John Angus put the artwork together. I thank Jack Bareilles, Gayle Olson-Raymer, and Delores McBroome for involving teachers in the project. My research would not have been possible without assistance from Julia Graham and the Interlibrary Loan Department of Humboldt State University.

NOTES

Introduction: Inventing a Past

1. For national narratives in other nations, see Stefan Berger, ed., *Writing the Nation: A Global Perspective* (New York: Palgrave Macmillan, 2007).
2. Although Trumbull's painting actually depicts the presentation of the Declaration to Congress by a five-man committee, which occurred on June 28, the date "July 4, 1776" was added to the title when it was placed in the Capitol Rotunda, giving the impression that the scene depicted the signing of the document, which supposedly occurred on that date. For when the Declaration of Independence was actually signed, see chapter 15.
3. Thomson quotations cited in Benjamin Rush to John Adams, February 12, 1812, *The Spur of Fame: Dialogues of John Adams and Benjamin Rush, 1805–1813*, John A. Schutz and Douglas Adair, eds. (San Marino, CA: Huntington Library, 1966), 210; Benjamin Rush, *Autobiography of Benjamin Rush*, George W. Corner, ed. (Princeton: Princeton University Press, 1948), 155, cited in J. Edwin Hendricks, *Charles Thomson and the Making of a New Nation, 1729–1824* (Rutherford, NJ: Fairleigh Dickinson University Press, 1979), 189. Thomson extended his idea of voluntary censorship to others: on one occasion, he urged David Ramsay, who was writing a history of the Revolution, to delete a story that was "too low for history" and to change some phrases "which did not please" and seemed "too common to comport with the dignity of history" (Hendricks, *Charles Thomson*, 164).
4. Noah Webster, *A Collection of Essays and Fugitive Writings* (Boston: I. Thomas and E.T. Andrews, 1790; reprint edition, Scholars' Facsimiles and Reprints, 1977), 23.
5. The text that includes virtually all of the tales is Joy Hakim's *A History of US* (New York: Oxford University Press, 2003). This is no accident, for Hakim, in undertaking the task of making history fun, has chosen stories for their appeal rather than their veracity.

In her keen desire to make history inclusive, however, she has managed to tell the story of African Americans and Native Americans at the time of our nation's founding much more extensively and accurately than in most other texts.

6. I do not mean, however, to include professional scholars within the "we" who still take these tales at face value and do whatever it takes to promote a sense of belonging. Some scholars have done an excellent job in deconstructing the traditional stories, and I draw on their work liberally, but I also extend their scope by examining not just one tale at a time but the entire rubric. We are dealing here not just with the ear of the elephant or its tail, but with the creature itself. The telling of history has been seriously skewed—more so, I think, than even most scholars have imagined.
7. I use the term "patriots" with some hesitation. At the time, loyalists as well as rebels would have considered themselves "patriots," for they too thought they were defending their country. But since the term has long denoted a particular group—those who opposed British policies and eventually the British army—I cede to common usage and call the rebels "patriots."
8. Ray Raphael, *The First American Revolution: Before Lexington and Concord* (New York: The New Press, 2002), 168.

1: Paul Revere's Ride

1. David Hackett Fischer, *Paul Revere's Ride* (New York: Oxford University Press, 1994), 331. This chapter draws extensively on Fischer's research.
2. The poem is reprinted in Edmund S. Morgan, ed., *Paul Revere's Three Accounts of His Famous Ride* (Boston: Massachusetts Historical Society, 1961).
3. Copley's portrait, in the Boston Museum of Fine Arts, is dated 1768–1770.
4. William E. Lincoln, ed., *The Journals of Each Provincial Congress of Massachusetts in 1774 and 1775, with an Appendix Containing the Proceedings of the County Conventions* (Boston: Dutton and Wentworth, 1838), 148.
5. Morgan, *Paul Revere's Three Accounts*, np.
6. *Pennsylvania Gazette*, June 7, 1775. Later in his article Gordon mentioned Revere by name, but only as a witness to the firing of the first shots at Lexington.
7. William Gordon, *The History of the Rise, Progress, and Establishment, of the Independence of the United States of America* (Freeport, NY: Books for Libraries Press, 1969; first published in 1788), 1: 477.
8. David Ramsay, *The History of the American Revolution* (Philadelphia: R. Aitken and Son, 1789; reprinted by Liberty Classics in 1990), 1: 187.
9. John Marshall, *The Life of George Washington* (New York: AMS Press, 1969; first published 1804–1807), 2: 211.
10. Mercy Otis Warren, *History of the Rise, Progress and Termination of the American Revolution, Interspersed with Biographical, Political and Moral Observations* (Boston: E. Larkin, 1805; reprinted by Liberty Classics in 1988), 1: 184. Warren's book has been transcribed for the Internet by Richard Seltzer, 2002, at www.samizdat.com/warren/.
11. Fischer, *Paul Revere's Ride*, 328.

12. Morgan, *Paul Revere's Three Accounts*, np.
13. Fischer, *Paul Revere's Ride*, 329.
14. Freeman Hunt, *American Anecdotes: Original and Select* (Boston: Putnam and Hunt, 1830).
15. Morgan, *Paul Revere's Three Accounts*, np.
16. Richard Frothingham, *History of the Siege of Boston, and of the Battles of Lexington, Concord, and Bunker Hill* (Boston: Little, Brown and Company, 1903; reprint edition, Da Capo Press, 1970; first published in 1849), 57–61.
17. Benson J. Lossing, *Pictorial Field-Book of the Revolution* (New York: Harper & Brothers, 1851), 1: 523.
18. George Bancroft, *History of the United States of America, from the Discovery of the Continent* (Boston: Little, Brown and Company, 1879; first published 1834–1874), 4: 517.
19. Bancroft and Lossing wrote approximately 1,500 pages each on the Revolution. Bancroft, who spins a coherent narrative, weaves in about one good ministory per page, while Lossing, who uses an entirely anecdotal approach, works in several per page. Lossing published 1,095 visual images, including several hundred portraits and signatures of famous revolutionaries, but he offered no image of Revere or his ride. For the treatment of history-as-anecdote in the antebellum nineteenth century, see chapter 15.
20. Although Longfellow believed strongly in abolitionism—in 1842 he published a book, *Poems on Slavery*, that reflected his abolitionist sentiments—he did not actively participate in any of the reform movements of the mid–nineteenth century. Instead of engaging with others toward common goals, he wrote poems and told stories with featured protagonists.
21. Fischer, *Paul Revere's Ride*, 90–112, 124–148.
22. Edward Eggleston, *A History of the United States and Its People, for the Use of Schools* (New York: D. Appleton and Co., 1888), 168.
23. Reuben Post Halleck, *History of Our Country, for Higher Grades* (New York: American Book Co., 1923), 179.
24. Ruth West and Willis Mason West, *The Story of Our Country* (Boston: Allyn and Bacon, 1935), 152; Gertrude Hartman, *America: Land of Freedom* (Boston: D.C. Heath and Co., 1946), 154–155.
25. John Fiske, *The American Revolution* (Boston and New York: Houghton Mifflin, 1891), 1:121. For Fiske as "the Bancroft of his generation," see Michael Kraus and Davis D. Joyce, *The Writing of American History* (Norman: University of Oklahoma Press, 1985), 181.
26. Fischer, *Paul Revere's Ride*, 337.
27. Esther Forbes, *Paul Revere and the World He Lived In* (Boston: Houghton Mifflin, 1942); Fischer, *Paul Revere's Ride*, 338.
28. Joy Hakim, *A History of US* (New York: Oxford University Press, 2003), 3: 71–73. Although Hakim does include Dawes and Prescott, she passes on the signal-light tale precisely as Longfellow conjured it: "Someone had to get a warning to those towns—and fast. It would help to know which way the redcoats would march. Would they go by the land route over the Boston Neck? Or would they take the shorter route—by boat across

the water to Charlestown and then on foot from there? . . . Paul Revere sent someone to spy on the British. 'Find out which way the redcoats will march,' the spy was told. 'Then climb into the high bell tower of the North Church and send a signal. Light one lantern if they go by land. Hang two lanterns if they go by sea.' Revere got in a boat and quietly rowed out into the Charles River. A horse was ready for him on the Charlestown shore. He waited—silently." At this point, Hakim shifts to Longfellow himself: "And lo! As he looks, on the belfry's height / A glimmer, and then a gleam of light! / He springs to the saddle, the bridle he turns, / But lingers and gazes, till full on his sight / A second lamp in the belfry burns!" Hakim then continues: "Now he knew! The redcoats would take the water route across the Charles River, just as Paul Revere was doing."

29. Michael J. Berson, ed., *United States History: Beginnings* (Orlando: Harcourt, 2003), 291.
30. Jesus Garcia et al., *Creating America: A History of the United States, Beginnings through Reconstruction* (Evanston, IL: McDougal Littell, 2002), 156–157.
31. Three is the upper limit, never a hint of any more. "Three men rode and gave warning of a British attack. One man was William Dawes. Who were the other two?" asks an online quiz. The choices: Dr. Samuel Prescott, Major John Pitcairn, Patrick Henry, Paul Revere. (Softschools.com: http://www.softschools.com/quizzes/social_studies/revolutionary_war/quiz414.html)
32. Thirteen texts displayed at the 2002 annual conference of the National Council for Social Studies in Phoenix, Arizona, all told the story. These included six elementary and middle-school texts: Sterling Stuckey and Linda Kerrigan Salvucci, *Call to Freedom* (Austin: Holt, Rinehart and Winston, 2003); Joyce Appleby et al., *The American Republic to 1877* (New York: Glencoe McGraw-Hill, 2003); Berson, *United States History: Beginnings*; James West Davidson, *The American Nation: Beginnings through 1877* (Upper Saddle River, NJ: Prentice Hall, 2003); Garcia, *Creating America: A History of the United States*; and Hakim, *A History of US*. The seven secondary-school texts are: Joyce Appleby et al., *The American Vision* (New York: Glencoe McGraw-Hill, 2003); Gerald A. Danzer et al., *The Americans* (Evanston, IL: McDougal Littell, 2003); Daniel J. Boorstin and Brooks Mather Kelley, *A History of the United States* (Upper Saddle River, NJ: Prentice Hall, 2002); David Goodfield et al., *The American Journey: A History of the United States* (Upper Saddle River, NJ: Prentice Hall, 2001); John Mack Faragher et al., *Out of Many: A History of the American People* (Upper Saddle River, NJ: Prentice Hall, 2003); Robert A. Divine et al., *America: Past and Present* (New York: Longman, 2003); and Paul Boyer, *American Nation* (Austin, TX: Holt, Rinehart and Winston, 2003). Newer editions incorporating versions of the Revere story include Emma J. Lapsansky-Werner, Peter B. Levy, Randy Roberts, Alan Taylor, *United States History*, Survey Edition (Upper Saddle River, NJ: Prentice Hall, 2013); James West Davidson and Michael B. Stoff, *America: History of Our Nation* (Upper Saddle River, NJ: Prentice Hall, 2014); Joyce Appleby, Alan Brinkley, Albert S. Broussard, James M. McPherson, and Donald A. Ritchie, *The American Journey* (Columbus, OH: Glencoe/McGraw-Hill, 2012); Michael J. Berson, Tyrone C. Howard, and Cinthia Salinas, *Harcourt Social Studies—United States: Making a New Nation* (Boston: Houghton Mifflin Harcourt,

2012); William Deverell and Deborah Gray White, *Holt McDougal United States History: Beginnings to 1877* (Boston: Houghton Mifflin Harcourt, 2012); Gerald A. Danzer, J. Jorge Klor de Alva, Larry S. Krieger, Louis E. Wilson, and Nancy Woloch, *The Americans* (Geneva, IL: Holt McDougal, 2012).

33. Lapsansky-Werner et al., *United States History*, 108. One recent secondary text comes closer to getting the story right. On April 18 Dr. Joseph Warren, upon receiving intelligence that British soldiers were preparing to march to Lexington and Concord, immediately sent for Revere, who "began to organize a network of riders who would spread the alarm." Then Revere, Dawes, and Prescott went forth and "the darkened countryside rang with church bells and gunshots—prearranged signals to warn the population that the Regulars were coming." This captures some of the truth but not all of it. Revere did not wait until the day the British were set to march to organize a network of riders; he and others had been doing this since early April, when they received news of British reinforcements. (Danzer et al., *The Americans*, 100–101.)
34. Jacqueline Jones, Peter H. Wood, Thomas Borstelmann, Elaine Tyler May, Vicki L. Ruiz, *Created Equal: A History of the United States*, vol. 1, Third Edition (Upper Saddle River, NJ: Pearson Longman, 2009), 195.
35. Davidson and Stoff, *America: History of Our Nation*, 153. See also a magazine-format college text by the same authors: "On the night of April 18 the sexton of Boston's Christ Church hung two lamps from its steeple. It was a signal the British troops had moved out of Boston and were marching toward the arms and ammunition stored by the provincial Congress in Concord. As the lamps flashed the signal, Revere and a comrade, William Dawes, rode out to arouse the countryside." (James West Davidson, Brian Delay, Christine Leigh Heyrman, Mark H. Lytle, and Michael B. Stoff, *U.S.: A Narrative History, Volume 1* [New York: McGraw-Hill, 2012)], 116–17).
36. Deverell and White, *United States History*, 114.
37. Appleby et al., *American Journey*, 135.
38. Berson et al., *United States: Making a New Nation*, 288–91, 314–15.
39. Howard H. Peckham, *The Toll of Independence: Engagements and Battle Casualties of the American Revolution* (Chicago: University of Chicago Press, 1974), 3.
40. For a list specifying the locations, dates, and purposes of Revere's various rides, including others I have not mentioned, see Fischer, *Paul Revere's Ride*, 299–300.

2: Sam Adams's Mob

1. A.J. Langguth, *Patriots: The Men Who Started the American Revolution* (New York: Simon & Schuster, 1988), 35, 57, 63, 89, 93.
2. Thomas Fleming, *Liberty! The American Revolution* (New York: Viking, 1997), 83.
3. Dennis B. Fradin, *The Signers: The Fifty-Six Stories Behind the Declaration of Independence* (New York: Walker and Company, 2002), 2.
4. Quoted in Pauline Maier, *The Old Revolutionaries: Political Lives in the Age of Samuel Adams* (New York: Alfred A. Knopf, 1980), 7.
5. For a wide assortment of contemporaneous comments on Samuel Adams, see John P.

Kaminski, ed., *The Founders on the Founders: Word Portraits from the American Revolutionary Era* (Charlottesville: University of Virginia Press, 2008), 61–80. The only use of "Sam" in these numerous selections are from Peter Oliver's diatribe against Adams in *Origin and Progress of the American Rebellion* (see note 6), a hearsay quote from Lord North, and informal "notes" taken by a third party on a conversation between Thomas Jefferson and Noah Webster in 1824.

6. Peter Oliver, *Origin and Progress of the American Rebellion*, Douglass Adair and John A. Schutz, eds. (Stanford: Stanford University Press, 1961), 65, 75.
7. Oliver, *Origin and Progress*, 28.
8. Thomas Hutchinson, *The History of the Colony and Province of Massachusetts-Bay* (Cambridge: Harvard University Press, 1936; first published, 1828), 3: 63.
9. Oliver, *Origin and Progress*, 39–41. Again, Hutchinson had a similar view of Adams, but he expressed this view less flamboyantly (see Hutchinson, *History of Massachusetts-Bay*, 3: 212).
10. John Andrews to William Barrell, August 11, 1774, in Massachusetts Historical Society, "Letters of John Andrews of Boston, 1772–1776," *Proceedings* 8 (1864–1865), 340.
11. Sylvester's affidavit, with its flamboyant accusations, is reprinted in James K. Hosmer, *Samuel Adams* (Boston and New York: Houghton Mifflin, 1885), 117–119, and Mary Caroline Crawford, *Old Boston Days and Ways* (Boston: Little, Brown, 1913), 253–255.
12. Stewart Beach, *Samuel Adams: The Fateful Years, 1764–1776* (New York: Dodd, Mead, and Co., 1965), 171–172. We do not know exactly why the charges were dismissed, but the attempt to frame Samuel Adams does not ring true: Adams's tone is uncharacteristic of his tone elsewhere; there is no evidence that he knew anyone named Sylvester; and it is implausible to think that Adams would have been visiting such a man frequently at his home. Sylvester attributed identical words to Benjamin Church, whom he was also trying to implicate as treasonous, and who would have been even less likely to say anything of the kind; at least later on, Church was an informer for the British.
13. George Bancroft, *History of the United States of America, from the Discovery of the Continent* (Boston: Little, Brown, 1879; first published, 1834–1874), 4: 109–110.
14. See, for example, William Deverell and Deborah Gray White, *Holt McDougal United States History: Beginnings to 1877* (Boston: Houghton Mifflin Harcourt, 2012), 101. A Google search (May 1, 2013) reveals 1,680 hits for "I look upon them as foreign enemies."
15. William Hallahan, *The Day the American Revolution Began* (New York: William Morrow, 2000), 65.
16. Samuel Adams to John Smith, December 20, 1765, in Harry Alonzo Cushing, ed., *The Writings of Samuel Adams* (New York: G.P. Putnam's Sons, 1904), 1: 60. Even college texts sometimes fail to distinguish between the two events: "In a carefully orchestrated series of mob action, Bostonians made certain that the Stamp Act would not be enforced. . . . Over a series of several days, the mob systematically vandalized the homes of several wealthy governmental loyalists, including Hutchinson. Although the mob consisted mostly of artisans and poor people, it had the support of Boston's merchant elite, for no one was ever punished." (James Oakes, Michael McGerr, Jan Ellen

Lewis, Nick Cullather, and Jeanne Boydston, *Of the People: A History of the United States*, vol. 1, Concise Edition [New York: Oxford University Press, 2011], 170.)

17. Louis Birnbaum, *Red Dawn at Lexington* (Boston: Houghton Mifflin, 1986), 25.
18. James West Davidson, Brian Delay, Christine Leigh Heyrman, Mark H. Lytle, and Michael B. Stoff, *U.S.: A Narrative History, Volume 1* (New York: McGraw-Hill, 2012), 113.
19. Hutchinson, *History of Massachusetts-Bay*, 3: 198–199.
20. John K. Alexander, *Samuel Adams: America's Revolutionary Politician* (Lanham, MD, Boulder, CO, and New York: Rowman & Littlefield, 2002), 83; Michael Burgan, *Samuel Adams: Patriot and Statesman* (Minneapolis: Compass Point, 2005), 55.
21. Birnbaum, *Red Dawn at Lexington*, 29. See also Langguth, *Patriots*, 179.
22. Although the author remains unknown, a manuscript from the Sewall papers in Ottawa is accepted by scholars as the most detailed authentic rendition of the meeting at Old South. After Rotch, one of the shipowners, reported that the governor would not let him return the tea to England, "Mr. Adams said that he could think of nothing further to be done," the account states. "About 10 or 15 minutes later," it continues, "I heard a hideous yelling in the Street at the S. West Corner of the Meeting House and in the Porch, as of an Hundred People, some imitating the Powaws of Indians and other the Whistle of a Boatswain, which was answered by some few in the House; on which Numbers hastened out as fast as possible while Mr. Adams, Mr. Hancock, Dr. Young with several others called out to the People to stay, for they said they had not quite done. . . . Mr. Adams addressed the Moderator in these Words, 'Mr. Moderator, I move that Dr. Young make (or be desired to make) a Speech'—which being approved of, Dr. Young made one accordingly of about 15 or 20 Minutes Length. . . . [W]hen he had done, the Audience paid him the usual Tribute of Bursts of Applause, Clapping, etc. and immediately Mr. Savage (the Moderator) dissolved the Meeting." (L.F.S. Upton, ed., "Proceeding of Ye Body Respecting the Tea," *William and Mary Quarterly*, Third Series, 22 [1965]: 297–298.) According to another firsthand account, "Mr. Samuel Adams cried out that it was a trick of their enemies to disturb the meeting, and requested the people to keep their places." (Francis S. Drake, ed., *Tea Leaves: Being a Collection of Letters and Documents relating to the Subject of Tea to the American Colonies in the year 1773* [Boston: A.O. Crane, 1884], LXX.) "An Impartial Observer" reported in both the *Boston Evening Post* and the *Boston Gazette* of December 20 that after the first "war-whoop" from the doorway, "silence was commanded, and a prudent and peaceable deportment again enjoined." A similar report appeared in the December 23 issue of the *Massachusetts Gazette and Boston Weekly News-Letter*.
23. Bancroft, *History of the United States*, 4: 280.
24. William V. Wells, *The Life and Public Services of Samuel Adams* (Freeport, NY: Books for Libraries Press, 1969; first published, 1865–1888), 2: iv, and 2: 122. The idea of a "signal" was first suggested by William Gordon in 1788. Writing in the present tense to bring his readers closer to the action, Gordon wrote that upon Rotch's announcement "there is a great deal of disputing, when a person disguised like an Indian, gives the war-whoop in

the front gallery, where there are few if any besides himself. Upon this signal it is moved and voted that the meeting be immediately dissolved. The people crowd out and run in numbers to Griffin's wharf." (*The History of the Rise, Progress, and Establishment, of the Independence of the United States of America* [Reprint edition: Freeport, NY: Books for Libraries Press, 1969], 1: 341.) In this rendition, it was not Adams who gave the alleged "signal" but an unnamed person with a war-whoop. While Gordon's timing, like Bancroft's and Wells's, is inconsistent with firsthand testimony, if there was some sort of "signal," a war-whoop seems a more plausible candidate than Adams's alleged coded message.

25. Sources suggesting that Adams advocated independence long before anyone else need to be examined critically. The most direct "evidence" comes from Joseph Galloway, a moderate at the First Continental Congress who turned Tory when his views did not prevail. According to Galloway, when independence was declared, Adams boasted that "he had laboured upwards of twenty years to accomplish the measure." (Galloway, *Historical and Political Reflections on the Rise and Progress of the American Revolution* [London: G. Wilkie, 1780], 109–110. Cited in Ralph V. Harlow, *Samuel Adams: Promoter of the American Revolution* [New York: Farrar, Straus and Giroux, 1975; first published in 1923], 288.) Galloway, who blamed his defeat on Adams, claimed also that Adams directed the "faction" at the Continental Congress as well as in Boston. (*Historical and Political Reflections*, 67.) Undoubtedly, declaring independence caused Samuel Adams to rejoice—just as it caused all ardent patriots to rejoice. Adams probably claimed some credit for the historic event, as did others; fueled by hindsight, he might have uttered some sort of "I-told-you-so," which Galloway naturally embellished. But even if Adams himself, glancing backward, saw his prior activities in a different light, we don't read history backward; what counts is what happened at the time. However Adams felt in 1776, we have no contemporaneous evidence from the 1760s that he preached the merits of independence at that time.

An Internet reference site, ABC-CLIO, www.abc-clio.com, includes in its list of famous quotations, "The country shall be independent, and we shall be satisfied with nothing short of it." These words, attributed to Samuel Adams on March 9, 1774, will doubtless be repeated in countless student papers, complete with name and date. The oft-cited quotation comes from William Gordon's early history, written in 1788. As a stylistic device, Gordon wrote in the present tense to simulate a contemporary narrative, and this passage appears under a conjured "entry" for March 9, 1774: "But there are a few in this colony who hanker after independency, and will be likely to bend their whole influence for the obtaining of it, whenever there is the least opening to encourage their efforts. At the head of these we must place Mr. Samuel Adams, who has long since said in small confidential companies—'the country shall be independent, and we will be satisfied with nothing short of it.' " (Gordon, *Rise, Progress, and Establishment of Independence*, 1: 347.) This artistic fabrication, combined with after-the-fact folklore, now passes for historical authenticity. In 1788 William Gordon said that other people had said in 1774 that Adams had said these words in private, at some undisclosed time in the past. There is no possible way of verifying Gordon's reporting of private conversations supposedly held "long since," presumably back in the 1760s—two decades before Gordon set them to paper. Although Adams himself left no writings dated March 9, 1774, this "source" has been accepted as valid simply because it is seen as "contemporary."

26. Maier, *Old Revolutionaries*, 21–26. Maier's entry for Samuel Adams in the updated (1999) *American National Biography* serves as a corrective for many of the traditional myths.
27. Adams to Reverend G.W., November 11, 1765, and Adams to John Smith, December 19, 1765, Cushing, *Writings*, 1: 28, 45. These sentiments are echoed in all his writings from 1765.
28. Adams, under the name of "Vindex," *Boston Gazette*, December 5, 1768, in Cushing, *Writings*, 1: 259.
29. Adams to Dennys De Berdt, October 3, 1768, in Cushing, *Writings*, 1: 249. Emphasis in original.
30. Adams, under the name of "Valerius Poplicola," *Boston Gazette*, October 28, 1771, in Cushing, *Writings*, 2: 262. By this time it was true that Samuel Adams was beginning to wonder: Will the rights of colonists ever be granted? In despair, he envisaged that "in some hereafter," when all appeals to reason had failed, "America herself under God must finally work out her own Salvations." (Adams to Arthur Lee, October 31, 1771, and Adams to Henry Merchant, January 7, 1772, in Cushing, *Writings*, 2: 267 and 309.) But in the words of historian Pauline Maier, this apocalyptic prediction, born of frustration, "fell short of advocacy." (Maier, *Old Revolutionaries*, 23.)
31. Adams to Arthur Lee, June 21, 1773, in Cushing, *Writings*, 3: 44.
32. Adams to Joseph Warren, September 25, 1774, in Cushing, *Writings*, 3: 158–159.
33. Adams to Samuel Cooper, April 3 and April 30, 1776; Adams to Joseph Hawley, April 15, 1776; in Cushing, *Writings*, 3: 276–285.
34. Adams to John Smith, December 20, 1765, in Cushing, *Writings*, 1: 60.
35. Adams, under the name "Determinatus," *Boston Gazette*, August 8, 1768, in Cushing, *Writings*, 1: 240. Emphasis in original.
36. Adams, under the name "Vindex," *Boston Gazette*, December 5, 1768, in Cushing, *Writings*, 1: 259. Emphasis in original.
37. Adams to Darius Sessions, January 2, 1773, in Cushing, *Writings*, 2: 398.
38. Adams to James Warren, May 21, 1774, *The Warren-Adams Letters* (Boston: Massachusetts Historical Society, 1917–1925), 1: 26. Pauline Maier states that this letter is misdated. (Maier, *Old Revolutionaries*, 28.)
39. Adams to Benjamin Kent, July 27, 1776, in Cushing, *Writings*, 3: 304.
40. Quoted in Alexander, *Samuel Adams: America's Revolutionary Politician*, 185.
41. For the less revolutionary meaning of "revolution" which prevailed before the turmoil of the French Revolution, see Garry Wills, *Inventing America: Jefferson's Declaration of Independence* (New York: Doubleday, 1978), 51–52.
42. David Ramsay, *The History of the American Revolution* (Philadelphia: R. Aitken & Son, 1789), 186, 321, 634. Here is Ramsay's list, along with a mention of clergy and printers who played prominent roles: "John Adams, and Samuel Adams, of Boston; Bland, of Virginia; John Dickinson, of Pennsylvania; Daniel Dulany, of Annapolis; William Henry Drayton, of South-Carolina; Dr. Franklin, of Philadelphia; John Jay, and

Alexander Hamilton, of New-York; Thomas Jefferson, and Arthur Lee of Virginia; Jonathan Hyman, of Connecticut; Governor Livingston, of New-Jersey; Dr. Mayhew, and James Otis, of Boston; Thomas Paine, Dr. Rush, Charles Thompson, and James Wilson, of Philadelphia; William Tennant, of South-Carolina; Josiah Quincy, and Dr. Warren, of Boston. These and many others laboured in enlightening their countrymen, on the subject of their political interests, and in animating them to a proper line of conduct, in defence of their liberties. To these individuals may be added, the great body of the clergy, especially in New-England. The printers of newspapers, had also much merit in the same way. Particularly Edes and Gill, of Boston; Holt, of New-York; Bradford, of Philadelphia; and Timothy, of South-Carolina." William Gordon, who also wrote a history in the late 1780s, did feature Adams but in ways that do not correspond to contemporaneous evidence from the 1760s and 1770s. See note 24.

43. Adams was allegedly the "chief manager" of the Tea Party and "Father of the Revolution." He was "the first to advocate independence" and therefore had to convince others, since "the people were slow to consider seriously that they must break from the mother country." (John Fiske, *A History of the United States* [Boston: Houghton Mifflin, 1899], 201; D.H. Montgomery, *Leading Facts of American History* [Boston: Ginn & Company, 1899], 155, 157; Wilbur F. Gordy, *A History of the United States for Schools* [New York: Charles Scribner's Sons, 1914], 139; William A. Mowry and Blanche S. Mowry, *Essentials of United States History* [Boston: Silver, Burdett and Company, 1914], 112.)
44. William A. Mowry and Arthur May Mowry, *First Steps in the History of Our Country* (Boston: Silver, Burdett and Company, 1899), 119–120.
45. Albert Bushnell Hart, *Essentials in American History* (New York: American Book Company, 1914), 156.
46. Thomas Rodney, "Characters of Some of the Members of Congress," post–March 8, 1781; Thomas Jefferson to Benjamin Waterhouse, January 31, 1819; John Adams to William Tudor, February 9, 1819, in John P. Kaminsiki, ed., *The Founders on the Founders: Word Portraits from the American Revolutionary Era* (Charlottesville: University of Virginia Press, 2008), 71, 79, 80.
47. John C. Miller, *Sam Adams: Pioneer in Propaganda* (Stanford: Stanford University Press, 1936), 53, 136–138, 141, 144–145.
48. Thomas A. Bailey, *The American Pageant* (Boston: Little, Brown and Company, 1956), 94, 981.
49. For the genesis of the Massachusetts committees of correspondence, see Ray Raphael, *Founders: The People Who Brought You a Nation* (New York: The New Press, 2009), 106–10.
50. Bailey, *The American Pageant*, 109, 147.
51. David M. Kennedy and Lizabeth Cohen, *The American Pageant*, Fifteenth Edition (Boston: Cengage Learning, 2014), 135, 170.
52. As cited in note 2, this quote comes not from the works of Hutchinson or Oliver but from the volume accompanying the PBS series *Liberty!*
53. George Bancroft, for all his professed belief in democracy, certainly followed this way

of thinking. " 'Make way for the committee!' was the shout of the multitude, as Adams came out from the council chamber and, baring his head, which was already becoming gray, moved through their ranks, inspiring confidence. . . . On ordinary occasions he seemed like ordinary men; but in moments of crisis, he rose naturally and unaffectedly to the highest dignity, and spoke as if the hopes of humanity hung on his words." (Bancroft, *History of the United States*, 4: 192.)

54. Matt Doeden, *The Boston Tea Party*, Charles Barnett III, ill. (Mankato, MN: Capstone, 2005), 5, 25.
55. John W. Tyler, *Smugglers and Patriots: Boston Merchants and the Advent of the American Revolution* (Boston: Northeastern University Press, 1986), 17.
56. Tyler, *Smugglers and Patriots*, 138–69.
57. Gordon, *Rise, Progress, and Establishment of Independence*, 1: 178.
58. There are two meanings attached to "Sons of Liberty" in Boston. The label can refer to the group meeting in John Marston's tavern in the late 1760s (and possibly earlier or later as well), or in a generic sense to all of Boston's most active patriots. Generally, in common usage, the latter sense is intended. We do not have any membership list for the Marston's tavern group, although we do know from extant letters written by active participants that they had "members" and "committees." Samuel Adams is not among the handful of known members, but that in no way establishes that he was not active in that group. Since at least forty-five people were, it seems likely that he was among them. See the correspondence between the "Sons of Liberty from the Town of Boston" and John Wilkes, Massachusetts Historical Society, *Proceedings*, 47: 190–211.
59. Wills, *Inventing America*, 20–24.
60. See Richard D. Brown, *Revolutionary Politics in Massachusetts: The Boston Committee of Correspondence and the Towns, 1772–1774* (New York: W.W. Norton, 1970), 48, 62–64; Raphael, *Founders*, 106–10.
61. Alfred F. Young, *Liberty Tree: Ordinary People and the American Revolution* (New York, New York University Press, 2006), 27–99.
62. For town meeting instructions, see Ray Raphael, "Instructions: The People's Voice in Revolutionary America," *Common-Place* 9:1 (October 2008): http://www.common-place.org/vol-09/no-01/raphael/
63. For the politicized population, see Ray Raphael, "The Democratic Moment: The Revolution in Popular Politics," in *The Oxford Handbook of the American Revolution*, Edward G. Gray and Jane Kamensky, eds. (New York: Oxford University Press, 2013), 121–28.
64. For a recent treatment that places Adams's effectiveness within this political rubric, see Alexander, *Samuel Adams: America's Revolutionary Politician*.
65. Mercy Otis Warren, *History of the Rise, Progress and Termination of the American Revolution, interspersed with Biographical, Political and Moral Observations* (Boston: E. Larkin, 1805; reprinted by Liberty Classics in 1988), 1: 211.

3: Molly Pitcher's Cannon

1. See Karin Wolf's entry for Betsy Ross in *American National Biography*, John A. Garraty and Mark C. Carnes, eds. (New York: Oxford University Press, 1999), 18: 900–901; and Laurel Thatcher Ulrich, "How Betsy Ross Became Famous," in *Common-Place* 8:1 (October 2007): http://www.common-place.org/vol-08/no-01/ulrich/.
2. Thomas Fleming—in his companion volume to the PBS program *Liberty!*—includes Abigail Adams's image as one of five key "portraits" of the American Revolution (Thomas Fleming, *Liberty! The American Revolution* [New York: Viking, 1997], 1–7). Joseph Ellis features Abigail Adams as one of his eight "Founding Brothers," despite the obvious gender incongruity. She was "one of the eight most prominent political leaders of the early republic," he claims. (Joseph Ellis, *Founding Brothers: The Revolutionary Generation* [New York: Alfred A. Knopf, 2001], 17, 162–205.)
3. Holly A. Mayer, *Belonging to the Army: Camp Followers and Community During the American Revolution* (Columbia: University of South Carolina Press, 1996), 20. For the most recent and thorough treatment of Deborah Sampson, see Alfred Young, *Masquerade: The Life and Times of Deborah Sampson, Continental Soldier* (New York: Alfred A. Knopf, 2004).
4. Sterling Stuckey and Linda Kerrigan Salvucci, *Call to Freedom* (Austin, TX: Holt, Rinehart and Winston, 2003), 168.
5. Gerald A. Danzer et al., *The Americans* (Evanston, IL: McDougal Littell, 2003), 117.
6. Joyce Appleby et al., *The American Republic to 1877* (New York: Glencoe McGraw-Hill, 2003), 164.
7. The six elementary and middle-school texts surveyed were all displayed at the annual convention of the National Council for Social Studies at Phoenix in November 2002. Those containing the Molly Pitcher story are Stuckey and Salvucci, *Call to Freedom*; Appleby, *The American Republic to 1877*; Michael J. Berson, ed., *United States History: Beginnings* (Orlando: Harcourt, 2003); James West Davidson, *The American Nation: Beginnings through 1877* (Upper Saddle River, NJ: Prentice Hall, 2003); and Joy Hakim, *A History of US* (New York: Oxford University Press, 2003). The one that made no mention of Molly Pitcher is Jesus Garcia et al., *Creating America: A History of the United States, Beginnings through Reconstruction* (Evanston, IL: McDougal Littell, 2002). Four secondary texts displayed at the NCSS conference also include the Molly Pitcher story: Joyce Appleby et al., *The American Vision* (New York: Glencoe McGraw-Hill, 2003); Danzer, *The Americans*; Daniel J. Boorstin and Brooks Mather Kelley, *A History of the United States* (Upper Saddle River, NJ: Prentice Hall, 2002); and David Goldfield, et al., *The American Journey: A History of the United States* (Upper Saddle River, NJ: Prentice Hall, 2001). Only *The American Journey* refers to Molly Pitcher as a legend; the others portray her as flesh and blood.
8. In the paperback edition of my own *People's History of the American Revolution* (New York: HarperCollins, 2002), which states that Molly Pitcher is a fictive creation, her dramatic presence on the front cover, leading the men into battle, belies my quibbles inside.

9. Augusta Stevenson, *Molly Pitcher: Young Patriot* (New York: Macmillan, 1986; originally published in 1960), 184–191.
10. The best known Revolutionary soldier in the years following the war, before the evolution of "Molly Pitcher," was in fact Deborah Sampson, who toured several states in 1802–1803, two decades after the war ended, as "The Celebrated Mrs. Gannett (Late Deborah Sampson), the American Heroine," recounting her story and performing "the manual exercise" for eager audiences. (Young, *Masquerade*, 167–224.)
11. Edward Hagaman Hall, *Margaret Corbin: Heroine of the Battle of Fort Washington, 16 November 1776* (New York: American Scenic and Historic Preservation Society, 1932), 14–15.
12. The "Waste Book for the Quartermaster Stores" and the "Letter Books of Captain William Price, Commissary of Ordinance and Military Stores," in the West Point library. The numerous tents she received were possibly turned into clothing. Captain Molly was unable to care for herself, and money for her support was paid directly to her caregiver. (Hall, *Margaret Corbin*, 24–30.)
13. Benson J. Lossing, *Pictorial Field-Book of the Revolution* (New York: Harper & Brothers, 1852), 2: 164.
14. Here is Waldo's full account, as reported by William Stryker well over a century later: "One of the camp women I must give a little praise to. Her gallant, whom she attended in battle, being shot down, she immediately took up his gun and cartridges and like a Spartan heroine fought with astonishing bravery, discharging the piece with as much regularity as any soldier present. This a wounded officer, whom I dressed, told me he did see himself, she being in his platoon, and assured me I might depend on its truth." (William S. Stryker, *The Battle of Monmouth* [Princeton: Princeton University Press, 1927], 189. Stryker's book was completed in 1899, although not published then.) Whether the "gun" in question was a cannon or a musket is not absolutely clear; both could be called a "piece," both were discharged by igniting cartridges, and both were fired at intervals that could be regular or irregular.
15. This is worrisome. The revised 1862 edition of Dr. James Thacher's *Military Journal of the American Revolution*, originally published decades earlier, contained some brand-new material—an account of Molly Pitcher—even though Thacher himself had died in 1844. Without further evidence, we cannot say whether Waldo's statement was contemporary to the time or whether it had been doctored to conform to a legend that emerged later, as Thacher's was.
16. Here is Martin's account: "One little incident happened, during the heat of the cannonade, which I was eye-witness to, and which I think would be unpardonable not to mention. A woman whose husband belonged to the Artillery, and who was then attached to a piece in the engagement, attended with her husband at the piece the whole time; while in the act of reaching a cartridge and having one of her feet as far before the other as she could step, a cannon shot from the enemy passed directly between her legs without doing any other damage than carrying away all the lower part of her petticoat,—looking at it with apparent unconcern, she observed, that it was lucky it did not pass a little higher, for in that case it might have carried away something else, and ended her and her

occupation." (Joseph Plumb Martin, *A Narrative of a Revolutionary Soldier* [New York: Signet, 2001; originally published in 1830], 115. In other reprints, Martin ends this piece not with "ended her and her occupation" but "continued her occupation.") Since Martin showed no surprise at a woman firing a cannon, this might well have been commonplace. He likely told the story for its ribald petticoat punch line.

17. Howard H. Peckham, *The Toll of Independence: Engagements & Battle Casualties of the American Revolution* (Chicago: University of Chicago Press, 1974), 52.
18. John Laffin, *Women in Battle* (London and New York: Abelard-Schuman, 1967), 38–43.
19. Freeman Hunt, *American Anecdotes: Original and Select* (Boston: Putnam and Hunt, 1830), 2: 275.
20. Emily Lewis Butterfield, "Lie There My Darling, While I Avenge Ye," in *Remembering the Revolution: Memory, History and Nation Making from Independence to the Civil War*, Michael McDonnell, Clare Corbould, Frances M. Clarke, and W. Fitzhugh Brundage, eds. (Amherst: University of Massachusetts Press, 2013), 201, 205. Butterfield cites two papers, "A Tale of '76," *Baltimore Gazette and Daily Advertiser*, July 9, 1830, and "A Tale of '76," *Charleston City Gazette*, July 15, 1830, and implies there were others. Here is the embellished 1837 piece: "MOLLY PITCHER— . . . At the commencement of the battle of Monmouth this intrepid woman contributed her aid by constantly carrying water from a spring to the battery where her husband was employed, as a cannonier, in loading and firing a gun. At length he was shot dead in her presence, just as she was leaving the spring; whereupon she flew to the spot—found her husband lifeless, and, at the moment, heard an officer, who rode up, order off the gun "for want of a man sufficiently dauntless to supply his place." Indignant at this order, and stung by the remark, she promptly opposed it—demanded the post of her slain husband to avenge his death—flew to the gun, and to the admiration and astonishment of all who saw her, assumed and ably discharged the duties of the thus vacated post of cannonier, to the end of the battle! For this sterling demonstration of genuine WHIG spirit, Washington gave her a lieutenant's commission upon the spot, which Congress afterwards ratified. And granted her a sword, and an epaulette, and half pay, as a lieutenant, for life! She wore the epaulette, received the pay, and was called 'Captain Molly!' ever afterwards." (Quoted in Marc Mappen, *There's More to New Jersey than the Sopranos* [Piscataway, NJ: Rutgers University Press, 2009], 31.)
21. George Washington Parke Custis, *Recollections and Private Memoirs of Washington* (New York: Derby & Jackson, 1860), 225. Custis began publishing his "recollections" of Washington serially in the 1820s. In 1840 these were gathered in the *National Intelligencer*, and in 1859, after his death, they appeared in book form. This is from the book edition, quoted in D.W. Thompson and Merri Lou Schaumann, "Goodbye, Molly Pitcher," *Cumberland County History 6* (1989), 11. It appeared in the *National Intelligencer*, February 22, 1840, and possibly in the *United States Gazette* in the late 1820s. Custis included a prologue to the story that has since been dropped: "At one of the guns of Proctor's battery, six men had been killed or wounded. It was deemed an unlucky gun and murmurs arose that it should be drawn back and abandoned." This was the cannon that Captain Molly would fire. After she had saved the day, Custis wrote, "the doomed

gun was no longer deemed unlucky." Thompson and Schaumann ("Goodbye, Molly Pitcher," 11–12) argue that this prologue is improbable on two counts: the lion's share of casualties among the artillery at Monmouth would have occurred at this one location, and the Americans rarely abandoned any of their cannons.

22. Pension application for Rebecca Clendenen, discussed and referenced in note 29.
23. Thompson and Schaumann, "Goodbye, Molly Pitcher," 15–16; Butterfield, "Lie There My Darling," 204.
24. For two different references, one from an oral tradition and the other printed in the *Pennsylvania Archives*, see Hall, *Margaret Corbin*, 34–35. A poem cited in 1905 uses "Moll" and "Molly" interchangeably (Carol Klaver, "An Introduction into the Legend of Molly Pitcher," *Minerva: Quarterly Report on Women and the Military* 12 [1994]: 52).
25. Butterfield, "Lie There My Darling," 206.
26. In his editorial notes to Custis's *Recollections and Private Memoirs of Washington* (Philadelphia: J.W. Bradley, 1861), Lossing refused to call Captain Molly by the name that was assuming greater popularity by that time: Molly Pitcher. "Art and Romance have confounded her with another character, Moll Pitcher," he stated (225–26). As recently as 1978, Michael Kammen, in his detailed study of how the Revolution was portrayed through American history, confused the protagonist of the play with the heroine of Monmouth (Michael Kammen, *A Season of Youth: The American Revolution and the Historical Imagination* [New York: Alfred A. Knopf, 1978], 111, 121, 132).
27. "Searching for Molly Pitcher Exhibit, 2001," Monmouth County Archives Internet site, accessed February 3, 2004; www.visitmonmouth.com/archives/.
28. Butterfield, "Lie There My Darling," 210.
29. In this manner, the Molly Pitcher legend parallels that of Betsy Ross: "There is really no point in arguing over who made the *first* flag because there wasn't one. The stars and stripes that we know today had multiple parents and dozens of siblings." (Ulrich, "How Betsy Ross Became Famous," www.common-place.org/vol-08/no-01/ulrich/.) People's motives for attaching themselves to the legend do not have to include fame; mere proximity will sometimes yield rewards. When Rebecca Clendenin applied for a war widow's pension in 1840, she tried to prove that her deceased husband had actually served at Monmouth by telling the story of a woman who had taken her husband's place at a cannon. Clendenin offered her version of a known "anecdote" as collaborative evidence; it gave her case an assumed authenticity, and it continues to do so today. Her testimony is sometimes used to affirm the existence of a real Molly Pitcher, even though anybody in the 1830s or 1840, including her husband, could have told the same story on the basis of what he or she had heard or read by that time. (Butterfield, "Lie There My Darling," 200.)
30. Thompson and Schaumann, "Goodbye, Molly Pitcher," 22.
31. Ibid., 21. A second obituary, although less low-key, likewise failed to acknowledge Mrs. McCauley as "Molly Pitcher."
32. Rev. George Swain, *Historical Discourse in Connection with the Presbyterian Church of Allentown and Vicinity, 1876* (Philadelphia: Kildare, 1877), 18; *Monmouth Inquirer*, March 26, 1876, in David George Martin, *A Molly Pitcher Sourcebook* (Hightstown, NJ:

Longstreet House, 2003), 38–40. Thanks to John Fabiano of the Allentown–Upper Freehold Historical Society for these references.

33. We don't know very much about her life before and during the Revolutionary War; in fact, there is some argument over the identity of the husband whom she supposedly accompanied into battle. Some historians claim he was John Casper Hays, who allegedly married Mary Ludwig on July 24, 1769; others say the marriage record actually lists the husband's name as William. John Hays first enlisted in the army in 1775, then reenlisted in 1777 in the Seventh Pennsylvania Regiment, which fought in the Battle of Monmouth Courthouse the following year. William Hays, who enlisted as a gunner in the artillery in 1777, was also reported at Monmouth. For the John Casper Hays version, see John B. Landis, "Investigation into American Tradition of Woman Known as Molly Pitcher," *Journal of American History* 5 (1911): 83–94, and John B. Landis, *A Short History of Molly Pitcher, the Heroine of the Battle of Monmouth* (Cumberland County, PA: Comman Printers, 1905), 10–14. For the William Hays version, see Thompson and Schaumann, "Goodbye, Molly Pitcher," 3–26. Thompson points to tax records for 1783, which show William and Mary Hays living with a three-year-old boy named John. Probate records confirm that young John was the son of William and Mary. If John Casper Hays lived in Carlisle after the war, he left no traces. In the revised *American National Biography*, published in 1999, John K. Alexander favors John over William, although he fails to explain John's mysterious disappearance after the war and the fact that subsequent records indicate that William was the father of Mary's son. It is certainly possible that Mary Hays was at Monmouth with her husband (whoever he might be), and it is conceivable, if she was with the army, that she helped the artillery team, but there is no written record for any of this.

After William Hays died in 1786, Mary Hays married John McCalla. (I render her surname as McCauley, perhaps the most common spelling, or Hays, her surname during the Revolution.) By 1810 John had either died or disappeared, and Mary, by then at least fifty-five years old, supported herself by whitewashing public buildings, cleaning, and laundering. (Thompson and Schaumann, "Goodbye, Molly Pitcher," 18–20; and Landis, *Short History of Molly Pitcher*, 17–20.)

In 1822, forty-four years after Monmouth, "Molly McKolly" was awarded a government pension amounting to a private's half-pay. The initial draft of the bill read "widow of a soldier," but the revised version read "for services rendered." (Thompson and Schaumann, "Goodbye, Molly Pitcher," 20.) The specific nature of those services was not stipulated, but might they have included her manning the cannon of her stricken husband? Later commentators have assumed so, but contemporary reports made no mention of such heroism, as newsworthy as it might have been. The Philadelphia *Chronicle* reported flatly, "It appeared satisfactory that this heroine had braved the hardships of the camp and dangers of the field with her husband who was a soldier of the Revolution." In New York, on the other hand, a press report added some embellishment, but nothing about firing her husband's cannon at Monmouth: "Molly Macauly, who received a pension from the state of Pennsylvania for service rendered during the Revolutionary War, was well-known to the general officers as a brave and patriotic woman. She was called Sgt. McCauly, and was wounded at some battle, supposed to be the Brandywine, where her sex was discovered. It was a common practice for her to swing her sable over her head, and huzza for 'Mad Anthony' as she termed Anthony Wayne. It was an unusual circumstance to find women in the ranks disguised as men, such was their order for independence. Elizabeth Canning was at a gun at Fort Washington when her husband was killed and she took his place immediately, loaded, primed and fired the cannon with which he was entrusted. She was wounded in the breast by a grapeshot." (*National Advocate*, March 7, 1822, quoted in Thompson and Schaumann, "Goodbye, Molly Pitcher," 20–21.) This account, offered during her lifetime but of dubious reliability, differed in almost every respect from the Molly Pitcher legend we know today.

34. *Carlisle Herald*, May 18, 1876, quoted in Linda Grant De Pauw, *Battle Cries and Lullabies: Women in War from Prehistory to the Present* (Norman: University of Oklahoma Press, 1998), 128.
35. *The* Cumberland Valley Chronicle*: Writings About Colonial Times and People*, in a packet of information put out by the Cumberland County Historical Society, states that the spelling on this headstone was actually "McCauly."
36. Klaver, "Legend of Molly Pitcher," 49.
37. Landis, *Short History of Molly Pitcher*, 24–25; Thompson and Schaumann, "Goodbye, Molly Pitcher," 24; Klaver, "Legend of Molly Pitcher," 42.
38. Landis, *Short History of Molly Pitcher*, 15.
39. Landis, "Investigation into Molly Pitcher," 83–96.
40. This was not necessarily "the very same pitcher carried by Molly Pitcher at the battle of Monmouth," the descendent admitted, but she claimed before a notary that the pitcher had belonged to her great-great-grandmother. A picture of the pitcher, along with a newspaper article announcing the gift to the Hamilton Library and the Cumberland County Historical Association, is included in the packet on Molly Pitcher available through the Cumberland County Historical Society.
41. Klaver, "Legend of Molly Pitcher," 49.
42. Stryker, *Battle of Monmouth*, 192. Amid all the fanfare, one man wasn't buying it. Jeremiah Zeamer, himself a resident of Carlisle, did not think it appropriate to honor a woman who had been described as vulgar and profane, while many "Revolutionary heroes who lived useful and respected lives" remained obscure. "Molly McCauley is neither the historical nor moral character to hold up to young Americans for emulation," he argued. Using careful genealogical research, he went on to shoot holes in the Molly-Pitcher-equals-Mary-Hays-McCauley equation. (Jeremiah Zeamer, "Molly McCauley Monument," *Carlisle Herald*, April 5, 1905, and "Molly Pitcher Story Analyzed," *Carlisle Volunteer*, February 20, 1907. The first is included in the Cumberland County Historical Society's Molly Pitcher packet; the second is cited in Klaver, "Legend of Molly Pitcher," 41–42.) But the public showed no concern for Jeremiah Zeamer's quibbles. Rather than scrap the legend, those who believed in their local heroine chose to change her image. Just as the vulgar Captain Molly had been transformed into a more genteel Molly Pitcher, so did Mary Hays McCauley take on a more gracious persona. The new monument placed by her grave in 1916 referred to her as an "army nurse" who became

known for "her many acts of kindness." Years later, a newspaper article described "Pennsylvania's Number One Revolutionary Heroine" as a "cheerful" person. (Molly Pitcher packet, Cumberland County Historical Society.) Mary was now fit to become a respectable heroine, an appropriate model for impressionable young girls.

43. Hall, *Margaret Corbin*, 38–43.
44. Dumas Malone, ed., *Dictionary of American Biography* (New York: Scribner's, 1948), 11: 574. Mary's alleged maiden name, Ludwig, has also been questioned, as has her date of birth, posited alternately as 1744 and 1754, but these issues do not relate directly to the Molly Pitcher story.
45. Henry Steele Commager and Richard B. Morris, *The Spirit of 'Seventy-Six: The Story of the American Revolution as Told by the Participants* (Indianapolis and New York: Bobbs-Merrill, 1958), 710, 714–715.
46. Klaver, "Legend of Molly Pitcher," 49.
47. John Todd White, "The Truth About Molly Pitcher," in *The American Revolution: Whose Revolution?* James Kirby Martin and Karen R. Stubaus, eds. (Huntington, NY: Krieger, 1977), 99–105; Linda Grant De Pauw and Conover Hunt, *Remember the Ladies: Women in America, 1750–1815* (New York: Viking, 1976), 90. De Pauw elaborated in "Women in Combat: The Revolutionary Experience," *Armed Forces and Society* 7 (198): 215, and *Battle Cries and Lullabies*, 126–131.
48. John A. Garraty and Mark C. Carnes, eds., *American National Biography* (New York: Oxford University Press, 1999), 17: 564–565; the author of the piece is John K. Alexander. All deeds ever attributed to "Molly Pitcher" are now attributed to Mary Hays as well. Benson Bobrick, in his 1997 *Angel in the Whirlwind: The Triumph of the American Revolution* (New York: Simon & Schuster, 1997), follows folkloric accounts picked up in the mid–nineteenth century when he writes, without citation, that "Mary Ludwig Hayes . . . had done equally brave service at Fort Clinton, where, in October 1777, she had actually fired the last shot before the fortress fell" (346).
49. "Supposedly": About.com Women's History, http://womenshistory.about.com/od/waramrevolution/a/Molly-Pitcher.htm. "May have" and "according to legend": Joyce Appleby, Alan Brinkley, Albert S. Broussard, James M. McPherson, and Donald A. Ritchie, *The American Journey* (New York: Macmillan/McGraw-Hill Glencoe, 2012), 164. "Legend says": Emma J. Lapsansky-Werner, Peter B. Levy, Randy Roberts, and Alan Taylor, *United States History*, Survey Edition (Upper Saddle River, NJ: Prentice Hall, 2013), 164, 119. "Is said to have": Jacqueline Jones, Peter H. Wood, Thomas Borstelmann, Elaine Tyrler May, and Vicki L. Ruiz, *Created Equal: A History of the United States*, vol. 1 (Upper Saddle River, NJ: Pearson Longman, 2009), 221.
50. "Legendary": James West Davidson, Michael B. Scott, *America: A History of Our Nation* (Upper Saddle River, NJ: Prentice Hall, 2014), 188. "Earning folk-legend status": Jones et al., *Created Equal*, 221.
51. Appleby et al., *American Journey*, 155.
52. Michael J. Berson, Tyrone C. Howard, and Cinthia Salinas, *Harcourt Social Studies—United States: Making a New Nation* (Boston: Houghton Mifflin Harcourt, 2012), 357.

53. Gerald A. Danzer, J. Jorge Klor de Alva, Larry S. Krieger, Louis E. Wilson, and Nancy Woloch, *The Americans* (Evanston, IL: Holt McDougal, 2012), 117.
54. Wikipedia, accessed April 7, 2013: http://en.wikipedia.org/wiki/Molly_Pitcher. The article further quotes *They Called Her Molly Pitcher*: "At one point, a British musket ball or cannon ball flew between her legs and tore off the bottom of her skirt. Mary supposedly said, 'Well, that could have been worse,' and went back to loading the cannon"—an age-appropriate translation of Joseph Plumb Martin's ribald tale. (See note 15.)
55. Stryker, *Battle of Monmouth*, 192.
56. For a discussion of women in the wagons, and Washington's general distaste for women in the army, see Ray Raphael, *A People's History of the American Revolution* (New York: The New Press, 2001, 121–123; reprinted by HarperCollins, 2002, 153–155).

4: The Shot Heard 'Round the World

1. David Hackett Fischer, *Paul Revere's Ride* (New York and Oxford: Oxford University Press 1994), 327.
2. A.J. Langguth, *Patriots: The Men Who Started the American Revolution* (New York: Simon & Schuster, 1988), 240.
3. Joy Hakim, *A History of US* (New York: Oxford University Press, 2003), 3: 73.
4. Alan Brinkley, *The Unfinished Nation: A Concise History of the American People, Volume 1*, Seventh Edition (New York: McGraw-Hill, 2014), 102. Emphases added.
5. Americans didn't call this controversial act of vandalism a "Tea Party" at the time. (Alfred F. Young, *The Shoemaker and the Tea Party* [Boston: Beacon Press, 1999], 108–113.) Public reception, even among those who opposed British policies, was divided. Washington, although he believed "the cause of America . . . ever will be the cause of America," chided Bostonians for "their conduct in destroying the tea." (Washington to George William Fairfax, June 10, 1774, *The Papers of George Washington*, W.W. Abbot and Dorothy Twohig, eds. [Charlottesville, University Press of Virginia, 1983; Colonial Series 10: 94–101].) Franklin and many others believed the East India Company should be compensated for the ruined merchandise.
6. David M. Kennedy and Lizabeth Cohen, *The American Pageant*, Volume 1, Fifteenth Edition (Boston: Cengage Learning, 2014), 118.
7. James West Davidson and Michael B. Scott, *America: History of Our Nation* (Upper Saddle River, NJ: Prentice Hall, 2014), 152.
8. William Deverell and Deborah Gray White, *Holt McDougal United States History: Beginnings to 1877* (Boston: Houghton Mifflin Harcourt, 2012), 112.
9. Much is made in many narratives about the "Day of Prayer and Fasting" held in Virginia, the most populous colony, on June 1, 1774. Supposedly, this revealed how devoted the Virginians were to the people of Massachusetts, since it caused the British to disband the Virginia House of Burgesses. In fact, many Virginians were acting in self-interest, not charity, when they decided on this course. The previous year, growers of tobacco (the basis of Virginia's economy) had announced that by 1775 they would withhold their

crops from the market. They hoped that British merchants would then buy tobacco at higher prices, anticipating the shortage to come. Since many tobacco planters were in debt, however, they feared that creditors would take them to court in retaliation, and if their scheme failed, the courts could seize their property. Supporting Boston with a "Day of Prayer and Fasting" and a pledge to boycott British trade solved all their problems. Not only did these actions give their market manipulation a patriotic cover, but they also caused the British government to dissolve the legislature—and since the legislature had not yet authorized the court fees, that meant the courts would have to close as well. The planters' plan worked: tobacco prices soared in anticipation of future shortages while growers sold out their crops before nonexportation was scheduled to take effect. Meanwhile, no British merchants could take any Virginians to court for unpaid bills.

Boston had asked other colonies to withdraw trade from both Britain and the West Indies. For the reasons just mentioned, Virginia planters were more than willing to comply with respect to Britain, but they refused to end their lucrative trade with the Indies. Similarly, South Carolina went along with much of the boycott but insisted on an exemption for rice, its main moneymaker. These actions, traditionally touted as sympathetic gestures of support, had decidedly self-serving overtones. (Woody Holton, *Forced Founders: Indians, Debtors, Slaves and the Making of the American Revolution in Virginia* [Chapel Hill: University of North Carolina Press, 1999], 115–129.)

10. A "revolution," according to the *Random House Webster's College Dictionary*, is "a complete and forcible overthrow and replacement of an established government or political system by the people governed." By this definition, the people of Massachusetts staged a textbook example of a revolution.
11. American Political Society, Records, American Antiquarian Society, Worcester; documents page of rayraphael.com: http://www.rayraphael.com/documents.htm.
12. Stephen Salisbury to Samuel Salisbury, July 22, 1774, Salisbury Family Papers, American Antiquarian Society, Worcester; Ray Raphael, *The First American Revolution: Before Lexington and Concord* (New York: The New Press, 2002), 108; documents page of rayraphael.com: http://www.rayraphael.com/documents.htm.
13. The story of the 1774 overthrow of British authority throughout Massachusetts, outlined in this and subsequent paragraphs, is told and referenced in Raphael, *First American Revolution*, 59–168.
14. Joseph Clarke to unknown recipient, August 30, 1774, in James R. Trumbull, *History of Northampton, Massachusetts, from its Settlement in 1654* (Northampton, MA: Gazette Printing Co., 1902), 346–348; reprinted in Raphael, *First American Revolution*, 98–101.
15. Gage to Secretary of State Lord Dartmouth, August 27, 1774, *Correspondence of General Thomas Gage*, Clarence E. Carter, ed. (New Haven: Yale University Press, 1931), 1: 366.
16. Raphael, *First American Revolution*, 130–138. Meanwhile, in Cambridge, some four thousand patriots forced the lieutenant governor of Massachusetts, the second highest official in the province, to resign his seat on the Council.
17. Ezra Stiles, *The Literary Diary of Ezra Stiles*, Franklin B. Dexter, ed. (New York: Charles Scribner's Sons, 1901), 479–481.

18. John Adams, *Diary and Autobiography*, L.H. Butterfield, ed. (Cambridge: Belknap Press, 1961), 2: 160.
19. Gage to Dartmouth, September 2, 1774, Gage, *Correspondence*, 1: 370.
20. American Political Society, Records.
21. Ebenezer Parkman, Diary, American Antiquarian Society; documents page of rayra phael.com: http://www.rayraphael.com/documents.htm.
22. Proceedings of the Worcester County Convention, September 6–7, William Lincoln, ed., *The Journals of Each Provincial Congress of Massachusetts in 1774 and 1775, and of the Committee of Safety, with an Appendix, containing the Proceedings of the County Conventions* (Boston: Dutton and Wentworth, 1838), 635. Access at documents page of rayraphael.com: http://www.rayraphael.com/documents.htm. From this source, with the Parkman diary, we can reconstruct the events of the day.
23. Lincoln, *Journals and Proceedings*, 637.
24. John Andrews to William Barrell, October 6, 1774, in Massachusetts Historical Society, "Letters of John Andrews of Boston, 1772–1776," *Proceedings 8* (1864–1865), 373–374.
25. Andrews to Barrell, August 29, 1774, in Andrews, "Letters," 348.
26. Proceedings, Worcester County Convention, September 20–21, 1774, Lincoln, *Journals and Proceedings*, 643.
27. Jonathan Judd Jr., Diary, vol. 2 (1773–1782), Forbes Library, Northampton, entry for September 7, 1774.
28. Worcester Town Records, Worcester City Hall, reprinted in Franklin P. Rice, ed., *Worcester Town Records from 1753 to 1783* (Worcester: Worcester Society of Antiquity, 1882), 244. These instructions can be viewed in Ray Raphael, "Instructions: The People's Voice in Revolutionary America," *Common-Place* 9:1 (October 2008), http://www.common-place.org/vol-09/no-01/raphael/ or on the documents page of rayraphael.com: http://www.rayraphael.com/documents.htm.
29. Samuel Adams to Joseph Warren, September 25, 1774, Harry Alonzo Cushing, ed., *Writings of Samuel Adams* (New York: G.P. Putnam & Sons, 1907), 3: 159.
30. John Adams to Joseph Palmer, September 26, 1774, and John Adams to William Tudor, October 7, 1774, in Robert J. Taylor, ed., *Papers of John Adams* (Cambridge: Harvard University Press, 1977), 2: 173 and 2: 187.
31. Journal of First Provincial Congress, Lincoln, *Journals and Proceedings*, 30.
32. A good account of the storming of Fort William and Mary appears in Fischer, *Paul Revere's Ride*, 52–58. Documentary sources are reprinted in Charles L. Parsons, "The Capture of Fort William and Mary, December 14 and 15, 1774," *New Hampshire Historical Society Proceedings* 4 (1890–1905), 18–47.
33. *Providence Gazette*, December 23, 1774; Fischer, *Paul Revere's Ride*, 57; J.L. Bell, *"Behold, the Guns Were Gone!": Four Brass Cannon and the Start of the American Revolution* (Boston: Massachusetts Historical Society, 2001).
34. L. Kinvin Wroth, ed., *Province in Rebellion: A Documentary History of the Founding of the Commonwealth of Massachusetts, 1774–1775* (Cambridge: Harvard University Press, 1975), document 671, page 1969. Benjamin Church, an informant who was a member of the Provincial Congress's key Committee of Safety, was the likely source of this

intelligence. Three days earlier, an intelligence report stated that "Twelve pieces of Brass Cannon mounted, are at Salem and lodged near the North River, on the back of the town." (Ibid., document 670, page 1968.)

35. Henry S. Commager and Richard B. Morris, eds., *The Spirit of 'Seventy-Six: The Story of the American Revolution as Told by the Participants* (Indianapolis and New York: Bobbs-Merrill, 1958), 1: 63–65.
36. Andrews, "Letters," 401.
37. Allen French, *General Gage's Informers* (New York: Greenwood Press, 1968), 15; "General Gage's Instructions of 22d February, 1775, to Captain Brown and Ensign D'Bernicre," and "Narrative, &c.," Massachusetts Historical Society *Collections* 4 (1916): 204–218.
38. James Warren to Mercy Otis Warren, April 6, 1775, *Warren-Adams Letters* (Boston: Massachusetts Historical Society, 1917), 1: 44–45.
39. *The Annual Register for the Year 1775* (London: J. Dodsley, 1776), 2–3, 16–17.
40. David Ramsay, *The History of the American Revolution* (Philadelphia: R. Aitken and Son, 1789; reprinted by Liberty Classics in 1990), 1: 106–107.
41. William Gordon, *The History of the Rise, Progress, and Establishment, of the Independence of the United States of America*, reprint edition (Freeport, NY: Books for Libraries Press, 1969; first published in 1788), 1: 382, 380, 377.
42. Mercy Otis Warren, *History of the Rise, Progress and Termination of the American Revolution, interspersed with Biographical, Political and Moral Observations* (Boston: E. Larkin, 1805; reprinted by Liberty Classics in 1988), 1: 145–146. In 1776 Samuel Adams himself took note of the dramatic turn of events "since the stopping of the Courts in Berkshire." In context, he seemed to be marking the beginning of the Revolution by this event. (Samuel Adams to Joseph Hawley, April 15, 1776, in Cushing, *Writings of Samuel Adams*, 3: 281.)
43. Paul Allen, *A History of the American Revolution: Comprising All the Principal Events Both in the Field and in the Cabinet* (Baltimore: John Hopkins, 1819), 1: 180–198.
44. Salma Hale, *History of the United States, from their First Settlement as Colonies, to the Close of the War with Great Britain in 1815* (New York: Collins and Hannay, 1830; first published in 1822), 142–144.
45. Charles A. Goodrich, *A History of the United States of America* (Hartford, CT: Barber and Robinson, 1823), 154.
46. Richard Snowden, *The American Revolution Written in the Style of Ancient History* (Philadelphia: Jones, Hoff and Derrick, 1793), 1: 14.
47. George Bancroft, *History of the United States of America* (Boston: Little, Brown, and Co., 1879; first published in 1854), 4: 379, 389, 390.
48. William V. Wells, *The Life and Public Services of Samuel Adams* (Freeport, NY: Books for Libraries Press, 1969; first published in 1865).
49. Commager and Morris, *The Spirit of 'Seventy-Six*, 31–38, 45–56, 66–97.
50. Here is one telling example. On a September evening in 1774, Abigail Adams, at home in Braintree, Massachusetts, observed from her window some two hundred men who had gathered to seize gunpowder from the local powder house and force the sheriff to

burn two warrants he was attempting to deliver. Some might call these men a "mob," but Adams observed otherwise. Successful in their missions, the men wanted to celebrate with a loud "huzzah." Normally they would, but there were extenuating circumstances this time. Should they, or should they not, disturb the Sabbath? "They call'd a vote," Abigail reported to John, who was in Philadelphia at the time attending the First Continental Congress, and "it being Sunday evening it passed in the negative." (Abigail Adams to John Adams, September 14, 1774, in Adams Family Correspondence, L.H. Butterfield, ed. [Cambridge, MA: Belknap Press of Harvard University Press, 1963], 1: 152.)

51. For the mislabeling of "Shays' Rebellion," see "Conclusion: Why We Tell Tall Tales."
52. French, *General Gage's Informers*, 20–21.
53. Fischer, *Paul Revere's Ride*, 249.
54. Some examples: As they mustered in the early morning hours at Wright's Tavern, Concord's farmers-turned-soldiers debated with each other the prospect of defending their town. When the Regulars finally reached Concord, no militiamen stood in the way; some had wanted to make a stand there, but they were outvoted. The younger, more impetuous minute men then sallied forth to the east, thinking they might face off against the Regulars from that stance, but upon viewing the enemy's vast numbers, they wisely retreated. Again on Meetinghouse Hill, with a commanding view of Main Street, the Concord militiamen debated whether to stand and fight or stage a strategic retreat, and again they settled on the wiser course, waiting for their numbers to grow. At the North Bridge they also consulted each other and debated the wisest course. These were collective strategic decisions, not knee-jerk individual responses. Fischer, *Paul Revere's Ride*, 204–205, 208–209.
55. Herbert T. Wade and Robert A. Lively, eds., *This Glorious Cause: The Adventures of Two Company Officers in George Washington's Army* (Princeton: Princeton University Press, 1958), 9.
56. Timothy Pickering, *An Easy Plan of Discipline for a Militia* (Boston: S. Hall, 1776), 9–10, quoted in Justin Florence, "Minutemen for Months: The Making of an American Revolutionary Army before George Washington, April 2–July 2, 1775," *Proceedings of the American Antiquarian Society*, 113: 1 (2003), 76–77.
57. John Shy, *A People Numerous and Armed: Reflections on the Military Struggle for American Independence* (Ann Arbor: University of Michigan Press, 1990), 238.

5: Winter at Valley Forge

1. F. Van Wyck Mason, *The Winter at Valley Forge* (New York: Random House, 1953), 1, 6, 7, 8. In full disclosure, this was among the first serious books I read; it had just come out, I was in fifth grade, and I loved it.
2. Howard Peckham, in his tabulation of battlefield casualties, lists only fifteen American deaths during the three winter months that the Continental Army was camped at Valley Forge—and not a single one of these occurred in Pennsylvania. The deadliest skirmish in this period was an Indian attack at Dunkard Creek, in western Virginia. (Peckham, *The Toll of Independence* [Chicago: University of Chicago Press, 1974], 46–48.)

3. Washington to John Hancock, September 24, 1776, in *The Writings of George Washington from the Original Manuscript Sources*, John C. Fitzpatrick, ed. (Washington, DC: United States Government Printing Office, 1931–1944), 6: 107–108.
4. John Shy, *A People Numerous and Armed: Reflections on the Military Struggle for American Independence* (Ann Arbor: University of Michigan Press, 1990), 173.
5. Soldiers John Brooks and Isaac Gibbs, cited in Wayne Bodle, *The Valley Forge Winter: Civilians and Soldiers in War* (University Park: Pennsylvania State University Press, 2002), 127, 202.
6. Cited from the diary of Albigence Waldo in Charles Royster, *A Revolutionary People at War: The Continental Army and the American Character, 1775–1783* (Chapel Hill: University of North Carolina Press, 1979), 191.
7. Bodle, *Valley Forge Winter*, 134.
8. Joseph Plumb Martin, *Narrative of a Revolutionary Soldier* (New York: Signet, 2001; originally published in 1830), 245.
9. Bodle, *Valley Forge Winter*, 165–169; Washington to Nathanael Greene, February 12, 1778, in Fitzpatrick, *Writings of George Washington*, 10: 454–455.
10. Martin, *Narrative*, 90.
11. Royster, *A Revolutionary People at War*, 196.
12. Bodle, *Valley Forge Winter*, 180; Washington to Thomas Wharton, February 12, 1778, in Fitzpatrick, *Writings of George Washington*, 10: 452–453.
13. Washington to the president of Congress, December 23, 1777, in Fitzpatrick, *Writings of George Washington*, 10: 193.
14. Washington to William Smallwood, February 16, 1778, and Washington to George Clinton, February 16, 1778, in Fitzpatrick, *Writings of George Washington*, 10: 467, 469.
15. Washington to John Banister, April 21, 1778, in Fitzpatrick, *Writings of George Washington*, 11: 285.
16. Thomas Fleming, *Liberty! The American Revolution* (New York: Viking, 1997), 20.
17. Edmund Lindop, *Birth of the Constitution* (Hillside, NJ: Enslow Publishers, 1987), 16.
18. Martin, *Narrative*, 157.
19. Ibid., 161–162.
20. David M. Ludlum, *The Weather Factor* (Boston: Houghton Mifflin, 1984), 50–51.
21. Temperatures for the winter of 1777–1778 come from Thomas Coombe, who resided in what is now West Philadelphia, near Sixty-Third Street and Market Street, about seventeen miles southeast of Valley Forge. Coombe took at least two readings every day from an outdoor thermometer, one at 8:00 a.m. and one at 2:00 or 3:00 p.m., roughly corresponding to the low and high temperatures of the day. Most evenings, he also recorded temperatures at 9:00 or 10:00. The vast majority of the "low" temperatures tabulated in this chart are from the 8:00 a.m. readings. (David M. Ludlum, *Early American Winters, 1604–1820* [Boston: American Meteorological Society, 1966], 1: 101.) The historic average comes from the low daily temperatures reported on the Internet by CityRatings .com.
22. Ludlum, *Weather Factor*, 57.
23. Joseph Lee Boyle, "The Weather and the Continental Army, August 1777–June 1778,"

unpublished manuscript, available electronically by contacting the Valley Forge National Historical Park, www.nps.gov/vafo/. Boyle's masterful work is a chronological compilation of primary sources that mention the weather and its impact on the army, for both the winter of 1777–1778 and the winter of 1779–1780. Because the manuscript is transmitted electronically, pagination is not reliable. Boyle's entries appear in chronological order, however, so citation should be easy to locate. The section on the 1779–1780 winter at Morristown appears at the end of the manuscript.

24. Boyle, "Weather and the Continental Army." In Elizabethtown, near Morristown, the *indoor* temperature in the morning never rose above freezing for the entire month. (See "The Hard Winter of 1779–1780," available electronically from the Morristown National Historical Park. www.nps.gov/morr/.)
25. Ludlum, *Weather Factor*, 57.
26. Ludlum, *Early American Winters*, 1: 115.
27. Ludlum, *Weather Factor*, 56.
28. Ludlum, *Early American Winters*, 1: 114–116; Ludlum, *Weather Factor*, 56–58; Boyle, "Weather and the Continental Army."
29. Martin, *Narrative*, 147–148.
30. Boyle, "Weather and the Continental Army."
31. Ibid.
32. Washington to magistrates of Virginia, January 8, 1780, in Fitzpatrick, *Writings of George Washington*, 17: 362–363; cited in Boyle, "Weather and the Continental Army."
33. Boyle, "Weather and the Continental Army."
34. Ibid.
35. Washington to Lafayette, March 18, 1780, in Fitzpatrick, *Writings of George Washington*, 18: 124–125. Cited in Ludlum, *The Weather Factor*, 59, and Boyle, "Weather and the Continental Army."
36. According to Eric P. Olsen, park ranger and historian at Morristown National Historical Park: "Parts of the Continental Army spent four winters around Morristown during the Revolutionary War. The first two winters featured General Washington and the bulk of the 'main' Continental Army. The later two winters did not include Washington and featured only small parts of the Continental Army. First winter, January 1777 to May 1777—Washington stays at Arnold's Tavern in Morristown [building no longer exists]. The troops stay in private homes and public buildings spread out from Princeton through Morristown to the Hudson Highlands. Second winter, December 1779 to June 1780—Washington stays at the Ford Mansion [part of Morristown NHP] and up to 13,000 soldiers camp 5 miles south of Morristown in Jockey Hollow [also part of Morristown NHP]. Third winter, November 1780 to January 1781—The Pennsylvania Line camps in Jockey Hollow while Washington is in New Windsor, NY. The Pennsylvania Line mutinies on January 1, 1780, and most of them leave Jockey Hollow. Later in January/February 1781 the Pennsylvania Line is replaced in Jockey Hollow by the New Jersey Brigade. The NJ Brigade had been camped further north in New Jersey and had also mutinied but their mutiny, unlike the PA Line mutiny, was suppressed. The NJ Brigade stays in Jockey Hollow until sometime in the Spring/Summer of 1781. Fourth

winter, 1781–1782—The New Jersey Brigade returns to Jockey Hollow for this winter." (Personal correspondence, September 2003.)

37. According to military historian Howard Peckham, about seven thousand American soldiers lost their lives in battle, while ten thousand American soldiers perished from disease. (Peckham, *Toll of Independence*, 130.)
38. Washington to Congress, December 22 and 23, 1777, Fitzpatrick, *Writings of George Washington*, 10: 183, 195–196.
39. Washington to Congress, December 22, 1777, Fitzpatrick, *Writings of George Washington*, 10: 183. Washington was also the source of the defining metaphor of the soldiers' plight: on April 21, 1778, he wrote that because the soldiers had no shoes, "their Marches might be traced by the blood from their feet." (Washington to John Banister, April 21, 1778, Fitzpatrick, *Writings of George Washington*, 11: 291.) William Gordon, in his 1788 history of the Revolution, claimed that Washington had told the story to him personally at a dinner party after the war: "Through the want of shoes and stockings, and the hard frozen ground, you might have tracked the army from White Marsh to Valley-forge by the blood of their feet." (William Gordon, *The History of the Rise, Progress, and Establishment, of the Independence of the United States of America*, reprint edition [Freeport, NY: Books for Libraries Press, 1969, first published in 1788], 3: 11–12.) Writers for over two centuries have followed Gordon's lead, using this catchy image to sum up the winter's experience. Lost in the translation has been a practical aspect of this quaint remark: tracking footprints in those days was a matter of military importance.
40. John Marshall, *Life of George Washington* (London and Philadelphia: Richard Phillips, 1804–1807), 3: 279–282.
41. Mercy Otis Warren, *History of the Rise, Progress and Termination of the American Revolution, interspersed with Biographical, Political and Moral Observations* (Boston: E. Larkin, 1805; reprinted by Liberty Classics in 1988), 1: 389; 3: 268–269.
42. Quoted in John Resch, *Suffering Soldiers: Revolutionary War Veterans, Moral Sentiment, and Political Culture in the Early Republic* (Amherst: University of Massachusetts Press, 1999), 72.
43. Mason L. Weems, *The Life of Washington* (Cambridge, MA: Belknap Press, 1962; reprint of ninth edition, 1809), 181–182. After the sixth edition, the story was included in all others.
44. Resch, *Suffering Soldiers*, 75.
45. Ibid., 73–74.
46. Salma Hale, *History of the United States, from their first Settlement as Colonies, to the Close of the War with Great Britain in 1815* (New York: Cothins and Hannay, 1830; first published in 1822), 188–189.
47. Charles A. Goodrich, *A History of the United States of America* (Hartford, CT: Barber and Robinson, 1823), 193.
48. From the *Tri-Weekly Post*, Springfield, MA, March 7, 1848. Cited in Boyle, "Weather at Valley Forge," Introduction.
49. Benson Lossing, *The Pictorial Field-Book of the Revolution* (New York: Harper & Brothers, 1851), 2: 331. George Bancroft, writing in the same era, cemented a place for Valley

Forge in America's collective memory. Bancroft devoted a full chapter to "Winter-Quarters at Valley Forge," but only half a paragraph to the winter camp of 1779–1780, without even mentioning Morristown by name. For Bancroft, the secret to the soldiers' success at Valley Forge was filial piety: "Washington's unsleeping vigilance . . . secured them against surprise; love of country and attachment to their general sustained them under their unparalleled hardships; with any other leader, the army would have dissolved and vanished." Bancroft played heavily on the contrast between the British and American armies: while Continental soldiers at Valley Forge starved and froze, the Redcoats in Philadelphia danced, gambled, and attended theatrical productions. (George Bancroft, *History of the United States of America, from the Discovery of the Continent* [Boston: Little, Brown, 1879; first published 1834–1874], 6: 41, 46.) Richard Hildreth, writing concurrently with Lossing and Bancroft, gave a more matter-of-fact rendering of the winter at Valley Forge, in keeping with his usual style. Although he detailed the shortages and bemoaned the need for soldiers to forage for their food, he did not glorify their suffering or use it to indulge in effusive displays of patriotism. (Richard Hildreth, *The History of the United States of America* [New York: Harper & Brothers, 1849; Augustus Kelly reprint of 1880 edition, 1969], 3: 231–232.)

50. Lorett Treese, *Valley Forge: Making and Remaking a National Symbol*, published on the Internet site for the Valley Forge National Historical Park, www.nps.gov/vafo/.
51. John Mack Faragher, Mari Jo Buhle, Daniel Czitrom, and Susan H. Armitage, *Out of Many: A History of the American People*, Seventh Edition (Upple Saddle River, NJ: Pearson/Prentice Hall, 2012), 165–67. Ironically, the text does mention one of the four winters at Morristown—but only the first winter there (1776–1777), not the notorious hard winter of 1779–1780—and it does so to contrast that earlier winter to "the hard winter at Valley Forge."
52. Allen Bowman, *The Morale of the American Revolutionary Army* (Port Washington, NY: Kennikat Press, 1943), 30; Broadus Mitchell, *The Price of Independence: A Realistic View of the American Revolution* (New York: Oxford University Press, 1974), 117–118.

6: Jefferson's Declaration

1. Thomas Fleming, *Liberty! The American Revolution* (New York: Viking, 1997), 170–171.
2. Joseph Ellis, *American Sphinx: The Character of Thomas Jefferson* (New York: Alfred A. Knopf, 1997), 56–59.
3. Locke was read by the more educated classes. Copies of the *Second Treatise on Government*, which patriots called "Liberty Books," circulated particularly among preachers, who contributed to the spread of Lockean ideas.
4. Woody Holton, *Forced Founders: Indians, Debtors, Slaves, and the Making of the American Revolution in Virginia* (Chapel Hill: University of North Carolina Press, 1999), 106–129, 191–205.
5. Michael A. McDonnell, *The Politics of War: Race, Class, and Conflict in Revolutionary Virginia* (Chapel Hill: University of North Carolina Press, 2007), 203; Holton, *Forced*

Founders, 200–205. The turnover in the fifth Virginia Convention was 38 percent, compared with only 4 percent for the third and fourth Virginia Conventions.

6. Charles Lee to Patrick Henry, May 7, 1776, in Holton, *Forced Founders*, 199.
7. Jefferson to Thomas Nelson, May 16, 1776, in Julian P. Boyd, ed., *Papers of Thomas Jefferson* (Princeton: Princeton University Press, 1950), 1: 292.
8. Mason's draft from *Pennsylvania Gazette*, June 12, 1776; Jefferson's draft from Pauline Maier, *American Scripture: Making the Declaration of Independence* (New York: Vintage, 1998; first published 1997), 236–241, with the ungrammatical "it's" for "its" left intact. Jefferson would certainly have scrutinized all the reports emanating from the Virginia Convention, particularly any matter relating to the issue of independence. At the time, Jefferson thought the work of the Virginia Convention in setting up a constitution for the newly independent state of Virginia was more important than the work of the Continental Congress, and he suggested Virginia recall its delegates so they could help with that state constitution. (Jefferson to Thomas Nelson, May 16, 1776, in Lyman H. Butterfield and Mina R. Bryan, eds., *Papers of Thomas Jefferson* [Princeton: Princeton University Press, 1950], 1: 292.)
9. A list of these documents appears in Maier, *American Scripture*, 217–223.
10. Peter Force, ed., *American Archives, Fourth Series: A Documentary History of the English Colonies in North America from the King's Message to Parliament of March 7, 1774, to the Declaration of Independence by the United States* (New York: Johnson Reprint Corporation, 1972; first published 1833–1846), 6: 933. For the practice of issuing instructions, see Ray Raphael, "Instructions: The People's Voice in Revolutionary America," Common-Place 9:1 (October 2008), http://www.common-place.org/vol-09/no-01/raphael/.
11. From the Congress of North Carolina, April 12, 1776, in Force, *American Archives, Fourth Series*, 5: 860.
12. Ibid., 6: 933.
13. Ibid., 5: 1208–1209.
14. Here, for instance, is a list of grievances from the "Declaration of the Delegates of Maryland":

    "The Parliament of Great Britain has of late claimed an uncontrollable right of binding these Colonies in all cases whatsoever. To enforce an unconditional submission to this claim, the Legislative and Executive powers of that state have invariably pursued for these ten years past a studied system of oppression, by passing many impolitick, severe, and cruel acts for raising a revenue from the Colonists; by depriving them in many cases of the trial by Jury; by altering the chartered Constitution of one Colony, and the entire stoppage of the trade of its Capital; by cutting off all intercourse between the Colonies; by restraining them from fishing on their own coasts; by extending the limits of, and erecting an arbitrary Government in the Province of Quebeck; by confiscating the property of the Colonists taken on the seas, and compelling the crews of their vessels, under the pain of death, to act against their native country and dearest friends; by declaring all seizures, detention, or destruction, of the persons or property of the Colonists, to be legal and just." (Force, *American Archives, Fourth Series*, 6: 1506.)

15. Ibid., 6: 557, 603. Although the other declarations varied in style and length, they were similar in their intent: the time had come for the United States to make a clean break. One example will stand for the rest:

> To the Honourable Representatives of the Province of New-York, in Provincial Congress convened. The humble Address of the General Committee of Mechanicks in union, of the City and County of New-York, in behalf of themselves and their constituents:
>
> GENTLEMEN: We, as a part of your constituents, and devoted friends to our bleeding country, beg leave, in a dutiful manner, at this time to approach unto you, our Representatives, and request your kind attention to this our humble address.
>
> When we cast a glance upon our beloved continent, where fair freedom, civil and religious, we have long enjoyed, whose fruitful fields have made the world glad, and whose trade has filled with plenty of all things, sorrow fills our hearts to behold her now struggling under the heavy load of oppression, tyranny, and death. But when we extend our sight a little farther, and view the iron hand that is lifted up against us, behold it is our King; he who by his oath and station, is bound to support and defend us in the quiet enjoyment of all our glorious rights as freemen, and whose dominions have been supported and made rich by our commerce. Shall we any longer sit silent, and contentedly continue the subjects of such a Prince, who is deaf to our petitions for interposing his Royal authority in our behalf, and for redressing our grievances, but, on the contrary, seems to take pleasure in our destruction? When we see that one whole year is not enough to satisfy the rage of a cruel Ministry, in burning our towns, seizing our vessels, and murdering our precious sons of liberty; making weeping widows for the loss of those who were dearer to them than life, and helpless orphans to bemoan the death of an affectionate father; but who are still carrying on the same bloody pursuit; and for no other reason than this, that we will not become their slaves, and be taxed by them without our consent,—therefore, as we would rather choose to be separate from, than to continue any longer in connection with such oppressors, We, the Committee of Mechanicks in union, do, for ourselves and our constituents, hereby publickly declare that, should you, gentlemen of the honourable Provincial Congress, think proper to instruct our most honourable Delegates in Continental Congress to use their utmost endeavors in that august assembly to cause these United Colonies to become independent of Great Britain, it would give us the highest satisfaction; and we hereby sincerely promise to endeavour to support the same with our lives and fortunes.
>
> Signed by order of the Committee,
>
> Lewis Thibou, Chairman.
>
> Mechanick-Hall, New York, May 29, 1776.
>
> (Force, *American Archives*, *Fourth Series*, 6: 614–615.)

16. Philip F. Detweiler, "The Changing Reputation of the Declaration of Independence: The First Fifty Years," *William and Mary Quarterly*, Third Series, 19 (1962): 559–561.
17. Maier, *American Scripture*, 165–167; Detweiler, "Changing Reputation," 561.
18. Lincoln-Douglas debate, Ottawa, IL, August 21, 1858, in Abraham Lincoln, *Political Writings and Speeches*, Terence Ball, ed. (Cambridge and New York: Cambridge University Press, 2013), xxvii.
19. Detweiler, "Changing Reputation," 562. Henry's speech on June 16, 1788, is most readily accessible at University of Chicago Press, *The Founders' Constitution*, Major Themes, chapter 14, document 39: http://press-pubs.uchicago.edu/founders/documents/v1ch14s39.html.
20. David Ramsay, *The History of the American Revolution* (Philadelphia: R. Aitken & Son, 1789; reprinted by Liberty Classics in 1990), 1: 340–346; William Gordon, *The History of the Rise, Progress, and Establishment, of the Independence of the United State of America* (Freeport, NY: Books for Libraries Press, 1969; first published in 1788), 2: 274–297.
21. Charles Warren, "Fourth of July Myths," *William and Mary Quarterly*, Third Series, 2 (1945): 263.
22. John Marshall, *The Life of George Washington* (New York, AMS Press, 1969; first published 1804–1807), 2: 405.
23. Ironically, Marshall, a leading Federalist, described the declaring of independence with a populist slant, highlighting "the people" rather than Jefferson. "American independence became the general theme of conversation, and, more and more, the general wish," he wrote. "The measures in Congress took their complexion from the temper of the people." Marshall, *Life of George Washington*, 2: 396–404.
24. Mercy Otis Warren, *History of the Rise, Progress and Termination of the American Revolution, interspersed with Biographical, Political and Moral Observations* (Boston: E. Larkin, 1805; reprinted by Liberty Classics in 1988), 3: 307–308. This appears in her concluding remarks. Earlier in the text, Warren wrote that the Declaration was "drawn by the ingenious and philosophic pen of Thomas Jefferson, Esquire." (1: 309.)
25. Irma B. Jaffe, *Trumbull: The Declaration of Independence* (New York: Viking, 1976), 69.
26. Maier, *American Scripture*, 175–176; Detweiler, "Changing Reputation," 572.
27. Jaffe, *Trumbull*, 62–66.
28. Maier, *American Scripture*, 186.
29. Jefferson to Dr. James Mease, September 26, 1825, in Paul Leicester Ford, ed., *Writings of Thomas Jefferson* (New York: G.P. Putnam's Sons, 1899), 10: 346.
30. John Adams to Benjamin Rush, June 21, 1811, in John A. Schutz and Douglass Adair, eds., *The Spur of Fame: Dialogues of John Adams and Benjamin Rush, 1805–1813* (San Marino, CA: Huntington Library, 1966), 182.
31. For Adams's most forceful statements of this argument, see his *Autobiography* and the accompanying letter to Timothy Pickering, August 6, 1822, in Charles Francis Adams, ed., *The Works of John Adams* (Boston: Charles Little and James Brown, 1850), 2: 510–515. Although Adams's memory of the committee was indeed flawed, the fact that the committee met, and that individual members made revisions, is suggested by Jefferson's own correspondence at the time. (See Robert E. McGlone, "Deciphering Memory: John

Adams and the Authorship of the Declaration of Independence," *Journal of American History* 85 [1998]: 411–438; and Maier, *American Scripture*, 101–102.) Here is the key piece of contemporary evidence: "Th. J. to Doctr. Franklyn. Friday morn. The inclosed paper has been read and with some small alterations approved of by the committee. Will Doctr. Franklyn be so good as to peruse it and suggest such alterations as his more enlarged view of the subject will dictate? The paper having been returned to me to change a particular sentiment or two, I propose laying it again before the committee tomorrow morning, if Doctr. Franklyn can think of it before that time." (Boyd, *Papers of Jefferson*, 1: 404.) There is no definitive proof that Jefferson's note to Franklin refers to the Declaration of Independence, but according to Julian Boyd, the editor, other possibilities are implausible, while all circumstantial and corroborating evidence points to the Declaration.

32. Jefferson to James Madison, August 30, 1823, in Ford, *Writings of Thomas Jefferson*, 10: 267. Jefferson further contended that the changes proffered by Franklin and Adams "were two or three only, and purely verbal." Even so, Jefferson laid no claim to the originality of his ideas. When Timothy Pickering, taking Adams's side, wrote that the Declaration "contained no new ideas, that it is a common-place compilation, its sentiments hacknied in Congress for two years before," Jefferson admitted that "may all be true," noting only, "I know only that I turned to neither book nor pamphlet in writing it."
33. Boyd, *Papers of Jefferson*, 1: 414.
34. "I did not consider it any part of my charge to invent new ideas altogether, and to offer no sentiment which had ever been expressed before." (Jefferson to Madison, August 30, 1823, Ford, *Writings of Thomas Jefferson*, 10: 267.)
35. Maier, *American Scripture*, 203–204.
36. Quoted in Garry Wills, *Inventing America: Jefferson's Declaration of Independence* (New York: Doubleday, 1978), xix–xx.
37. Maier, *American Scripture*, 202.
38. Force, *American Archives, Fourth Series*, 6: 514.
39. Ibid., 5: 1206.
40. Wills, *Inventing America*, xxi. Lincoln's argument would have been stronger had Jefferson stayed with Mason's phrase "equally free and independent," instead of paraphrasing the words of James Wilson, who had argued several years before that "all men are, by nature, equal and free." To Lincoln's contemporary critics, the vague and undefined notion of "equality" was preposterous: people were obviously not equal with respect to all sorts of physical attributes, let alone social position or political standing. Mason's terminology would have eliminated this glib rebuttal: "equally free and independent" makes it clear that people are to be considered equal precisely because they are free and independent. This would have provided a much more forceful argument against slavery, although Mason, like Jefferson, probably had not intended his words to be used to this end. Mason's Declaration of Rights, however, had lost its luster—not because of inferior wording, but because the congressional Declaration had supplanted it in the public mind and its primary author had become president.
41. For Jefferson's attitudes on miscegenation, see his *Notes on the State of Virginia* (Chapel Hill: University of North Carolina Press, 1955; written in 1781), 138–140. Jefferson's

breeding of slaves for profit can be deduced from his letters. On January 17, 1819, Jefferson wrote to his plantation overseer: "I consider the labor of a breeding woman as no object, and that a child raised every 2 years is of more profit than the crop of the best laboring man." The following year he reiterated this little piece of fiscal philosophy: "I consider a woman who brings a child every two years as more profitable than the best man of the farm. What she produces is an addition to capital, while his labors disappear in mere consumption." (Jefferson to Joel Yancy, January 17, 1819, and Jefferson to John W. Eppes, June 30, 1820, in Edwin Morris Betts, ed., *Thomas Jefferson's Farm Book* [Charlottesville: University Press of Virginia, 1976] 43, 46. Whenever Jefferson ran into debt, which was often, he could and did sell slaves to meet the demands of his creditors. (Betts, *Jefferson's Farm Book*, 5.) Compromised ethically and politically, Jefferson tried to conceal these embarrassing transactions in human flesh: "I do not (while in public life) like to have my name annexed in the public papers to the sale of property," he wrote—the "property," in this case, being a euphemism for slaves. (Jefferson to Bowling Clarke, September 21, 1792, in Betts, *Jefferson's Farm Book*, 13.)

42. For a discussion of the relation of Lincoln to others who made this argument before him, see Maier, *American Scripture*, xix–xx, 202–203.
43. Vivian Bernstein, *America's History: Land of Liberty—Beginning to 1877* (Austin, TX: Steck-Vaughn, 1997), 81.
44. Joy Hakim, *A History of US* (New York: Oxford University Press, 2003) 3: 98–100. This is the cornerstone of Hakim's treatment of the American Revolution. The cover copy for volume 3, *From Colonies to Country*, reads: "Read all about it! How the people in thirteen small colonies beat a great and very powerful nation, became free, and went on to write some astounding words that inspired the whole world."
45. James West Davidson and Michael B. Scott, *America: History of Our Nation* (Upper Saddle River, NJ: Prentice Hall, 2014), 171; William Deverell and Deborah Gray White, *Holt McDougal United States History: Beginnings to 1877* (Boston: Houghton Mifflin Harcourt, 2012), 110.
46. Although *Common Sense* circulated widely and certainly made its mark, only scant print records and no sales records survive, so we simply do not know how many copies were sold. The three numbers most often cited (100,000 and 120,000 and 150,000) were offered by Paine himself, who had no way of ascertaining the information but a great deal of interest in exaggerating his impact. The estimate of half a million was first posited by a biographer more than a century later. None of these estimates are realistic, given the demographics of the country, the state of the print industry, the location of the twenty-five known contemporary printings, and distribution patterns at that time. For the full story, see Trish Loughran, *The Republic in Print: Print Culture in the Age of U. S. Nation Building, 1770–1870* (New York: Columbia University Press, 2007), 40–58 and 253–261. For a brief rendition, see Ray Raphael, "Thomas Paine's Inflated Numbers," in *Journal of the American Revolution* (online), March 20, 2013: http://allthingsliberty.com/2013/03/thomas-paines-inflated-numbers./ The biography that posited 500,000 is Moncure Daniel Conway's *The Life of Thomas Paine: With a History of His Literary,*

Political, and Religious Career in America, France, and England (New York: G.P. Putnam's Sons, 1892) 1: 69 (chapter 6).

47. Jefferson to Henry Lee, May 8, 1825, in Ford, *Writings of Thomas Jefferson*, 10: 343. See also Jefferson to James Madison, August 30, 1823, in Ford, *Writings of Thomas Jefferson*, 10: 268.
48. Jefferson to Dr. James Mease, September 26, 1825, in Ford, *Writings of Thomas Jefferson*, 10: 346.

7: An Assembly of Demigods

1. Alexander Hamilton, James Madison, and John Jay, *The Federalist Papers* (originally titled *The Federalist*), Yale Law School, Avalon Project: http://avalon.law.yale.edu/18th_century/fed02.asp.
2. Lester Jesse Cappon, ed., *The Adams-Jefferson Letters: The Complete Correspondence between Thomas Jefferson and Abigail and John Adams* (Chapel Hill: University of North Carolina Press, 1959), 1: 194–196.
3. John Robert Irelan, *The Republic, or, A History of the United States of America* (Chicago: Fairbanks and Palmer, 1888), 15: 164.
4. Charles A. Beard, *An Economic Interpretation of the Constitution* (New York: Macmillan, 1913).
5. James Madison, *Notes of Debates in the Federal Convention of 1787*, Adrienne Koch, ed. (New York: W.W. Norton, 1987), May 30. On the Internet: Avalon Project, Yale Law School, http://avalon.law.yale.edu/subject_menus/debcont.asp. In this chapter I cite dates rather than page numbers since there are so many different editions of Madison's *Notes*. All quotations from the Federal Convention with identifying dates in my text are from Madison, unless otherwise specified. In several places my treatment of the debates here follows the line I took in *Constitutional Myths: What We Get Wrong and How to Get It Right* (New York: The New Press, 2013), 35–55, and, where noted, in *Mr. President: How and Why the Founders Created a Chief Executive* (New York: Alfred A. Knopf, 2012).
6. Ibid., June 29. For the political challenge, see Clinton Rossiter, *1787: The Grand Convention* (New York: Macmillan, 1966), 182–96.
7. Ibid., June 30. Five days later, on July 5, Bedford offered a nonapology apology that did nothing to lessen the small-state, large-state divide: "He found that what he had said as to the small States being taken by the hand, had been misunderstood; and he rose to explain. He did not mean that the small States would court the aid & interposition of foreign powers. He meant that they would not consider the federal compact as dissolved untill it should be so by the Acts of the large States. In this case The consequence of the breach of faith on their part, and the readiness of the small States to fulfill their engagements, would be that foreign Nations having demands on this Country would find it their interest to take the small States by the hand, in order to do themselves justice. This was what he meant. But no man can foresee to what extremities the small States may be driven by

oppression. He observed also in apology that some allowance ought to be made for the habits of his profession [Bedford was a lawyer] in which warmth was natural & sometimes necessary. But is there not an apology in what was said by [Mr. Govr. Morris] that the sword is to unite: by Mr. Ghorum that Delaware must be annexed to Penna. and N. Jersey divided between Penna. and N. York. To hear such language without emotion, would be to renounce the feelings of a man and the duty of a Citizen."

8. Ibid., July 5.
9. Ibid., June 29.
10. Many commentators suggest that Franklin was using the ploy to bring his colleagues to their senses. For a thoroughly researched discussion, see William G. Carr, *The Oldest Delegate: Franklin in the Constitutional Convention* (Newark: University of Delaware Press, 1990), 96–101.
11. Ibid., June 29.
12. Washington to Hamilton, July 10, 1787, W.W. Abbot and Dorothy Twohig, eds., *The Papers of George Washington* (Charlottesville: University Press of Virginia, 1983–), Confederation Series, 5: 257. Hamilton left the Convention because he was consistently outvoted by his New York colleagues Robert Yates and John Lansing Jr.
13. Madison, *Notes of Debates*, July 14 (Martin) and July 12 (Davie).
14. As with any vote on multiple issues, it is difficult to dissect the returns, but judging from previous and subsequent positions, it appears that a bloc of small states was happy to achieve equal representation in the second branch whereas Virginia and Pennsylvania, not ready to compromise, refused to concede and voted against the measure. South Carolina and perhaps Georgia also resisted compromise, with at least some delegates holding out for full slave representation. Delegates from Massachusetts were divided over the slavery compromise, while three of the four North Carolina delegates thought compromise on all issues was in order. At first glance the five-to-four tally might have seemed inconclusive, subject to being overturned in the future. But two states were not present, and both likely would have approved: New Hampshire because it was a small state and New York because it appeared to give the states legal representation in Congress. Tiny Rhode Island, not present at the Convention, would also have favored equal representation for small states, and Georgia, had all its delegates been present, might well have voted yes rather than no. The vote was not as close as it might appear. (Richard Beeman, *Plain, Honest Men: The Making of the American Constitution* [New York: Random House, 2010], 219–22.)
15. Madison, *Notes of Debates*, July 16.
16. Ibid., August 24.
17. Not all small-state delegates agreed with Dayton. Delegates from New Hampshire and Delaware, thinking that separate ballots would prove too cumbersome, broke ranks with their small-state brethren.
18. For Morris's opposition to legislative selection of the president see Raphael, *Mr. President*, 78–120 and 281–85, and for the devious methods used by Morris and the New Jersey delegation to get the matter into committee, see ibid., 101–6.
19. For the work of the committee and the creation of the electoral college, see ibid., 106–10.

20. Madison, *Notes of Debates*, September 4 and 5. On September 5, committee member Rufus King "observed that the influence of the small States in the Senate was somewhat balanced by the influence of the large States in bringing forward the candidates; and also by the concurrence of the small States in the Committee in the clause vesting the exclusive origination of money bills in the House of Representatives." To this observation Madison appended a footnote: "This explains the compromise mentioned above by Mr. Govr. Morris. Col. Masson, Mr. Gerry & other members from large States set great value on this privilege of originating money bills. Of this the members from the small States, with some from the large States who wished a high mounted Govt endeavored to avail themselves, by making that privilege, the price of arrangements in the constitution favorable to the small States, and to the elevation of the Government."
21. Samuel Tilden in 1876, Benjamin Harrison in 1888, and Albert Gore in 2000 won the popular vote but lost in the electoral college. Andrew Jackson won a plurality of votes in 1824, but since no candidate received a majority of electoral votes, the presidency was decided in the House of Representatives, which chose John Quincy Adams over Jackson.
22. Although this compromise passed Congress by a substantial majority, it failed to receive unanimous approval from the separate state legislatures, as required for any amendment to the Articles of Confederation.
23. Madison, *Notes of Debates*, August 21.
24. Ibid., August 21 and 22.
25. Failure to require a two-thirds majority for navigation laws was among the main reasons George Mason and Edmund Randolph of Virginia refused to sign the Constitution. Mason argued: "By requiring only a majority to make all commercial and navigation laws, the five Southern States, whose produce and circumstances are totally different from that of the eight Northern and Eastern States, may be ruined, for such rigid and premature regulations may be made as will enable the merchants of the Northern and Eastern States not only to demand an exhorbitant freight, but to monopolize the purchase of the commodities at their own price, for many years, to the great injury of the landed interest, and impoverishment of the people; and the danger is the greater as the gain on one side will be in proportion to the loss on the other." (Merrill Jensen et al., eds., *Documentary History of the Ratification of the Constitution* [Madison: State Historical Society of Wisconsin, 1976], 8: 45 or 13: 350.) Toward the end of the Convention, Randolph declared there were "features so odious in the constitution as it now stands, that he doubted whether he should be able to agree to it," and failure to require a supermajority for navigation laws "would compleat the deformity of the system." Randolph was not above compromise, but he had been left out of this one. (Madison, *Notes of Debates*, August 29.)
26. Ibid., August 22.
27. Ibid., August 8.
28. Washington to Patrick Henry, Benjamin Harrison, and Thomas Nelson (former governors of Virginia), September 24, 1787, Jensen et al., *Documentary History of the Ratification of the Constitution*, 8: 15.

8: American Aristocracy

1. Gordon Wood, "The Greatest Generation," *New York Review of Books*, March 29, 2001.
2. David McCullough, "The Argonauts of 1776," *New York Times*, July 4, 2002.
3. Joseph Ellis, *Founding Brothers: The Revolutionary Generation* (New York: Alfred A. Knopf, 2001), 13, 17.
4. Gordon Wood perceives the need to apply some sort of standard. In his "Greatest Generation" essay (see note 1), he first attests to the founders' foibles: "Certainly they were not immune to temptations of self-interest that attracted most ordinary human beings. They wanted wealth and position and often speculated heavily in order to realize their aims. They were not democrats, certainly not democrats in any modern manner. They were never embarrassed by talk of their being an elite, and they never hid their superiority to ordinary folk." So what makes these elitists, in Wood's estimation, the greatest generation? "They struggled to internalize the new liberal man-made standards that had come to define what it meant to be truly civilized—politeness, taste, sociability, learning, compassion, and benevolence—and what it meant to be good political leaders—virtue, disinterestedness, and an aversion to corruption and courtier-like behavior. Of course, they often did not live up to such standards; but once internalized, these enlightened and classically republican ideals and values to some degree circumscribed and controlled their behavior. Members of this revolutionary generation sought, often unsuccessfully, to be what Jefferson called 'natural aristocrats'—aristocrats who measured their status not by birth or family but by enlightened values and benevolent behavior. It meant, in short, having all the characteristics that we today sum up in the idea of a liberal arts education." Wood's standards are minimal: the founders were "great" because they internalized the values of a liberal arts education and externalized the manners of a finishing school. The thrill is gone. Do members of "the greatest generation" deserve our adulation simply because they tried (but often failed) to be virtuous?
5. To develop standards, perhaps we should follow the lead of the Catholic Church, which has established very precisely who can be called a "saint." To qualify, a candidate must endure the scrutiny first of a specially convened tribunal, then, in succession, of the Congregation for the Causes of Saints; a committee of nine theologians; a committee of cardinals and bishops; and finally the Pope. If these officials all certify that the candidate possessed both the theological virtues (faith, hope, and charity) and the cardinal virtues (prudence, justice, temperance, and fortitude), he or she can be called a "Servant of God." Certification by these deliberative bodies that the Servant of God performed a miracle earns the title of "Blessed," and finally, certification that the Blessed performed a miracle after she or he had died warrants the title of "Saint." It's all cut and dried. To be fair and precise, shouldn't we require candidates for historical greatness to undergo some sort of scrutiny like this? Such a notion is admittedly absurd, revealing the futility of applying the term "great" in an objective manner.
6. American Heritage, *Great Minds of History: Interviews with Roger Mudd* (New York: Wiley, 1999).
7. Charles Murray, in *Human Accomplishment: The Pursuit of Excellence in the Arts and*

Sciences, 800 B.C. to 1950 (New York: HarperCollins, 2003), attempts to quantify and rank people who "have achieved great things." By examining how many times people are mentioned in standard reference works and indexes, Murray claims to distinguish "great accomplishment from lesser achievement." Only by equating "greatness" with "influence" could this method claim any objective validity. It is no accident that Murray does not extend his analysis to the political arena. If he did, Hitler would certainly emerge as one of history's greatest humans.

8. Ellis, *Founding Brothers*, 13. Ellis assumes that whatever occurs within the narrow and contained world inhabited by "central players" must be "historically significant." Fame and significance, however, are not synonymous. Ellis opens his masterfully written book with an intriguing story of a duel between two fading political figures, Alexander Hamilton and Aaron Burr, in 1804—a tragic personal drama of little historical import. He follows with a tale about a dinner party in which a major deal was supposedly struck; this intimacy in the political arena makes for a good story, but Ellis himself admits that the deal was discussed in other venues as well, and his dinner party scenario "vastly oversimplifies the history that was happening at that propitious moment." Another tale features the "silence" of the first federal Congress over the question of slavery; here indeed was an issue of great national importance, yet Ellis's claim that debates within Congress over the question of slavery were "central" while the experiences of the slaves themselves were not is disingenuous. The final story eulogizes the friendship between John Adams and Thomas Jefferson during their later years. This reconciliation between elder statesmen affords a poignant conclusion to the book, but it was hardly central to the founding of our nation or "the subsequent history of the United States, including our own time." The story of the Adams-Jefferson friendship, like that of the Burr-Hamilton duel, appears significant only because the characters had participated in other important events at previous times. Ellis includes these episodes not because they are crucial to the history of the United States, but because they can be turned into interesting stories. The lives of heroes and giants, from birth to death, will always make for a good read—but biographical sketches of famous personalities should not be presented as "significant" history.

   Ironically, since Ellis's stories do not relate to the actual founding of our nation, they are all "marginal or peripheral" to "the central events and achievements of the revolutionary era." Ellis refers to the two "founding moments" in American history, the Declaration of Independence in 1776 and the adoption of a Constitution in 1787–1788, yet he addresses neither of these, for his book commences in the year 1790. There is nothing wrong in this, save for the false packaging. He titles his book *Founding Brothers: The Revolutionary Generation* to give the stories added weight and significance, even though he addresses neither the "Founding" nor the "Revolution." Like so many others, he rides the coattails of America's most special time: the act of national creation.

9. Before accepting the position of superintendent of finance, Morris insisted that he have the absolute power to dismiss, on his own authority alone, any officer at all involved in federal expenditures. After his appointment, Congress placed all money borrowed from foreign governments directly in his hands. It permitted him to import or export goods on the nation's tab, with no oversight. It allowed him to issue private contracts to supply

the army, and it placed the entire Marine Department under his control. It granted him the authority to deal with foreign ministers, thereby allowing him to operate his own department of foreign affairs. Meanwhile, the state of Pennsylvania, the nation's most prominent commercial center, granted Morris the authority to run its official business more or less by himself.

10. For Morris's central roles in the founding of the nation, see Ray Raphael, *Founders: The People Who Brought You a Nation* (New York: The New Press, 2009), and Charles Rappleye, *Robert Morris: Financier of the American Revolution* (New York: Simon & Schuster, 2011).
11. McCullough, "Argonauts of 1776," July 4, 2002.
12. Ibid.
13. David McCullough, *John Adams* (New York: Simon & Schuster, 2001), 78, 90. McCullough also notes that delegates for six states in the Continental Congress "were under specific instructions not to vote for independence." This was true in the early spring of 1776, but over the course of the next few months, all states except New York either instructed their delegates to vote for independence or permitted them to do so. These changed instructions were not due to debates within Congress, but to pressure from without.
14. John Adams to Benjamin Rush, March 19, 1812, in the Rare Books and Manuscripts Department, ms no. 229 (44), Boston Public Library. The words deleted are: "Mr Gerry, Mr Lovel was not there. Gerry not till 1776. Lovel not till 1777."
15. Adams to Jefferson, November 12, 1813, John Adams, *Works of John Adams*, Charles Francis Adams, ed. (Boston: Little, Brown and Company, 1850–1856), 10: 78–79.
16. John Adams, with his handy breakdown of one-third, one-third, and one-third, is often cited as the definitive source on the strength of Tories, patriots, and neutrals during the American Revolution. In 1815, writing to James Lloyd, he stated that a "full one third were averse to the Revolution. . . . An opposite third conceived a hatred of the English. . . . The middle third . . . were rather lukewarm." (Charles Francis Adams, ed., *The Works of John Adams* [Boston: Charles Little and James Brown, 1850], 10: 110.) Here, however, Adams was speaking not about the American Revolution but about the political split in 1797 between Americans who supported the French Revolution and those who supported Britain, France's enemy at that time. Words usually deleted would make this clear: "rather lukewarm *to both England and France*." In 1908 historian Sydney George Fisher misinterpreted Adams's reminiscence, thinking it applied to the numbers of patriots and loyalists in the American Revolution, and that mistaken notion has been passed along. Adams showed a penchant for breaking down the population into thirds; writers of history texts, in turn, have shown a penchant for accepting as fact these quick and easy assessments, set to paper several decades later by an aging man and taken totally out of context.
17. McCullough, *John Adams*, jacket copy (written by McCullough).
18. John Adams to Abigail Adams, July 3, 1776, in Charles Francis Adams, ed., *Familiar Letters of John Adams and his Wife Abigail Adams, during the Revolution* (Boston: Houghton Mifflin, 1875), 193.

19. Chase to Adams, June 28, 1776, *Papers of John Adams*, Robert J. Taylor, ed. (Cambridge, MA: Belknap Press, 1977), 4: 351
20. McCullough, *John Adams*, 129.
21. Overpromoting the individual agency of their subjects is an occupational hazard of biographers. Since the importance of their stories is determined in part by the importance of their protagonists, they have a vested interest in endowing their subjects with as much historical significance as the record will bear—and sometimes more. The very nature of their enterprise entices them to portray their chosen heroes as prime movers of history.
22. John Ferling, *Setting the World Ablaze: Washington, Adams, Jefferson, and the American Revolution* (New York: Oxford University Press, 2000), 306. Here is the entire quotation, the closing paragraph of Ferling's book: "Washington and Adams achieved historical greatness in the American Revolution. In some ways, Adams's achievement was the more impressive. His was the more lonely struggle. Before 1778 he battled for unpopular, but necessary, ends against a recalcitrant Congress. Later, when faced with a menacing isolation in Europe, he struggled against America's most popular diplomat and citizen and refused to quail before an imperious ally in whose clutches the very survival of the American Revolution seemed to rest. He was a 'bold spirit,' as Daniel Webster stated in an address at Faneuil Hall in Boston shortly after Adams's death, a 'manly and energetic' leader who possessed the qualities of 'natural talent and natural temperament' which the Revolutionary crisis demanded. The Revolutionary generation was indeed fortunate to have had Washington and Adams as its greatest stewards and shepherds."
23. Ellis, *Founding Brothers*, 16.

9: "Give Me Liberty or Give Me Death!"

1. William Wirt, *Sketches of the Life and Character of Patrick Henry* (Philadelphia: James Webster, 1818), 121–123. Paragraph delineations added, and Wirt's descriptive interludes omitted. Emphasis in original.
2. Richard R. Beeman, *Patrick Henry: A Biography* (New York: McGraw-Hill, 1974), xi; Andrew Burstein, *America's Jubilee* (New York: Alfred A. Knopf, 2001), 35, 39. Wirt continued: "[T]he style of the narrative, fettered by a scrupulous regard to real facts, is to me the most difficult in the world. It is like attempting to run, tied up in a bag. My pen wants perpetually to career and frolic it away."
3. Wirt to Adams, January 12, 1818, in Burstein, *America's Jubilee*, 46.
4. Citations here are based on the third edition, published in 1818 by James Webster in Philadelphia.
5. A list of several of these editions appears in Judy Hample, "The Textual and Cultural Authenticity of Patrick Henry's 'Liberty or Death' Speech," *Quarterly Journal of Speech* 63 (1977): 299. The speech itself was actually excerpted a few months prior to publication of the book in *Port Folio*, December 1816.
6. Wirt to Tucker, August 16, 1815, *William and Mary Quarterly*, First Series, 22 (1914), 252. Cited in Hample, "Textual Authenticity," 300. Unfortunately, the term "verbatim"

in this sentence is unclear: does it refer to the speech itself, or merely to the effect it had on Tucker, which Wirt did in fact include in a footnote to his biography? (Wirt, *Patrick Henry*, 122.)

7. Hample, "Textual Authenticity," 298–310; Stephen T. Olsen, "A Study in Disputed Authorship: the 'Liberty or Death' Speech," PhD dissertation, Pennsylvania State University, 1976; Charles I. Cohen, "The 'Liberty or Death' Speech: A Note on Religion and Revolutionary Rhetoric," *William and Mary Quarterly*, Third Series, 38 (1981), 702–717; David A. McCants, "The Authenticity of William Wirt's Version of Patrick Henry's 'Liberty or Death' Speech," *Virginia Magazine of History and Biography* 87 (1979), 387–402.
8. Moses Coit Tyler, *Patrick Henry* (Boston: Houghton Mifflin, 1887), 126; Hample, "Textual Authenticity," 301.
9. Thanks to the written record (and in this case, the audio and visual record as well), we do know the exact words of Kennedy's exciting conclusion: "My fellow citizens: let no one doubt that this is a difficult and dangerous effort on which we have set out. No one can foresee precisely what course it will take or what costs or casualties will be incurred. Many months of sacrifice and self-discipline lie ahead—months in which both our patience and our will will be tested—months in which many threats and denunciations will keep us aware of our dangers. But the greatest danger of all would be to do nothing. The path we have chosen for the present is full of hazards, as all paths are—but it is the one most consistent with our character and courage as a nation and our commitments around the world. The cost of freedom is always high—but Americans have always paid it. And one path we shall never choose, and that's the path of surrender or submission. Our goal is not the victory of might, but the vindication of right—not peace at the expense of freedom, but both peace and freedom, here in this hemisphere, and we hope, around the world. God willing, that goal will be achieved. Thank you and good night."
10. Hample, "Textual Authenticity," 308. The letter was originally published in *Magazine of History*, March 1906, 158.
11. From the *South Carolina Gazette and Country Journal*, June 6, 1775, cited in Woody Holton, "Rebel Against Rebel: Enslaved Virginians and the Coming of the American Revolution," *Virginia Magazine of History and Biography* 105 (1997): 171, 176; Woody Holton, *Forced Founders: Indians, Debtors, Slaves, and the Making of the American Revolution in Virginia* (Chapel Hill: University of North Carolina Press, 1999), 149–151; Peter Wood, " 'Taking Care of Business' in Revolutionary South Carolina: Republicanism and the Slave Society," in Jeffrey J. Crow and Larry E. Tise, eds., *Southern Experience in the American Revolution* (Chapel Hill: University of North Carolina Press, 1978), 282; Ray Raphael, *People's History of the American Revolution: How Common People Shaped the Fight for Independence* (New York: The New Press, 2001), 246.
12. William J. Van Schreeven, Robert L. Scribner, and Brent Tarter, eds., *Revolutionary Virginia: The Road to Independence, a Documentary Record* (Charlottesville: University Press of Virginia, 1973–1983), 3: 6.
13. Holton, "Rebel Against Rebel," 174.
14. According to the 1787 and 1788 tax records, Patrick Henry owned sixty-six slaves in the

years following the Revolution. (Jackson T. Main, "The One Hundred," *William and Mary Quarterly*, Third Series, 11 [1954], 376, 383.)

15. Holton, "Rebel Against Rebel," 174; Beeman, *Patrick Henry*, 70.
16. A photocopy of Henry's warning is reprinted in Beeman, *Patrick Henry*, insert between pp. 57 and 59. Some historians portray Henry as being soft on slavery, based on a single letter he wrote in 1773: "Is it not amazing, that at a time, when ye Rights of Humanity are defined & understood with precision, in a Country above all others fond of Liberty, that in such an Age, & such a Country we find Men, professing a Religion ye most humane, mild, meek, gentle & generous; adopting a Principle as repugnant to humanity as it is inconsistent with the Bible and destructive to Liberty? . . . Would any one believe that I am Master of Slaves of my own purchase! I am drawn by ye general inconvenience of living without them, I will not, I cannot justify it. However culpable my Conduct, I will so far pay my devoir to Virtue, as to own the excellence & rectitude of her Precepts, & to lament my want of conforming to them." (Robert D. Meade, *Patrick Henry: Patriot in the Making* [Philadelphia and New York: J.B. Lippincott Co., 1957], 299–300.) Clearly, Henry understood the inherent evils of slavery, but over the course of three decades of public service—as a state legislator, governor, and representative to the Continental Congress—he made no moves to further the sentiments he voiced in 1773, while he did take actions to defend the institution of slavery. In May 1776, Henry served on the committee that drafted the Virginia Declaration of Rights, which stated in its first article that "all men are born equally free and independent." Some of the more astute delegates were distressed by these dangerous words, which they feared could be used in the future to justify the abolition of slavery. The bill was sent back to committee "to vary the language, as not to involve the necessity of emancipating the slaves." The committee soon reported back: although all men are born free and independent, they can claim their rights only "when they enter into a state of society"—and slaves, of course, were not "part of the society to which the declaration applied." Apparently, this bit of sophistry quieted the dissent. (Henry Mayer, *Son of Thunder* [New York: Franklin Watts, 1986], 300–301; Beeman, *Patrick Henry*, 101–102.)

    Henry did oppose the African slave trade, but this position, supported by most Virginia slaveholders, served their economic interests: since Virginia was the primary supplier of slaves to the rest of the states, they naturally opposed foreign competition. In 1785 Patrick Henry supported a bill prohibiting slave importation; this bill, passed by and for the Virginia gentry, included one provision which prevented slaves from testifying in court and another which allowed them to be punished "with stripes" for gathering in groups or leaving home without a pass. The net effect was to tighten control over the slaves that were already there.

    In 1788, during the ratification debates, Henry complained that the proposed Constitution did not provide adequate safeguards against emancipation. Slavery, he insisted, was strictly a local issue, yet the Constitution failed to guarantee that it would be treated that way. Under the "necessary and proper" clause, he feared, Congress could tax slavery so heavily that masters would be forced to free their slaves.

    In his will, Henry allowed his wife Dolly, "if she chooses," to "set free one or two of my slaves"—cautious words indeed from such a flamboyant defender of freedom (Henry Mayer, *Son of Thunder*, 473). By contrast, Patrick's sister Elizabeth stated as her last wishes: "Whereas by the wrongdoing of man it hath been the unfortunate lot of the following negroes to be Slaves for life, to wit, Nina, Adam, Nancy senr, Nancy, Kitty and Selah. And whereas believing the same have come unto my possession by the direction of providence, and conceiving from the clearest conviction of my conscience aided by the power of a good and just God, that it is both sinful and unjust, as they are by nature equally free with myself, to continue them in Slavery I do therefore by these presents, under the influence of a duty I not only owe my own conscience, but the just God who made us all, make free the said Negroes, hoping while they are free of man they will faithfully serve their MAKER through the merits of CHRIST." (Meade, *Patrick Henry*, 312–313.) Here was some fire, the sort of passion that her brother managed to muster only for the "liberty" of free whites.

17. Holton, "Rebel Against Rebel," 173.
18. William Wirt Henry, *Patrick Henry: Life, Correspondence and Speeches* (New York: Charles Scribner's Sons, 1891), 1: 121; Holton, *Forced Founders*, 10, 32, 37–38.
19. Randolph C. Downes, *Council Fires on the Upper Ohio: A Narrative of Indian Affairs in the Upper Ohio Valley until 1795* (Pittsburgh: University of Pittsburgh Press, 1968), 209; Louise P. Kellogg, ed., *Frontier Advance on the Upper Ohio, 1778–1779* (Madison: State Historical Society of Wisconsin, 1916), 100.
20. Colin C. Calloway, *The American Revolution in Indian Country* (New York: Cambridge University Press, 1995), 202.
21. Beeman, *Patrick Henry*, 123.
22. Wirt, *Patrick Henry*, 65.
23. McCants, *Patrick Henry*, 121–122.
24. Joy Hakim, *A History of US* (New York: Oxford University Press, 2003), 3: 62. Hakim's dramatic rendering is based on a secondhand account, a conversation with a man over ninety years of age, who allegedly recalled the event fifty-nine years after the fact. Hakim and many others have accepted this account, at face value, as trustworthy and accurate. By 1834, when the conversation was reported, Wirt had successfully established an official "memory" of the speech, which clearly influenced the informant, John Roane. (Tyler, *Patrick Henry*, 129–133; Hample, "Textual Authenticity," 301–302.)

10: The Whites of Their Eyes

1. Richard Frothingham, *History of the Siege of Boston, and of the Battles of Lexington, Concord, and Bunker Hill* (Boston: Little, Brown, and Company, 1903; reprint edition, Da Capo Press, 1970; first published in 1849), 140. Nineteenth-century sources often used "white of their eyes" instead of "whites of their eyes."
2. Paul F. Boller Jr. and John George, *They Never Said It* (New York: Oxford University Press, 1989), 106; Tom Burnham, *Dictionary of Misinformation* (New York: Crowell, 1975), 69–70; Lyman C. Draper, *King's Mountain and Its Heroes* (Cincinnati: Peter G. Thomson, 1881), 107.

3. David K. Wilson, *The Southern Strategy: Britain's Conquest of South Carolina and Georgia, 1775–1780* (Columbia, SC: University of South Carolina Press, 2005), 254; James Piecuch, "Massacre or Myth: Banastre Tarleton at the Waxhaws, May 29, 1780," *Southern Campaigns of the American Revolution* 1: 2 (October, 2004): http://www.southerncampaign.org/newsletter/v1n2.pdf.
4. Howard H. Peckham, *Toll of Independence: Engagements & Battle Casualties of the American Revolution* (Chicago: University of Chicago Press, 1974), 130–134.
5. Charles Royster, *A Revolutionary People at War: The Continental Army and American Character, 1775–1783* (Chapel Hill: University of North Carolina Press, 1979), 225.
6. William Moultrie, *Memoirs of the American Revolution* (New York: David Longworth, 1802), 2: 96–97; quoted in John Buchanan, *The Road to Guillford Courthouse: The American Revolution in the Carolinas* (New York: John Wiley and Sons, 1997), 69.
7. Joseph Plumb Martin, *A Narrative of a Revolutionary Soldier* (New York: Signet, 2001; originally published in 1830), 79–80.
8. John Chester to Joseph Fish, July 22, 1775, in Frothingham, *Siege of Boston*, 391.
9. Peter Brown to his mother, June 25, 1775, in Frothingham, *Siege of Boston*, 392.
10. William Prescott to John Adams, August 25, 1775, in Frothingham, *Siege of Boston*, 395.
11. William Tudor to John Adams, June 26, 1775, in Frothingham, *Siege of Boston*, 396.
12. Issachar Bates, *The Revolutionary War* (Old Chatham, NY: Shaker Museum Foundation, 1960; originally published in 1833), np.
13. Ray Raphael, *A People's History of the American Revolution: How Common People Shaped the Fight for Independence* (New York: The New Press, 2001), 161.
14. Bates, *The Revolutionary War*, np.
15. "Lieut. Dana tells me he was the first man that fired, and that he did it singly, and with a view to draw the enemy's fire, and he obtained his end fully, without any damage to our party." (John Chester to Joseph Fish, July 22, 1775, in Frothingham, *Siege of Boston*, 390.)
16. Peter Brown to his mother, June 25, 1775, ibid., 393.
17. These figures are from the official British returns. Ibid., 389.
18. Ibid., 382–384.
19. Ibid., 140–143.
20. John Marshall, *The Life of George Washington* (New York: AMS Press, 196; first published 1804–1807), 2: 239.
21. David Humphreys, *An Essay on the Life of the Honorable Major Israel Putnam* (Hartford, CT: Hudson and Goodwin, 1788), 103. Putnam, at the time, was almost as renowned as Washington. This was the first biography of an American written by an American.
22. Mason L. Weems, *The Life of George Washington* (Cambridge, MA: Belknap Press, 1962; reprint of ninth edition, published in 1809), 74–75. Emphasis in original. Weems did not have to invent this story; very likely, it was already part of folkloric tradition. Major General Israel Putnam, the protagonist of this tale, was a legendary hero, one of the most famous men in America. Not only had "Old Put" served with distinction in the French and Indian War, people said, but he had also been shipwrecked near Havana, held prisoner by the French, and nearly burned at the stake by Indians.

23. Paul Allen, *A History of the American Revolution, Comprising all the Principal Events both in the Field and the Cabinet* (Baltimore: Johns Hopkins, 1819), I: 259; Charles A. Goodrich, *History of the United States of America* (Hartford, CT: Barber and Robinson, 1823), 158; Salma Hale, *History of the United States, from their First Settlement as Colonies, to the Close of the War with Great Britain in 1815* (New York: Collins and Hannay, 1822), 151; Noah Webster, *History of the United States* (New Haven, CT: Durric & Peck, 1833); Richard Hildreth, *The History of the United States of America* (New York: Harper & Brothers, 1880, first published 1849), 3: 83; George Bancroft, *History of the United States of America, from the Discovery of the Continent* (Boston: Little, Brown, and Company, 1879; first published 1834–1874), 4: 615.
24. Frothingham, *Siege of Boston*, 154–164.
25. Those not wishing to show a preference as to the identity of the commander attributed these words to both the leading candidates. In his 1858 biography of Israel Putnam, George Canning Hill wrote: "Putnam told the men, as he passed hastily along the lines, dusty and perspiring, not to waste their fire, for powder was very scarce. 'Wait,' said he, 'till you see the whites of their eyes.' " Not wishing to offend the Prescott fans, he then added: "Prescott gave the same orders to those within the redoubt." (George Canning Hill, *American Biography: General Israel Putnam* [Boston: E O. Libby and Co., 1858], 148.)
26. David Saville Muzzey, *The United States of America* (Boston: Ginn and Co., 1933), 1: 111. Muzzey was the most widely read textbook writer of his, or perhaps any, generation.
27. John A. Garraty and Mark C. Carnes, *American National Biography* (New York: Oxford University Press, 1999), 18: 11–12 and 17: 564–564. The Putnam entry was written by Bruce Daniels, the Prescott entry by William Fowler. In popular histories the confusion continues, but so does the story. Louis Birnbaum, in *Red Dawn at Lexington*, goes with Prescott: "Men, you are all marksmen; do not any of you fire until you can see the whites of their eyes." Robert Leckie, in *George Washington's War*, writes with equal certainty: "Burly Israel Putnam rode up and down the lines roaring the immortal words, 'Don't fire until you see the white of their eyes! Then, fire low.' " A.J. Langguth in *Patriots* and Thomas Fleming in *Liberty!* also weigh in with Putnam. Benson Bobrick, in *Angel in the Whirlwind*, hedges. By using the generic term "officers" and writing in the passive voice, he manages to tell the story without favoritism: "Those on the front line were now exhorted by their officers 'to be cool' and to reserve their fire until the enemy 'were near enough for us to see the white of their eyes.' " (Contrary to appearances, this is not a direct quotation from a participant, but only a literary device.) Even so, since Bobrick wants to place Putnam at the heart of the action, he has him uttering further commands: "Fire low—take aim at the waistbands—pick off the commanders—aim at the handsome coats." (Louis Birnbaum, *Red Dawn at Lexington* [Boston: Houghton Mifflin, 1986], 241; Robert Lieke, *George Washington's War: The Saga of the American Revolution* [New York: HarperCollins, 1992], 159; A.J. Langguth, *Patriots: The Men Who Started the American Revolution* [New York: Simon & Schuster, 1988], 281; Fleming, *Liberty!*, 140; Benson Bobrick, *Angel in the Whirlwind: The Triumph of the American Revolution* [New York: Simon & Schuster, 1997], 141.) Both Langguth and Fleming note that the command had been used in the past.

28. The entry for Putnam says nothing about it, while that for Prescott states only that the British were "within close range." Writers during the second half of the twentieth century who stated the distance generally shortened it greatly. Richard Ketchum and Francis Russell, for instance, listed it at fifty feet, or three rods—down considerably from the ten to twelve rods of the Committee of Safety. (Ketchum and Russell, *Lexington, Concord, and Bunker Hill* [New York: Harper and Row, 1963], 108.) Even at fifty feet, however, patriots could not have seen the whites of the eyes of the advancing Redcoats.

11: Patriotic Slaves

1. For a discussion of Dunmore proclamation, see Ray Raphael, *A People's History of the American Revolution: How Common People Shaped the Fight for Independence* (New York: The New Press, 2001), 254–261.
2. For a discussion of Clinton's offer and the response it triggered, see Raphael, *People's History of the American Revolution*, 261–270.
3. Contemporary estimates placed the "loss" of slaves in South Carolina at 20,000–25,000. See Abbott Hall, Custom House Report, December 31, 1784, *Papers of Thomas Jefferson*, Julian P. Boyd, ed. (Princeton: Princeton University Press, 1950), 8: 199; David Ramsay, *History of the Revolution in South Carolina* (Trenton: Isaac Collins, 1785), 2: 382. These figures were probably exaggerated. According to estimates by patriots after the war, 60,000 slaves fled to the British from three states (Ray Raphael, *A People's History of the American Revolution* [New York: The New Pess, 2001], 261–62), but these figures were likely exaggerated to highlight the losses of their masters, who were trying to avoid payment of debts to British merchants by claiming that the British had "stolen" their property. The estimates were also very rough: Jefferson, for instance, recalled that thirty slaves fled from his own plantation, and twenty-seven of these had died of smallpox; by adding a seemingly arbitrary number of zeroes, this led him to conjecture that in Virginia as a whole, 30,000 had fled and 27,000 had died. (Cassandra Pybus, "Thomas Jefferson's Faulty Math: The Question of Slave Defections in the American Revolution," *William and Mary Quarterly*, 3rd ser., 62 [2005], 243–47.) Despite these exaggerations, even the most conservative estimates by modern scholars suggest that around 20,000 slaves fled to the British in search of freedom, while the total number of blacks who served in the Continental army was only about 5,000—and many of these, perhaps most, were freeman, not slaves. (Pybus, "Jefferson's Faulty Math," 261; Allan Kulikoff, "Uprooted Peoples: Black Migrants in the Age of the American Revolution, 1790–1820," in Ira Berlin and Ronald Hoffman, eds., *Slavery and Freedom in the Age of the American Revolution* [Charlottesville: University Press of Virginia, 1983], 143–145.)
4. W.W. Abbot and Dorothy Twohig, eds., *Papers of George Washington* (Charlottesville: University Press of Virginia, 1983), Revolutionary War Series, 2: 125, 354.
5. George D. Massay, "The Limits of Antislavery Thought in the Revolutionary Lower South: John Laurens and Henry Laurens," *Journal of Southern History* 63 (1997): 517.
6. Rachel N. Klein, *Unification of a Slave State: The Rise of the Planter Class in the South*

Carolina Backcountry, 1760–1808 (Chapel Hill: University of North Carolina Press, 1990), 107.

7. Michael A. McDonnell, *The Politics of War: Race, Class, and Conflict in Revolutionary Virginia* (Chapel Hill: University of North Carolina Press, 2007), 393.
8. The average term for blacks who served was actually four and a half years, not the single year implied by this notice. (Robert Ewell Greene, *Black Courage, 1775–1783: Documentation of Black Participation in the American Revolution* [Washington, DC: Daughters of the American Revolution, 1984], 2, cited in Charles Patrick Neimeyer, *America Goes to War: A Social History of the Continental Army* [New York: New York University Press, 1996], 82.)
9. For the names and ages of seventeen people enslaved to Washington who fled in 1781, see Raphael, *People's History of the American Revolution*, 262, 361. For additional information and sources concerning these and other enslaved people who left Washington's plantations, see Cassandra Pybus, *Epic Journeys: Runaway Slaves of the American Revolution and Their Global Quest for Liberty* (Boston: Beacon Press, 2006), 45–47, 230–231; and Charles Lincoln, ed., *Naval Documents of the American Revolution* (Washington, DC: Government Printing Office, 1906), 5: 1250–1251. For the number of slaves Washington owned, see Jackson T. Main, "The One Hundred," *William and Mary Quarterly*, Third Series, 11 (1954). For in-depth investigations into Washington and slavery, see Fritz Hirschfield, *George Washington and Slavery: A Documentary Portrayal* (Columbia: University of Missouri Press, 1997), and Henry Wiencek, *An Imperfect God: George Washington, His Slaves, and the Creation of America* (New York: Farrar, Straus and Giroux, 2003).
10. Benson Lossing, *Pictorial Field-Book of the Revolution* (New York: Harper Brothers, 1851), 2: 779. See also Ramsay, *History of the Revolution in South Carolina*, 2: 382.
11. William C. Nell, *Colored Patriots of the American Revolution* (Boston: Robert F. Wallcut, 1855; Arno Press and *New York Times* reprint edition, 1968), 7–8. Phillips's remarks were written as an introduction to an earlier draft of Nell's work, published as a pamphlet in 1852.
12. Nell, *Colored Patriots*, 5–6.
13. Ibid., 236–237.
14. The views of committed abolitionists were echoed by George Bancroft, who always gave a Northern slant to his history of the Revolution. Bancroft reported that "more than seven hundred black Americans fought side by side with the white" at Monmouth, and he made a special point of including blacks in his treatment of Bunker Hill: "Nor should history forget to record that, as in the army at Cambridge, so also in this gallant band, the free negroes of the colony had their representatives; for the right of free negroes to bear arms in the public defence was, at that day, as little disputed in New England as their other rights. They took their place not in a separate corps, but in the ranks with the white men; and their names may be read on the pension roles of the country, side by side with those of other soldiers of the revolution." (George Bancroft, *History of the United States of America, from the Discovery of the Continent* [Boston: Little, Brown, and Company, 1879; first published 1834–1874], 6: 142, and 4: 614.) Bancroft probably based

his Monmouth numbers on the returns of Alexander Scammell, adjutant general of the Continental Army, for August 24, 1778, which identified 755 black soldiers. (Neimeyer, *America Goes to War*, 83].) Bancroft's regional pride was unabashed: while slavery prevailed in the South, the rights of "free negroes" were never questioned in his native New England. But Bancroft failed to mention the next chapter in this saga: within a month of the heroic performance of African American soldiers at Bunker Hill, Horatio Gates, the adjutant general for the rebel forces, prohibited the recruitment of "any stroller, Negro, or vagabond." (Benjamin Quarles, *The Negro in the American Revolution* [Chapel Hill: University of North Carolina Press], 15.)

15. John Fiske, *The American Revolution* (Boston: Houghton Mifflin, 1891), 1: 178.
16. Edward Eggleston, *The Ultimate Solution of the American Negro Problem* (Boston: Gorham Press, 1913), 127–128.
17. Edward Eggleston, *A History of the United States and Its People* (New York: D. Appleton, 1888) and *The New Century History of the United States* (New York: American Book Company, 1904).
18. These are the texts available at the University of California's Northern Regional Library Facility in Richmond: D.H. Montgomery, *The Leading Fact of American History* (Boston: Ginn and Co., 1891); D.H. Montgomery, *The Student's American History* (Boston: Ginn and Co., 1897); D H. Montgomery, *The Beginner's American History* (Boston: Ginn and Co., 1899); Roscoe Lewis Ashley, *American History, for Use in Secondary Schools* (New York: Macmillan, 1907); David Saville Muzzey, *An American History* (Boston: Ginn and Co., 1911); Willis Mason West, *American History and Government* (Boston: Allyn and Bacon, 1913); Henry Eldridge Bourne and Elbert Jay Benton, *A History of the United States* (Boston: D C. Heath and Co., 1913); William Backus Guitteau, *Our United States: A History* (New York: Silver, Burdett and Co., 1919); Reuben Post Halleck, *History of Our Country for Higher Grades* (New York: American Book Company, 1923); Rolla Tryon and Charles R. Lingley, *The American People and Nation* (Boston: Ginn and Co., 1927); William A. Hamm, Henry Eldridge Bourne, and Elbert Jay Benton, *A Unit History of the United States* (Boston: D.C. Heath and Co., 1932); David Saville Muzzey, *The United States of America* (Boston: Ginn and Co., 1933); David Saville Muzzey, *An American History* (Boston: Ginn and Co., 1933); David Saville Muzzey, *History of the American People* (Boston: Ginn and Co., 1934); Harold Underwood Faulkner and Tyler Kepner, *America: Its History and People* (New York: Harper & Brothers, 1934); Ruth West and Willis Mason West, *The Story of Our Country* (Boston: Allyn and Bacon, 1935); James Truslow Adams and Charles Garrett Vannest, *The Record of America* (New York: Charles Scribner's Sons, 1935); Harold Rugg and Louise Krueger, *The Building of America* (Boston: Ginn and Co., 1936); William A. Hamm, *The American People* (Boston: D.C. Heath and Co., 1942); George Earl Freeland and James Truslow Adams, *America's Progress in Civilization* (New York: Charles Scribner's Sons, 1942); Gertrude Hartman, *America: Land of Freedom* (Boston: D.C. Heath and Co., 1946); Robert E. Riegel and Helen Haugh, *United States of America: A History* (New York: Charles Scribner's Sons, 1953).
19. The lack of attention given to blacks during the early years of Jim Crow comes as no

surprise, but it is astonishing that the silence continued in the subsequent writings of the Progressives. Despite their interest in the social "revolution" fought on the home front, historians such as Carl Becker, Charles and Mary Beard, and John Franklin Jameson paid little attention to the most fundamental class conflict of all: that between enslaved people and their masters. The Beards chronicled the "desperate struggle" in Virginia "between planters on the seaboard and small farmers of the interior, a struggle which involved nothing less than a revolution in the social order of the Old Dominion"—but enslaved people must have sat that revolution out, for they are not included in the tale. The fact that the institution of slavery rigidified in the South ran counter to the Beardses' thesis that the American Revolution had brought about "the opening of a new humane epoch." (Charles A. Beard and Mary R. Beard, *The Rise of American Civilization* [New York: Macmillan, 1927] 1: 267, 296.) In a similar vein, Jameson stated that "very substantial progress was made" during the Revolution toward "the removal or amelioration of slavery." (J. Franklin Jameson, *The American Revolution Considered as a Social Movement* [Princeton: Princeton University Press, 1940; first published in 1926], 26.) The flight of enslaved people to the British was not included as part of the "amelioration" of slavery or the "new human epoch." Although the Northern version of the black Revolutionary tale made occasional cameo appearances, the Southern version was entirely left out.

20. George W. Williams, *History of the Negro Race in America, from 1619 to 1880* (New York: G.P. Putnam's Sons, 1883; reprint edition, Arno Press, 1968), 326. Between the work of Nell and Williams, one other black historian gained some readership. In 1867 William Wells Brown recapitulated Nell's work in a book titled *The Negro in the American Rebellion: His Heroism and His Fidelity* (Boston: Lee and Shepard, 1867). Like Nell, Brown ingratiated himself to a white audience by pointing to the patriotic service of blacks; his only major change was to use the term "Negro" instead of "colored."
21. Williams, *History of Negro Race*, 1: 355–359. Although he did include David Ramsay's claim that 25,000 slaves had fled to the British in South Carolina and Thomas Jefferson's exaggerated estimate that 30,000 had escaped in Virginia, Williams accepted at face value Jefferson's version of the story: those who escaped were cruelly mistreated by the British.
22. Ibid., 1: 384.
23. Carter G. Woodson, *The Negro in Our History* (Washington, DC: Associated Publishers, 1922), 60–61.
24. Ibid., 71.
25. W.E.B. Du Bois, *The Gift of Black Folk: The Negroes in the Making of America* (Boston: Stratford Co., 1924; reprint edition, 1975), 82.
26. John Hope Franklin, *From Slavery to Freedom: A History of American Negroes* (New York: Alfred A. Knopf, 1947), 132–134.
27. Benjamin Quarles, *The Negro in the American Revolution* (Chapel Hill: University of North Carolina Press, 1961).
28. Gary Nash, personal communication, November 2003. For the importance of Quarles's book, see Nash's introduction to the 1996 reprint, published by University of North Carolina Press.

29. For estimates of slaves fleeing to the British, see note 3 above.
30. In the words of historian John Shy, "By 1783, Southern slave owners, previously content to run a system more flexible and less harsh in practice than it appeared in the statute books, realized as never before how fragile and vulnerable the system actually was, and how little they could depend on the [alleged] cowardice, ignorance, and gratitude of their slaves. Troubled by the agitation, even within themselves, created against slavery by the rhetorical justification of the Revolution, slaveowners set about giving legal and institutional expression to a new level of anxiety about the system. New rules regarding slavery and a new articulation of racist attitudes may have been one of the most important, enduring and paradoxical legacies of the Revolutionary War." (*A People Numerous and Armed: Reflections on the Military Struggle for American Independence* [Ann Arbor: University of Michigan Press, 1990], 257.)
31. The texts surveyed were displayed at the 2002 annual conference of the National Council for Social Studies in Phoenix, Arizona. They included six elementary and middle-school texts: Sterling Stuckey and Linda Kerrigan Salvucci, *Call to Freedom* (Austin, TX: Holt, Rinehart and Winston, 2003); Joyce Appleby et al., *The American Republic to 1877* (New York: Glencoe McGraw-Hill, 2003); Michael J. Berson, *United States History: Beginnings* (Orlando: Harcourt, 2003); James West Davidson, *The American Nation: Beginnings through 1877* (Upper Saddle River, NJ: Prentice Hall, 2003); Jesus Garcia, *Creating America: A History of the United States* (Evanston, IL: McDougal Littell, 2003); and Hakim, *A History of US*. The seven secondary-school texts are: Joyce Appleby et al., *The American Vision* (New York, Glencoe McGraw-Hill, 2003); Gerald A. Danzer et al., *The Americans* (Evanston, IL: McDougal Littell, 2003); Daniel J. Boorstin and Brooks Mather Kelley, *A History of the United States* (Upper Saddle River, NJ: Prentice Hall, 2002); David Goodfield et al., *The American Journey: A History of the United States* (Upper Saddle River, NJ: Prentice Hall, 2001); John Mack Faragher et al., *Out of Many: A History of the American People* (Upper Saddle River, NJ: Prentice Hall, 2003); Robert A. Divine et al., *America: Past and Present* (New York: Longman, 2003); and Paul Boyer, *American Nation* (Austin, TX: Holt, Rinehart and Winston, 2003).
32. For black patriots who were sent back into slavery at war's end, see Raphael, *People's History of the American Revolution*, 284–292.
33. Emma J. Lapsansky-Werner, Peter B. Levy, Randy Roberts, and Alan Taylor, *United States History*, Survey Edition (Upper Saddle River, NJ: Prentice Hall, 2013), 111, 127.
34. Michael J. Berson, Tyrone C. Howard, and Cinthia Salinas, *Harcourt Social Studies—United States: Making a New Nation* (Boston: Houghton Mifflin Harcourt, 2012), 342.
35. Joyce Appleby, Alan Brinkley, Albert S. Broussard, James M. McPherson, and Donald A. Ritchie, *The American Journey* (New York: Macmillan/McGraw-Hill Glencoe, 2012), 157.
36. Quarles, *The Negro in the American Revolution*, 15; *The Papers of George Washington*, Revolutionary War series, W.W. Abbot and Dorothy Twohig, eds. (Charlottesville: University Press of Virginia, 1983), 2: 125, 354, 620, 623, 625.
37. Mark C. Carnes and John A. Garraty, *The American Nation: A History of the United States*, Fourteenth Edition (Upper Saddle River, NJ: Pearson, 2012), 132.

38. Raphael, *People's History of the American Revolution*, 293–295.
39. Ibid., 284–288.
40. The preceding four paragraphs are adapted from ibid., 267–268.
41. Boston: Beacon Press, 2006.
42. Boston King's narrative, which originally appeared in 1798, is reprinted in Vincent Carretta, ed., *Unchained Voices: An Anthology of Black Authors in the English-Speaking World of the Eighteenth Century* (Lexington: University of Kentucky Press, 1996), 351–366. Sections dealing specifically with the American Revolution are reprinted in Raphael, *People's History of the American Revolution*, 272–276. David George's narrative, which originally appeared in 1793, is also reprinted in Carretta, *Unchained Voices*, 333–346. Sections dealing specifically with the American Revolution are reprinted in Raphael, *People's History of the American Revolution*, 276–280. For an in-depth treatment of Thomas Peters, see Gary B. Nash, "Thomas Peters: Millwright and Deliverer," in *Struggle and Survival in Colonial America*, David G. Sweet and Gary B. Nash, eds. (Berkeley: University of California Press, 1981), 69–85; reprinted in Gary B. Nash, *Race, Class, and Politics: Essays on American Colonial and Revolutionary Society* (Urbana: University of Illinois Press, 1986), 269–282. Nash bases his story on two studies of blacks who sided with Britain: Ellen Gibson Wilson, *The Loyal Blacks* (New York: Capricorn, 1976), and James W. St. G. Walker, *The Black Loyalists: The Search for a Promised Land in Nova Scotia and Sierra Leone, 1783–1870* (New York: Africana, 1976).
43. Thomas Fleming, *Liberty! The American Revolution* (New York: Viking, 1997), 1–2, 6.
44. Harry Washington's story is told in Cassandra Pybus, "Mary Perth, Harry Washington, and Moses Wilkinson: Black Methodists Who Escaped from Slavery and Founded a Nation," in *Revolutionary Founders: Rebels, Radicals, and Reformers in the Making of the Nation*, Alfred F. Young, Gary B. Nash, and Ray Raphael, eds. (New York: Alfred A. Knopf, 2001), 155–168; and Pybus, *Epic Journeys*, 3, 5, 20, 26–27, 32, 40–42, 59–61, 69, 150, 199, 201, 218.
45. A handful of college texts now feature Harry Washington, Thomas Peters, or Boston King. Of twenty-three recent (2011–2014) college texts surveyed, four feature Harry (aka Henry) Washington: James West Davidson, Brian DeLay, Christine Leigh Heyrman, Mark H. Lytle, and Michael B. Stoff, *Experience History: Interpreting America's Past*, vol. 1 (New York: McGraw-Hill, 2011), 182; Carol Berkin, Christopher L. Miller, Robert W. Cherny, James L. Gormly, Douglas Egerton, and Kelly Woestman, *Making America: A History of the United States*, Brief Sixth Edition (Boston: Wadsworth/Cengage Learning, 2014), 146; Eric Foner, *Give Me Liberty! An American History*, Third Edition (New York: W.W. Norton, 2011), 242; James West Davidson, Brian DeLay, Christine Leigh Heyrman, Mark. H. Lytle, and Michael B. Stoff, *U.S.: A Narrative History* (New York: McGraw-Hill, 2012), 136. Two feature Thomas Peters: Nancy Hewitt and Steven F. Lawson, *Exploring American History: A Brief Survey with Sources* (New York: Bedford/St. Martin's, 2013), 183; Jacqueline Jones, Peter H. Wood, Thomas Borstelmann, Elaine Tyler May, Vicki L. Ruiz, *Created Equal: A History of the United States*, vol. 1, Third Edition (Upper Saddle River, NJ: Pearson Longman, 2009), 202–203. One features Boston King: James Roark, Michael Johnson, Patricia Cline Cohen, Sarah

Stage, Alan Lawson, and Susan M. Hartmann, *The American Promise: A History of the United States*, Fourth Edition (New York: Bedford/St. Martin's, 2009), 221. This is a positive development. Texts for lower grades, however, have not yet wished to tell the Harry Washington/George Washington story, which is founded on a relationship they would rather not feature. This is regrettable. Even texts for elementary students do address the problematic issue of slavery, so there is no reason to shy from a balanced presentation of the history of enslaved people during the American Revolution.

12: Brutal British

1. John Buchanan, *The Road to Guilford Courthouse: The American Revolution in the Carolinas* (New York: John Wiley and Sons, 1997), 60, 81–84.
2. Robert M. Weir, " 'The Violent Spirit': The Reestablishment of Order, and the Continuity of Leadership in Post-Revolutionary South Carolina," in *An Uncivil War: The Southern Backcountry during the American Revolution*, Ronald Hoffman, Thad W. Tate, and Peter J. Albert, eds. (Charlottesville: University Press of Virginia, 1985), 74. Tarleton later explained the butchery at the Waxhaws by the fact that he had gone down when his horse was shot from under him, "which stimulated the soldiers to a vindictive asperity not easily restrained." (Buchanan, *Road to Guilford Courthouse*, 85.)
3. Kevin Phillips, *The Cousins' Wars: Religion, Politics, and the Triumph of Anglo-America* (New York: Basic Books, 1999), 162, 638.
4. A. Roger Ekirch, "Whig Authority and Public Order in Backcountry North Carolina," in Hoffman, Tate, and Albert, *Uncivil War*, 107–108.
5. William Pierce to St. George Tucker, July 20, 1781, in Sylvia R. Frey, *Water from the Rock: Black Resistance in a Revolutionary Age* (Princeton: Princeton University Press, 1991), 133.
6. John C. Dann, ed., *The Revolution Remembered: Eyewitness Accounts of the War of Independence* (Ann Arbor: University of Michigan Press, 1990), 188–9. This punishment, called "spicketing," was a brutal variation of the common practice of "picketing," in which the prisoner, like a horse, was merely tied to a stake in the ground.
7. Edward J. Cashin, *The King's Ranger: Thomas Brown and the American Revolution on the Southern Frontier* (Athens: University of Georgia Press, 1989), 27–28.
8. Dann, *Revolution Remembered*, 202–3.
9. Buchanan, *Road to Guilford Courthouse*, 237.
10. Shelby's statement, taken from conversations in 1815 and 1819, appears in Lyman C. Draper, *King's Mountain and its Heroes* (Cincinnati: Peter G. Thomson, 1881), 545. Draper reprints Shelby's complete narrative, as well as the diary of a Huguenot Tory from New York, Lieutenant Anthony Allaire, who recorded the hanging and the trampled prisoners. (Draper, *King's Mountain*, 511–513.)
11. William Gordon, *The History of the Rise, Progress, and Establishment, of the Independence of the United States of America* (Freeport, NY: Books for Libraries Press, 1969; first published in 1788), 3: 231, 456.
12. Ibid., 2: 293, 324.

13. David Ramsay, *History of the Revolution in South Carolina* (Trenton: Isaac Collins, 1785).
14. Cashin, *The King's Ranger*, 120, 127, 219.
15. David Ramsay, *The History of the American Revolution* (Philadelphia: R. Aitken & Son, 1789; reprinted by Liberty Classics in 1990), 2: 249.
16. Ibid., 2: 293, 324.
17. Mercy Otis Warren, *History of the Rise, Progress and Termination of the American Revolution, interspersed with Biographical, Political and Moral Observations* (Boston: E. Larkin, 1805; reprinted by Liberty Classics in 1988), 3: 428–429. For a discussion of Warren's treatment of barbarities, with additional citations, see William Raymond Smith, *History as Argument: Three Patriot Historians of the American Revolution* (The Hague: Mouton and Co., 1966), 87–88.
18. Salma Hale, *History of the United States, from their First Settlement as Colonies, to the Close of the War with Great Britain in 1815* (New York: Collins and Hannay, 1830; first published in 1822), 210.
19. John Frost, *History of the United States of North America* (London: Charles Tilt, 1838), 261.
20. George Bancroft, *History of the United States of America, from the Discovery of the Continent* (Boston: Little, Brown, and Company, 1879; first published 1834–1874), 6: 458, 427, 295, 289, 293.
21. Richard Hildreth, *The History of the United States of America* (New York: Harper & Brothers, 1880; first published in 1849), 3: 329.
22. John Fiske, *The American Revolution* (Boston: Houghton Mifflin, 1891), 2: 182.
23. Claude Halstead Van Tyne, *The American Revolution, 1776–1783* (New York: Harper & Brothers, 1905), 255. This is volume 9 of a twenty-seven-volume series titled *The American Nation*, edited by Albert Bushnell Hart.
24. Cited in Gary B. Nash, "The Concept of Inevitability in the History of European-Indian Relations," in *Inequality in Early America*, Carla Gardina Pestana and Sharon V. Salinger, eds. (Hanover, NH: University Press of New England, 1999), 280.
25. David Hackett Fischer, "*The Patriot* Is to History as Godzilla Was to Biology," *Minneapolis Star Tribune*, July 4, 2000. Originally published in the *New York Times*.
26. Thomas Fleming, *Liberty! The American Revolution* (New York: Viking, 1997), 311. As in *The Patriot*, Fleming focuses much of his attention on Banastre Tarleton, whom he refers to as Britain's most potent "weapon."
27. For a deconstruction of this and other Thomas Brown mythologies, see Cashin, *The King's Ranger*, 120–121, 127, 219–228.
28. Robert Leckie, *George Washington's War: The Saga of the American Revolution* (New York: HarperCollins, 1992), 587–588.
29. Ibid., 583–584.
30. James West Davidson and Michael B. Stoff, *America: History of Our Nation* (Upper Saddle River, NJ: Prentice Hall, 2014), 191–192.
31. William Deverell and Deborah Gray White, *Holt McDougal United States History: Beginnings to 1877* (Boston: Houghton Mifflin Harcourt, 2012), 135.

32. David M. Kennedy and Lizabeth Cohen, *The American Pageant*, volume 1, Fifteenth Edition (Boston: Cengage Learning, 2014), 142.
33. Thomas Bailey, *The American Pageant: A History of the Republic* (Boston: Little, Brown and Company, 1956), 118.
34. James Oakes, Michael McGeer, Jan Ellen Lewis, Nick Cullather, and Jeanne Boydston, *Of the People: A History of the United States* (New York: Oxford University Press, 2011), 194.
35. Nancy A. Hewitt and Steven Lawson, *Exploring American Histories: A Brief Survey with Sources* (Boston: Bedford/St. Martin's, 2013), 179.

13: The Final Battle: Yorktown

1. Cornwallis offered to surrender two days earlier, on October 17, so that date is sometimes used.
2. Joy Hakim, *A History of US* (New York: Oxford University Press, 2003), 3: 146.
3. A.J. Langguth, *Patriots: The Men Who Started the American Revolution* (New York: Simon & Schuster, 1988), 544. Emphasis added.
4. Quoted in Robert Harvey, *A Few Bloody Noses: The American War of Independence* (London: John Murray, 2001), 412.
5. Washington to president of Congress, October 27, 1781, in *The Writings of George Washington, from the Original Manuscript Sources*, John C. Fitzpatrick, ed. (Washington, DC: United States Government Printing Office, 1931–1944), 23: 297.
6. Fitzpatrick, *Writings of George Washington*, 23: 271, 297, 302, 347, 352, 359, 361, 365, 367, 390, 443, 447, 477.
7. Washington to Nathanael Greene, November 16, 1781, in Fitzpatrick, *Writings of George Washington*, 23: 347.
8. Douglas Southall Freeman, *George Washington: A Biography* (New York: Charles Scribner's Sons, 1952), 5: 405, 415.
9. Ibid., 415.
10. Fitzpatrick, *Writings of George Washington*, 24: 315.
11. On August 10, 1782, Washington wrote to Chevalier de Chastellux, "The enemy talk loudly, and very confidently of Peace; but whether they are in earnest, or whether it is to amuse and while away the time till they can prepare for a more vigorous prosecution of the War, time will evince." (Fitzpatrick, *Writings of George Washington*, 24: 496.)
12. Ibid., 25: 42.
13. Washington to James McHenry, September 12, 1782, in Fitzpatrick, *Writings of George Washington*, 25: 151. Four days later he wrote again, "I have no doubt on my Mind of the Kings wishes to prosecute the War . . . as long as the Nation will vote Men or Money to carry it on." (Washington to John Mitchell, September 16, 1782, in Fitzpatrick, *Writings of George Washington*, 25: 166.)
14. Ibid., 25: 265.
15. Freeman, *George Washington*, 438; Washington to Chevalier de la Luzerne, March 19,

1783, in Fitzpatrick, *Writings of George Washington*, 26: 236; Washington to president of Congress, March 19, 1783, in Fitzpatrick, *Writings of George Washington*, 26: 238.

16. Piers Mackesy, *The War for America, 1775–1783* (Cambridge, MA: Harvard University Press, 1965), 524–25; Freeman, *George Washington*, 5: 513.
17. Mackesy, *War for America*, 404; Washington to Marquis de Lafayette, November 15, 1781, in Fitzpatrick, *Writings of George Washington*, 23: 341.
18. Mackesy, *War for America*, 461.
19. Howard H. Peckham, *The Toll of Independence: Engagements and Battle Casualties of the American Revolution* (Chicago: University of Chicago Press, 1974), 3–16, 91–92.
20. Mackesy, *War for America*, 524–525.
21. A full rendering of Britain's global contest is in Mackesy, *War for America*.
22. *The Annual Register, or a View of the History, Politics, and Literature, for the Year 1782* (London: J. Dodsley, 1783), 25: 96.
23. "The Speech of the Right Honourable William Pitt, in the House of Commons, on Friday, February 21, 1783" (London: J. Debrett, 1783), 13–35: http://www.archive.org/stream/speechrighthono00pittgoog#page/n43/mode/2up.
24. Mackesy, *War for America*, 498–500.
25. Winthrop D. Jordan, Miriam Greenblatt, and John S. Bowes, *The Americans: A History* (Boston: McDougal Littell/Houghton Mifflin, 1996), 115. Although this text is old, it is still in use in many financially strapped schools.
26. William Gordon, *The History of the Rise, Progress, and Establishment, of the Independence of the United States of America* (Freeport, NY: Books for Libraries Press, 1969; first published in 1788), 4: 196–392.
27. David Ramsay, *The History of the American Revolution* (Philadelphia: R. Aitken & Son, 1789; reprinted by Liberty Classics in 1990), 2: 290, 293.
28. Mercy Otis Warren, *History of the Rise, Progress and Termination of the American Revolution, interspersed with Biographical, Political and Moral Observations* (Boston: E. Larkin, 1805; reprinted by Liberty Classics in 1988), 3: 42–436.
29. John Marshall, *The Life of George Washington* (New York: AMS Press, 1969; first published 1804–1807), 4: 532–537.
30. These four early historians understood well that what started as America's War for Independence had extended to the West Indies and even to Gibraltar, that it had come to involve the major powers of Europe, and that the conclusion to that war could only be understood in this wider context. Strangely, only Gordon, who published in England, included a running account of events in East India; that was simply too far away, even though it seriously impacted British policies with respect to the United States.
31. Mason L. Weems, *The Life of Washington* (Cambridge, MA: Belknap Press, 1962; reprint of ninth edition, 1809), 113.
32. Noah Webster, *History of the United States* (New Haven: Durrie & Peck, 1833), 242.
33. John Frost, *History of the United States of North America* (London: Charles Tilt, 1838), 255–257. Although the book was published in London, Frost was an American from Philadelphia.
34. George Bancroft, *History of the United States of America, from the Discovery of the*

Continent (Boston: Little, Brown, and Company, 1879; first published 1834–1874), 6: 432–484.

35. I surveyed twenty-three textbooks, published between 1890 and 1955, available at the University of California's Northern Regional Library Facility in Richmond: D.H. Montgomery, *The Leading Fact of American History* (Boston: Ginn and Co., 1891); D.H. Montgomery, *The Student's American History* (Boston: Ginn and Co., 1897); D.H. Montgomery, *The Beginner's American History* (Boston: Ginn and Co., 1899); Edward Eggleston, *The New Century History of the United States* (New York: American Book Company, 1904); Roscoe Lewis Ashley, *American History, for Use in Secondary Schools* (New York: Macmillan, 1907); David Saville Muzzey, *An American History* (Boston: Ginn and Co., 1911); Willis Mason West, *American History and Government* (Boston: Allyn and Bacon, 1913); Henry Eldridge Bourne and Elbert Jay Benton, *A History of the United States* (Boston: D.C. Heath and Co., 1913); William Backus Guitteau, *Our United States: A History* (New York: Silver, Burdett and Co., 1919); Reuben Post Halleck, *History of Our Country for Higher Grades* (New York: American Book Company, 1923); Rolla Tryon and Charles R. Lingley, *The American People and Nation* (Boston: Ginn and Co., 1927); William A. Hamm, Henry Eldridge Bourne, and Elbert Jay Benton, *A Unit History of the United States* (Boston: D.C. Heath and Co., 1932); David Saville Muzzey, *The United States of America* (Boston: Ginn and Co., 1933); David Saville Muzzey, *An American History* (Boston: Ginn and Co., 1933); David Saville Muzzey, *History of the American People* (Boston: Ginn and Co., 1934); Harold Underwood Faulkner and Tyler Kepner, *America: Its History and People* (New York: Harper & Brothers, 1934); Ruth West and Willis Mason West, *The Story of Our Country* (Boston: Allyn and Bacon, 1935); James Truslow Adams and Charles Garrett Vannest, *The Record of America* (New York: Charles Scribner's Sons, 1935); Harold Rugg and Louise Krueger, *The Building of America* (Boston: Ginn and Co., 1936); William A. Hamm, *The American People* (Boston: D.C. Heath and Co., 1942); George Earl Freeland and James Truslow Adams, *America's Progress in Civilization* (New York: Charles Scribner's Sons, 1942); Gertrude Hartman, *America: Land of Freedom* (Boston: D.C. Heath and Co., 1946); Robert E. Riegel and Helen Haugh, *United States of America: A History* (New York: Charles Scribner's Sons, 1953).

36. Bourne and Benton, *A History of the United States*, 220.

37. West and West, *The Story of Our Country*, 171.

38. Thomas A. Bailey, *The American Pageant: A History of the Republic* (Boston: Little, Brown and Company, 1956), 116–17, 121.

39. The thirteen texts surveyed were displayed at the 2002 annual conference of the National Council for Social Studies in Phoenix, Arizona. They included six elementary and middle-school texts: Sterling Stuckey and Linda Kerrigan Salvucci, *Call to Freedom* (Austin, TX: Holt, Rinehart and Winston, 2003); Joyce Appleby et al., *The American Republic to 1877* (New York: Glencoe McGraw-Hill, 2003); Michael J. Berson, *United States History: Beginnings* (Orlando: Harcourt, 2003); James West Davidson, *The American Nation: Beginnings through 1877* (Upper Saddle River, NJ: Prentice Hall, 2003); Jesus Garcia et al., *Creating America: A History of the United States* (Evanston, IL: McDougal

Littell, 2007); and Hakim, *A History of US*. The seven secondary-school texts are: Joyce Appleby et al., *The American Vision* (New York: Glencoe McGraw-Hill, 2003); Gerald A. Danzer et al., *The Americans* (Evanston, IL: McDougal Littell, 2003); Daniel J. Boorstin and Brooks Mather Kelley, *A History of the United States* (Upper Saddle River, NJ: Prentice Hall, 2002); David Goodfield et al, *The American Journey: A History of the United States* (Upper Saddle River, NJ: Prentice Hall, 2001); John Mack Faragher et al., *Out of Many: A History of the American People* (Upper Saddle River, NJ: Prentice Hall, 2003); Robert A. Divine et al., *America: Past and Present* (New York: Longman, 2003); and Paul Boyer, *American Nation* (Austin, TX: Holt, Rinehart and Winston, 2003).

40. Boyer, *American Nation*, 129.
41. Boorstin and Kelley, *A History of the United States*, 97.
42. One of these is the latest edition of *American Pageant*, unchanged in this respect for more than half a century despite new authors on the cover: David M. Kennedy and Lizabeth Cohen, *The American Pageant*, volume 1, Fifteenth Edition (Boston: Cengage Learning, 2014). Two others share the same authors, with overlapping texts geared for different markets: James West Davidson, Brian DeLay, Christine Leigh Heyrman, Mark H. Lytle, and Michael B. Stoff, *U.S.: A Narrative History* (New York: McGraw-Hill, 2012), and *Experience History: Interpreting America's Past*, vol. 1 (New York: McGraw-Hill, 2011). One short paragraph here reveals how easily authors can convey the global context, even in a brief survey: "It need not have ended at Yorktown, but timing made all the difference. At the end of 1781 and early in 1782, the British army received setbacks in the other theaters of the war: India, the West Indies, and Florida. The French and the Spanish were everywhere in Europe as well, gathering in the English Channel, preparing a major offensive against Gibraltar. The cost of fighting was already enormous. British leaders recognized that the rest of the empire was at stake and set about cutting their losses in America." (*Experience History*, 180.) The remaining two texts are Jacqueline Jones, Peter H. Wood, Thomas Borstelmann, Elaine Tyler May, and Vicki L. Ruiz, *Created Equal: A History of the United States*, vol. 1, Third Edition (New York: Pearson Longman, 2009); and John Mack Faragher, Mari Jo Buhle, Daniel Czitrom, Susan H. Armitage, *Out of Many: A History of the American People*, Seventh Edition (Upper Saddle River, NJ: Pearson/Prentice Hall, 2012).
43. Eric Foner, *Give Me Liberty! An American History*, Third Edition (New York: W.W. Norton, 2011); David Goldfield, Carl Abbott, Virginia DeJohn Anderson, Jo Ann E. Argersinger, Peter H. Argersinger, William L. Barney, Robert M. Weir, *The American Journey: A History of the United States*, Brief Sixth Edition (Upper Saddle River, NJ: Prentice Hall, 2011); Alan Brinkley, *American History: Connecting With the Past*, vol. 1, Fourteenth Edition (New York: McGraw-Hill, 2012).
44. Texts with no mention of British military involvement elsewhere: Mark C. Carnes and John A. Garraty, *The American Nation: A History of the United States*, Fourteenth Edition (Upper Saddle River, NJ: Pearson, 2012); Kevin M. Schultz, *HIST-3*, volume 1 (Boston: Cengage Learning, 2014); Nancy Hewitt and Steven F. Lawson, *Exploring American History: A Brief Survey with Sources* (New York: Bedford/St. Martin's, 2013); James Oakes, Michael McGerr, Jan Ellen Lewis, Nick Cullather, and Jeanne Boydston,

Of the People: A History of the United States, vol. 1, Concise Edition (New York: Oxford University Press, 2011); Robert A. Divine, T.H. Breen, George M. Fredrickson, R. Hal Williams, Ariela J. Gross, H.W. Brands, *America: Past and Present*, Ninth Edition (New York: Pearson/Longman, 2011); H.W. Brands, T.H. Breen, R. Hal Williams, and Ariela J. Gross, *American Stories: A History of the United States*, Second Edition (Upper Saddle River, NJ: Pearson, 2012); Mary Beth Norton, David M. Katzman, David W. Blight, Howard P. Chudacoff, Fredrik Logevall, Beth Bailey, Thomas Paterson, and William M. Tuttle Jr., *A People and a Nation: A History of the United States* (Boston: Houghton Mifflin, 2007); James Henretta, Rebecca Edwards, and Robert Self, *America: A Concise History*, Fifth Edition (New York: Bedford/St. Martin's, 2012); James Roark, Michael Johnson, Patricia Cline Cohen, Sarah Stage, Alan Lawson, and Susan M. Hartmann, *The American Promise: A History of the United States*, Fourth Edition (New York: Bedford/St. Martin's, 2009); Michael Schaller, Robert D. Schulzinger, John Bezis-Selfa, Janette Thomas Greenwood, Andrew Kirk, Sarah J. Purcell, and Aaron Sheehan-Dean, *American Horizons: U.S. History in a Global Context*, Concise Edition (New York: Oxford University Press, 2013); Jennifer D. Keene, Saul Cornell, Edward T. O'Donnell, *Visions of America: A History of the United States*, Second Edition (Upper Saddle River, NJ: Pearson, 2013); Joseph R. Conlin, *The American Past: A Survey of American History*, Tenth Edition (Boston: Wadsworth/Cengage Learning, 2014); Carol Berkin, Christopher L. Miller, Robert W. Cherny, James L. Gormly, Douglas Egerton, and Kelly Woestman, *Making America: A History of the United States*, Brief Sixth Edition (Boston: Wadsworth/Cengage Learning, 2014); Paul S. Boyer, Clifford E. Clark Jr., Karen Halttunen, Joseph F. Kett, Neal Salisbury, Harvard Sitkoff, and Nancy Woloch, *The Enduring Vision: A History of the American People*, Eighth Edition (Boston: Wadsworth/Cengage Learning, 2014); Alan Brinkley, *The Unfinished Nation: A Concise History of the American People*, vol. 1, Seventh Edition (New York: McGraw-Hill, 2014).

45. Conlin, *American Past*, 162.
46. Even within the scholarly community, despite so much attention paid to "the Atlantic World," little attention is paid to how the global context of British military commitments affected that nation's military performance at the end of the war and its decision not to pursue the war in the rebellious United States after March 1782. One well-received recent book, Andrew Jackson O'Shaughnessy's *The Men Who Lost America: British Leadership, the American Revolution, and the Fate of the Empire* (New Haven: Yale University Press, 2013), in 361 pages, devotes but a single paragraph (on page 358) to the impact of Britain's overreach on its withdrawal from the war with the United States.
47. Schaller et al., *American Horizons: U.S. History in a Global Context*, 273.
48. Hewitt and Lawson, *Exploring American History*, 181.

14: March of the American People

1. Henry S. Commager and Richard B. Morris, *The Spirit of 'Seventy-Six: The Story of the American Revolution as Told by the Participants* (Indianapolis and New York: Bobbs-Merrill, 1958), 1295.

2. Gerald A. Danzer, J. Jorge Klor de Alva, Larry S. Krieger, Louis E. Wilson, and Nancy Woloch, *The Americans* (Evanston, IL: Holt McDougal, 2012), 117.
3. This phrase comes from Daniel K. Richter, *Facing East from Indian Country* (Cambridge, MA: Harvard University Press, 2001).
4. For a referenced treatment of the internal politics of the Iroquois during the Revolution, see Ray Raphael, *People's History of the American Revolution: How Common People Shaped the Fight for Independence* (New York: The New Press, 2001), 193–209.
5. James H. Merrell, "Declarations of Independence: Indian-White Relations in the New Nation," in *The American Revolution: Its Character and Limits*, Jack P. Greene, ed. (New York: New York University Press, 1987), 198.
6. Frederick Cook, ed., *Journals of the Military Expedition of Major General John Sullivan against the Six Nations of Indians in 1779* (Auburn, NY: Knapp, Peck, and Thomson, 1887), 303. This volume contains several firsthand accounts against the "war on vegetables" staged by Sullivan's forces (112–113, 70–77, 172–175). Sullivan follows contemporary usage when he refers to the Iroquois as "the Five nations," ignoring the incorporation of the Tuscaroras in the early eighteenth century.
7. C.A. Weslager, *The Delaware Indians: A History* (New Brunswick, NJ: Rutgers University Press, 1972), 305. The full text of the treaty that offered this alluring suggestion is reprinted in Colin G. Calloway, ed., *The World Turned Upside Down: Indian Voices from Early America* (Boston: St. Martin's Press, 1994), 190–193.
8. For a referenced treatment of the Delaware and Shawnee during the Revolution, see Raphael, *People's History of the American Revolution*, 209–220.
9. Raphael, *People's History of the American Revolution*, 221–222.
10. Cited in Tom Hatley, *The Dividing Paths: Cherokees and South Carolinians through the Era of Revolution* (New York and Oxford: Oxford University Press, 1993), 199–200.
11. William Drayton to Francis Salvador, July 24, 1776, in R. W. Gibbes, ed., *Documentary History of the American Revolution* (New York: D. Appleton, 1857), 2: 29.
12. Williamson to Drayton, August 22, 1776, in Gibbes, *Documentary History*, 2: 32.
13. John W. Caughey, *McGillivray of the Creeks* (Norman: University of Oklahoma Press, 1938), 91–92.
14. *A Brief History of the United States for Schools*, n.a. (New York: A.A. Barnes and Company, 1875), 128–29; David B. Scott, *A School History of the United States* (New York: Harper & Brothers, 1874), 195; D.H. Montgomery, *The Leading Facts of American History* (Boston: Ginn and Co., 1899), 181.
15. Charles A. Goodrich, *A History of the United States of America* (Hartford, CT: Barber and Robinson, 1823), 200.
16. *Brief History of the United States* (Barnes), 130–31.
17. Montgomery, *Leading Facts of American History*, 181. A revised edition of the same text in 1910 elaborated on Clark's tale. Before "drove the British out," Montgomery inserted: "He and his little band of stalwart backwoodsmen set out to capture the enemy's forts (1778–1779). They endured terrible hardships and sufferings in crossing the 'Drowned Lands' where the Wabash River, in Indiana, had overflowed the country. Often they had to push forward for miles through ice-cold water waist-deep. But neither

hunger, cold, nor exhaustion could force them to turn back. They literally waded to victory." (163.)

18. These are the texts available at the University of California's Northern Regional Library Facility in Richmond: D.H. Montgomery, *The Leading Fact of American History* (Boston: Ginn and Co., 1891); D.H. Montgomery, *The Student's American History* (Boston: Ginn and Co., 1897); D.H. Montgomery, *The Beginner's American History* (Boston: Ginn and Co., 1899); Edward Eggleston, *The New Century History of the United States* (New York: American Book Company, 1904); Roscoe Lewis Ashley, *American History, for Use in Secondary Schools* (New York: Macmillan, 1907); David Saville Muzzey, *An American History* (Boston: Ginn and Co., 1911); Willis Mason West, *American History and Government* (Boston: Allyn and Bacon, 1913); Henry Eldridge Bourne and Elbert Jay Benton, *A History of the United States* (Boston: D.C. Heath and Co., 1913); William Backus Guitteau, *Our United States: A History* (New York: Silver, Burdett and Co., 1919); Reuben Post Halleck, *History of Our Country for Higher Grades* (New York: American Book Company, 1923); Rolla Tryon and Charles R. Lingley, *The American People and Nation* (Boston: Ginn and Co., 1927); William A. Hamm, Henry Eldridge Bourne, and Elbert Jay Benton, *A Unit History of the United States* (Boston: D.C. Heath and Co., 1932); David Saville Muzzey, *The United States of America* (Boston: Ginn and Co., 1933); David Saville Muzzey, *An American History* (Boston: Ginn and Co., 1933); David Saville Muzzey, *History of the American People* (Boston: Ginn and Co., 1934); Harold Underwood Faulkner and Tyler Kepner, *America: Its History and People* (New York: Harper & Brothers, 1934); Ruth West and Willis Mason West, *The Story of Our Country* (Boston: Allyn and Bacon, 1935); James Truslow Adams and Charles Garrett Vannest, *The Record of America* (New York: Charles Scribner's Sons, 1935); Harold Rugg and Louise Krueger, *The Building of America* (Boston: Ginn and Co., 1936); William A. Hamm, *The American People* (Boston: D.C. Heath and Co., 1942); George Earl Freeland and James Truslow Adams, *America's Progress in Civilization* (New York: Charles Scribner's Sons, 1942); Gertrude Hartman, *America: Land of Freedom* (Boston: D.C. Heath and Co., 1946); Robert E. Riegel and Helen Haugh, *United States of America: A History* (New York: Charles Scribner's Sons, 1953). The three that mention Sullivan are Eggleston (1904), Guitteau (1919), and Halleck (1923). The latter two devote only a single sentence; only Eggleston describes the nature of Sullivan's campaign.
19. Halleck, *History of Our Country*, 206.
20. Muzzey, *History of the American People*, 145.
21. Freeland and Adams, *America's Progress in Civilization*, 189.
22. Guitteau, *Our United States*, 191.
23. The elementary and middle-school texts: Sterling Stuckey and Linda Kerrigan Salvucci, *Call to Freedom* (Austin, TX: Holt, Rinehart and Winston, 2003); Joyce Appleby et al., *The American Republic to 1877* (New York: Glencoe McGraw-Hill, 2003); Michael J. Berson, *United States History: Beginnings* (Orlando: Harcourt, 2003); James West Davidson, *The American Nation: Beginnings through 1877* (Upper Saddle River, NJ: Prentice Hall, 2003); Jesus Garcia et al., *Creating America: A History of the United States*; and Hakim, *A History of US*. The seven secondary-school texts: Joyce Appleby et al., *The American*

Vision (New York, Glencoe McGraw-Hill, 2003); Gerald A. Danzer et al., *The Americans* (Evanston, IL: McDougal Littell, 2003); Daniel J. Boorstin and Brooks Mather Kelley, *A History of the United States* (Upper Saddle River, NJ: Prentice Hall, 2002); David Goodfield et al., *The American Journey: A History of the United States* (Upper Saddle River, NJ: Prentice Hall, 2001); John Mack Faragher et al., *Out of Many: A History of the American People* (Upper Saddle River, NJ: Prentice Hall, 2003); Robert A. Divine et al., *America: Past and Present* (New York: Longman, 2003); and Paul Boyer, *American Nation* (Austin, TX: Holt, Rinehart and Winston, 2003).

Of three college texts surveyed at that time, all described the Sullivan campaign in gruesome detail, while only one mentioned the frontier heroics of George Rogers Clark. (James L. Roark et al., *The American Promise: A History of the United States* [Boston: Bedford/St. Martin's, 2002]; Gary B. Nash and Julie Roy Jeffrey, *The American People: Creating a Nation and a Society* [New York: Addison Wesley, 2001]; and Mary Beth Norton et al., *A People and a Nation: A History of the United States* [Boston: Houghton Mifflin, 1990].) These texts did not sugarcoat the truth. According to *The American Promise*, "Continental army troops under the command of General John Sullivan carried out a planned campaign of terror and destruction. . . . Forty well-established Indian towns met with total destruction; the soldiers looted and torched the dwellings, then burned cornfields and fruit orchards. In a few towns women and children were slaughtered." (205.) Such honesty was admirable and it has continued in current college texts, but it also gives cause for wonder: If this is what really happened, why do only twenty-year-olds who take history in college learn about it? We certainly expect German children to learn about the Holocaust long before they enter the university, so why are American children in such need of protection?

24. Richard White, *The Middle Ground: Indians, Empires, and Republics in the Great Lakes Region, 1650–1815* (Cambridge and New York: Cambridge University Press, 1991), 376. Cited from Clark's *Memoir*. A slightly modified version of the *Memoir* has recently been published under the title *The Conquest of the Illinois*, Milo Milton Quaffe, ed. (Carbondale and Edwardsville: Southern Illinois University Press, 2001), 147.
25. Colin G. Calloway, *The American Revolution in Indian Country: Crisis and Diversity in Native American Communities* (Cambridge and New York: Cambridge University Press, 1995), 54.
26. The question and correct answer are on wiki.answers: http://wiki.answers.com/Q/Who_defended_settlers_in_the_western_landes.
27. Bourne and Benton, *History of the United States*, 211.
28. Montgomery, *Beginner's American History*, 131.
29. Appleby et al., *American Republic*, 196.
30. Hakim, *History of US*, 3: 151.
31. Technically, the act applied only to land "which has been purchased of the Indian inhabitants." This requirement was repeatedly and increasingly ignored. In 1851, for instance, when government agents in California negotiated eighteen treaties to purchase Indian land, the treaties were unanimously rejected by the Senate. The land already belonged to the government, opponents of the treaty argued, by a treaty with Mexico, which had

supposedly relinquished territory it never settled or even controlled. Since government ownership was simply *assumed*, land could be divided and sold at will. (See Ray Raphael, *Little White Father: Redick McKee on the California Frontier* [Eureka, CA: Humboldt Country Historical Society, 1993].)

32. These were the texts from the 2002 NCSS conference, as listed in note 23. One, *The American Journey* (Prentice Hall), did mention Alexander McGillivray, but only as an ally of Spain. The authors engaged in a lengthy discussion of the struggles between Spain and the United States over control of the Mississippi, but other than the brief mention of McGillivray, they make no mention of Indians or their attempts to keep their lands.
33. Michael J. Berson, Tyrone C. Howard, and Cinthia Salinas, *Harcourt Social Studies—United States: Making a New Nation* (Boston: Houghton Mifflin Harcourt, 2012), 367–368.
34. Emma J. Lapsansky-Werner, Peter B. Levy, Randy Roberts, and Alan Taylor, *United States History*, Survey Edition (Upper Saddle River, NJ: Prentice Hall, 2013), 138.
35. James West Davidson, Brian DeLay, Christine Leigh Heyrman, Mark H. Lytle, and Michael B. Stoff, *Experience History: Interpreting America's Past*, vol. 1 (New York: McGraw-Hill, 2011), 174.
36. James West Davidson and Michael B. Stoff, *America: History of Our Nation* (Upper Saddle River, NJ: Prentice Hall, 2014), 189. Other texts retreat in different ways. After being "badly defeated" by Native forces and local loyalists one text states, "Sullivan took revenge by burning forty Indians villages. It was an act of violence and cruelty that deeply shocked and shamed General Washington." (Carol Berkin, Christopher L. Miller, Robert W. Cherny, James L. Gormly, Douglas Egerton, and Kelly Woestman, *Making America: A History of the United States*, Brief Sixth Edition [Boston: Wadsworth/Cengage Learning, 2014], 136.) In fact, Washington ordered and fully approved of the expedition. On May 31, 1779, General Washington issued specific instructions to Sullivan "to lay waste" to Indian towns "in the most effectual manner, that the country may be not merely overrun, but destroyed." Washington minced no words, and his orders evidenced a hateful tone: "The expedition you are appointed to command is to be directed against the hostile tribes of the Six Nations of Indians, with their associates and adherents. The immediate objects are the total destruction and devastation of their settlements, and the capture of as many prisoners of every age and sex as possible. It will be essential to ruin their crops now in the ground and prevent their planting more . . . You will not by any means listen to any overture of peace before the total ruinment of their settlements is effected. Our future security will be in their inability to injure us and in the terror . . . [and] severity of the chastisement they receive." (George Washington to John Sullivan, May 31, 1779, in *The Writings of George Washington from the Original Manuscript Sources, 1745–1799*, John C. Fitzpatrick, ed. [Washington, DC: U. S. Government Printing Office, 1931–1944], 15:189–193.

15: Storybook Nation

1. See Michael McDonnell, "National Identity and the American War for Independence: A Reappraisal," *Australasian Journal of American Studies* 20 (2001), 3–17.
2. John Shy, *A People Numerous and Armed: Reflections on the Military Struggle for American Independence* (Ann Arbor: University of Michigan Press, 1990), 26.
3. John Adams to Abigail Adams, July 3, 1776, in Adams, *Familiar Letters of John Adams and his Wife Abigail Adams, during the Revolution*, Charles Francis Adams, ed. (Boston: Houghton Mifflin, 1875), 193–194.
4. Charles Warren, "Fourth of July Myths," *William and Mary Quarterly*, Third Series, 2 (1945): 246. Here are the original journal entries, not included in the first printed version: "July 19. 1776. Resolved That the Declaration passed on the fourth be fairly engrossed on parchment with the title and stile of 'The Unanimous Declaration of the 13 United States of America' and that the same when engrossed be signed by every member of Congress.—Aug. 2. 1776. The declaration of Independence being engrossed & compared at the table was signed by the Members." (John H. Hazelton, *The Declaration of Independence: Its History* [New York: Dodd, Mead and Co., 1906], 204.) The original manuscript of the minutes, in the journals of the Continental Congress, was first consulted by Mellen Chamberlain in 1884. (Warren, "Fourth of July Myths," 245.) The printed version in the journals of the Continental Congress that appears on the Library of Congress website, edited by Worthington Chauncey Ford in 1906 (http://memory.loc.gov/ammem/amlaw/lwjc.html), reflects the original manuscript for July 19 and August 2, but the July 4 entry is still doctored by inserting the engrossed, signed copy, the "official" one the nation has celebrated since 1777.
5. At least seven signers, and possibly several others, were not present on August 2: Matthew Thornton, Thomas McKean, Elbridge Gerry, Oliver Wolcott, Lewis Morris, Richard Henry Lee, and George Wythe. (Hazelton, *Declaration of Independence*, 210–219.) Thomas McKean, the last man to sign, offered convincing testimony that a single act of signing never took place. (McKean to John Adams, January 1814, *The Works of John Adams*, Charles Francis Adams, ed. [Boston: Little, Brown and Co., 1856], 10: 87–89.) There is some question about whether George Wythe ever signed his own name. "It is unlikely that he personally signed it on his return in the fall, as some delegates did; he had probably authorized a clerk to do so for him when the document was engrossed," writes Robert Kirtland in *American National Biography* (24: 93).
6. John A. Garraty and Mark C. Carnes, eds., *American National Biography* (New York: Oxford University Press, 1999), 4: 468; 11: 146; 13: 772; 15: 903–904; 18: 911–912; 19: 73; 21: 609; 23: 514, 721; 24: 93; Dumas Malone, ed., *Dictionary of American Biography* (New York: Scribner's, 1943), 4: 235; 17: 284; 18: 325. Even today, all these names appear as signers of the Declaration of Independence in the July 4, 1776, entry of the Library of Congress's *Journals of the Continental Congress, 1774–1789*: http://memory.loc.gov/cgi-bin/query/r?ammem/hlaw:@field(DOCID+@lit(jc00525)).

   In the case of Samuel Chase of Maryland, the notion that these men signed the Declaration on July 4, 1776, created an interesting folktale. A few days earlier, Chase had been in Maryland, attending the state convention. Because he supposedly signed the Declaration of Independence on July 4, people thought he must have engaged in a heroic ride that is still immortalized today: "In the next two days he rode one hundred miles and arrived in Philadelphia just in time to sign the Declaration of Independence." (Margaret Horsnell's entry for Samuel Chase, in Garraty and Carnes, *American National Biography*, 4: 743.) In fact, Chase had fallen ill and didn't arrive back in Philadelphia until July 17. (James Haw, Francis F. Beirne, Rosamond R. Beirne, R. Samuel Jett, *Stormy Patriot: The Life of Samuel Chase* [Baltimore: Maryland Historical Society, 1980], 68.)

7. Garry Wills, *Inventing America: Jefferson's Declaration of Independence* (New York: Doubleday, 1978), 341.
8. *Independent Gazetteer*, July 11, 1789; cited in Len Travers, *Celebrating the Fourth: Independence Day and the Rites of Nationalism in the Early Republic* (Amherst: University of Massachusetts Press, 1997), 43.
9. Travers, *Celebrating the Fourth*, 49. These orations were generally placed in print, and some became bestsellers.
10. *Independent Gazetteer*, July 8, 1786; cited in Travers, *Celebrating the Fourth*, 56–57.
11. Sarah J. Purcell, *Sealed with Blood: War, Sacrifice, and Memory in Revolutionary America* (Philadelphia: University of Pennsylvania Press, 2002), 20.
12. William Gordon, *The History of the Rise, Progress, and Establishment, of the Independence of the United States of America*, reprint edition (Freeport, NY: Books for Libraries Press, 1969; first published in 1788). Although he did not arrive in Boston until 1770, Gordon was an ardent advocate of republican principles. In 1772 he was elected minister for the Roxbury congregation, in 1774 he preached the Thanksgiving Day sermon for the Massachusetts Provincial Congress, and the following year he was chosen as its official chaplain. His rise to prominence within patriotic circles was meteoric—too much so for John Adams. "Parson Gordon, of Roxbury, spent the evening here," Adams wrote in his diary on September 16, 1775. "I fear his indiscreet prate will do harm in this city. He is an eternal talker, and somewhat vain, and not accurate nor judicious; very zealous in the cause, and a well-meaning man, but incautious, and . . . fond of being thought a man of influence at headquarters, and with our Council and House, and with the general officers of the army, and also with gentlemen in this city and other Colonies." (Adams, *Works of John Adams*, 2: 423–424.) Gordon took copious notes throughout the war, always with the intent of publication. Ambitious and talkative, he placed his networking energies at the service of history: he wrote and spoke incessantly with "those in the know," then incorporated what they told him within his narrative. When Gordon finished his work in the mid-1780s, Boston printers vied for the rights to publish the first locally produced chronicle of the War for Independence. But the author chose to publish his magnum opus in England instead of America, and he drew the wrath of both jealous printers and unforgiving ideologues. "A mercenary scribbler," one critic called him. (David D. Van Tassel, *Recording America's Past: An Interpretation of the Development of Historical Studies in America, 1607–1884* [Chicago: University of Chicago Press, 1960], 40.) Having alienated his American audience, Gordon failed to excite a British readership. His history was a flop—but it was not without influence. Later generations of writers and

historians would cite William Gordon as an authoritative source. Since Gordon had lived through the Revolution and talked to all the right people, his words would be accepted as faithful and accurate representations of actual events.

13. David Ramsay, *The History of the American Revolution* (Philadelphia: R. Aitken & Son, 1789; reprinted by Liberty Classics in 1990). Ramsay was not only a writer but also a Revolutionary activist and politician. He served as a South Carolina state legislator, the president of the state senate, and a delegate to the Continental Congress in the 1780s.
14. David Ramsay, *History of the Revolution in South Carolina* (Trenton: Isaac Collins, 1785), 1: 231; cited in William Raymond Smith, *History as Argument: Three Patriot Historians of the American Revolution* (The Hague: Mouton & Co., 1966), 56.
15. John Marshall, *The Life of George Washington* (New York: AMS Press, 1969; first published 1804–1807).
16. Mercy Otis Warren, *History of the Rise, Progress and Termination of the American Revolution, interspersed with Biographical, Political and Moral Observations* (Boston: E. Larkin, 1805; reprinted by Liberty Classics in 1988).
17. *Columbian*, IV (March 1789), 50, cited in Van Tassel, *Recording America's Past*, 36.
18. Van Tassel, *Recording America's Past*, 39; Harvey Wish, *The American Historian: A Social-Intellectual History of the Writing of the American Past* (New York: Oxford University Press, 1960), 41; Michael Krause and Davis D. Joyce, *The Writing of American History* (Norman: University of Oklahoma Press, 1985), 56–60; George H. Callcott, *History in the United States, 1800–1860: Its Practice and Purpose* (Baltimore: Johns Hopkins Press, 1970), 134–138.
19. Marshall did better than the others, perhaps because his title led people to believe they would be reading about the much-idolized Washington. Critics, however, took him to task for wasting two full volumes before getting to the subject promised by the title.
20. Sydney Fisher, "Legendary and Myth-making Process in Histories of the American Revolution," *American Philosophical Society Proceedings*, 51 (1912): 64.
21. Mason L. Weems, *The Life of Washington* (Cambridge, MA: Belknap Press, 1962; reprint of ninth edition, 1809), Introduction by Marcus Cunliffe, xiv.
22. Cunliffe introduction to Weems, *Life of Washington*, xiv; Van Tassel, *Recording America's Past*, 71.
23. There is some controversy as to whether the first edition of his pamphlet was *The Life and Memorable Actions of George Washington*, printed by George Keating of Baltimore, or *A History of the Life and Death, Virtues and Exploits of General George Washington*, printed in Georgetown "for the Rev. M.L. Weems of Lodge No. 50, Dumfries." (Lewis Leary, *The Book Peddling Parson* [Chapel Hill: Algonquin Books, 1984], 84.)
24. Lester H. Cohen, *The Revolutionary Histories: Contemporary Narratives of the American Revolution* (Ithaca, NY: Cornell University Press, 1980), 166.
25. Fisher, "Myth-making Process," 65. Fisher continued: "Reckless in statement, indifferent to facts and research, his books are full of popular heroism, religion and morality, which you at first call trash and cant and then, finding it extremely entertaining, you declare with a laugh, what a clever rogue."

26. Weems, *Life of Washington*, 109–110.
27. David Ramsay, *The Life of George Washington* (Boston: D. Mallory and Co., 1811; first published in 1807).
28. Charleston: A.E. Miller, 1828.
29. Anonymous, *Stories of the Revolution; Comprising a Complete Anecdotal History of that Great National Event* (Philadelphia: Grigg and Elliot, 1847).
30. Fisher, "Myth-making Process," 56; John Spencer Basset, *The Middle Group of American Historians* (New York: Macmillan, 1917), 103.
31. Noah Webster, *A Collection of Essays and Fugitive Writings* (Boston: I. Thomas and E.T. Andrews, 1790; reprint edition, Scholars' Facsimiles & Reprints, 1977), 24–5.
32. Richard Snowden, *The American Revolution Written in the Style of Ancient History* (Philadelphia: Jones, Hoff & Derrick, 1793), 2 volumes.
33. Van Tassel, *Recording America's Past*, 90.
34. Salma Hale, *A History of the United States from their first Settlement as Colonies, to the Close of the War with Great Britain in 1815* (New York: Collins and Hannay, 1830; first published in 1822), preface.
35. Wills, *Inventing America*, 51–52. Wills quoted one of the entries of the 1741 *Chambers Cyclopaedia*: "The REVOLUTION, used by way of eminence, denotes the great turn of affairs in England in 1688."
36. Paul Allen, *A History of the American Revolution, Comprising all the Principal Events both in the Field and the Cabinet* (Baltimore: Johns Hopkins, 1819), I: iv–v.
37. Benson Lossing, *The Pictorial Field-Book of the Revolution* (New York: Harper & Brothers, 1851), 1: iv–v.
38. Peter Force and M. St. Clair Clarke, *American Archives* (Washington, DC, 1833–1853).
39. George Bancroft, *History of the United States of America, from the Discovery of the Continent* (Boston: Little, Brown, and Company, 1879; first published 1834–1875).
40. Richard Hildreth, *The History of the United States of America* (New York: Harper & Brothers, 1880; first published in 1849), 1: introductory "advertisement."
41. John Fiske, *The American Revolution* (Boston: Houghton Mifflin, 1891), 1: vii.
42. Ann Arnold Hunter, *A Century of Service: The Story of the DAR* (Washington, DC: National Society Daughters of the American Revolution, 1991), 15–16.
43. Cited in Arthur Johnston, *Myths and Facts of the American Revolution* (Toronto: William Briggs, 1908), 27–28.

Conclusion: Why We Tell Tall Tales

1. David Harlan, quoted in Peter Seixas, "Schweigen! Die Kinder! or Does Postmodern History Have a Place in the Schools," in *Knowing, Teaching, and Learning History: National and International Perspectives*, Peter N. Stearns, Peter Seixas, and Sam Wineburg, eds. (New York: New York University Press, 2000), 27. Harlan also calls the past polysemous, or having multiple meanings.
2. Ray Raphael, *Constitutional Myths: What We Get Wrong and How to Get It Right* (New York: The New Press, 2013), 77–102. Similarly, authors try to define Jefferson's view of

slavery, as if that were some fixed entity impervious to the influence of external events. In fact, Jefferson's public and private life intersected with the institution of slavery on many levels across the years. In 1769 he tried to make it easier for masters to free their slaves. In 1776 he proposed that "no person hereafter coming into this country [Virginia] shall be held in slavery under any pretext." In 1783 he advocated the gradual emancipation of all slaves in Virginia after 1800. In 1784 he advocated the exclusion of slavery in the West. But he also argued that blacks were inherently inferior to whites (*Notes on the State of Virginia*, drafted in 1781 and published in 1785), tightened Virginia's slave codes, offered a slave as a bounty for any white man who joined the army, claimed ownership of over six hundred human beings during his lifetime (about two hundred at a given moment), bred slaves for profit ("I consider the labor of a breeding woman as no object, and that a child raised every 2 years is of more profit than the crop of the best laboring man," he wrote to his plantation manager in 1819), sold more than a hundred men, women, and children to finance his architectural schemes at Monticello, and in 1820 vigorously opposed the Missouri Compromise because it invoked federal power to prohibit slavery in the Northwest. To establish consistency within all of this is simply not possible. Jefferson's "position" on slavery was certainly affected by external events and by changes in his personal circumstances over time. He did not exactly drive this engine of history, but was driven by it.

3. The iconic treatment of Lexington and Concord also conceals what was happening in Boston preceding the British march. Residents there were flocking from the city in droves, hoping to avoid the military rule that was sure to accompany outright conflict. Active patriots tried to remove valuable property before it was confiscated, while even people who had taken no special part in the conflict feared they might soon be subjected to the hazards of war should Boston itself become a battlefield. On April 11 Boston merchant John Andrews noted "the streets and neck lin'd with waggons carrying off the effects of the inhabitants . . . imagining to themselves that they shall be liable to every evil that can be enumerated, if they tarry in town." Three days after that, the Provincial Congress recommended that donations intended for relief of the poor in Boston be used to help evacuate the city. (John Andrews, "Letters of John Andrews of Boston, 1772–1776," Massachusetts Historical Society, *Proceedings*, 8 [1864–1865], 402; William Lincoln, ed., *The Journals of Each Provincial Congress of Massachusetts in 1774 and 1775, and of the Committee of Safety, with an Appendix, containing the Proceedings of the County Conventions* [Boston: Dutton and Wentworth, 1838], 142–143. See also *Massachusetts Gazette and Boston Post-Boy*, April 10, 1775.)
4. Alan Brinkley, *The Unfinished Nation: A Concise History of the American People*, Seventh Edition (New York: McGraw-Hill, 2014), 107. For the May 10 resolution of Congress, see *JCC* 4: 342.
5. Brinkley, *Unfinished Nation*, 93, 135, 137. The author does admit that "many people contributed to the Constitution," which makes his claim of individual agency all the more striking. Madison was the "most important," he proclaims, although ascribing the supreme importance of a single individual is optional, not necessary, to the narrative of the Constitutional Convention. (Ibid., 135.)

6. Shays himself recognized this when he said to General Rufus Putnam, one of his adversaries: "I am not . . . I never had any appointment but that at Springfield, nor did I ever take command of any men but those of the county of Hampshire; no, General Putnam, you are deceived, I never had half so much to do in the matter as you think." (Robert A. Feer, *Shays's Rebellion* [New York: Garland, 1988; reprint of PhD dissertation, Harvard University, 1958], 212.)
7. Brinkley, *Unfinished Nation*, 129, and Alan Brinkley, *American History: Connecting With the Past*, vol. 1, Fourteenth Edition (New York: McGraw-Hill, 2012), 157; Michael Schaller, Robert D. Schulzinger, John Bezis-Selfa, Janette Thomas Greenwood, Andrew Kirk, Sarah J. Purcell, and Aaron Sheehan-Dean, *American Horizons: U.S. History in a Global Context*, Concise Edition (New York: Oxford University Press, 2013), 279.
8. The term "Regulators" had been used by popular uprising in South Carolina in the late 1760s and North Carolina in the early 1770s. For a more accurate treatment of the Massachusetts Regulators' movement on 1786–1787, see Gregory Nobles, " 'Satan, Smith, Shattuck, and Shays': The People's Leaders in the Massachusetts Regulation of 1786," in Alfred F. Young, Gary B. Nash, and Ray Raphael, *Revolutionary Founders: Rebels, Radicals, and Reformers in the Making of the Nation* (New York: Alfred A. Knopf, 2011), 215–31.
9. This model is espoused in Linda Grant DePauw, "Politicizing the Politically Inert," in *The American Revolution: Changing Perspectives*, William M. Fowler Jr. and Wallace Coyle, eds. (Boston: Northeastern University Press, 1979), 3–25.
10. Stuart Murray, *American Revolution* (New York: DK Eyewitness Books, 2005).
11. California: Fifth Grade Standards, Performance Standard CA 5.5.4., National History Education Clearinghouse: http://teachinghistory.org/teaching-materials/state-standards/california/5.

Afterword: Which Myths Persist, and Why

1. Nancy Hewitt and Steven F. Lawson, *Exploring American History: A Brief Survey with Sources* (Boston: Bedford/St. Martin's, 2013), 185–191.
2. One author, attempting to set the record straight, points out the differences between Longfellow's poem and the historical record: "Longfellow omits any mention of *the other* rider, William Dawes." (Emphasis added.) That's all there were, just the two of them, the fate of the nation still on their shoulders alone. James Cross Giblin, *The Many Rides of Paul Revere* (New York: Scholastic Press, 2007), 73.
3. James West Davidson and Michael B. Stoff, *America: History of Our Nation* (Upper Saddle River, NJ: Prentice Hall, 2014), 171. This is a middle-school text.
4. Hewitt and Lawson, *Exploring American History*, 165.
5. James Oakes, Michael McGerr, Jan Ellen Lewis, Nick Cullather, and Jeanne Boydston, *Of the People: A History of the United States*, vol. 1, Concise Edition (New York: Oxford University Press, 2011), 188.
6. See chapter 4. Although none yet include Worcester's declaration, textbooks for high

school and college are beginning to take some notice of the Massachusetts Revolution of 1774. Several now describe the Massachusetts Government Act in greater detail, noting that it "terminated the long history of self-rule by communities in the colony of Massachusetts" or calling it the "most detested" of the Coercive Acts. Some stop there, but others continue with brief renditions of the revolt that erupted throughout the colony, highlighting one or two of the incidents. A select few offer more extensive accounts.

Massachusetts Government Act: John Mack Faragher, Mari Jo Buhle, Daniel Czitrom, and Susan H. Armitage, *Out of Many: A History of the American People*, Seventh Edition (Upper Saddle River, NJ: Pearson/Prentice Hall, 2012), 151; David Goldfield, Carl Abbott, Virginia DeJohn Anderson, Jo Ann E. Argersinger, Peter H. Argersinger, William L. Barney, and Robert M. Weir, *The American Journey: A History of the United States*, Brief Sixth Edition (Upper Saddle River, NJ: Prentice Hall, 2011), 132; Joyce Appleby, Alan Brinkley, Albert S. Broussard, James M. McPherson, and Donald A. Ritchie, *The American Journey* (New York: Macmillan/McGraw-Hill Glencoe, 2012), 129.

Brief renditions highlighting one or two of the incidents: Eric Foner, *Give Me Liberty! An American History*, Third Edition (New York: W.W. Norton, 2011), 195; James Henretta, Rebecca Edwards, and Robert Self, *America: A Concise History*, Fifth Edition (New York: Bedford/St. Martin's, 2012), 154; James Oakes, Michael McGerr, Jan Ellen Lewis, Nick Cullather, and Jeanne Boydston, *Of the People: A History of the United States*, vol. 1, Concise Edition (New York: Oxford University Press, 2011), 178; Emma J. Lapsansky-Werner, Peter B. Levy, Randy Roberts, and Alan Taylor, *United States History*, Survey Edition (Upper Saddle River, NJ: Prentice Hall, 2013), 104, 108. Not all these texts convey the democratic character of the rebellion, however: "John Hancock, Samuel Adams, and other colonial leaders then convened a Provincial Congress to govern Massachusetts without Gage." (Lapsansky-Werner, 108.) Samuel Adams was in Philadelphia at the time, and the push for a Provincial Congress was initiated by a multicounty meeting of committees of correspondence in late August, convened at the request of Worcester County, not Hancock, Adams, or other leaders from Boston (Raphael, *First American Revolution*, 84–84).

More extensive accounts: James Roark, Michael Johnson, Patricia Cline Cohen, Sarah Stage, Alan Lawson, and Susan M. Hartmann, *The American Promise: A History of the United States*, Fourth Edition (New York: Bedford/St. Martin's, 2009), 168–69, 171; Gary B. Nash, *The Unknown American Revolution: The Unruly Birth of Democracy and the Struggle to Create America* (New York: Viking, 2005), 178–182. Nash's book is not a text in the standard sense, but it is used as a basic text in several college courses. A key primary source from the Massachusetts Revolution of 1774 is included in Howard Zinn and Anthony Arnove, *Voices of a People's History of the United States* (New York: Seven Stories Press, 2004), 93–95, a readings book that accompanies Zinn's widely used *A People's History of the United States*.

7. The text can be viewed digitally at: http://www.rayraphael.com/documents/decloration_independence.htm or http://www.common-place.org/vol-09/no-01/raphael/. The monographic treatment of this period, which provides the context for the Worcester Declaration, is Ray Raphael, *The First American Revolution: Before Lexington*

and Concord (New York: The New Press, 2002). Contextual documentary evidence is collected in microfiche form in L. Kinvin Wroth, ed., *Province in Rebellion: A Documentary History of the Founding of the Commonwealth of Massachusetts, 1774–1775* (Cambridge, MA: Harvard University Press, 1975) and in other sources referenced in *First American Revolution*. Pauline Maier readily embraced the Worcester Declaration. (Talk given to the Massachusetts Historical Society, September 24, 2012.)

8. Jacqueline Jones, Peter H. Wood, Thomas Borstelmann, Elaine Tyler May, and Vicki L. Ruiz, *Created Equal: A History of the United States*, vol. 1, Third Edition (New York: Pearson Longman, 2009), 188.
9. David M. Kennedy and Lizabeth Cohen, *The American Pageant*, Fifteenth Edition (Boston: Cengage Learning, 2014), 19, 125.
10. http://www.thefreedictionary.com/Molly+Pitcher.
11. http://en.wikipedia.org/wiki/Molly_Pitcher.
12. Type in a brief passage on a Google search—"by every member present except Mr. Dickinson"—and you will find several thousand matches, quotations from Thomas Jefferson dated 1819 or 1821. Each time, Jefferson stated that the Declaration of Independence was signed on July 4 by all delegates to the Continental Congress except Dickinson. Casual readers surfing the Net will likely assume that Jefferson remembered well and knew what he is talking about, since he wrote the document himself. In fact, we have no record dating from the time of the event that anybody other than President Hancock and Secretary Thomson signed on July 4; several members present on the Fourth, in addition to Dickinson, never did sign. We do have clear documentation that an engrossed copy of the Declaration was signed by many members on August 2, and fourteen signers were not even present on July 4—but none of this contemporaneous evidence is revealed on the Google search so it carries no weight. In this manner, historical distortions due to the bending of memory easily take hold. Forty-three years after the fact, even Thomas Jefferson found himself influenced by the myth of a Fourth of July signing, purposely contrived by Congress, that had established firm roots in American culture. (See chapter 15.)
13. Recently, for example, I noticed something suspicious about an army recruiting poster alleged to date from 1776 and reproduced in many textbooks. The poster opened: "To all brave, healthy, able bodied, and well disposed young men, in this neighborhood, who have any inclination to join the troops now raising under General Washington, for the defence of the liberties and independence of the United States." This appears to be an artifact of the Revolutionary War, but the very small print following the bold introduction raised doubts in my mind: "Against the hostile designs of foreign enemies." Just who were those "foreign enemies" with "hostile designs" in 1776? Americans at that time considered the British as their "Brethren" and "common kindred," as they proclaimed in the Declaration of Independence. They looked upon belligerent Indians as "savages" rather than foreign powers. Although they certainly regarded the Hessian soldiers contracted by King George III as "foreign," they characterized those auxiliary troops as mercenaries motivated by money, not by "hostile designs." Did this poster really date from the Revolutionary War?

Thanks to the Internet, the answer came quickly. The names of three officers were listed on the poster, along with the regiment for which they were recruiting. A series of simple Google searches revealed that these three men did in fact serve together in the designated regiment in 1798, when General Washington was the titular head of the so-called "Additional Army" raised in anticipation of a war with France. Further searches revealed that these men also served during the Revolutionary War, but at no time during that war did they all hold the offices listed on the poster, nor did they serve in the designated regiment. Twenty years ago, I would have had to travel far or request diverse documents from distant repositories to acquire the relevant information, but a colleague and I resolved the matter within two or three hours, working from our office computers. Further, this work can be easily replicated and checked by other investigators. Historical research has been revolutionized and democratized. (Ray Raphael and Benjamin H. Irvin, "Take Notice: The Not-So-1776 Recruiting Poster," in *Journal of the American Revolution: Collectors Edition*, vol. 1, Todd Andrlik, Hugh T. Harrington, and Don N. Hagist, eds. (Yellow Springs, OH: Ertel Publishing, 2013).

14. See, for example, the prodigious output of the online *Journal of the American Revolution*, http://allthingsliberty.com/.
15. *Common Core State Standards Initiative*, English Language Arts Standards—Reading: Informational Text, Grade 5, RI 5.6; English Language Arts Standards—History/Social Studies, Grade 6–8, RH 6–8.6; English Language Arts Standards—History/Social Studies, Grade 11–12, RH 11–12.6 and RH 11–12.8: http://www.corestandards.org/ELA-Literacy.
16. According to Common Core's "publishers' criteria," there should be as little context as possible: "Text-dependent questions do not require information or evidence from outside the text or texts; they establish what follows and what does not follow from the text itself. Eighty to ninety percent of the Reading Standards in each grade require text-dependent analysis; accordingly, aligned curriculum materials should have a similar percentage of text-dependent questions. When examining a complex text in depth, tasks should require careful scrutiny of the text and specific references to evidence from the text itself to support responses." (*Revised Publishers' Criteria for the Common Core State Standards in English Language Arts and Literacy, Grades 3–12*, page 6: http://www.corestandards.org/assets/Publishers_Criteria_for_3-12.pdf).

The rationale for such an approach is clear: students should focus on the material at hand, independent of extraneous information or misinformation that might color their reading. Unfortunately, though, it is impossible to achieve Common Core goals without paying significant attention to context. How can middle-school students determine the "avoidance of particular facts" without knowing what those facts are and bringing them into play? How can juniors and seniors corroborate or challenge an author's "claims, reasoning, or evidence" with "other information" if no other information is to be considered? Common Core standards suggest that juniors and seniors examine Madison's use of the term "faction" in *The Federalist* No. 10, but how could they possibly glean what he meant by "a rage for paper money . . . or for any other improper or wicked project" without examining what was happening in state legislatures at the time and how that played into the creation of a new Constitution?

17. "AP United States History 2005 Scoring Guidelines" PDF, accessed October 1, 2013. http://www.mpsaz.org/rmhs/staff/jxcollums/class1/ap2/files/ap_2005_dbq_revolution.pdf. Among the "outside information" students might wish to bring to bear on this document, the Scoring Guidelines says, is "Molly Pitcher."
18. Molly Gutridge, Broadside, 1779. Evans Early American Imprints document 43671, repository New-York Historical Society. National Humanities Center website, accessed October 1, 2013. http://nationalhumanitiescenter.org/pds/makingrev/war/text7/touchonthetimes.pdf.
19. Here is a set of questions we might ask of any document:
    - Who is/are the authors, and how do we know that? When and where was the document created? In professional terms, what is the provenance?
    - Why just then? What else was happening at that very moment? We need strict chronology to establish context, paying close attention to the date of proximate events.
    - Has there been a lapse of time between events described in the document and reporting about them? If so, what public discourse might have influenced the author's memory and presentation?
    - What are the broad parameters of the issues/problems/events being addressed?
    - What were the acceptable limits of discussion at that time, within which this is presented?
    - What are the specific issues/problems/events being addressed? Again, we need to pay attention to chronology—specifics might change day by day.
    - Why might the author(s) be addressing these issues right at this particular moment? Who is the audience—public or private? Friend, foe, or other? What is the venue of communication—letter, diary, newspaper, book, etc.? Why does/do the author(s) even bother? Is this an attempt to convince? Strategize? Report? Inform? Describe? Express emotion?
    - What other sources might help determine the overarching goal and how this fits within it? Do other sources corroborate or contradict the author(s)? Do other authors offer similar or different accounts, claims, or arguments?

PHOTO CREDITS

Introduction and chapters 2, 5, 10, and 12 are taken from John Grafton, *The American Revolution, a Picture Sourcebook: 411 Copyright-Free Illustrations* (New York: Dover, 1975).

Chapter 1 is from *Harper's Weekly*, June 29, 1867, reproduced in Alfred F. Young and Terry J. Fife, *We the People: Voices and Images of the New Nation* (Philadelphia: Temple University Press, 1993).

Chapter 4 is from Benson J. Lossing, *The Pictorial Field-Book of the Revolution* (New York: Harper and Brothers, 1851–1852).

Chapter 7, by Barry Faulkner, is from the National Archives, Washington, D.C.

Chapters 3, 6, 9, 11, 13, 14, and 15 are from the Granger Collection, New York.

INDEX

Note: Page numbers in **boldface** represent images.